A MEASURE OF FREEDOM

A Measure of Freedom

IAN CARTER

OXFORD
UNIVERSITY PRESS

Oxford University Press, Great Clarendon Street, Oxford OX2 6DP
Oxford New York
Athens Auckland Bangkok Bogotá Buenos Aires Calcutta
Cape Town Chennai Dar es Salaam Delhi Florence Hong Kong Istanbul
Karachi Kuala Lumpur Madrid Melbourne Mexico City Mumbai
Nairobi Paris São Paulo Singapore Taipei Tokyo Toronto Warsaw
and associated companies in Berlin Ibadan

Oxford is a registered trade mark of Oxford University Press

Published in the United States
by Oxford University Press Inc., New York

British Library Cataloguing in Publication Data
Data available

Library of Congress Cataloging in Publication Data
Carter, Ian.
A measure of freedom / Ian Carter.
Includes bibliographical references.
1. Library. II. Title.
JC585.C335 1999 323.44—dc21   98–37478
ISBN 0–19–829453–0

1 3 5 7 9 10 8 6 4 2

Typeset in 10½/12½pt Times
by Graphicraft Limited, Hong Kong
Printed in Great Britain
on acid-free paper by
Biddles Ltd, Guildford and King's Lynn

To the memory of my father

FRANK CARTER

ACKNOWLEDGEMENTS

I SHOULD like to acknowledge the support of a number of institutions which have made possible the completion of this book. They are: the Department of Education and Science and the European University Institute (doctoral grants, 1988–91), the Institute for Humane Studies (Claude R. Lambe Fellowship, 1991–2), the Leverhulme Trust (Study Abroad Grant, 1993–5), and the University of Pavia (Postdoctoral Fellowship, 1995–7).

Parts of the present work draw on previously published articles. In particular, s. 1.5 draws on 'Una replica', *Quaderni di Scienza Politica*, 2 (1995), 462–7; parts of Chapter 2 draw on 'The Independent Value of Freedom', *Ethics*, 105 (1995), 819–45 (© 1995 by the University of Chicago); and parts of Chapter 5 draw on 'Interpersonal Comparisons of Freedom', *Economics and Philosophy*, 11 (1995), 1–23. My thanks to the publishers for permission to use this material.

I am grateful to all the colleagues in Florence, Manchester, Pavia, and elsewhere from whom I have received insights, criticism, and other sorts of help in writing this book. In particular, for useful feedback either on draft chapters or on earlier efforts, I should like to thank Carla Bagnoli, Francesco Battegazzorre, Marco Clementi, Jerry Cohen, Geert Demuijnck, Giorgio Fedel, Luca Ferrero, Maurice Glasman, Tim Gray, Martin van Hees, Ian Holliday, Janos Kis, Kristján Kristjánsson, Will Kymlicka, Veronica Muñoz Dardé, Marco Negri, Onora O'Neill, Mario Ricciardi, Amartya Sen, John Stanton Ife, Mario Stoppino, and Jo Wolff. Simon Caney, Serena Olsaretti, and Felix Oppenheim read a draft of the whole book, and I thank them for their detailed and challenging comments.

Four other people deserve a special mention. At the European University, in Florence, Steven Lukes and Philippe Van Parijs supervised the doctoral thesis out of which this book eventually grew. I am extremely grateful to them for all their support and constructive criticism. In more recent years, at the University of Pavia, Salvatore Veca has been an invaluable source of encouragement and stimulation. In further refining my ideas, I have benefited greatly from his critical advice. Finally, it remains for me to thank Hillel Steiner, a patient reader and friendly critic of my work on freedom ever since I began it under his supervision at Manchester. Much of my thinking on political philosophy has been influenced by his, and although he does not agree with everything I say in this book, the size of my intellectual debt to him will be clear to anyone who reads it.

I.C.

Pavia
June 1998

CONTENTS

PART II: VALUE-BASED FREEDOM

PART III: EMPIRICAL FREEDOM

Introduction

A GROUP of political thinkers is engaged in an unashamedly transhistorical discussion about freedom. They do not all agree with each other. They have been listening to Thomas Hobbes explaining how 'liberty is in some places *more*, and in some *less*, and in some times *more*, in other times *less*, according as they that have the sovereignty shall think most convenient'.[1] But where and when *has* liberty been 'more', and where and when has it been 'less'? Isaiah Berlin is quite sure that 'the average subject of the King of Sweden is on the whole a good deal freer than the average citizen of . . . Albania'.[2] While not disagreeing with him, Roger Scruton feels he should emphasize that it is in Great Britain that we find 'more freedom . . . of every kind than in most other countries of the world'.[3] Their compatriot Bryan Magee, on the other hand, is more ready to praise the United States, believing that 'there is more freedom for the individual there than here'. His favourite state is California. 'There can be few more attractive places to live in, and few where the individual is freer to do his own thing.'[4] But all over America people are, he declares, 'extraordinarily free'.[5] Christopher Caudwell does not concur. As a Marxist, it is his firm belief that 'as Russia shows, even in the dictatorship of the proletariat, man is already freer'.[6] And in John Somerville's view we should at least note that 'in the communist world, there is more freedom from the power of private money, from the influence of religious institutions, and from periodic unemployment'.[7] Even if capitalism leaves some people poorer, however, this is not enough to persuade Friedrich von Hayek that it makes them less free. Even 'the poor in a competitive society' are in his view

---

[1] T. Hobbes, *Leviathan* (London: Penguin, 1985), ch. 21, 271. Like most English-speaking philosophers, I use the terms 'liberty' and 'freedom' interchangeably.

[2] I. Berlin, *Four Essays on Liberty* (Oxford: Oxford University Press, 1969), 130. Berlin was writing in 1969.

[3] R. Scruton, *The Meaning of Conservatism* (Harmondsworth: Penguin, 1980), 19.

[4] Except where they refer to actual individuals, I use the terms 'his' and 'her' interchangeably; likewise, 'he' and 'she', 'him' and 'her', 'man' and 'person'.

[5] B. Magee, article in the *Guardian* (Weekend), 22 Sept. 1990.

[6] C. Caudwell, *The Concept of Freedom* (London: Lawrence & Wishart, 1965), 74.

[7] J. Somerville, 'Toward a Consistent Definition of Freedom and its Relation to Value', in C. J. Friedrich (ed.), *Liberty* (New York: Atherton Press, 1962), 300.

'much more free than a person commanding much greater material comfort in a different type of society'.[8] In a more conciliatory mood, though speaking at a later date, Nicholas Ashford points out that 'the Soviet Union is already a freer place than it was a year ago', while 'some people would question whether Great Britain still deserves its top rank position in the light of recent repressive moves by Mrs. Thatcher's government'.[9]

Is *more* freedom *better*? *Should* the freest society really be given a 'top rank position'? Not everyone thinks so. Adolf Hitler suggests that 'a very large measure of individual liberty is not necessarily the sign of a high degree of civilization'.[10] Similarly, Peregrine Worsthorne complains that contemporary politicians have given too much importance to freedom: many of today's problems, he says, 'stem, not from a diminution of liberty, but from its unbridled growth'.[11] Expressing a more balanced view, Samuel Johnson clarifies matters helpfully: 'we are all agreed as to our *own* liberty', he says; 'we would have as much of it as we can get; but we are not agreed as to the liberty of *others*: for in proportion as we take, others must lose.'[12]

What limits should be placed on government intervention if we are each interested in having 'as much liberty as we can get'? In the view of Cesare Beccaria, no government should limit the liberty of an individual beyond removing 'the least possible portion [of that liberty] that suffices to induce others to defend it'. Only 'the aggregate of these least possible portions constitutes the right [of governments] to punish'.[13] John Rawls agrees, suggesting that 'liberty . . . be restricted only for the sake of liberty',[14] as does Hayek, who endorses the same principle in his own words: 'we should accept only the prevention of more severe coercion as the justification for the use of coercion by the government.'[15] For Hayek, this principle implies keeping state intervention to a minimum. But 'of course', he is wrong, says Bertrand Russell, because 'it is obvious that freedom is not to be increased by a mere diminution of government'.[16] For 'without a fair measure of economic equality', chips

---

[8] F. von Hayek, *The Road to Serfdom* (London: Routledge & Kegan Paul, 1944), 76.

[9] N. Ashford, article in the *Independent*, 28 Jan. 1989.

[10] A. Hitler, *Hitler's Table Talk*, trans. N. Cameron and R. H. Stevens (Oxford: Oxford University Press, 1988), 423.

[11] P. Worsthorne, 'Too Much Freedom', in M. Cowling (ed.), *Conservative Essays* (London: Cassell, 1978), 148.

[12] J. Boswell, *The Life of Samuel Johnson LL.D.* (London: Everyman, 1906), 8 Apr. 1779, 272, my emphasis.

[13] C. Beccaria, *On Crimes and Punishments*, trans. H. Paolucci (Indianapolis: Bobbs-Merrill, 1963), 12–13.

[14] J. Rawls, *A Theory of Justice* (Cambridge, Mass.: Harvard University Press, 1971), 302.

[15] F. von Hayek, *The Constitution of Liberty* (London: Routledge & Kegan Paul, 1960), 44.

[16] B. Russell, 'Freedom in Society', in *Sceptical Essays* (London: Allen & Unwin, 1935), 173.

in Roy Hattersley, 'the equal rights of every citizen to the greatest amount of freedom . . . is impossible'.[17]

How are we to judge between the conflicting claims of these political thinkers? The best strategy is to begin by looking at what views and assumptions they hold in common—at what it is that allows them to understand each other, and to recognize their agreements and disagreements as such. Something they manifestly hold in common is the view that it is important to be able to say *how free* an individual or society is—sometimes absolutely, sometimes comparatively, but nearly always in an 'overall' or 'on-balance' sense. Behind that view lies the assumption that we can make sense of the idea of freedom as a *quantitative attribute*. A quantitative attribute is an attribute that can in principle be measured. It is not merely possessed or lacked but, rather, possessed or lacked *to a certain degree*.

The subject of this book is the quantitative attribution of freedom. It should be made clear from the outset, however, that it is not the primary aim of this book to assess the truth value of the claims of the above thinkers (with the exception, perhaps, of those of Hitler, Worsthorne, and Johnson). Assessing the majority of those claims will actually involve measuring freedom, and that is not something that I aim to do. The primary aim of this book is, and must be, more fundamental than that. For crucial though those claims are, no sufficient analysis has yet been given of their *meaning*.

Consider a simple analogy: that of the quantitative attribute 'weight'. We should hardly judge it acceptable for you to say that you weigh more than me and then go on in the same breath to admit that you have never in your life set eyes on a pair of scales, or that you have yet to understand the real meaning of the expression 'is heavier than'. Yet this is so often what happens, in an analogous way, in the case of freedom. Neglect of the question of what it would mean to measure freedom, and indeed of whether or how far freedom is measurable at all, represents a great hole in the ever expanding political and philosophical literature on freedom. With few exceptions, the tendency to date among political theorists has been to concentrate only on the meaning of the claim that a person is free to do a specific thing, and not at all on the meaning of the claim that one person or group is, in an overall sense, 'freer' than another. At the same time, adjectives like 'more', 'less', 'expanded', 'diminished', 'equal', and 'maximal' continue to be used as qualifiers of 'freedom' in politics, in everyday life, and in political and social philosophy.

The ultimate aim of this book, then, is to remedy the above shortcoming. It is to see how far and in what ways we can render meaningful the kind of

---

[17] R. Hattersley, *Choose Freedom: The Future for Democratic Socialism* (London: Joseph, 1986), 75.

quantitative attributions of freedom that we should like to be able to make, by asking whether, and if so in what ways, freedom is a measurable attribute.

My first task, however, must be to justify such an aim more fully. Before asking whether and in what ways freedom is a measurable attribute, we ought first to show how and why it is *important* that freedom be seen as a measurable attribute. We need, in other words, to establish what kind of quantitative attributions of freedom we should indeed like to be able to make, and how relevant they are to our wider moral and political concerns. That, broadly speaking, is the aim of Part I of this book. In particular, the question is central to Chapters 2 and 3. In order to answer it, we shall need to provide an analysis of the different ways in which freedom is *valuable*. Some ways of attributing value to freedom imply an interest in quantifying freedom, while others do not. I shall argue that the former play a fundamental role in contemporary liberal thought. The idea of 'more' and 'less' freedom is indeed an ineradicable part of liberal discourse and theorizing.

As will become clear in Part I, I believe it would be a mistake to divorce our reasoning about the nature of freedom (as a quantitative attribute) from our reasoning about other goods—in particular, from our reasoning about societal *justice*. This is not to say that freedom should be *defined* (even partly) in terms of justice; rather, it is to say that we should take account of the *demands* made on the concept of freedom by our ideas about justice. My interest in the measurement of freedom indeed arises directly out of an interest in justice. It arises out of the idea that justice consists, in part, in a distribution of freedom that is either maximal or in some sense fair—in other words, that justice means, in part, 'maximal freedom' or 'equal freedom' or 'a minimum of freedom for all' or something of the sort, or perhaps some combination of these principles. If this is part of what justice means, then our conception of justice presupposes certain powers of measuring freedom.

The basic idea running through this book is that we implicitly conceive of freedom in a non-specific way as well as in a specific way. When we think of freedom in a specific way, we have in mind the freedom to do a specific thing or set of things. When we think of freedom in a non-specific way, we have in mind freedom as a quantitative attribute—as something an agent has more or less of in an overall sense—without concentrating on any one specific thing that the agent is free to do. In Chapter 1, I argue that freedom in this non-specific, purely quantitative sense is indeed an *attribute of agents*. In Chapter 2, I argue that freedom in this non-specific, purely quantitative sense is *valuable*. In Chapter 3, I look at different ways of *distributing* freedom in this non-specific, purely quantitative sense, and the powers of measuring freedom that these require. Later chapters of the book work out further implications of this idea for the way we should define and measure freedom.

Before turning briefly to the subject matter of those later chapters, I should say a word about how we should understand the terms 'freedom' and 'measurement'. To begin with the latter, it is clear that freedom might be measurable on more than one kind of scale, and unless otherwise stated, I use the term 'measurement' in a broad sense, to cover any of these scales. When our demands are at their least, ordinal comparisons of freedom may suffice—as they would appear to, for example, in verifying Magee's claim that few places are 'freer' than California. When our demands are at their greatest, cardinal comparisons will be required—as they are, for example, by Beccaria's prescription that governments remove only 'the aggregate' of the 'least possible portions' of individuals' freedom. In addition, our demands might be for interpersonal or intrapersonal comparisons, for greater or lesser degrees of precision, and for greater or lesser degrees of completeness. It is also worth making one other distinction at this early stage: some of the above demands might be more easily satisfied at the level of purely conceptual analysis than at a more 'realistic' level, where we take into account practical difficulties of measurement. This being a work of political philosophy, my main concern is with the former, conceptual level of analysis. Only in the final chapter will I have something to say about the search for 'realistic' metrics of freedom, and even there my only aim will be to suggest the direction that such a search should take in the light of my conceptual analysis.

I shall turn to the question of how 'freedom' should be defined in Chapter 1. Nevertheless, I shall limit myself at that early stage to describing the general 'concept' of freedom. I shall assume, in line with a broadly liberal view, that freedom is the absence of preventing conditions on agents' possible actions. Various 'conceptions' of freedom will then be considered in Parts II and III, as the argument of the book unfolds. These more precise conceptions of freedom involve particular interpretations of the terms 'agent', 'preventing condition', and 'possible actions' in so far as they relate to freedom. The reason I do not discriminate between such interpretations in Part I is that I believe the question of their validity to depend, in part, on our arguments about the ways in which overall freedom can and should be measured—arguments that will not get under way until Parts II and III. And the reason for this last belief is that I see our thinking about the definition of freedom as linked to our thinking about the nature of justice in the way just mentioned: justice places demands on our powers of *measuring* freedom, and our powers of measuring freedom are in turn partly determined by the *nature* of freedom. Arguments about the nature of freedom and arguments about its measurement are indeed interdependent. It will not do, then, simply to give the 'correct' definition of freedom at the outset and subsequently to ask whether and how far freedom, on that definition alone, is measurable. Rather, we need to place the concept of freedom within the wider context of a theory of justice, and to seek a kind of 'reflective equilibrium' involving the two. One way of looking at the problem of measurability is by saying that if freedom turns out to be unmeasurable, then we cannot endorse a theory of justice that presupposes its measurability. Alternatively, it might be said that if our theory of justice presupposes the measurability of freedom, we cannot endorse a definition of freedom that excludes such measurability. Each of these points of view is arbitrarily one-sided. A reflective-equilibrium approach combines them. The notion of reflective equilibrium is examined in Chapter 4, which might be called the methodological chapter of this book.

Still on the definition of freedom, I should also say something about so-called 'negative' and 'positive' freedom, since debates about freedom have often been couched in these terms. In this book I shall refer very little to 'negative' and 'positive' freedom, as I think greater conceptual clarity is achieved by seeing both of these kinds of freedom as exemplifying the absence of preventing conditions on agents' possible actions. Although Berlin's famous distinction has some important uses, it is not especially relevant to our present concerns—except in so far as 'positive freedom' means 'self-mastery', understood as the dominance of an 'authentic' self over a merely empirical self. And in this case, in order to avoid confusion, I prefer where possible to use the term 'self-mastery'. Many theorists have taken 'positive freedom' to mean something quite different from self-mastery, namely 'ability' or 'capability' in a much broader sense; and to make matters worse, yet others have called this last meaning of freedom 'negative'. The meaning of 'overall freedom' that I shall eventually arrive at ought in any case to be compatible both with what is most commonly meant by those in the 'negative' camp—the idea of freedom as the absence of constraints imposed by other humans—and with the idea of freedom as ability: some differences between conceptions of freedom are not affected by problems of measurement, and this last difference appears to be one of them. Moreover, although I shall eventually exclude 'self-mastery' from my account of the criteria that are relevant to overall-freedom judgements (Chapter 6), this will not itself imply a lack of interest, on the part of liberals, in self-mastery.

Part II of this book is concerned with what I see as a mistaken account of judgements about degrees of overall freedom, and Part III with my own alternative account. The first I call the 'value-based' account of freedom; the second, the 'empirical' account. The value-based account, which sees degree-of-freedom judgements as normative, in the sense of being inevitably bound up with goods other than freedom, is by far the most popular among those philosophers who have had something to say on the subject. Nevertheless, I shall argue (in Chapter 5) that the value-based view is self-defeating, because it contradicts the reasons set out in Part I for being interested in the first place in assessing people's degrees of freedom. In particular, it contradicts the view, defended earlier on, that freedom is 'non-specifically valuable'. On the 'empirical approach' to measuring freedom—the approach I intend to defend—we maintain a clear distinction between freedom and other goods, so that the extent of a person's freedom is a function of nothing other than the sheer extent of her available action (an idea to be examined and defended at some length in Chapter 7). One of the reasons for the initial attractiveness of the value-based approach seems to be the view that a purely empirical conception of freedom somehow ignores the important senses in which freedom is valuable. I shall reverse this claim, and argue that it is *only* the empirical conception of freedom that entails *respecting* all of the important senses in which freedom is valuable.

There are many other issues to be dealt with along the way. For example, there is the question of whether or how far different kinds of constraints on freedom (physical prevention, coercion, difficulty) are commensurable in terms of overall degrees of unfreedom (Chapter 8). There is also the question of whether the overall freedom of a group or society is something more than the freedom of its individual members combined (Chapter 9). In answering these and other questions, we must continually bear in mind the central concern mentioned above—that is to say, the concern to provide an account of overall freedom which not only fits in with our intuitions about the nature of freedom, but which also lives up, in reflective equilibrium, to the demands made by our ideas about the value of freedom and its just distribution.

My overall aim is to provide a coherent conception of freedom that allows the idea of 'more or less freedom' to play a useful role in a liberal theory of justice—a conception, in other words, which gives meaning to the assertion that people ought to be accorded *a measure of freedom*.

PART I

Justice and Overall Freedom

1

The Concept of Overall Freedom

THERE is an important controversy among liberal political philosophers which has yet to be clarified satisfactorily. This chapter and the next are aimed at providing such a clarification, as well as defending one side against the other. The division turns on the question, does liberty play a fundamental role in liberal thinking? The initial reaction of many liberals—and I count myself among them—is to say 'yes'. How, indeed, could it not be part of the *essence* of liberalism to see freedom as a fundamental, if not *the* fundamental, component in one's system of values? But is this initial thought borne out by a careful, close analysis of the idea of freedom and of the reasons we have for valuing it? There is a recent tendency among liberal theorists to deny this initial thought, and therefore to deny that freedom is a fundamental good for liberals. There is no such thing as 'freedom' *tout court*, they say; there are only specific *freedoms*, like the freedom to speak one's mind on political matters or the freedom to leave the country or the freedom to practise a certain religion. According to these theorists, liberals stand up for specific freedoms, not freedom as such, and each specific freedom needs to be justified by reference to other goods of a more fundamental nature—goods which do not themselves include freedom. Therefore, freedom is not itself a fundamental good for liberals.

Which side one takes in this disagreement depends on whether one is interested only in specific freedoms, or also in *overall* freedom, where one's overall freedom is the amount of freedom one has in either absolute or relative terms, and represents some kind of an aggregation over one's specific freedoms. The theorists mentioned above, who are sceptical about freedom having value 'as such', are interested only in specific freedoms. They endorse what I shall call the *specific-freedom thesis*. By contrast, those whom I shall later dub 'freedom-based liberals' believe that people have a right to (or at least a fundamental interest in having) *a measure of freedom*. They believe that freedom as such *is* a fundamental good for liberals, and that liberals should therefore care about 'how much freedom' people have. They endorse what I shall call the *overall-freedom thesis*. According to the specific-freedom thesis, a person's specific freedoms are all that we need worry about. According to the overall-freedom thesis, a person's overall degree of freedom matters too,

	Free or not free	Free to a degree
With reference to specific freedoms	(*a*)	(*b*)
In an overall sense	(*c*)	(*d*)

Fig. 1

and so the justification of a particular set of specific freedoms must make reference, among other things, to 'how much freedom' those specific freedoms jointly constitute.

These two theses are in need of some unpacking, as they can each take different forms and be defended for different reasons. Before we turn to that task, however, we need to be clearer about the meaning of the terms 'specific freedoms' and 'overall freedom'.

1.1 SPECIFIC FREEDOMS AND OVERALL FREEDOM

There are different ways of attributing freedom to an agent. One way is by saying simply that she is free. Another way is by saying that she is free to a certain degree or, in other words, that she has a certain amount of freedom (in either relative or absolute terms). Moreover, each of these ways of attributing freedom can be taken to refer either to the agent's overall freedom, or to some specific freedom (or freedoms). Thus, a person may be described as 'free' or 'not free', either *tout court* or with reference to the possibility of doing a specific thing (or set of things). And a person may be described as free to a certain degree either in an overall sense, or with reference to the possibility of doing a specific thing (or set of things). In these terms, we can distinguish four ways in which an agent may be said to have freedom (see Fig. 1).

I shall not concern myself further here with the meaning of statements of type (*c*) in Fig. 1. Our political theorizing demands more of us than the ability to say that a person simply is or is not free in an overall sense; we require ourselves not only to be able to distinguish between the presence or absence of the quality 'freedom', but also to be able to distinguish between the different degrees to which it is present. 'Complete freedom' is, as Bertrand Russell says, 'only possible for omnipotence; partial freedom is a matter of degree'.[1] Indeed, when we place them in their linguistic contexts, we can see that

---

[1] B. Russell, 'Freedom and Government', in R. Anshen (ed.), *Freedom: Its Meaning* (London: Allen & Unwin, 1942), 231.

statements of type (c) are in most cases nothing more than vague versions of statements of type (d), or elliptical references to the set of the most important specific freedoms (and therefore reducible to sets of statements of type (a) or type (b)). The latter interpretation has been suggested by Gerald MacCallum.[2] Joel Feinberg sees both interpretations as possible: when a person says he is 'free' *simpliciter*, Feinberg says, he 'may intend to convey that he is on the whole free, or at liberty, to do a great many things, or to do most of the things that are worth doing, or perhaps to do a greater percentage of the worthwhile things than are open to most people'.[3] Later on, in Chapter 8, I shall also argue that we can dispense with statements of type (b), though for now we may classify (a) and (b) together as designating one kind of statement—the kind that refers to a specific freedom or to a set of specific freedoms. For now, then, I shall concern myself solely with the distinction between attributions of the freedom to do a specific thing or set of things (types (a) or (b)) and attributions of degrees of overall freedom (type (d)).

Having eliminated statements of type (c), we may take the expressions 'overall freedom', 'freedom *tout court*', and 'freedom as such' to mean the same thing. This can at least be so for the purpose of the present investigation, where what matters is that none of these three expressions specifies the *actions* that the agent is free, unfree, or more or less free to perform. The only difference is that the expression 'overall' freedom (as opposed to the expressions 'freedom *tout court*' and 'freedom as such') makes clear the fact that when one is talking of an agent's 'freedom', rather than (at least implicitly) of her 'freedom to do x' or her 'freedom to do y', one is referring to some kind of *aggregation* over her specific freedoms.

Two further qualifications are necessary before moving on. First, we should note that the term 'specific freedom' can refer either to the freedom to perform an act-*type* or to the freedom to perform an act-*token*—a point of some importance for Part III of this book. Clearly, a 'specific freedom' can be more or less specific. An example of a specific freedom might be said to be 'freedom of speech'. This *is* an example of a specific freedom (in my terms), inasmuch as it refers to a specific freedom-type, despite the fact that one can also talk of the freedom to speak one's mind on religious matters, or of the freedom to do so on Tuesday mornings, which are clearly progressively more specific freedom-types. I shall leave open the question of how specific a 'specific freedom' is for now, and shall not return to that question until Chapter 7. The important point to bear in mind here is that 'specific freedom', as I am using the term, contrasts with 'overall freedom', and not with 'freedom-type'.

---

[2] G. MacCallum, 'Negative and Positive Freedom', *Philosophical Review*, 76 (1967), s. 4.
[3] J. Feinberg, *Social Philosophy* (Englewood Cliffs, NJ: Prentice-Hall, 1979), 18.

What the terms 'specific freedom' and 'freedom-type' have in common, in contrast to 'overall freedom' (or 'freedom *tout court*' or 'freedom as such'), is the fact that they are used to refer to *specific actions or types of action* which the agent is free to perform.

Secondly, when I talk in an unqualified way of 'the measurement of freedom', I mean to refer to the measurement of *overall* freedom. Looking back at the 'transhistorical discussion' set out at the beginning of this book, we can see that some writers have presupposed comparisons of degrees of freedom of a *specific* kind. For example, we saw John Somerville claim that in the Soviet Union there was more freedom 'from periodic unemployment' than in the West, and we saw Roger Scruton claim that in Britain there was more freedom 'of every kind' than in other countries. However, my central concern in this book is not with questions of degrees of specific freedoms, but with the question of 'how free' people are *tout court*. It is arguable that to take an interest in the former question just *is* to take an interest in the latter question, as I hope will become clear in the next chapter (see in particular s. 2.7). In any case, our present focus is on claims like that of Berlin, who believes the average Swede to be 'a good deal freer' than the average Albanian, or like that of Magee, who sees the American people as 'extraordinarily free', or like that of Hattersley, for whom every citizen has an equal right to 'the greatest amount of freedom'. The *reason* for this focus lies in the view that freedom is 'non-specifically' as well as 'specifically' valuable—a view to be explained and defended in the next chapter.

1.2 DEFINING FREEDOM

To provide a complete definition of freedom is to specify all of the necessary and sufficient conditions for 'having or lacking freedom'. We have now seen, however, that 'having or lacking freedom' is an ambiguous term. It might mean 'having or lacking the freedom to do a specific thing, or set of things', or it might mean 'having more or less freedom overall'. Therefore, 'defining' freedom might be said to involve either of two things. It might be said to involve specifying necessary and sufficient conditions for having or lacking 'the freedom to do specific things', or it might be said to involve specifying necessary and sufficient conditions for having 'more or less' of the quantitative attribute 'freedom'.

Clearly, the importance of the definition of *overall* freedom is that it refers to conditions not necessarily present in the definition of 'a specific freedom' regarding the variables according to which we should measure freedom. It is certainly true that the two kinds of freedom are closely related. For example, if it is said that a necessary condition for having the freedom to do x is that one desires to do x, then it will follow that our 'overall freedom' is affected by the number of desirable things we are unconstrained from doing, and perhaps by the degree of their desirability. However, there clearly remains an *underdetermination* of our definition of 'overall freedom' by our definition of 'a specific freedom'. We may know that a person's overall freedom consists in some kind of aggregation over her particular freedoms, but *the rules of aggregation are not themselves provided by the definition of 'a specific freedom'.* How are we to arrive at a summation of specific freedoms? Can they just be counted, or should they each be weighted in some way? And how are we to compare different kinds of constraints on freedom in terms of the degree to which they restrict overall freedom? It is a symptom of the neglect by political philosophers of questions relating to overall freedom that the debates which have taken place over the last decades on the definition of freedom have focused almost exclusively on the problem of specifying necessary and sufficient conditions for having a specific freedom. Much of my work in the rest of this book, in particular in Parts II and III, will therefore consist in attempting to infer plausible definitions of overall freedom from plausible definitions of specific freedoms, where the latter underdetermine the former.

It would be wrong for me to supply a *precise* definition at this stage either of specific freedoms or of overall freedom. The search for a precise definition is a complex task, and one to which much of this book is devoted: as we shall see more clearly in Chapter 4, we need an account of overall freedom that can play an adequate role in a liberal theory of justice, as well as fulfilling the requirements of coherence and of consistency with our intuitions. Only a broadly defined *concept* of freedom will therefore be assumed at this stage. It is common for theorists of freedom to apply John Rawls's distinction between a 'concept' and its rival 'conceptions' to the case of freedom, and I shall do the same here.[4] In line with the now canonical analysis of Gerald MacCallum, we can say that the concept of freedom is that of the absence of certain preventing conditions on agents' possibile actions.[5] (For convenience, we can say that actions not subject to preventing conditions are 'available', where the latter term is also taken to be synonymous with 'unprevented' or 'unconstrained' or 'unimpeded'. In addition, I shall sometimes refer to available actions as 'options'.) Applying the distinction between a concept and its rival conceptions,

---

[4] Rawls, *A Theory of Justice*, 5. On the application to freedom, see e.g. T. Gray, *Freedom* (London: Macmillan, 1991), ch. 1.

[5] MacCallum, 'Negative and Positive Freedom'. This triadic formula was in a sense anticipated by Felix Oppenheim in *Dimensions of Freedom: An Analysis* (New York: St Martin's Press, 1961). However, Oppenheim did not have in mind a concept of freedom that would cover all possible definitions.

we can say that the various conceptions of the concept of freedom differ in the way they interpret the meaning of the three terms 'agent', 'preventing condition', and 'action'.[6] Must an obstacle render an action physically impossible in order to count as a preventing condition and therefore as a case of unfreedom? Or do threats also count as preventing conditions? Can an agent be unfree because she suffers from 'internal' constraints? Must constraints on freedom be obstacles that are imposed by human beings, or do natural obstacles count too? And what about the relevant actions? Do these actions consist in what the agent desires to do? Or do they also include what the agent does not desire to do? These are some of the questions to which a conception of freedom ought to provide answers.

To be more precise, the triadic relation mentioned above serves to define the concept of a *specific* freedom. The concept of overall freedom can in turn be defined as quantifying over specific freedoms, where the latter are defined at the level of the concept (see s. 1.5, below). The arguments of Part I of this book (in particular, of Chapters 1 to 3) refer to the idea of freedom (in both the specific and the overall sense) only at the more general level of the concept. My hope is that the appeal of those arguments will be fairly broad among liberals. Only later, in Parts II and III of this book, should it become apparent that their acceptance also points to certain particular interpretations of the three elements of MacCallum's formula. Although some of these particular interpretations might appear rather controversial if presented here and now, I believe that they will be much less so in the light of the arguments of the whole of Part I.

I assume the *concept* of a specific freedom, as defined above, to be something on which all liberals, in a broad sense, can agree. Under the umbrella of 'liberalism in the broad sense' I mean to include at least libertarians like Friedrich von Hayek and Robert Nozick and liberal egalitarians like John Rawls and Ronald Dworkin. It is to liberals in this broad sense that the arguments of this book are directed. I need not therefore claim, as MacCallum does, that his triadic formula is all-inclusive as far as rival conceptions of freedom are concerned. In fact, those familiar with MacCallum's analysis will already have noticed that my own definition of the concept is narrower than his, as it refers only to possible actions, and not also, as in his definition, to possible 'becomings'. I make no apology for this restriction of the concept of freedom, the justification of which is simply that my starting point is a *liberal* concept. When liberals talk about freedom, they do not normally refer to possible 'becomings'—only to possible 'doings'. Thus, a number of traditionally

---

[6] A concise overview of the spectrum of possible conceptions is provided in S. Lukes, *Marxism and Morality* (Oxford: Clarendon Press, 1985), 72–5.

non-liberal conceptions of freedom can already be seen as lying outside the scope of our investigation. An example is provided by the Marxist view (on a literal interpretation) that communism offers the possibility of attaining a 'higher' kind of freedom, where man is no longer 'alienated', but becomes a 'species being'.

1.3 INTUITIONS AND COMMON-SENSE COMPARISONS

We have seen that the definition of freedom can be a definition either of 'a specific freedom' or of 'overall freedom'—that it can stipulate either what it is to be free to do a specific thing (or specific type of thing), or what it is to be more or less free overall (i.e. more or less free *tout court*). Now this distinction clearly also applies to our *intuitions* about freedom—that is to say, to our pre-theoretical ideas about what it is to have freedom. When theorists construct a definition of freedom, they generally appeal, among other things, to our linguistic intuitions about freedom. They appeal to the judgements that common sense normally sanctions. They present us with examples, and ask us whether we would 'really want to say' that a certain person in a given example is free to do this or that. A popular example is that of a locked room. A person unintentionally locks you in a room. Some have claimed that only intentionally imposed obstacles restrict freedom. But 'do you really want to say' here that you are 'free' to leave such a room? Would that not be counter-intuitive? Here, an example is being used to appeal to a linguistic intuition about a specific freedom (i.e. the freedom to leave a room), in order to make a general point about the relevance of intention to the existence of constraints on specific freedoms.

As I have said, theorists have tended to concentrate on the definition of a specific freedom, and have thus tended to appeal to intuitions about the presence or absence of specific freedoms. However, this is not to deny that there is also a wealth of examples, both in politics and in everyday life, of expressions of intuitive judgements about 'how free' people are. Most of the empirical claims in the 'transhistorical discussion' presented earlier are based on intuitive judgements of this kind. If we are to construct a definition of overall freedom, we should presumably take these intuitions into account in a similar way.

I shall call our intuitions about degrees of overall freedom our *common-sense comparisons* of freedom. Some of our common-sense comparisons of freedom are purely hypothetical ('you would be much freer if...'), whereas others refer to actual degrees of freedom ('the British are now freer than the Chinese'; 'the average American is less free than the average Swede';

'Nelson Mandela has much more freedom now than he had fifteen years ago'). In these last cases, the comparison arises out of a combination of impressionistic empirical observations (or assumed circumstances of given individuals or groups) and certain linguistic intuitions about the meaning of freedom. In calling these intuitions 'comparisons', I am implying that they are always intuitions about *relative* degrees of overall freedom (either interpersonal or intrapersonal). Absolute assessments of degrees of overall freedom do not, in my view, figure in people's intuitions abut 'how free' they are (although the ability to make them may be presupposed by certain of their *normative* intuitions—their ideas about 'how free' people *ought* to be: for example, where it is felt that 'everyone ought to have at least a minimum degree of freedom'). Only by actually measuring freedom can we conceivably arrive at assessments made in absolute terms, since for these we require a *unit* of measurement, and our pre-theoretical intuitions do not appear themselves to include the notion of such a unit. This is not to say, on the other hand, that absolute measurements of freedom are impossible; only that their possibility depends on our having passed through the stage of *theorizing* about the meaning of overall freedom. I shall have more to say about this in Chapter 4, where we shall take a closer look at the relationship between intuitions, definitions, and measurement.

1.4 THE SPECIFIC-FREEDOM THESIS

Now that we have a reasonably clear idea of the distinction between overall freedom and specific freedoms, we can move on to an examination of the views of those authors who are sceptical about the usefulness or possibility of defining or evaluating or measuring overall freedom. Let us begin by taking a fairly indiscriminate look at some examples of this 'specific-freedom thesis', before attempting to sort them into different categories.

At its most extreme, endorsing the specific-freedom thesis means holding the belief that all talk of 'increasing', 'expanding', 'equalizing', or 'maximizing' freedom in some overall sense is simply nonsense. This appears to be the view of Ronald Dworkin. According to Dworkin, liberty cannot be some sort of 'commodity', as if we could say that one restriction of freedom were more undesirable than another on the grounds 'that in the first case the amount of that commodity taken away . . . is, for some reason, either greater in amount or greater in its import than in the second'. That would be 'bizzare'.[7] For

---

[7] R. Dworkin, 'We Do Not Have a Right to Liberty', in R. L. Cunningham (ed.), *Liberty and the Rule of Law* (College Station: Texas A. & M. University Press, 1979), 172; id., *Taking Rights Seriously* (London: Duckworth, 1977), 270.

liberty is not something which can be taken to be 'even roughly measurable'.[8] Felix Oppenheim is sympathetic to this last point. It might just make sense, Oppenheim says, to claim that in the United States there is more freedom of speech than in the Soviet Union. But what would it mean to say that in the United States there is 'more freedom',[9] or that in Italy 'there is freedom'?[10] The most important reason why such claims do not make sense is, according to Oppenheim, the fact that 'there is no such thing as freedom'.[11] By this he means that there is no such thing as freedom *tout court*, or overall freedom. There are only specific freedoms. This is because 'freedom' is a relational concept: the term expresses a relation between a *specific* agent who is free with respect to another *specific* agent to perform a *specific* action (or at most a relation between specific *kinds* of agent and specific *kinds* of action). To imagine that various specific freedom relations can somehow be combined into overall measures of freedom is to treat liberty like a 'commodity' or a 'substance'. But, as S. I. Benn and R. S. Peters state, 'liberty is not a commodity to be weighed and measured. I am free to do x, y, and z, but not p, q, and r—but there is no substance called "freedom" of which I can therefore possess more or less.'[12]

Dworkin believes that the claim that there is no such thing as overall freedom provides him with ammunition for his polemic against libertarians who assert that there is a general 'right to liberty', as if liberty 'trumped' all other interests *as such*. If there is no such thing as liberty as such, then liberty as such is not something we can have a right to, and so cannot be one of the constitutive ideals of liberalism. Similarly, the specific-freedom thesis undermines the libertarian claim that the policies favoured by egalitarians 'conflict with liberty'. If there is no such thing as liberty as such, then liberty as such is not something with which egalitarian policies can conflict. On the other hand, this is not to say that Dworkin believes we must abandon the cause of liberty altogether. For we are still in his view able to make sense of the term *liberties*. At this point the question becomes 'Which specific liberties?', and is naturally to be answered by reference to those ideals which *are* constitutive

---

[8] R. Dworkin, *A Matter of Principle* (Cambridge, Mass.: Harvard University Press, 1985), 189.

[9] Oppenheim, *Dimensions of Freedom*, ch. 8, s. III c; cf. id., *Political Concepts: A Reconstruction* (Oxford: Blackwell, 1981).

[10] Oppenheim, 'Si può misurare la libertà complessiva? Nota critica agli scritti di Ian Carter', *Quaderni di Scienza Politica*, 2 (1995), 456.

[11] Ibid. 461; cf. id., 'Social Freedom and its Parameters', *Journal of Theoretical Politics*, 7 (1995); id., *Dimensions of Freedom*, 127.

[12] S. I. Benn and R. S. Peters, *Social Principles and the Democratic State* (London: Allen & Unwin, 1959), 214. Cf. J. B. S. Haldane, 'A Comparative Study of Freedom', in Anshen (ed.), *Freedom*, 94; N. Bobbio, *Left and Right: The Significance of a Political Distinction*, trans. A. Cameron (Chicago: Chicago University Press, 1996), 76.

of liberalism and which for Dworkin consist in treating people with equal concern and respect. While there is no sense in talking about individuals as having more or less freedom *as such*, then, liberals should also recognize that this is no cause for concern. For an interest in freedom as such is superfluous to the pursuit of the ideals of liberalism. We should simply concentrate on giving people the right 'liberties'.

Will Kymlicka agrees with Dworkin that freedom as such is not one of the foundational values of liberalism. Again, the emphasis is on giving individuals the freedom to do certain specific things, which, given that we cannot appeal to freedom as such, we must seek to justify by reference to values other than freedom: 'We don't answer [the] question [of how valuable specific liberties are] by determining which liberties contain more or less of a single commodity called "freedom". . . . For the reason it is important to be free in a particular situation is not the amount of freedom it provides, but the importance of the various interests it serves. . . . The idea of freedom as such, and lesser or greater amounts of it, does no work in political argument.'[13]

And the same idea appears also to be present in the work of the later Rawls. Despite Rawls's initial arguments in favour of 'the most extensive liberty', and the rule that 'liberty can be restricted only for the sake of liberty',[14] he has since claimed only to have been interested in defending a list of specific liberties—those which he has all along called the 'basic' liberties. 'No priority is assigned to liberty as such, as if something called "liberty" has a pre-eminent value and is the main if not the sole end of political and social justice.'[15] This revision (or clarification) appears to have come largely in response to H. L. A. Hart's claim that measuring freedom in order to assess which hypothetical set of liberties is the 'most extensive' will rarely be possible, and that where it is possible, the 'extent' of liberty will not be what matters.[16] A similar stance has been taken by other liberals who have faced up to this problem of measurement. For example, according to Onora O'Neill, not only is it true that 'liberty has no metric'; it is also fortunately the case that 'obligations of justice . . . can be constructed without assuming a metric . . . for liberty'.[17] And in the

[13] W. Kymlicka, *Contemporary Political Philosophy* (Oxford: Oxford University Press, 1990), 145–51.

[14] Rawls, *A Theory of Justice*, 302.

[15] J. Rawls, *Political Liberalism* (New York: Columbia University Press, 1993), 191–2.

[16] H. L. A. Hart, 'Rawls on Liberty and its Priority', in N. Daniels (ed.), *Reading Rawls* (Oxford: Blackwell, 1975). For a more detailed sceptical argument, see O. O'Neill, 'The Most Extensive Liberty', *Proceedings of the Aristotelian Society*, 80 (1980).

[17] O. O'Neill, *Constructions of Reason: Explorations of Kant's Practical Philosophy* (Cambridge: Cambridge University Press, 1989), 214–15. Cf. id., *Towards Justice and Virtue: A Constructivist Account of Practical Reasoning* (Cambridge: Cambridge University Press, 1996), 161–2, 171.

view of Peter de Marneffe, 'the idea of constitutional democracy that has been central to the liberal tradition . . . recognizes no general right to liberty; rather it recognizes rights to specific basic liberties'.[18]

Let us now try to unpack the specific-freedom thesis, by separating out some of the lines of thought mentioned above. On closer inspection, we can see that there are three different ways in which one can express scepticism about the notion of overall freedom. These are represented by the following three claims.

1. There is no such thing as overall freedom.
2. Overall freedom cannot be measured.
3. There is no point in measuring overall freedom.

It will be useful to provide names for each of these versions of the specific-freedom thesis. Let us say, then, that the first claim represents the *ontological* version of that thesis, the second claim its *epistemic* version, and the third claim its *normative* version. Correspondingly, we can call the *denial* of (1), (2), and (3), respectively, the ontological version, the epistemic version, and the normative version of the *overall*-freedom thesis. The ontological version of the specific-freedom thesis says that specific freedoms are the only things that count because specific freedoms are the only things that there are; the epistemic version says that while there may be such a thing as overall freedom, we cannot know very much about it (given insuperable problems of measurement); and the normative version says that even if there is such a thing as overall freedom, and even if we can know how free people are overall, this is of no great importance, given our aims and values. To assert the overall-freedom thesis is to deny one or more of these claims.

The authors cited above do not usually explicitly recognize the distinction between the three versions of the specific-freedom thesis. Dworkin certainly has in mind both the epistemic (or ontological?) version *and* the normative version when he says that talk of overall freedom cannot make sense, and that freedom as such is not a fundamental value for liberals. Clearly, however, it is one thing to say that liberal values do or do not presuppose a commitment to making sense of claims about 'how free' people are, and another to say that those claims can or cannot be made sense of (either existentially, or because of problems of measurement).

The distinction which gets blurred most easily is that between the ontological and epistemic versions of the specific-freedom thesis. If we look more closely at defences of the epistemic version of the specific-freedom thesis, we

---

[18] P. de Marneffe, 'Liberalism, Liberty, and Neutrality', *Philosophy and Public Affairs*, 19 (1990), 273–4.

can see that these can in fact be based on two kinds of reason: the practical kind and the conceptual kind. Practical reasons, such as the difficulty of gathering the necessary information, are not the main concern of this book. My main concern is with conceptual reasons, like the problems involved in the very idea of combining different kinds of freedom or different kinds of constraints. And it is exactly these reasons which appear to blur the distinction between (1) and (2). Often, the conceptual problems of measurement referred to in (2) can be very radical. For example, it might be said that there is something mistaken about the very idea of 'counting' the options open to a person —that to do so is theoretically impossible—and that as a result the idea of overall freedom is meaningless. Or again, such a notion might be said to be problematic because there are so many different ways of constraining freedom (e.g. by preventing, obstructing, threatening, or punishing) which do not appear to be combinable into overall judgements. Saying this much seems tantamount to saying that there is 'no such thing' as overall freedom.

However, we can see the sense in which claims (1) and (2) are nevertheless distinct when we notice that a number of authors in the 'specific-freedom' camp have said that overall freedom cannot be measured except in exceptional circumstances. Some have suggested, for example, that given the problem of combining different kinds of freedom, or of 'counting' options, we can only say for sure that agent A is freer than agent B if the set of actions available to B is a subset of the set of actions available to A.[19] This is to give a conceptual reason for saying that we are very rarely able to say who is freer than whom, but it is not to deny that there is such a thing as overall freedom. On the contrary, the suggestion depends for its intelligibility on our *having* certain degrees of overall freedom. The suggestion is that degrees of overall freedom are 'out there', but that we cannot do much to compare them. After all, once it is agreed that A can be judged freer than B where the above-mentioned 'subset rule' applies, it can hardly be denied that A and B have a certain degree of overall freedom even where that rule does not apply. The most that can be said is that A's and B's degrees of freedom are incomparable. Acceptance or rejection of the 'subset rule' appears indeed to be a good test of one's view of the ontological version of the specific-freedom thesis. Those who are sceptical about the possibility of measuring freedom but who accept the subset rule can be said to endorse the specific-freedom thesis in its epistemic but not in its ontological form.

---

[19] Cf. M. Taylor, *Community, Anarchy and Liberty* (London: Cambridge University Press, 1982), 151–2; M. J. Gorr, *Coercion, Freedom and Exploitation* (New York: Peter Lang, 1989), 97–8; R. J. Arneson, 'Freedom and Desire', *Canadian Journal of Philosophy*, 3 (1985). Depending on our account of what it is to perform 'the same action', it may be that this 'subset rule' only allows for intrapersonal comparisons of freedom.

It seems to me that the best way of tackling these different versions of the specific-freedom thesis is by taking them on in the order (1), (3), (2)—that is, by first taking on the ontological version, then the normative version, and finally the epistemic version. Clearly we should deal with the ontological version before the normative version, because there will be no point in arguing about whether liberals are committed to ensuring that people have a measure of overall freedom (maximal freedom, equal freedom, or whatever) if there is in any case no such thing as overall freedom. On the other hand, it seems reasonable to argue against the normative version before tackling problems of measurement, as the former task will justify our interest in the latter.

The theorist who has provided the most serious defence of the ontological version of the specific-freedom thesis is Oppenheim, and his position will be dealt with in the remainder of this chapter. This should help in providing further clarification of the concept of overall freedom—in particular, of how that concept can be defined in terms of the concept of a specific freedom. The normative version, which I shall turn to in the next chapter, is what I take to be the most important of the objections raised by Dworkin and Kymlicka. The normative specific-freedom thesis assumes a certain view of the *value* of freedom, and concludes from this that we are not committed to knowing how free people are in an overall sense. If I am successful in refuting this view, the sceptic may as a result retreat to the epistemic version of the specific-freedom thesis. But it is only later (above all, in Part III of this book) that I shall turn to the issues raised by a possible retreat of that kind.

To recapitulate, then, this book defends the overall-freedom thesis from an ontological point of view (in the remainder of this chapter), from a normative point of view (for the most part, in Chapter 2) and from an epistemic point of view (above all, in Part III).

1.5 IS THERE SUCH A THING AS OVERALL FREEDOM?

A collection of papers by Heidegger was published in English under the title *The Question of Being*. When a philosopher asked for a copy at a shop, the shop girl said, 'The question of being what?' Ryle on being told of this incident said, 'That girl should be found and given a Ph.D'.[20]

The reaction of the shop girl in this story reminds one of Oppenheim's reaction to statements referring explicitly or implicitly to overall freedom. If someone declares that they have 'freedom', Oppenheim will ask, 'Freedom to do what?', and 'Freedom with respect to whom?' 'Freedom', on its own,

---

[20] W. Charlton, *The Analytic Ambition* (Oxford: Blackwell, 1991), 56.

does not refer to anything. In this connection, Oppenheim has explicitly con-trasted my account of freedom as a quantitative attribute with his own account of freedom as a triadic *relation*: agent R is, with respect to agent P, free or unfree to do *x*. On this point Oppenheim appears to have an ally in Kristján Kristjánsson, who agrees that 'freedom is a *relation* and not a *property*': 'freedom is not something that one happens to possess or stumble across like a chest of gold, it is a relation between agents.'[21]

For present purposes we can follow Oppenheim in stipulating that R is free with respect to P to do *x* if P does not impose preventing conditions on R's doing *x*, and R is unfree with respect to P to do *x* if P does impose pre-venting conditions on R's doing *x*. Notice that we here assume that the only 'preventing conditions' relevant to an agent's freedom and unfreedom are those imposed by other agents. For Oppenheim, moreover, these preventing con-ditions are restricted to 'impossibility' and 'punishability'. But nothing turns on the validity of this interpretation of the relevant preventing conditions as far as the present argument is concerned. In broader terms, freedom might be conceived of as consisting in a relation between an agent and any number of other preventing conditions, including those that are of natural origin rather than brought about by other agents (although, as Oppenheim and Kristjánsson would be quick to point out, we would then no longer be dealing with the concept of 'social freedom' but, rather, with what Oppenheim calls 'freedom of action'). In other words, we could if we wanted simply remove agent P from Oppenheim's triadic formula and refer instead to 'preventing conditions' in the widest sense, thus bringing us closer to MacCallum's formula (see s. 1.2). While the argument that follows could be adapted to fit this inter-pretation, for simplicity's sake I shall here adopt Oppenheim's formula, and shall refer to the presence of a preventing condition by saying that 'P prevents R from doing *x*'.

We have seen that according to Oppenheim, the most important reason for seeing attributions of degrees of freedom *tout court* as fruitless is that there is 'no such thing as freedom': because the word 'freedom' describes a rela-tion between agents, it should not be taken to refer to a *thing*. There is not 'something' in the world called freedom, and to say that there is would be to commit 'the fallacy of reification',[22] where to commit such a fallacy is to be 'misled by verbal form into thinking simply because some noun has a use, there must be something to which it refers'.[23] What Oppenheim seems to have

---

[21] K. Kristjánsson, *Social Freedom: The Responsibility View* (Cambridge: Cambridge University Press, 1996), 11, emphasis in original.

[22] Oppenheim, 'Si può misurare la libertà complessiva?', 456.

[23] S. Blackburn, *The Oxford Dictionary of Philosophy* (Oxford: Oxford University Press, 1994), 325.

in mind here is that my account of overall freedom as a quantitative attribute goes against ontological parsimony—that such a view of freedom implies what Quine would call an 'overpopulated universe'.[24] Calling freedom a 'thing' of which there is more or less is, to put it bluntly, seeing things.

It is not clear whether Ryle would have awarded Oppenheim a Ph.D. for this observation, or whether he would instead have seen the predicate 'is very free' as sufficiently precise to be meaningful. (Perhaps even 'is free' would for Ryle have qualified as meaningful, despite its meaning being extremely vague, as we saw in s. 1.1. After all, it is still a more precise predicate than just 'is'.) In any case, Oppenheim's point of view does seem to have its roots in a respectable ontological theory, even if today such a theory is less fashionable than it once was. I have in mind the theory of logical atomism, according to which, in A. J. Ayer's words, 'the world consists of simple particulars, which have only simple qualities, in the sense that any complex qualities which they may have are analysable into simple ones, and which stand in simple relations to one another'.[25] Even though Oppenheim has not explicitly embraced this theory, something like it surely lies behind his objection to the idea of overall freedom:[26] freedom is not a particular; neither is it a property (a point on which, as we have seen, Kristjánsson agrees); instead, it is a *simple relation*—a triadic relation of which the elements are two specific agents and a specific action.

Now I do not think that anyone would want to say that freedom is a 'thing', if by a 'thing' we mean a 'particular' in the sense in which that word is used above. In this respect, 'freedom' is obviously not like 'atom' or 'quark' or 'butter' or 'banana'. Having accepted this straightforward point, however, it does not seem to me to be a mistake to call freedom a 'thing' that we can 'possess' *in virtue of its being a quantitative attribute* (or property, or quality—I use these three terms interchangeably). Nor indeed does this position seem to me to be incompatible with the view of freedom as a *relational* concept. Let us first take a look at the distinction between a relation and an attribute (or property or quality), and then move on to the idea of freedom as a 'thing'.

Kristjánsson partly justifies his claim that 'being free' is a relation and not a property by means of an analogy with 'being tall': 'Although "I am free" may look like "I am alive"', he says, 'it is surely more akin to "I am tall"—and since Frege we have a clear sense of relational predicates which Plato,

---

[24] W. V. O. Quine, *From a Logical Point of View* (Cambridge, Mass.: Harvard University Press, 1953), 4. Quine is of course referring not to 'overall freedom', but to 'possible entities'.
[25] A. J. Ayer, *Russell and Moore: The Analytical Heritage* (London: Macmillan, 1971), 54. Cf. B. Russell, *Logic and Knowledge* (London: Routledge, 1988), esp. 189–207.
[26] I should emphasize that this is only *my* view of what lies behind Oppenheim's position, and that Oppenheim might still be consistent in disagreeing with such a view.

for instance, lacked when he tried to understand tallness as a property.'[27] What Kristjánsson overlooks in drawing this analogy is the fact that tallness (unlike freedom) *presupposes* the existence of a certain property—in this case, vertical extension—and involves the comparison of two or more instances of that property. 'Is tall' is therefore a relational predicate in a way that 'is free' is not, for the former refers to a relation between two or more instances of a certain quantitative attribute found in two or more individuals. We should be careful not to confuse the two sense of 'relational' that are at work when we say that freedom on the one hand, and tallness on the other, are relational concepts. Let us clarify these two senses of 'relational' by saying that tallness expresses a *comparative* relation. (An exception occurs in expressions like 'how tall are you?' But here even Kristjánsson would not call tallness a relational concept.)

What I want to suggest is that 'being free', or 'being free to do x' can be described as a property in the same way as 'having vertical extension' can be so described. It is true that 'being tall', inasmuch as it means 'being taller than Smith' (or 'being taller than average'), refers to a relation. However, the relation in question is a comparative one: it is a relation between two instances of vertical extension. The correct analogy, then, is not between 'being tall' and 'being free', but between 'being tall' and 'being freer than Jones' (or 'being freer than average'), for here we are dealing with two *comparative* relational concepts. My aim is not to question the idea that concepts (like that of tallness) which at least implicitly presuppose interpersonal comparisons of certain properties (like that of vertical extension) are expressions of relations. Rather, my concern is with the prior question of the existence of the properties to be compared. My claim is that social freedom is such a property. It is true that social freedom is also a (non-comparative) relational concept in a way that vertical extension is not, inasmuch as one's social freedom is a function of what other people prevent one from doing. This is the sense in which Kristjánsson rightly sees 'is free' as relational. It is my view, however, that on the basis of this (non-comparative) relation we can also talk of freedom as a property, and that this property 'freedom' is something that we can then go on to compare interpersonally by talking about people as 'more or less free', in the same way as we compare vertical extension interpersonally when we talk about people as 'more or less tall'.

To see how social freedom can be considered a property of a person, consider first a more straightforward relation: that of fatherhood. The concept of fatherhood, like that of freedom, expresses a relation, though a diadic rather than a triadic one: A is the father of B. However, on the basis of there being

---

[27] Kristjánsson, *Social Freedom*, 11.

such a relation between A and B, it also makes sense to say that 'fatherhood' is a property of A. (This kind of property is sometimes called 'extrinsic'.) Notice, moreover, that we do not need to say that A is the father of a *specific* person in order to say meaningfully that A has the property of being a father. When we say 'A is a father', without even an implicit reference to A's off-spring, then there is generally an implicit understanding that we are making use of the existential quantifier in reference to 'B' in the diadic relation of fatherhood: 'A is a father' is true, we implicitly assume, if A is male and has procreated '*some* person' (or '*at least one* person'), B. Thus, the statement 'A is a father' is not in itself in need of any further specification in order to be meaningful. If I announce, 'Yesterday I became a father', it is not appropriate to answer, 'The father of whom?' It might be thought polite to ask me for further information about my new offspring, but such a request would not be seen as having been provoked by an inadequacy in my original announcement, such that I have 'failed' to specify of whom I am the father; what my announcement refers to is not a relation I have with some specific person (even if it implies the existence of such a relation) but, rather, a newly acquired attribute of mine. (There *would* be an inadequacy in my announcement if I had instead said, 'I am *the* father', and it was not clear from the context to whom I was referring.)

The relational concept of freedom is less straightforward than that of fatherhood, because it expresses a triadic rather than a diadic relation: R is, with respect to P, free to do x. But the way in which we can arrive at the idea of freedom as an attribute (on the basis of this relation) is the same as in the case of fatherhood: what we need to do is to quantify over one or more of the elements of the relation.

First, by quantifying over 'P' in the triadic freedom relation, we arrive at the idea of *a specific freedom of a specific agent*—that is, the freedom of R to do x. It is perfectly comprehensible to attribute to an agent the freedom or unfreedom to do x without specifying *who* leaves the agent free to do x or renders her unfree to do x. As in the case of B in the relation of father-hood, the element P in the definition of 'unfreedom to do x' gets interpreted here as referring to '*some* person', or '*at least one* person' (i.e. we use the existential quantifier). Similarly, in the definition of 'freedom to do x', we interpret 'P' as meaning 'every other agent'. (Here, we use the universal quantifier.) In this way, we can say simply that 'R is free to do x' or that 'R is unfree to do x': she is *free* to do it if *every* other agent *refrains* from preventing her from doing it, and she is *un*free to do it if *some* other agent *prevents* her from doing it.

From here we can move on to the case of *overall* freedom—to the case, not of R's freedom to do x, but of R's freedom *tout court*. 'R is free to do x'

expresses a relation between R and x, but, as we have seen, also expresses an attribute which R has in virtue of a complex relation between R and all other Ps. (I say 'complex' relation to distinguish that relation from the 'simple' relation between R and a specific P, but nothing turns here on my use of the terms 'complex' and 'simple'.) The difference between the attribution of the freedom to do x and the attribution of overall freedom lies in the fact that in this second case we also use the universal quantifier in referring to x. We can indeed say that specific freedoms are the more simple attributes in terms of which the more complex quantitative attribute 'overall freedom' is analysable. Overall freedom can be defined in terms of specific freedoms in the following way: R is free overall *to the extent that* R has *all* of the specific freedoms that R can conceivably have. The use, here, of the expression 'to the extent that' makes explicit the sense in which overall freedom is a *quantitative* attribute. Admittedly, it is not yet obvious how we are to understand the expression 'all of the specific freedoms that R can conceivably have'. But the above definition of overall freedom will serve our purposes for now, until I come to refine it in Chapter 7. Given this definition, an agent's overall freedom can be expressed as a *fraction*, which represents the proportion of conceivable actions which the agent is not prevented (by *any* other agent) from performing.[28] (Notice that nothing I have said here implies that it is ever possible, even logically speaking, for a person to be free with respect to everybody to do anything—i.e. for her overall freedom to be 1/1, or 'complete', as was literally implied by statements of type (*c*) in Fig. 1 in s. 1.1.)

In order further to clarify the notion of overall freedom, let us return to our comparison between the concepts of freedom and of fatherhood. We have seen that, like the concept of fatherhood, the concept of freedom expresses a relation, although a triadic rather than a diadic one. We have also seen that freedom, like fatherhood, can be a property. An important difference arising from the fact that fatherhood expresses a merely diadic relation is that, in contrast to the concept of freedom, fatherhood is not a *quantitative* attribute. We do not say that a person is 'more father' than another on the grounds that he has more offspring, just as we do not say that a person is 'more unfree' than another because she is unfree with respect to a greater number of other agents. What is lacking in the concept of fatherhood is the third element, the element x in the freedom relation, over which we quantify, in the case of the freedom relation, in order to make judgements about agents' degrees of *overall* freedom. It may of course be suggested that such quantification is impossible, or extremely difficult, or leads to counter-intuitive results. But this suggestion

---

[28] The idea that overall freedom should be expressed in terms of a fraction was first put forward by Hillel Steiner. See s. 7.1.

moves the goalposts: we shall no longer be talking about the ontological version of the specific-freedom thesis, but about its epistemic version. Such objections may therefore be legitimately put aside until later in this book. For now, the relevant point is that it makes sense to derive the idea of freedom as a quantitative attribute from the idea of freedom as a specific relation, and therefore that if specific-freedom relations are 'out there', then so too is over-all freedom. Given this point, it is not clear to me why there should be any incoherence in the idea that freedom is both a relation and an attribute, or why the idea of overall freedom as a quantitative attribute need be seen as mysterious or somehow 'metaphysical', whatever our disagreements over how to aggregate over specific freedoms in order to make sense of that idea.

We now come, thirdly and finally, to claims like 'There is freedom in Italy.' According to Oppenheim, claims like this ought to be dispensed with, because they refer to a 'thing' that is not really there. But are such claims necessarily so mysterious? Once it has been conceded that freedom is a quant-itative attribute of agents, there is surely nothing inappropriate in simply refer-ring to its presence in certain parts of the world. Consider another analogy. If I say that there is more red in today's sunset than in yesterday's, I am unlikely to be interpreted as having asserted the presence of some *substance* that is supposedly contained in greater measure in today's sunset than in yesterday's. Neither is it likely that my claim will be seen as having no referent at all. Instead, I am likely to be understood to have meant that a greater proportion of the sky is red this evening than yesterday evening, and in this sense to have referred to the existence of a greater quantity of the quantitative attrib-ute 'red' in today's sunset than in yesterday's.

The statement 'there is (more or less) freedom' refers in exactly the same way as does the statement 'there is (more or less) red'. In the case of freedom, we can make sense of this assertion by interpreting it as quantifying over *all three* elements of the freedom relation—as quantifying not only over 'P' and x, but also over 'R'. Of course, the claim that 'there is freedom in Italy' either does not say very much or is very vague. Interpreted as a precise but banal proposition, it means that in Italy there is 'some person' (or 'at least one person') who has the property of being free to do at least one thing. Inter-preted as a vague but more interesting proposition, it probably means that Italy is such that all or most or a large number of its inhabitants or citizens have a degree of freedom that is not particularly low or is around average. But this banality or vagueness does not imply that the proposition has no referent, and it might be avoided by specifying degrees of freedom more accurately, if that indeed turns out to be possible.

The logical atomist might still object that claims like 'There is more red in today's sunset', or 'There is more freedom in Italy', are inappropriate ontologically speaking, and that to make them is to fail to distinguish clearly between particulars, properties, and relations. For my part, I am making the fairly standard assumption that, when it comes to analysing concepts, one legitimate court of appeal is our ordinary language and the habits, rules, and conventions which govern its use.[29] This court of appeal clearly overrules the above objection: according to our linguistic habits, rules, and conventions, simple particulars are not the only 'things' in the world. I should add that another court of appeal, at least for social and political philosophers, consists in the social and political purposes for which the concepts that we analyse are used. As Oppenheim himself says, our definitions of concepts 'cannot be either true or false, but only more or less fruitful—fruitful, here, in the context of social and moral philosophy'.[30] It seems to me that the idea of overall freedom as a quantitative attribute can indeed be fruitful in this sense, given that a fundamental normative premiss for many liberal philosophers is that freedom is valuable *as such* or what I call 'non-specifically' valuable. Our next task will be the examination of that normative premiss.

[29] Cf. P. Strawson, *Logico-linguistic Papers* (London: Methuen, 1971), 9; J. L. Austin, *Philosophical Papers* (Oxford: Oxford University Press, 1979), 182–7.
[30] Oppenheim, 'Si può misurare la libertà complessiva?', 445.

2

The Value of Freedom

Now that we know there to be such a thing as overall freedom, we can ask whether this matters to us and, if so, why. The central question of this chapter, then, is whether liberals should be content with a list of specific liberties, or whether they should also take an interest in 'how free' people are in an overall sense. I shall argue for the latter position. In other words, I shall put forward a liberal case for what I have called 'the normative version of the overall-freedom thesis'.

As should already be clear, there is a logical relation between our degree of interest in the concept of overall freedom and the reasons we give for *valuing* freedom: some reasons for seeing freedom as valuable imply an interest in its overall quantifiability, while others do not. Those that do can be categorized as reasons for seeing freedom as valuable as such, or what I shall call *non-specifically* valuable. Thus, the main purpose of this chapter is to analyse and justify the claim that freedom is non-specifically valuable. If and only if freedom is non-specifically valuable, people have a right to (or at least an interest in having) a measure of overall freedom, and the normative version of the specific-freedom thesis is mistaken.

In the course of this chapter, we shall see how our political discourse and theorizing place *demands* on us regarding the quantification of the attribute 'freedom'. These may be said to be demands for greater or lesser *powers of measurement*. I say 'greater or lesser' powers, because the answer to the question of whether freedom *is* measurable is not likely to be a straightforward 'yes' or 'no'. Powers of measurement admit of degrees, and different principles of distributive justice require different powers of measurement. The nature of these required powers will be one of the main concerns of Chapter 3. For now, my aim is simply to demonstrate that liberals have an interest in being able to measure people's overall freedom, in at least the weakest sense of 'measurement'. I aim to show that the impossibility of measuring overall freedom, in at least the weakest sense of 'measurement', would imply a cost for liberalism which, other things being equal, liberals would be better off not paying.

2.1 THE IDEA OF NON-SPECIFIC VALUE

That the love of liberty can be something more than just the love of being free to do certain specific things is initially best made clear by means of an extreme example: think of how a prisoner feels on suddenly being released, or of the sentiment of a people on overthrowing an oppressor. Isaiah Berlin employs this example in an argument directed against MacCallum's explication of freedom as a triadic relation. MacCallum sees any claim about freedom as referring at least implicitly to three elements: an agent, X, who is free from constraints, Y, to do or be a certain thing, Z (see s. 1.2). But, says Berlin, it is quite conceivable for an individual or a people to strive to be free of their oppressor —to desire to be rid of their chains—without aiming towards any particular Z.[1] Berlin has certainly hit on something here. However, I think he is wrong to see this example as creating a problem for MacCallum's explication of freedom. In support of Berlin, John Gray has suggested that 'if a man may wish to be rid of his chains, without having in mind any ulterior end apart from the freedom he gains in attaining this, it seems that freedom must be regarded as basically a dyadic rather than as a triadic concept'.[2] I hold the antecedent in this suggestion to be true, but I reject the consequent, according to which we must abandon the idea of freedom as a triadic relation. I agree with MacCallum and Oppenheim that it does not make sense to talk of an agent (X) being free from constraints (Y) without at least implicit reference to the things (Z) that the agent is free to do or be. However, I believe that there is an alternative way of capturing Berlin's insight without abandoning MacCallum's triadic formula, namely, by interpreting the 'Z' in MacCallum's formula as *non-specific* in nature. The oppressed people in Berlin's example do care about the fact that once they are rid of their chains there will be many new things that they are free to do; the point is that their minds are not focused on any of those things in particular. They value 'being free to do things' in a general, rather than in any specific sense. If they did not value the freedom to do things in at least this general sense, then it would indeed be difficult to explain their dislike for their chains.

In this chapter I intend to show that liberals have good reasons for valuing freedom in exactly this non-specific way. Such reasons identify a quantitative attribute whose measurement depends on our being able to quantify over Zs in the way outlined in the previous chapter (s. 1.5). They are reasons, that is, for wanting to be able to measure overall freedom.

[1] Berlin, *Four Essays on Liberty*, p. xliii.
[2] J. Gray, *Liberalisms* (London: Routledge, 1989), 49.

I should point out that there are in fact two ways of arguing for the importance of being able to measure overall freedom. One way is by showing freedom to be non-specifically valuable. Another consists in demonstrating the usefulness of degree-of-freedom assessments for *social science*—the importance, in *explaining* events, of being able to make correlations between degrees of freedom and degrees, say, of political stability. In this second case, a neutral attitude is taken towards the value of freedom, but overall freedom is still seen as a useful indicator for political science. This is the sort of reply to Dworkin and Kymlicka that one might have expected from Oppenheim: given his interest in neutral political science, one might have expected Oppenheim to take a prima facie interest in overall freedom as one among many potential explanatory phenomena, were this not precluded by his belief that such a phenomenon does not exist. I shall not concern myself here with this second kind of interest in measuring freedom. My aim, rather, is to oppose the normative version of the specific-freedom thesis with a similarly normative argument.

In this normative argument I shall try to show that one of the interests served by the presence of specific freedoms is an interest people have in freedom itself. Thus, while Rawls claims that throughout the history of democratic thought 'the focus has been on achieving certain specific liberties',[3] my point is that this focus has been motivated by, among other things, an interest in freedom *as such*. Again, while Kymlicka states that the value of any set of specific freedoms should be assessed by reference to the various interests it serves, my point is that freedom is *itself* one of our interests. If freedom is itself one of our interests, then when we ask how much a specific set of freedoms contributes to the fulfilment of our interests, *one* of the things we must be asking is *how much that specific set of freedoms contributes to our freedom*. And once we ask this last question, we are assuming an interest in freedom as something of which we can have more or less.

The difference between my view and that of Dworkin and Kymlicka, then, is that their view entails denying that our freedoms have value *independently of the value we attach to the specific things they leave us free to do*. Hence my use of the term 'non-specific value'.[4] The 'non-specific value' of a freedom

---

[3] Rawls, *Political Liberalism*, 292.

[4] In previous work, I have used a different term to refer to non-specific value, namely, 'independent value'. See my two articles 'The Independent Value of Freedom', *Ethics*, 105 (1995), and 'The Concept of Freedom in the Work of Amartya Sen: An Alternative Analysis Consistent with Freedom's Independent Value', *Notizie di Politeia*, 43–4 (1996). While continuing to believe that the term 'independent value' captures much of what I have in mind, I now prefer the term 'non-specific value'. As well as making the contrast with the specific-freedom thesis much clearer, this helps to avoid the confusion of 'independent value' with 'intrinsic value'. Another reason for this preference lies in the tendency of some to interpret 'independent value' as meaning 'objective value'. I remain agnostic here over whether freedom has objective value.

or set of freedoms is its value in terms of the good 'freedom'. If freedom is 'non-specifically valuable', then we attach value to our freedom not only because of the specific things it allows us to do, but also because of the mere fact of our having freedom. To say that freedom is non-specifically valuable is to say that it is valuable 'as such'.

We may define the non-specific value of a phenomenon (or the value that that phenomenon has 'as such') in the following way:

> A phenomenon, x, has non-specific value (is valuable as such) iff the value of x cannot be described wholly in terms of a good brought about or contributed to by a specific instance of x or set of specific instances of x.

Perhaps the idea of non-specific value will become clearer if we try applying the above definition to the substance 'gold'. Is gold valuable only in the form of a gold ring or a gold watch or a gold bracelet (certain specific 'instances' of gold)? The answer is clearly 'no'. Gold is also valuable independently of the particular form it takes. We might value having a gold ring more than having a gold nugget, even if the former constitutes a smaller quantity of gold than the latter, but this is not to deny that we also take an interest in 'how much gold' we have. It is not to deny that we take an interest in gold 'as such'. As a matter of fact, we do take such an interest; we do see gold as non-specifically valuable. Similarly, to say that the attribute 'freedom' is non-specifically valuable is to say that its value cannot be described wholly in terms of the valuable phenomena other than freedom which are brought about by or partly constituted by certain specific freedoms, such as the freedom to leave one's country or the freedom to practise Catholicism or the freedom to drive one's car faster than 100 miles per hour.

Dworkin and Kymlicka do not think that freedom has non-specific value. Indeed, they would no doubt say that the analogy I have just drawn with gold is typical of the oversimplistic, 'single commodity' view of freedom that I hold (although this of course caricatures my own position; liberty is only a 'commodity' in the sense—if there is one—in which beauty or well-being are commodities). For Dworkin and Kymlicka, the only kind of value that freedom has is what we may call *specific* value. This means that, in their view, the value, for example, of my being free to play basketball on Tuesday, football on Wednesday, and cricket on Thursday is simply a function of the value of my playing basketball on Tuesday, football on Wednesday, and cricket on Thursday. 'How free' these three specific freedoms make me in comparison with some other set of specific freedoms is a question which, even if intelligible, is of no normative import.

In the course of this chapter I shall distinguish between four different kinds of non-specific value. These I shall call 'unconditional value', 'intrinsic value', 'non-specific instrumental value', and 'non-specific constitutive value', where the last two are species of instrumental value and constitutive value respectively. It is important to make these distinctions, because the normative version of the specific-freedom thesis often rests on a confusion of one of these kinds of value with another when attributed to freedom. Definitions of these different kinds of value will be supplied along the way, and will be collected together to provide an overview at the end of this chapter (in ss. 2.9 and 2.10). At this point, only a few preliminary words of explanation are necessary.

First, it should be pointed out that, despite first appearances, to say that freedom is non-specifically valuable is not necessarily to say that freedom is *intrinsically* valuable. The non-specific value of freedom might be intrinsic or, say, instrumental value, depending on one's normative point of view. The difference between freedom being instrumentally valuable and it being intrinsically valuable lies, rather, in the *ultimate reducibility or irreducibility* of freedom to some other good. If freedom is merely instrumentally valuable, its value may at least in theory be reduced to that of another phenomenon—the end to which it is a means (say, for example, happiness). If freedom is intrinsically valuable, on the other hand, its value cannot conceivably be 'reduced away' in this sense, because freedom is an end in itself. That freedom is intrinsically valuable is what we may take people to mean implicitly when they refer to freedom as itself 'a value', rather than as simply 'valuable', or 'a good'. Notice that I have been careful to define 'non-specific value' in such a way as to avoid its identification with 'intrinsic value'. I have not said that freedom has non-specific value if it has value 'in addition to', or 'over and above', the value of the other phenomena which specific freedoms bring about or contribute to, since this would seem to imply that freedom has intrinsic value.

Intrinsic value is necessarily non-specific in nature. But this is not to say that instrumental value must always be specific in nature. Instrumental value can be either specific or non-specific. Thus, to return to the example of gold, a reason I might have for valuing gold intrinsically might be that I like its colour, or that I enjoy the feeling of touching it; a reason I might have for valuing gold in a specific instrumental way might be that I like to have gold moulded in a particular shape around the third finger of my left hand because I want to use a traditional symbol to communicate to the world that I am married; and a reason I might have for valuing gold in a non-specific instrumental way might be that I am planning to have my gold rings, bracelets, and nuggets melted down and made into some other gold object (which I have yet to decide on).

How, it will now be asked, can *freedom* be non-specifically valuable and yet only instrumentally so? The answer lies in our ignorance about the nature of the ultimate good being realized, so that this ultimate good is not characterizable in terms of the instrumental values of specific freedoms. The easiest way to grasp this point is by means of an analogy with the value we attach to money. Most of us do not see money as intrinsically valuable; most of us see it only as a means to certain ends. However, when asked to specify those ends, we often find that we are unable to do so. We say that we would like to win the national lottery, and yet when asked how we would spend the money we are often not able to give a clear answer. This does not make our desire to win the lottery irrational. The point is, rather, that we do not value money only as a means to buying the latest recording of Mozart's symphonies or as a means to eating a bar of chocolate, but also as a means to satisfying whatever our future desires may turn out to be. That is why even those of us who like Mozart and chocolate more than anything else still prefer money to record tokens and chocolate rations. Freedom, like money, can be thought of in the same way as 'non-specifically' instrumentally valuable—as being valuable not because certain specific freedoms help to bring about a certain specific end or set of ends, but simply because our ends (which we are not able at present to *specify*) are better promoted by there being more freedom than by there being less. (I shall expand on the money analogy in s. 2.4.)[5]

Having explained and defended the non-specific instrumental value of freedom, I shall turn to the possibility of its having 'constitutive value' (s. 2.5). As I shall define the expression, to say that freedom is 'constitutively valuable' is to say that freedom is a constitutive part of some other good, where this other good is itself intrinsically valuable. To say that freedom is constitutively valuable in this way is to say something stronger than that freedom is merely instrumentally valuable, yet weaker than that freedom is intrinsically valuable. It is to say that freedom is a necessary condition for some other good in an analytical rather than a causal sense. As we shall see, constitutive value, like instrumental value, can be either 'specific' or 'non-specific'.

It must be emphasized that none of the different kinds of non-specific value that we shall examine need provide an *exclusive* answer to the question of how freedom is valuable. It is quite consistent, for example, to see freedoms as having value both instrumentally (in either or both senses of 'instrumentally') *and* intrinsically. It is indeed quite consistent (as well as plausible) to say that freedom has both non-specific value and specific value. My aim here is not to deny that freedom has specific value, but to argue that it also has non-specific value. The *share* of freedom's value which is assigned to the category of non-specific value will determine the *degree of importance* of the need to be able to measure overall freedom.

---

[5] The analogy with money *is* only an analogy; despite the fact that money normally gives us freedom, money and freedom are not the same thing (see ss. 8.5 and 10.3).

More precisely still, when I say that my aim is to argue that freedom has non-specific value as well as specific value, I take the expression 'having non-specific value' to be short for 'having more specific value than non-specific *dis*value'. There may be reasons for *dis*valuing freedom in a non-specific way, and it is only if freedom turns out to be non-specifically valuable on balance (at least up to some point of satiation) that my argument against the (normative) specific-freedom thesis will go through. But I shall set aside these arguments about disvalue for now, and will only turn to them (in s. 2.6) once I have examined the various kinds of value.

Intrinsic value, non-specific instrumental value, and non-specific constitutive value are all kinds of non-specific value which can plausibly be assigned to freedom. However, there is one further kind of non-specific value—a stronger kind of value—which it is much more difficult to see freedom as having: this is what I shall call 'unconditional' value. Unfortunately, some of the arguments that have been presented in favour of the (normative) specific-freedom thesis have confused unconditional value with the other kinds of non-specific value, and so we need first to examine this category, if only as a means to showing exactly what is *not* being argued for.

2.2 UNCONDITIONAL VALUE

An intrinsically valuable thing may or may not in addition be unconditionally valuable. An intrinsically valuable thing has value in addition to the value (or disvalue) it gets from its consequences, and is thus good *ceteris paribus*. An unconditionally valuable thing has more value than any other thing *regardless* of the value of its consequences, and is thus good *in any possible world*. Another way of putting this is by saying that an unconditionally valuable thing is 'lexically prior', in value, to merely intrinsically valuable things.

The set of unconditionally valuable things is only a subset of the set of intrinsically valuable things (which is in turn only a subset of the set of non-specifically valuable things). To say that a property is intrinsically good is not to say that all of the objects or events possessing that property are good on balance, since any of those objects or events may possess some other property that is intrinsically bad. Even if the freedom provided by alternative A is more intrinsically valuable than (i.e. is itself a greater amount of freedom than) that provided by alternative B, there is no logical reason why alternative B should not be better than alternative A on balance. This will be so if alternative B is more valuable in terms of some other intrinsically good property, G, and the gain in G provided by B is better than the gain in freedom provided by A. Only if we say that freedom is unconditionally valuable do

we make the additional claim that alternative A *must* be better than alternative B, regardless of the worth of G.

Social democrats commonly represent libertarians or conservatives as holding freedom to be unconditionally valuable. For example, according to Philip
Pettit, libertarians hold freedom to be 'the only important value'.[6] The claim
can be found in 'right-wing' thought, if not as often as its opponents would
like us to believe: take, for example, Milton Friedman's claim that 'freedom
should be given priority over every other social value',[7] or the remark of Senator
Barry Goldwater, in the 1964 US presidential campaign, that 'extremism in
the pursuit of liberty is no vice'.[8]

Notice that the claim that freedom is unconditionally valuable is not necessarily identical in meaning to the deceptively straightforward claim that 'more
freedom is always better than less'. This point is worth making, given that
the normative version of the overall-freedom thesis has sometimes been couched
in these terms by its critics.[9] The 'always' in 'more freedom is *always* better
than less' could have one of two meanings. First, it might mean that there is
no *ceteris paribus* clause to be added, in the way I have already explained,
to the claim that it is good to have more freedom. In this case, the word 'always'
means that freedom 'trumps' other goods when it comes into conflict with
them. Secondly, it might mean that fulfilling people's interest in freedom is,
as Joseph Raz would put it, an 'insatiable principle'.[10] In this case, the word
'always' refers not to conflicts between freedom and other goods, but, rather,
to the scale of more and less freedom itself, and implies that freedom is not
one of those things that it is possible to have enough of. In other words, in
the second case, the word 'always' means that no matter *how much* freedom
one already has, it is always better to have an additional unit of freedom.
Henceforth, I shall refer to the first meaning of 'always better' by saying that
something is always better 'in the non-*ceteris paribus* sense', and to the second meaning by saying that it is always better 'in the non-satiable sense'. It
is quite possible for the claim that 'more freedom is always better than less'
to mean 'always' in both of these senses. The point, however, is that conflicts
with other goods on the one hand, and satiation on the other, represent different kinds of reasons for the permissibility of restricting freedom. It is also

    [6] P. Pettit, 'A Definition of Negative Liberty', *Ratio*, NS 2 (1989), 153.

    [7] Cited in A. Hirsch and N. de Marchi, *Milton Friedman* (London: Harvester Wheatsheaf,
1990), 281.

    [8] Quoted in B. I. Page, *Choices and Echoes in Presidential Elections* (Chicago: University
of Chicago Press, 1978), 127.

    [9] See, for example, Gerald Dworkin's *The Theory and Practice of Autonomy* (Cambridge:
Cambridge University Press, 1988), ch. 5 (in particular, the citations of Rawls and Nozick at
p. 64).

    [10] J. Raz, *The Morality of Freedom* (Oxford: Clarendon Press, 1986), 235–6.

quite coherent, then, to say that 'more freedom is always better than less' in only one of these senses. For instance, it is conceivable that increases in freedom be non-satiating, but still only good *ceteris paribus*. It seems reasonable to assume that the view that freedom is 'unconditionally valuable' means that more freedom is always better than less in both senses of 'always better'. We shall return to the distinction between the satiability clause and the *ceteris paribus* clause in Chapter 3, when we look at the justification of various principles for the distribution of freedom.

The notion of 'unconditional value' may therefore be defined as follows:

A phenomenon, *x*, has unconditional value iff *x* is intrinsically valuable and more *x* is always better than less *x* both in terms of increasing quantities of *x* and in terms of the choice between *x* and other phenomena.[11]

Those who argue for the specific-freedom thesis often appear to believe that the thesis can be vindicated through a denial of the claim that freedom is unconditionally valuable. Kymlicka argues against the idea that freedom of choice is 'intrinsically valuable' in the following way:

Saying that [1] freedom of choice is intrinsically valuable suggests that [2a] the more we exercise our capacity for choice, [2b] the more free we are, and hence [3] the more valuable our lives are.[12] [The component phrases have been numbered for ease of reference.]

Therefore freedom cannot be intrinsically valuable, Kymlicka goes on, because to say so would be to deny the truth that 'a valuable life, for most of us', is 'filled with commitments and relationships', which, precisely, 'aren't the sort of thing that we question every day'. Now this last point may be quite true, but it is not contradicted by the idea that freedom is intrinsically valuable. For one thing, the inference from (1) to (2a)+(2b) only appears plausible because it plays on an ambiguity in the word 'choice'. 'Having choice' is not the same as 'choosing'. To choose (i.e. to exercise one's capacity for choice) is to *exercise* one's freedom. One can have freedom (i.e. *have* some choice) without choosing. One can be free to choose to question one's commitments without choosing to question them, and the former can be a good thing even if doing the latter would be bad. Furthermore—and here we come to the distinction between intrinsic and unconditional value—the view that freedom is intrinsically valuable does not even contradict one's valuing one's commitments

---

[11] This definition allows us to remain agnostic over the question of whether there is more than one unconditionally valuable thing. The definition may be logically satisfied by any two or more goods which never conflict with one another.

[12] W. Kymlicka, 'Liberalism and Communitarianism', *Canadian Journal of Philosophy*, 18 (1988), 187; id., *Liberalism, Community and Culture* (Oxford: Oxford University Press, 1989), 49.

more highly than one's *having* choice. For if by (1) Kymlicka really means that 'freedom of choice is intrinsically valuable [and not unconditionally valuable]', then (2*b*) implies (3) only *ceteris paribus*, and not in any possible world. And (2*b*) implying (3) only *ceteris paribus* is not contradicted by our valuing our commitments more than we value our freedom of choice. If on the other hand by (1) Kymlicka really means, as he appears to, that 'freedom of choice is unconditionally valuable', then although (2*b*) will imply (3) in any possible world, a fact which will indeed be contradicted by our valuing our commitments more highly than our freedom of choice, the argument is no longer one against freedom of choice being intrinsically valuable.

Ronald Dworkin too appears at times to identify intrinsic and unconditional value in his argument to the effect that there is no 'right to liberty'. Dworkin points out that anything worthy of being called a right must be a claim that can be upheld even against the public interest, and goes on to suggest that because certain specific liberties *are* rightly denied us in the name of the public interest —such as the liberty to drive uptown on Lexington Avenue—we cannot therefore have a right to liberty.[13] However, there is no reason why a 'right to liberty' need imply a right to any *specific* liberties, unless it is interpreted as a right to *unlimited* liberty, rather than as a right to a certain degree of liberty. Dworkin appears to assume that if rights are 'trumps', then a right to liberty must assign liberty the status of a trump among values. But this implication does not hold. It is possible to call 'the right to liberty' a trump without calling 'liberty' itself a trump. This one can do by claiming that the right to liberty is the right to a certain *degree* of liberty (specified in either relative or absolute terms). Dworkin's rejection of the right to liberty appears to rest on the assumption that either we have a right to *all possible* liberties (including the right to drive uptown on Lexington Avenue)—a position which seems to imply that liberty is unconditionally valuable—or else we have no right to liberty at all. He therefore assumes exactly what he needs to prove in order for his rejection of the right to liberty to go through: that liberty is not a quantitative attribute.

It is perhaps their eagerness to distance themselves from libertarians—a factor contributing to their blindness to the distinction between unconditional and intrinsic value—that serves in part to explain the hostility shown by Dworkin and Kymlicka to the view that freedom is non-specifically valuable. Whether or not it is fair to represent libertarians as seeing freedom as unconditionally valuable, and whether or not seeing freedom as unconditionally valuable implies libertarianism, it is certainly not true that the view that freedom is *intrinsically* valuable (let alone the view that freedom is non-specifically valuable) implies libertarianism. Nor, therefore, need Rawlsian liberals deny such a view in order to distinguish that ideology from their own.

---

[13] Dworkin, 'We Do Not Have a Right to Liberty', 170–1; id., *Taking Rights Seriously*, 269–70.

Fears of libertarianism aside, there may also be a less ideological explanation for the apparently widespread confusion of intrinsic value with unconditional value, and that is the tendency to confuse two different levels at which we can ask the question 'What is the value of freedom?' At one level we may be taken to be asking whether 'the value of freedom' is something which depends wholly on its consequences, or whether freedom also has value in itself. At another level we may be asking how valuable freedom is in relation to other goods. Answering at the first of these levels that freedom is intrinsically valuable may give the false impression that an answer has been given at the second level, to the effect that all other goods are subordinate to that of freedom.

I shall not give any reasons here for seeing freedom as unconditionally valuable, because I have not found any in the literature on freedom (even in the *libertarian* literature), and I cannot think of any myself. I shall therefore now turn directly to the view that freedom is *merely* intrinsically valuable.

2.3 INTRINSIC VALUE

In line with the remarks made in s. 2.1, the notion of intrinsic value can be defined in the following way:

> A phenomenon, *x*, has intrinsic value iff *x* is an end in itself (that is, if *x* has a positive overall value which is not reducible to the value of any other phenomenon).

How might we defend the claim that freedom is intrinsically valuable? There is a difficulty involved in the very idea of 'arguing' that something is intrinsically valuable, since it is normal to argue for the value of a thing by reference to the value of other things which it brings about or which necessarily accompany it, and the concept of intrinsic value excludes that possibility by definition. J. S. Mill recognized this as a problem for utilitarians who wish to argue that happiness is intrinsically valuable, and admitted that ultimately he could do no more than point out that people do as a matter of fact desire happiness for its own sake: 'If the end which the utilitarian doctrine proposes to itself were not, in theory and practice, acknowledged to be an end, nothing could ever convince any person that it was so. No reason can be given why the general happiness is desirable, except that each person so far as he believes it to be attainable, desires his own happiness.'[14] Similarly, in the case of freedom, while the fact of people desiring freedom as an end in itself would not *prove* the thesis of freedom's intrinsic value, we may take it that this fact would at least affect the *plausibility* of such a thesis.

[14] J. S. Mill, *Collected Works* (London: Routledge & Kegan Paul, 1969), x. 234.

Kymlicka does not believe that people as a matter of fact value freedom for its own sake. 'Freedom of choice . . . isn't pursued for its own sake', he says, 'but as a precondition for pursuing those projects and tasks that *are* valued for their own sake.'[15] This is an empirical claim, and is as difficult to disprove as it is to prove. However, what can be said is that it is unnecessarily dogmatic. Consider an example put forward by Thomas Hurka. In situation S1 we have only two options, whereas in situation S2 we have those same two options plus eight more (i.e. a total of ten options). Now imagine that the two options in S1 are also the best two options in S2, and that in either situation we can only choose one option. Although we will probably make the same choice in S2 as in S1, we will still often prefer S2 to S1, simply because it gives us 'more choice'. (Notice that I do not say we will 'always' prefer it. It is unlikely that we will always prefer it unless more freedom is always better than less in the non-*ceteris paribus* as well as the non-satiable sense.) Hurka suggests that this kind of example is the key test for the view that having choice is intrinsically valuable. Had any one of the options in S2 been more valuable than either of those in S1, our reason for preferring S2 would not necessarily have been that S2 gave us more choice. In the above example, on the other hand, this would appear to be the *only* possible reason for preferring S2. We see a difference between our choice in S1 and our choice in S2 (despite the fact that they are equally adequate as a means to obtaining our preferred outcome) because, as Hurka puts it, when we choose to bring about *x* in S2, we are choosing not only to bring about *x*, but also *not* to bring about *y*, *z*, *a*, *b*, and so on: 'To have ten options rather than just the best among them is to be able to say no as well as yes. It is to be able to say no nine times, and to be responsible for the fact that no was said.'[16]

To give the example more real-life content, imagine a situation in which one person has ten feasible career options, including those of becoming a teacher, lawyer, politician, or accountant, and in which another person only has the choice of becoming a teacher or doing nothing. And imagine that both of them prefer teaching to any other occupation. 'If we ask why these people are teachers our answer may at one level be the same. But if we ask why they are not lawyers, politicians, or accountants the answers will be different.'[17]

What Hurka's example illustrates is the value we place on our *agency*—on our ability to make an impact on the world, by intervening in the causal chains which bring about events and states of affairs. A necessary condition for our being able to intervene in this way is that we be able to say no as

---

[15] Kymlicka, 'Liberalism and Communitarianism', 187; cf. id., *Liberalism, Community and Culture*, 148.

[16] T. Hurka, 'Why Value Autonomy?', *Social Theory and Practice*, 13 (1987), 376.

[17] Ibid. 366.

well as yes. And, as the example suggests, as a result of this fact, we value having *more* choice rather than *less*. The more times we are able to say no, the more impact we will have on the world when we *do* choose, and hence the more value there is in our situation.

Gerald Dworkin has suggested that arguments like that of Hurka have a counter-intuitive implication: if having choice is intrinsically valuable, then where doing A is preferred to doing B, and doing B to doing C, there must be some values for A, B, and C such that the option set {B, C} would be preferable to the option set {A}.[18] A similar counter-argument has been put forward by Giuliano Pontara, according to whom one need only increase the value of the best option in S1 by an infinitesimal amount in order to make it at least less than obvious that S2 is preferable to S1.[19] Another intuitive case against the idea of freedom's intrinsic value might be thought to be made by pointing out that the numbers of options in Hurka's example are particularly low. Perhaps we would be more indifferent between S1 and S2 if S1 were to contain 2 million options and S2 were to contain 10 million. This objection rests on the plausible assumption that if a phenomenon is intrinsically valuable,[20] then more of that phenomenon is always better than less in the non-satiable sense.

For some, these counter-arguments may weaken Hurka's claim that freedom has intrinsic value. But they do not seem to me to be decisive. Certainly, as Keith Dowding points out, Gerald Dworkin has not succeeded in showing the preference for option set {B, C} over option set {A} to be 'irrational',[21] and for my part I can imagine certain situations in which I would indeed prefer the set with the less valuable but greater number of options simply *because* I value freedom intrinsically. In a sense, then, the above objections seem to beg the question in favour of freedom not being intrinsically valuable. Appeals to basic intuitions about value can only take us so far in persuading others about which objects have intrinsic value.

2.4 INSTRUMENTAL VALUE

Hurka's example at least makes it understandable for someone to claim that freedom is intrinsically valuable. It is unnecessarily dogmatic to say that we 'do not' value freedom as one of our ends, simply because we can see that

---

[18] Dworkin, *The Theory and Practice of Autonomy*, 80.
[19] G. Pontara, *Filosofia pratica* (Milan: Il Saggiatore, 1988), 320–1.
[20] And if that phenomenon is itself a 'non-satiating good' (on which point, see s. 3.2, below).
[21] K. Dowding, 'Choice: Its Increase and its Value', *British Journal of Political Science*, 22 (1992), 305.

some people *might* value freedom in this way, and it is difficult to see on what basis such people can be called irrational. What is less clear is whether those who agree with Hurka's evaluation of the choice sets in S1 and S2 must *necessarily* admit that freedom is *intrinsically* valuable. For it might plausibly be objected that the mere fact of our preferring larger choice sets to smaller choice sets (with identical best options) does not contradict the idea that we prefer them because they bring about some other good, and that freedom is therefore only instrumentally valuable. Hurka may have demonstrated that we value a greater degree of choice more highly than a lesser degree of choice. But has he thereby shown that 'more choice' is one of our *ends*? Might there not be some more distant end, as distinct from those directly attained through the choices in question, to which we see the existence of 'more choice' as contributing to a greater degree than that of 'less choice'?

Fortunately, this objection need not detain us here, since we can still argue that our preference for the choice set in S2 over that in S1 demonstrates freedom's *non-specific* value. As I tried to make clear at the outset, we do not need to see freedom as intrinsically valuable in order to see freedom as non-specifically valuable. It is quite coherent to see freedom as having only instrumental value—as being a good thing only because it is a means to some other good—and nevertheless see freedom as being valuable as such. Given the difficulty of arguing that freedom is intrinsically valuable, then, we may just as well move on now to the arguments for freedom's instrumental value.

Instrumental value can be defined straightforwardly, in terms of the means–ends relation:

A phenomenon, x, has instrumental value iff x is a means to some other valuable phenomenon, y (and therefore the value of x is reducible to the value of y).

And, within the concept of instrumental value, we can distinguish the 'non-specific' from the 'specific' variety in the following way:

A phenomenon, x, has non-specific instrumental value iff x, without regard to the nature of its specific instances, is a means to some other valuable phenomenon, y.

A phenomenon, x, has specific instrumental value iff a certain specific instance (or set of instances) of x is a means to some other valuable phenomenon, y.

That freedom has specific instrumental value may be what Kymlicka means when he says that 'freedom of choice . . . isn't pursued for its own sake, but as a precondition for pursuing those projects and tasks that *are* valued for their own sake' (cited in the previous section). If we say that freedom is specifically instrumentally valuable, what we mean is that a certain kind of behaviour, x, is valuable, for whatever reason (e.g. because it is valuable in itself or because it has good consequences or because it is a constitutive part of something that is valuable in itself), and that having the freedom to do x is a necessary precondition for doing x. (There will of course be other necessary preconditions for doing x.) Should we say that freedom's instrumental value is *wholly* 'specific' in the above sense? It seems to me that this would be a gross error, and that an extremely important part of freedom's instrumental value is of a non-specific nature. What explains the non-specific instrumental value of freedom is the unavoidability of *human ignorance and fallibility*. Put crudely, an important kind of reason for our preferring the choice set offered in S2 to that offered in S1 is that we are not *sure* about the values of the various options.

As human beings, we are necessarily uncertain about the instrumental values of specific options. On the other hand, we do know that *some* specific option or set of options (we just do not know which) will serve some specific end—an end the exact nature of which has yet to become clear, or an end which we are aware might change in the future. Now the point here is not just that some freedoms have specific value while others do not, and that we do not yet know which freedoms fall into the first category and which into the second; our lack of knowledge in the present, about which specific freedoms will (with hindsight) turn out to have served our ends, also implies that *at present* freedom is *non*-specifically valuable. To see this, consider an analogy with judgements of probability. Suppose that it is true at time t that the probability of event x occurring at $t+1$ is 0.5. And suppose that at $t+1$ x does not in fact occur. We shall then be able to say with hindsight that, at t, x was not in fact going to occur. But this does not invalidate the probability judgement originally made at t. It remains true that at time t the probability of x occurring at $t+1$ was 0.5. Similarly, it might turn out at time $t+1$ that the freedom we had at time t to perform action a at $t+1$ was of no value in pursuing the ends that we in fact turned out (at $t+1$) to have. But this does not invalidate a judgement made at time t according to which the freedom to do a *was* valuable because we could not know at t whether or not it would serve our ends. Our ignorance about the future gives value to specific freedoms in the present that otherwise would not have value. Those freedoms have value *in virtue of* our ignorance.

The justifications of freedom's non-specific instrumental value can be usefully categorized under two headings. Freedom may be seen as non-specifically valuable (*a*) as a means to some social goal or (*b*) as a means to individual well-being.

(a) *Freedom as a means to a social goal*

Hayek is an example of a thinker who should in my view be classified as seeing freedom as non-specifically instrumentally valuable as a means to a social goal. For Hayek, the ultimate human value appears to be 'progress', rather than freedom.[22] Progress is the improvement of the 'condition of mankind'. It involves 'a process of adaptation and learning', and 'consists in the discovery of the not yet known'.[23] The best means a society has of attaining progress is, according to Hayek, that of granting freedom to its individual members. And it is our very ignorance of the direction in which progress will lead us that makes this so. Since freedom is only a means to this end, 'if there were omniscient men, if we could know not only all that affects the attainment of our present wishes but also our future wants and desires, there would be little case for liberty'. As it turns out, however, 'the advance and even the preservation of civilization are dependent upon a maximum of opportunity for accidents to happen'.[24] Now, because the concrete nature of our ends is not known to us, it has to be admitted, as Norman Barry puts it, that 'the benefits of liberty are not measurable'.[25] And this means that it is not possible to say of any one particular liberty how valuable it is in terms of the degree of progress to which it is a means. 'We shall not achieve our ends if we confine liberty to the particular instances where we know it will do good . . . If we knew how freedom would be used, the case for it would largely disappear.'[26] Because of our lack of knowledge of future events and desires (and because of a government's ignorance even of most people's *present* desires), the value of liberty is reducible to that of progress *only in a generalized sense*. All that we know is the truth of the *empirical generalization* that if there is more liberty, greater progress is likely to result.

J. S. Mill appears to be making a similar point to that of Hayek where he defends liberty of thought and expression on the grounds that it is the best means to attaining the truth (since freedom of expression leads to 'the clearer perception and livelier impression of truth, provided by its collision with error'), and where he defends the liberty to experiment with different ways of living as a means to assessing their worth (since 'the worth of different modes of life should be proved *practically*').[27] Mill's position appears to be

---

[22] Hayek, *The Constitution of Liberty*, chs. 1–3; id., *Law, Legislation and Liberty* (London: Routledge & Kegan Paul, 1982), ch. 7.

[23] Hayek, *The Constitution of Liberty*, 40.   [24] Ibid. 29.

[25] N. Barry, 'Hayek on Liberty', in Z. Pelczynski and J. Gray (eds.), *Conceptions of Liberty in Political Philosophy* (London: Athlone Press, 1984), 278.

[26] Hayek, *The Constitution of Liberty*, 31. The reference here to freedom's value 'largely disappearing' suggests that for Hayek freedom's value is almost *exclusively* of the non-specific kind.

[27] Mill, *On Liberty*, ch. 3, *Collected Works*, xviii. 260, my emphasis.

very close to that of Hayek where, in a famous passage in *On Liberty*, he attempts to justify the pursuit of liberty as such by suggesting that one ought to pursue utility in a *general* sense—that is, utility as 'progress': 'it must be utility in the largest sense, grounded on the permanent interests of man as a progressive being.'[28] Given this, it seems to me that the most plausible interpretation of Mill on the value of liberty is that he saw liberty's value as at least including non-specific instrumental value.[29] This interpretation may go some way towards helping to resolve the problem of the oft-noted apparent contradiction in Mill over the question of whether it is liberty or utility that has supreme value.[30] The non-specificity of freedom's value allows the utilitarian consistently to promote certain specific freedoms even where, *as far as we can see*, the exercise of those specific freedoms would lead to an overall reduction in utility. For those specific freedoms will also have value in terms of utility in a more general sense, in virtue of our ignorance and fallibility. Treating freedom as non-specifically valuable as a means to utility may give the false impression that one sees freedom as a value that competes with utility, as another intrinsic good rather than as a good which ultimately reduces to it. Some of Mill's stronger pro-freedom rhetoric might therefore have been wrongly interpreted as implying freedom's intrinsic value when it was only intended to imply freedom's non-specific instrumental value.

The arguments of Mill and Hayek can of course be disputed on empirical grounds. One might object that freedom does *not* provide the best means to progress or to 'utility in the largest sense', or one might deny that progress or 'utility in the largest sense' have value in the first place. I shall not attempt here to improve on the arguments of Mill and Hayek; my main interest is in classifying those arguments as arguments for the non-specific value of freedom. On the other hand, it is worth expanding somewhat on the importance that arguments of this kind have had within the liberal tradition, for this appears to have been overlooked by a number of today's critics of liberalism.

The idea that freedom provides a necessary means to a value called social or economic progress has in particular been overlooked by Alastair MacIntyre in his critique of the 'Enlightenment tradition'. MacIntyre accuses Enlightenment thinkers and their contemporary liberal descendants of having abandoned the Aristotelian idea that man has a *telos*—that human beings naturally aim towards some end—and of having failed, as a result, to provide a justificatory bridge

[28] Ibid., ch. 1, *Collected Works*, xviii. 224.

[29] While Mill's position appears to lean towards Hayek's regarding the definition of 'utility', Hayek's appears to lean away from Mill's regarding the definition of 'progress'. For according to Hayek, progress is 'movement for movement's sake', and is not reducible to utility because 'often it makes us sadder men' (*The Constitution of Liberty*, 41).

[30] See, for example, Isaiah Berlin's 'John Stuart Mill and the Ends of Life', in his *Four Essays on Liberty*, 128, 178.

linking 'man-as-he-is' to 'man-as-he-ought-to-be'. According to MacIntyre, because they lacked a notion of a human *telos*, Enlightenment thinkers also lacked a basis on which to engage in rational discussions about the validity of their moral principles, and this is a theoretical inadequacy which contemporary liberalism has inherited.[31]

This criticism of the Enlightenment tradition collapses once we focus on the ideals of perfectibility and progress. For it is clear that within this tradition moral principles *can* be justified teleologically, and that the relevant *telos* for most Enlightenment thinkers, no less than for Aristotle, was human perfectibility. There are, of course, differences between the Aristotelian and Enlightenment notions of human perfectibility, not the least of which, for our present purposes, is the degree of *specificity of content* in the two notions. The Enlightenment notion seems to lack a specific content, and this, as I see it, must be what lies behind MacIntyre's erroneous claim that Enlightenment thinking allows for *no telos*. When we come to examine the Enlightenment notion of perfectibility, it is not at all clear which particular ends, in concrete terms, this notion implies. Despite first appearances, however, the lack of specificity of content in the Enlightenment notion of human perfectibility does not prevent it from grounding specific moral principles. Indeed, it is this very difference between the Aristotelian notion of man's *telos* and the Enlightenment notion of perfectibility—the difference in terms of specificity of content —that allows the Enlightenment thinker, unlike the Aristotelian, to assert the non-specific value of freedom.

Perhaps the clearest illustration of the above point is to be found in the ideal of perfectibility as expounded by Condorcet. If we look at Condorcet's notion of perfectibility, we can see that it is indeterminate along two dimensions. To visualize these two dimensions, imagine a signpost pointing out the path to perfection. This is no ordinary signpost, for it tells us that perfection is indefinitely many miles away, and it points in innumerable directions. Regarding the *distance* to perfection, Condorcet talks approvingly of 'the doctrine of the *indefinite* perfectibility of the human race'.[32] The reason for man's perfectibility being 'truly indefinite' lies partly in the fact that the human mind can never gain knowledge of all the facts of nature, and partly in the fact that 'the actual number of truths may always increase'. In the words of Kant, 'no one can or ought to decide what the highest degree may be at which mankind may have to stop progressing'.[33] Similarly, in connection with the

---

[31] A. MacIntyre, *After Virtue: A Study in Moral Theory* (London: Duckworth, 1981), ch. 5.

[32] M. J. A. N. Condorcet, *Sketch for a Historical Picture of the Progress of the Human Mind*, trans. J. Barraclough (Westport, Conn.: Hyperion Press, 1955), 142, my emphasis.

[33] I. Kant, *Appendix from 'The Critique of Pure Reason'*, in his *Political Writings*, trans. H. B. Nisbet (Cambridge: Cambridge University Press, 1991), 191.

direction in which our progress towards perfection will take us, Condorcet recognizes that the nature of progress is by definition something that cannot be specified substantively: 'It is impossible to pronounce about the likelihood of an event that will occur only when the human species will have necessarily acquired a degree of knowledge of which we can have no inkling.'[34]

In the 'Aristotelian tradition' inherited by contemporary communitarians, man's *telos* has neither of the above indeterminacies. Or rather, it has them to a much lesser extent. Thus, if we imagine a spectrum of degrees of specificity of man's end (along the two dimensions mentioned above), we can say that the Enlightenment tradition falls at the less specific end of the spectrum, and the Aristotelian tradition at the more specific end. For Enlightenment thinkers, man has a relatively indeterminate end, though it is given some content by reference to the abstract concepts of reason, knowledge, and happiness. For Aristotle, man has a relatively specific end—one which we can at present know, and which we can describe in concrete terms, if only by means of general concepts. As MacIntyre says, for Aristotle the nature of humans 'is such that they have certain aims and goals, such that they move by nature towards a *specific* telos'.[35] Thus, the 'virtues are, on Aristotle's view, dispositions to act in *specific* ways for *specific* reasons'.[36] While Aristotle begins by defining the good life by means of the abstract term *eudaimonia*, he nevertheless goes on to suggest that it is better realized through a life of contemplation than through a life of action. And in his *Politics* we learn that we are each born into certain general roles—those of man, woman, or slave, for example—and that some of these are naturally subordinate to others. Each of these roles, and each of the more specific roles we find ourselves best fitted to—those of carpenter, statesman, or philosopher—has its natural function in the *polis*, its own specific *telos*, which we can discover by observing and contemplating the nature of the role itself. A more abstract, modern notion of perfectibility does not involve taking these further steps towards specifying the content of the good life for individuals.

John Passmore distinguishes between the Aristotelian and post-Renaissance views of perfectibility by underlining the tendency of the latter 'to value the journey more than the arrival, the process of finding out more than the truth arrived at, the doing rather than the having'.[37] For Aristotle, in contrast, 'to perfect oneself . . . is to *achieve* an end, a *specific* end'.[38] The reference to achievement here shows how we can also contrast the two notions of perfectibility in

---

[34] Condorcet, *Sketch*, 184–8.   [35] MacIntyre, *After Virtue*, 148, my emphasis.
[36] A. MacIntyre, *Whose Justice? Which Rationality?* (London: Duckworth, 1988), 109, my emphasis.
[37] J. Passmore, *The Perfectibility of Man* (London: Duckworth, 1970), 48.
[38] Ibid. 46, my emphasis.

terms of the difference between the terminal and the non-terminal—between a reachable goal and one that is indefinitely far off. As Horace Kallen says, the Enlightenment notion of progress contains no *terminus ad quem*. At most, it involves movement away from something, such as scarcity or ignorance —a *terminus a quo*. The idea of a goal is taken over by a sense 'of the road *opened*, of pursuit *unhindered* . . . This, in part, accounts for the illogic of "infinite perfectibility". The phrase embodies the Enlightenment's unexpressed feeling that *distance from*, not *distance to*, gives the span of Progress, that hence the going is the goal.'[39]

It is useful, then, to draw a broad distinction between man's end being conceived of on the one hand in terms of an indeterminate, non-terminal notion of perfectibility, and on the other hand in terms of a specific terminus. The contrast between these more and less determinate notions of perfectibility is of course alive in contemporary political ideologies. The tendency to think about human perfection in terms of a specific terminus has continued into the nineteenth and twentieth centuries and has, unlike the non-specific, non-terminal view, come into sharp conflict with the modern ideal of liberty. This might be put down in part to the fact that it is more plausible to justify sacrificing people's present freedoms in the name of a clearly reachable and substantive societal goal than in the name of an indefinitely far off and unspecified one. But there is also a more positive reason for saying that the non-specific, non-terminal conception of perfectibility goes hand in hand with liberty, and that consists in the empirical correlation between progress and liberty made so clear by Mill and Hayek: the more our notion of perfectibility is indeterminate, the more liberty becomes a necessary precondition for its attainment. MacIntyre is blinded to this kind of teleological justification for providing individuals with a measure of freedom, because he fails to see how a relatively indeterminate *telos* can nevertheless generate a relatively determinate moral principle. It is only once we have grasped the notion of non-specific instrumental value that such a justification becomes comprehensible.

(b) *Freedom as a means to individual well-being*

It is not only as a means to a social goal like progress or collective utility that freedom can have non-specific instrumental value. Individual freedom can also have non-specific instrumental value from the point of view of the individual herself. This will be especially so if individual well-being is seen, as it sometimes is by contemporary utilitarians, as the satisfaction of informed desires. For it is arguable that a rational individual, while valuing freedom as

---

[39] H. M. Kallen, *Patterns of Progress* (New York: Columbia University Press, 1950), 27, emphasis in the original.

merely instrumental to the satisfaction of certain needs or desires, nevertheless desires as a consequence to have 'as much freedom as possible' (at least *ceteris paribus*). Why should this be so, if freedom is merely instrumentally valuable? The answer to this question can be made clear by reference to the analogy drawn earlier with money (in s. 2.1). As we saw there, money is not normally considered to be intrinsically valuable; most individuals desire it merely as a means to obtaining other goods (although there is a small minority of 'Scrooges', who come to see money as intrinsically valuable). Nevertheless, because the world is an unpredictable place, and we cannot be sure even of the nature of our own future desires and needs, let alone of the nature of future supply and demand, it is prudent to prefer money to other commodities. Imagine that one wished to present a view of the value of money analogous to the view of freedom implied by the (normative) specific-freedom thesis. Imagine, in other words, an argument aimed at showing that the instrumental value of money is wholly 'specific' in nature. Presumably, such an argument would have to look something like this:

We don't desire money for its own sake, but as a means to other things that we do value for their own sake. Therefore, there is no need to quantify money. Rather, what people desire is certain specific 'moneys', or specific 'kinds of money', such as food rations, record tokens, and petrol vouchers, according to the ends which they see money as serving.[40]

Clearly, this argument against the need to quantify money fails to deal with the objection outlined above. Because our preferences over 'moneys' are based on less than perfect knowledge of the future, it is rational to desire money in a general sense. Hence money acquires a value which is independent of that of the specific things which it is a means to possessing, and we have not merely record tokens and petrol vouchers, but dollars, pounds, and roubles. This is not to say that money is intrinsically valuable, but merely that it is non-specifically valuable. Scrooges are not the only people in this world interested in money in a non-specific sense, and who are therefore interested in 'how much money' they have. Preferring money to sweet rations does not make one a Scrooge, even if one strongly desires to eat sweets.

A similar case can be made out for the non-specific instrumental value of freedom. Since we cannot be sure of our future desires or needs, we do not value freedom merely as one of the necessary means to our doing *x*, *y*, and *z*, but rather, as one of the means by which we may satisfy whatever our needs and desires may be. Once again, the value of liberty turns out to be reducible *only in a generalized sense* to that of the ends it serves. Once again, we can

---

[40] Not a \$10 record token or a £10 petrol voucher but, rather, a *one-record* record token or a *six-gallon* petrol voucher.

only be sure (or as sure as possible) of attaining the ends liberty serves by making sure that there is as much liberty as possible (at least *ceteris paribus*). Here, as before, the instrumental value of liberty is of a non-specific kind. The value of liberty lies in that which liberty allows us to do, but (given the lack of certain kinds of knowledge) does not consist in the value of any of the specific things that specific liberties allow us to do.

Apart from the straightforward satisfaction of desires, there is another typically liberal conception of individual well-being which implies freedom's non-specific instrumental value, and it is worth noting that this is a particular conception of well-being in which Kymlicka himself believes. We have seen that the idea of freedom as non-specifically valuable is incompatible with Kymlicka's conclusions about the role of freedom in liberal political theory. Nevertheless, the idea is in keeping with one of his fundamental premisses, and it may only be his failure to embrace that premiss wholeheartedly that prevents him from perceiving freedom's non-specific value. I have in mind the liberal commitment to what L. T. Hobhouse called 'personal growth'.

The concept of growth can be traced back to Mill and Humboldt, both of whom compared the development of the individual personality to that of a plant.[41] Growth can be seen as another of the 'unmeasurable benefits' of liberty. As in the case of Hayekian-Millian progress, the motivation for taking an interest in individual growth lies in the inadequacy of the policy of merely allowing people to do or to have only that which they at present desire, or which is at present judged (by them or others) to be in their interests. For advocates of growth, however, this motivation arises not out of an ultimate interest in social progress, but simply out of the belief that an individual's well-being depends on her being in a position to change, develop, and determine her *own* desires and interests. Since the very concept of 'growth' suggests that the source of such changes must lie 'within' the individual herself, the recognition of growth as a good thing must carry with it the idea that individuals should be granted the 'space' in which to determine their own ends: 'Human personality is that within which lives and grows, which can be destroyed but cannot be made, . . . but can be placed under conditions in which it will flourish and expand . . . The foundation of liberty is the idea of growth.'[42]

Something similar to Hobhouse's and Mill's ideal of growth can also be found in Kant, who, in Charles Larmore's words, shares with Mill the view that 'we should always maintain a contingent allegiance, revisable on reflection, to any substantial view of the good life', and that given forms of life are valuable 'only if we understand them as ones we choose, or would choose,

---

[41] See Mill, *On Liberty*, ch. 3 (*Collected Works*, xviii), and W. von Humboldt, *The Limits of State Action* (Indianapolis: Liberty Classics, 1993), ch. 2.

[42] L. T. Hobhouse, *Liberalism* (London: Greenwood Press, 1911), 121–2.

from a position of critical detachment, in something like an experimental spirit'.[43] On this view, the good life for an individual is such that it can never be decided on by some external agency, such as a 'paternal government', since this would be to treat people 'as immature children', who are 'obliged to behave purely passively', and would therefore be 'the greatest conceivable despotism'.[44] The proper concern of politics must be with 'developing a legal framework which will allow individuals to lead a moral life and thus be true to their innate humanity'.[45]

Kymlicka follows in this liberal tradition, agreeing that the reason for our interest in 'liberties' is that the means to living 'a good life' involves not only deliberation about which courses of action maximize given values, but also deliberation about those values themselves. The good life, however objective, is not necessarily that which we currently *believe* to be the good life. And since the values which determine what is a good life for me must be values which I endorse, 'my life only goes better if I'm leading it from the *inside*, according to my beliefs about value. Liberty is needed precisely to find out what is valuable in life—to question, re-examine, and revise our beliefs about value.'[46] But since growth is something which Kymlicka believes must come from within, and cannot therefore be doled out by governments in any fair or unfair manner, his position lacks the ingredients it needs if it is to have the 'liberal' egalitarian consequences he desires. If growth is a good for every individual, and as liberal egalitarians we are unable directly to accord equal *growth* to all, then we ought surely to accord the *means* to growth equally to all. And since, as Kant, Humboldt, Mill, Hobhouse, and Kymlicka argue, an essential means to growth is liberty, such a commitment ought surely to imply a policy of 'equal liberty'.

Kymlicka may object that the concept of growth does not imply the importance of the freedom to perform actions *per se*, but of the freedom to perform actions that are meaningful, like the options listed in Hurka's example in s. 2.2. The importance of growth implies that different alternative *meaningful* options—such as being a Catholic or a Muslim, a teacher or a musician—should be open to any one individual. Not all options are meaningful, and those that are can be specified. Therefore, the instrumental value of freedom

[43] C. Larmore, *The Morals of Modernity* (Cambridge: Cambridge University Press, 1996), 128. Larmore criticizes this Kantian-Millian ideal on the grounds that it is itself an object of reasonable disagreement. My own argument for the non-specific value of liberty does not depend on such an ideal but only cites it as one possible justification.

[44] Kant, 'On the Common Saying: "This May be True in Theory, but it does not Apply in Practice"', in *Political Writings*, 74.

[45] Reiss, postscript to Kant's *Political Writings*, 259.

[46] Kymlicka, 'Liberalism and Communitarianism', 185. Cf. id., *Liberalism, Community and Culture*, 10–13.

remains specific to those meaningful options. But this objection surely assumes too static an understanding of what is 'meaningful'.[47] The idea that it is important for us to have options we see as meaningful represents a part of the truth about freedom's value, but not the whole truth. For why should the relevant list of options be restricted to those that different agents *at present* see as meaningful? Is not one of the reasons we see freedom as valuable the fact that free social intercourse, together with the 'experiments in living' talked of by Mill, lead new meanings to be created? How are we to say which options human creativity might in the future lead individuals to judge to be meaningful? It is true, given the argument from growth, that freedom is instrumentally valuable as a means to performing meaningful actions. But part of this instrumental value is of a non-specific nature, given that we are unwarranted in ruling out any particular available actions as 'non-meaningful'. The degree of instrumental value of a set of freedoms cannot therefore be assessed wholly by reference to the meaningfulness of the actions it makes available.

2.5 CONSTITUTIVE VALUE

There is a particular view of the value of freedom which is not adequately captured by the means–ends dichotomy suggested by the terms 'intrinsic' and 'instrumental' (as I have defined them). That view consists in saying that freedom is not intrinsically valuable, but nevertheless forms a *constitutive part* of some intrinsically valuable thing. In our analysis so far, we have been assuming that when we ask 'why' a thing is valuable, the 'because' in our answer must imply a causal process. We have been assuming, in other words, that if there is a reason for x being valuable, that reason must consist in the fact that x 'causes', or 'brings about', some other valuable thing. If on the other hand x is a constitutive part of an intrinsically valuable thing, then it is possible to say why x is valuable simply by reference to this fact, and thus without saying *either* that it is a means to some other good, *or* that it is an end in itself.

This last alternative may prove attractive to those who see freedom as having value independently of the value of the specific things it allows us to do, but who feel intuitively both that the idea of freedom as instrumentally valuable is too weak, and that the idea of freedom as intrinsically valuable is too strong. On the one hand, such people will dislike the idea that freedom is no more than a means to an end, such as happiness or progress or personal

---

[47] Such an assumption seems indeed to underlie Kymlicka's belief that in order to make meaningful choices, and thus in order for one's liberty to have value, one is completely dependent on the particular culture of which one is a member. Cf. Kymlicka, *Liberalism, Community and Culture*.

growth. On the other hand, they might see the idea that freedom has intrinsic value as a form of fetishism.[48] They would not like to say that freedom is a good thing *in isolation* from other valuable things—that freedom would be a good thing even if there were no other good things.[49] A solution to this problem is to see freedom as a constitutive part of some intrinsically valuable complex of phenomena. For in this case, it will be that complex of phenomena that is valuable in isolation, rather than freedom itself. On the other hand, it will also be true that that complex of phenomena has less, little, or no intrinsic value where it does not include freedom. Indeed, strictly speaking, the particular complex that includes freedom will not be present if freedom is not itself present, since it will be part of the *definition* of the complex that it includes freedom. This is what is meant by saying that freedom is a 'constitutive part' of the complex.

Constitutive value, like instrumental value, can be either specific or non-specific. If freedom has specific constitutive value, this is because a certain specific freedom is a constitutive part of a certain intrinsically valuable phenomenon, whereas if freedom has non-specific constitutive value, it is freedom *tout court* (most likely, *a certain degree of freedom*) that is required for the existence of that intrinsically valuable phenomenon. Clearly, it is only the non-specific constitutive value of freedom that implies an interest in the question of 'how free' people are.

We may define the two kinds of constitutive value in the following way:

A phenomenon, *x*, has non-specific constitutive value iff *x*, without regard to the nature of its specific instances, is a constitutive part of some other phenomenon, *y*, and *y* is intrinsically valuable.

A phenomenon, *x*, has specific constitutive value iff a certain specific instance (or set of instances) of *x* is a constitutive part of some other phenomenon, *y*, and *y* is intrinsically valuable.

To say that freedom is specifically constitutively valuable is, from a liberal point of view, unambitious, though certainly plausible. The most obvious sense in which freedom is specifically constitutively valuable is as a constitutive part of any valuable specific *action*. It is commonly said that action, as opposed to mere behaviour, is necessarily freely chosen, at least in the minimal sense that in order to have *acted* in doing *x* one must have been free to do not-*x*.

---

[48] John Gray rightly or wrongly uses the term 'fetish' to describe the attachment of free-marketeers to the value of individual choice. See e.g. his *Enlightenment's Wake: Politics and Culture at the Close of the Modern Age* (London: Routledge, 1993), 90.

[49] This remark is meant to reflect the fact that some philosophers have defined 'intrinsic value' in terms of goodness *in isolation*. Cf. G. E. Moore, *Ethics* (London: Oxford University Press, 1965), 68; R. M. Chisholm, 'Intrinsic Value', in A. I. Goldman and J. Kim (eds.), *Values and Morals* (Dordrecht: Reidel, 1978).

This line of reasoning may indeed provide a better interpretation than that provided in s. 2.4 of Kymlicka's claim that 'freedom of choice . . . isn't pursued for its own sake, but as a precondition for pursuing those projects and tasks that *are* valued for their own sake' (though in this case one should not say that it is a *pre*condition). On this alternative interpretation, we no longer say that the freedom to do *x* is *instrumentally* valuable because it is a *causally* necessary condition for 'doing *x*' but, rather, that the freedom to do *x* and the freedom to do not-*x* are *constitutively* valuable because they are (jointly) a *logically* necessary condition for 'doing *x*', where '*x*' is a freely chosen action.

An example of the claim that freedom is specifically constitutively valuable can be found in the work of Amartya Sen. There is an element of ambiguity in Sen's writings on the value of freedom. In a number of places, he has explicitly claimed that freedom is 'intrinsically' valuable. He says, for example, that we have an interest in ranking opportunity sets in terms of the freedom they make available, and that this is different from ranking such sets in terms of the values of their member options: 'if freedom is of some intrinsic value in a person's life, then the valuation of a capability set need not coincide with the evaluation of the chosen element of it. The substantive problem . . . is whether we value freedom *over and above* its instrumental role, i.e., what freedom permits us to achieve.'[50]

The claim that freedom has value 'over and above [the value of] . . . what freedom permits us to achieve' certainly fits well with my own understanding of intrinsic value. However, the examples Sen gives in defence of this view seem to me to be more suited to supporting the view that freedom is specifically constitutively valuable. A recurrent example in Sen's writings is that of the difference between starving and fasting. Sen points out that fasting necessarily results from a choice (food or no food), whereas starving simply results from a lack of food. Given that some individuals value fasting but not starving, and given the fact that the behaviour of those individuals is the same regardless of whether they are given the choice whether or not to eat (i.e. they do not eat), it must be the case, Sen says, that freedom is intrinsically valuable. Sen's reason for drawing this conclusion may appear to be the same as that of Hurka in the example cited earlier (in s. 2.3): the degree of freedom present in two situations gets isolated as the only difference between them, and therefore as the only basis we can possibly have for preferring one situation to the other. However, while Sen's example clearly shows that freedom has a certain kind of value, it does not seem to me to be appropriate to

---

[50] A. Sen, 'Freedom of Choice: Concept and Content', *European Economic Review*, 32 (1988), 290, emphasis in original.

call that kind of value *intrinsic* value. It is not freedom as such that is valued by the fasting individual in Sen's example, but the freedom to eat. The freedom to eat is valuable for those interested in fasting because the freedom to eat (and not freedom as such) is a constitutive part of the practice of fasting. If this is all that Sen has in mind when he says, for example, that 'the good life is inter alia a life of freedom',[51] then it would be more consistent of him to say that while he indeed sees freedom as having value over and above *its instrumental role* (see the above citation), it is not true that he sees it as having value over and above the value of the specific possible achievements for which it is a necessary condition.

The latter interpretation indeed seems to me to be more in keeping with Sen's general theory of individual well-being, which, despite its influence in bringing the importance of freedom to the attention of welfare economists, has less liberal implications than might at first appear. Sen's basic concern is with the possibilities people have of 'functioning' in the right way. As Martha Nussbaum has pointed out, the idea that human well-being consists in the achievement of certain 'functionings' can be traced back to Aristotle.[52] The valuable functionings are said by Nussbaum and Sen to include eating, walking, living a long life, 'affiliating', 'enjoying humour', and so on. For Sen, taking an interest in people's functionings represents an important improvement on welfarism, which assesses people's well-being purely in terms of their utility levels. We can imagine a cripple who, despite his disability, has an unusually cheerful disposition, and is thus very efficient at converting resources into utility. Welfarism may well imply that this cripple is 'better off' than an able-bodied person who happens to be very inefficient at converting resources into utility (say, because he is grumpy or has expensive tastes), and there seems to be something wrong with that. Surely a more objective way of assessing how well off people are would be by looking at their functionings.

This is not the place to judge whether or how far the above view is indeed an improvement on welfarism. What does need pointing out, however, is that, on the face of it, employing Aristotelian functional concepts hardly provides a promising start for the construction of a *liberal* theory of individual well-being. This, indeed, partly accounts for my criticism of MacIntyre in the previous section. Is it not excessively paternalist to insist that people do or be certain specific things in order to achieve their own personal *telos*? Would we still be pursuing their *telos* if we removed their freedom to *avoid* these

---

[51] A. Sen, 'Well-Being, Agency and Freedom', *Journal of Philosophy*, 82 (1985), 202.

[52] See M. Nussbaum, 'Nature, Function, and Capability: Aristotle on Political Distribution', *Oxford Studies in Ancient Philosophy*, Suppl. Vol. (1988), in particular at 153–5 and 175–6. See also her 'Non-relative Virtues: An Aristotelian Approach', in M. Nussbaum and A. Sen (eds.), *The Quality of Life* (Oxford: Clarendon Press, 1993).

functionings? Sen and Nussbaum implicitly answer this objection by saying that theirs is a *liberal* theory of functionings: their version of the Aristotelian theory incorporates freedom of choice as an important element of individual well-being.[53] Freedom gets included in their account of well-being through the stipulation that it is only valuable for a person to achieve a certain set of functionings if she has the freedom *not* to achieve that set of functionings —if, in other words, her achievements result from her own choices. Thus, our conclusion about the difference in value between fasting and starving gets extended to cover all valuable functionings, and in line with this Sen says that he would like to concentrate on 'capabilities', rather than on functionings, where a person's capability set reflects her *freedom* to choose among valuable functionings.[54] However, the perception Sen and Nussbaum have of the high value liberals assign to freedom does not appear to have gone as far as distinguishing between specific and non-specific value. As a result, their concession to liberalism turns out to be a minimal one. What matters to them is still only the 'freedom *to choose what is valuable*'.[55] All that is implied by their concession is that freedom has a form of specific value, namely, specific constitutive value: freedom is valuable as a constitutive part of valuable functionings.

If Sen and Nussbaum were to be bolder (i.e. more liberal) about the value of freedom, and certainly if they were to remain true to Sen's perception of the value freedom has 'over and above [and not merely as a constitutive part of] . . . what freedom permits us to achieve', they would place value not only on the capability to achieve valuable functionings (like fasting), but also on capability as such. They would at least say that the latter, as well as the former, is a constitutive part of individual well-being, and therefore that an individual's well-being is also contributed to by the mere fact of her being capable of doing more things rather than fewer.

Why is this so? Why should freedom also be seen as *non*-specifically constitutively valuable? One answer can be found in what is perhaps the most plausible reinterpretation of the argument of Hurka examined in s. 2.3. For Hurka, freedom is valuable because human agency is valuable: the more freedom we have, the greater the sense in which we can be called agents, and thus responsible for what we do, because the greater the number of times that we can say 'no'. To put this argument in Sen's terms, it is valuable for an agent not

[53] On the difference with Aristotle here, see D. Charles, 'Perfectionism in Aristotle's Political Theory: Reply to Martha Nussbaum', *Oxford Studies in Ancient Philosophy*, Suppl. Vol. (1988), 202–4.

[54] See e.g. A. Sen, 'Capability and Well-Being', in Nussbaum and Sen (eds.), *The Quality of Life*, 33.

[55] M. Nussbaum, 'Reply to David Charles', *Oxford Studies in Ancient Philosophy*, Suppl. Vol. (1988), 213, my emphasis.

just to be able to say 'no' to a particular functioning, but also to be able to say 'no' more times rather than fewer. And since these 'noes' can be 'noes' to any functionings whatsoever, many of them of *not* valuable, the kind of value we are dealing with here is clearly 'non-specific'. Why should it be non-specific *constitutive* value (rather than intrinsic value or non-specific instrumental value)? There is no decisive argument here, but the idea surely has some plausibility. As I pointed out earlier (in s. 2.4), Hurka's argument does not demonstrate decisively that freedom is an end in itself. Neither, on the other hand, need it be taken to imply that freedom is a 'means' to agency. To say that freedom would have no value were it not for agency is not necessarily to say that freedom is a means to agency. For it might be said to be analytically rather than causally true that freedom is a necessary condition for agency.

In a similar vein, Lawrence Crocker has argued that freedom is a 'non-causal necessary condition' for the 'autonomy complex'. This 'autonomy complex' includes certain kinds of human behaviour which we value 'in many cases where their consequences are negligible or even unfortunate'.[56] Among these kinds of behaviour Crocker includes 'many acts of risk taking, holding to principle, sacrificing, compromising, admitting mistakes, and struggling through',[57] a list to which we might add the characteristic of individual spontaneity—one which Mill claimed to have 'intrinsic worth . . . deserving . . . regard on its own account'.[58] Of all of these kinds of behaviour, it can be said that freedom is a necessary condition. True, they are all *specific* kinds of behaviour. However, they are also kinds of behaviour that can cover any possible aim or action. Any specific purpose can conceivably be sacrificed, compromised, mistakenly chosen, struggled towards, and so on. Moreover, these kinds of behaviour do not only cover specifically valuable purposes if, as Crocker says, their consequences can be 'negligible or even unfortunate'. Therefore, it seems correct to categorize the kind of value singled out by Crocker as non-specific. Why non-specific *constitutive* value? Like Mill in the case of spontaneity, Crocker himself claims that the above kind of value is 'intrinsic' value. But this seems to me to be a mistake. Crocker's argument makes the value of freedom depend on that of another phenomenon; freedom would not have value were it not for the value of the 'autonomy complex'. On the other hand, his explanation of freedom's value is, as he says, 'non-causal'. It is analytically, not contingently true that freedom is a necessary condition for the autonomy complex. It therefore seems to me that on his view, an autonomous person is by definition *inter alia* a person who does things like 'admitting mistakes' and 'struggling through', and that a person who does things like that is by definition *inter*

---

[56] L. Crocker, *Positive Liberty* (London: Nijhoff, 1980), 115.   [57] Ibid.
[58] Mill, *On Liberty*, ch. 3, *Collected Works*, xviii. 261.

alia a person with a certain degree of freedom. This makes freedom non-specifically valuable as a constitutive part of the 'autonomy complex'.

Yet another account of freedom's non-specific constitutive value might consist in saying that agency and autonomy are in turn part of 'the social bases for self-respect', which together form one of Rawls's so-called 'primary goods' —'perhaps the most important primary good'[59]—where it is self-respect that is ultimately of intrinsic value. Or perhaps it could be said that liberty is a necessary condition for having self-respect in a more direct sense. Rawls himself claims, in any case, that liberty is one of the bases of self-respect.[60] According to Henry Shue, this implies seeing liberty as a 'causally effective means' to self-respect.[61] But if the argument presented above is correct, then this need not follow. An alternative meaning of the claim that freedom forms one of the 'bases' for self-respect is that people's self-respect is in part a *function* of their freedom—that it is analytically, not causally true, that a person needs a certain degree of freedom in order to have self-respect.

Rawlsians might object that what has 'constitutive value' for them is not liberty as such but, rather, 'the basic liberties', and therefore that liberty for them has only specific constitutive value. However, for such an objection to go through, it must be the case that Rawlsians see the basic liberties as contributing to self-respect (or whatever other intrinsically good thing) *only* because of the value of the kinds of things the basic liberties let us do, and not at all because of the simple fact that the basic liberties are *liberties*. Once the notion of 'basic liberty' gets unpacked in this way, the above objection loses its central motivation. One need not deny the non-specific value of liberty in order to give the Rawlsian basic liberties priority over other liberties. Reasons for such a priority might indeed have to do with the specific constitutive value of the basic liberties. But such reasons do not prevent us from also seeing liberty *itself* as constitutively valuable (liberty itself being the characteristic the basic liberties have in common with the non-basic liberties). They do not prevent it from being an important question 'how free' one set of specific basic liberties makes one when compared with another set of specific basic liberties (or indeed, how free people are in terms of their specific non-basic liberties— something which might still be of interest to Rawlsians where two people 'tie' in terms of their basic liberties). We can still be interested in people having 'the most extensive basic liberty' (within the limits of satiation), and one possible reason for this lies in the non-specific constitutive value of liberty.[62]

---

[59] Rawls, *A Theory of Justice*, 440.   [60] Ibid. 544–5.

[61] H. Shue, 'Liberty and Self Respect', *Ethics*, 85 (1975), 197.

[62] The priority of maximal basic liberty *is* incompatible with the idea that liberty as such is *unconditionally* valuable (unless it is the case, as a matter of fact, that a maximally free person always has, *inter alia*, maximal basic liberty).

2.6 NON-SPECIFIC VALUE AND NON-SPECIFIC DISVALUE

We must be honest about freedom's disvalue as well as its value. Something therefore needs to be said about the objections put forward by Gerald Dworkin, who has presented some convincing arguments against the idea that having more choice is always better than having less. Gerald Dworkin points out that even in an example such as that of Hurka (where larger and smaller choice sets have identical best options), having more choice may not be better than having less, given the costs attached to having more choice. These costs may be of two kinds, reflecting 'either general features of choice, or intrinsic features of particular choices'.[63] Presumably, if the second kind of cost is different from the first, 'intrinsic features of particular choices' are not features of choice as such but, rather, features determined by the nature of the specific things one can choose to do in specific situations. Among the costs attached to choice as such Gerald Dworkin notes the burden of acquiring the information necessary for informed choice and the costs in time and effort of making choices.[64] Among the costs attached to certain specific examples of choices, he notes the burden of responsibility attached to the choice of whether or not to bring a Down's syndrome infant into the world, and the possible decrease in welfare brought about by allowing the free choice of marriage partners.

Now we need not deny the existence of these costs of freedom in order for the central argument of this chapter to go through. We need not even deny that certain kinds of costs can outweigh the benefits outlined so far in certain ways. Only a certain kind of cost, and a certain kind of outweighing of benefits, can contradict my thesis about the value of freedom. As we shall now see, this fact considerably weakens the force of Gerald Dworkin's objections.

The additional complication brought about by the introduction of costs into our analysis means that we need to distinguish, for the sake of clarity, between a thing having value (or being valuable), and that thing having value (or being valuable) *on balance*. Freedom has non-specific value *on balance* if freedom's non-specific value outweighs freedom's non-specific disvalue. The burden of this chapter has been to suggest not merely that freedom is non-specifically valuable, but that it is non-specifically valuable *on balance*; where I have previously claimed that 'freedom is non-specifically valuable', I should therefore be taken to have meant implicitly that it is non-specifically valuable on balance. Otherwise, it would not have been implied that we have an interest in freedom as such, and in giving people a measure of freedom. This implicit meaning fits in with ordinary language usage; the idea that something

---

[63] Dworkin, *The Theory and Practice of Autonomy*, 65.   [64] Ibid. 66–7, cf. 72–3.

is 'intrinsically valuable' is usually taken to mean that it has more intrinsic value than intrinsic disvalue.[65] The only kind of non-specific value in the case of which this additional clarification is not needed is that of unconditional value. Where we say that a thing has unconditional value, we are already saying that its value trumps its disvalue, and vice versa where we say that it has unconditional disvalue. They very idea of weighing up costs and benefits is ruled out by the notion of unconditionality.

As we have seen, Gerald Dworkin identifies two kinds of disvalue of freedom. The first is its non-specific disvalue (the costs attached to 'general features of choice') and the second is its specific disvalue (the costs attached to certain specific choices). However, the second of these kinds of disvalue is not relevant to the question of whether freedom of choice is non-specifically valuable (on balance). Freedom of choice is non-specifically valuable (on balance) if its non-specific value outweighs its non-specific disvalue. Only if we see freedom as unconditionally valuable will we need to deal with arguments about the disvalue of specific choices. Only then will we have to say that we would *always* (in the non-*ceteris paribus* sense) prefer the choice set S2 in Hurka's example, whatever the contents of sets S1 and S2. If freedom is merely non-specifically valuable (on balance), then the benefits of having choice must always outweigh *certain* costs—those costs which reflect, as Gerald Dworkin puts it, 'general features of choice'.

Notice, moreover, that for my central thesis about the value of freedom to be defeated, it is not enough that freedom's non-specific disvalue outweigh its non-specific value once we have reached a particularly high degree of freedom. Rather, the former must outweigh the latter all the way down the scale. Otherwise, the presence of non-specific disvalue would only contradict the claim that more freedom is better than less in the non-satiable sense, and not the claim—for which I have been arguing—that more freedom is better than less at least up to a point of satiation. This seems to me to dispose of the example referring to the burden of choice in terms of the time and effort needed to process large quantities of information about available alternatives.

It might of course turn out that the assertion of freedom's on-balance non-specific value (and therefore of the need to measure freedom) is of little importance for another reason, the source of that reason being Gerald Dworkin's arguments for the specific instrumental disvalue of having choice. This might be so if, as a consequence of his arguments, most sets of freedoms, in most situations, are seen as having more on-balance specific disvalue than on-balance non-specific value, and therefore (at the level of value in general)

---

[65] See, for example, Roderick Chisholm's definition of 'intrinsically valuable', in his 'Intrinsic Value', 126.

as having disvalue (on balance) all the way down the scale. I think that the likelihood of a liberal accepting this claim is very low. To those who disagree, I can only repeat my admission that the *share* of freedom's positive value which is assigned to the category of non-specific value determines the degree of importance of the need to be able to measure freedom (see the end of s. 2.1), and place my own arguments for freedom's non-specific value alongside Gerald Dworkin's arguments (duly distinguished) for its non-specific and specific disvalue.

2.7 DEGREES OF OVERALL FREEDOM TO DO VALUABLE THINGS

Suppose the advocate of the specific-freedom thesis puts forward the following objection: 'I accept your arguments to the effect that we are committed to knowing "how much freedom" people have (be this in relative or absolute terms), but this does not imply that I must take an interest in freedom *as such*. I can still hang on to the specific-freedom thesis, since all I need admit is that we should take an interest in how much of *this* specific freedom a person has, how much of *that* specific freedom she has, and so on.'

This objection is in need of some clarification. Consider the expression 'how much of a certain specific freedom'. The role of this expression in the objection seems to be such as to imply that there can be a certain specific freedom-*type* that is particularly valuable, and that as a consequence we should be interested in maximizing, or (say) in guaranteeing a fair amount of the *tokens* of, that freedom-type. But where is such an interest supposed to come from? The source must be a composite value, made up of (*a*) *there being certain specific freedom-types* and (*b*) *there being a measure of freedom*. And what the objector seems to want to add is that part (*b*) of this composite value has value only when combined with part (*a*). There is certainly nothing logically incoherent about saying this. Neither does it conflict with my own view that having a measure of freedom is one good among many, or with the idea that we should measure freedom in accordance with the approach defended in Part III of this book. But it does conflict with my view that we should take an interest in people's *overall* freedom.

Is this logically sound halfway position convincing from a *normative* point of view? I think not. Such a position involves assigning too weak a value to (*b*) compared to that assigned to (*a*). For, if we reflect carefully on this question, we can see that it is very difficult to find a good reason for saying that (*b*) is valuable only in combination with (*a*). The only reason I can see for wanting to quantify *only* over the tokens of a specific freedom-type (rather than over these *and also* over all other freedom-tokens) is that freedom is non-specifically valuable *only within that freedom-type*—i.e. that different tokens of the freedom to perform act-type *x* are valuable independently of *which* particular tokens they are of the freedom to perform act-type *x*, but not independently of the fact that they *are* tokens of the freedom to perform act-type *x* (rather than of the freedom to perform act-type *y* or act-type *z*). However, if one starts to appeal to the idea of non-specific value within certain freedom-types, then one would seem to have no way of resisting the further arguments presented in this chapter for the *wholly* non-specific value of freedom. We saw this happen, for example, to the position of Kymlicka at the end of s. 2.4: once it was admitted that freedom was valuable as a means to personal growth, it was seen to be illegitimate to confine this value to certain 'meaningful' options. Similarly, where freedom was seen as valuable as a constitutive part of agency or of the 'autonomy complex', we saw that this kind of value must include non-valuable options as well as valuable ones. It seems then that the only reasons there are for saying that (*b*) is valuable are reasons for saying that (*b*) is valuable independently of (*a*). If this is indeed so, then we must either affirm the value of (*b*) independently of (*a*) or else deny it altogether. In other words, if one accepts that people should have a measure of freedom, one accepts that that measure is a measure of freedom as such, and not simply a measure of that portion of their freedom that is made up of specifically valuable freedom-types. I can think of no normative reason for wanting to measure only the amount of freedom provided by specifically valuable freedom-types.

2.8 EXTREME DIFFERENCES IN SPECIFIC VALUE

It seems to me that a major factor contributing to the initial plausibility of the normative version of the specific-freedom thesis is the tendency of authors to concentrate our attention on examples of *specific* freedoms that have *an extremely high or low degree of specific value*. An old favourite is the example which juxtaposes freedom from restrictions on religious practices with freedom from the regulations imposed by traffic lights.[66] Similarly, we might be asked to compare the freedom to turn up at work wearing a skullcap with the freedom to turn up at work wearing a V-neck sweater.[67] To take this argumentative

---

[66] The example comes from Charles Taylor's 'What's Wrong with Negative Liberty', in A. Ryan (ed.), *The Idea of Freedom* (London: Oxford University Press, 1979). Taylor does not himself argue for the specific-freedom thesis in any of its forms. On the contrary, he assumes an interest in quantifying overall freedom. I take a close look at Taylor's conception of freedom in Chs. 5 and 6.

[67] This example was put to me by Kymlicka (in personal correspondence).

strategy even further, we might be asked to compare a particularly valuable specific freedom with the freedom to perform a clearly vicious action: say, the freedom to perform cold-blooded murder. These examples are intended to provide extreme contrasts between the specific values of two specific freedoms, where the 'amount of freedom' each provides (given the empirical approach to measuring freedom defended later in this book) nevertheless appears to be roughly the same, or perhaps even greater in the case of the less specifically valuable specific freedom. The specific-freedom theorists tell us that in such examples the one kind of freedom matters a great deal more than the other kind, *and that therefore* the number of actions available to a person (the sheer number of 'open doors'), in purely quantitative terms, cannot in itself be a very important thing. But this implication does not hold. Such examples do *not* constitute a case against the non-specific value of freedom. All that they imply is that freedom has *specific* value, and that the variations between specific freedoms in terms of *this* kind of value can be very great. Concentrating on examples where the differences in specific value are extreme can blind us to the *other* important kinds of value that can come into play. One could be forgiven, indeed, for attributing to Ronald Dworkin and Will Kymlicka the belief that to assert the non-specific value of freedom is to *deny* the great differences between the specific values of the specific freedoms in the above examples. It would certainly be foolish to deny such differences, but there remains the fact that specific value is not the only kind of value that freedoms can have or lack, since freedom also has value as such.

Those initially persuaded by the specific-freedom thesis would do well to put aside for a moment such examples, take a look around themselves, and experience the phenomenon of *overall* freedom—the simple fact of there being a greater or lesser number of doors open to them. Our awareness of this phenomenon is most acute when it is subject to major or sudden increases or decreases. But the phenomenon does not go away after the passing of such moments, and the fact of it being present to a greater rather than a lesser degree remains valuable (subject to various qualifications), for the reasons I have set out in this chapter. What Kymlicka calls the 'neutral counting' of freedoms[68] *does* matter for those reasons, and is *not* intended by its advocates (or at least need not be intended) to substitute the idea of discriminating between specific freedoms in terms of their specific values. And if, in practice, having more freedom is sometimes found to be incompatible with having a set of specific freedoms with a high degree of specific instrumental value, this is a conflict which must be faced up to rather than ignored.

---

[68] W. Kymlicka, *Contemporary Political Philosophy* (Oxford: Oxford University Press, 1990), 137–41.

1. Freedom has unconditional value ⎫
2. Freedom has intrinsic value ⎪ freedom has
3. Freedom has non-specific constitutive value ⎬ non-specific value
4. Freedom has non-specific instrumental value ⎭

5. Freedom has specific constitutive value ⎫ freedom has
6. Freedom has specific instrumental value ⎭ specific value

FIG. 2

2.9 SUMMARY

For the sake of clarity, it is worth mapping out the different kinds of value that we have encountered in this chapter (together with their definitions, set out in the next section). The claims about freedom set out in Fig. 2 can be said to vary, roughly speaking, from the stronger to the weaker as we progress down from claim (1) to claim (6). As should now be clear, we need take no interest in measuring overall freedom if (5) and (6) are the only true claims about its value. However, we have seen that while it would be unwise to deny claims (5) and (6), liberals also have strong reasons at least for making claims (4) and (3). They may, in addition, wish to make claim (2), and despite (2) being difficult to argue for, it is no less difficult to argue against. Liberals have no good reason for making claim (1), but that is far from being a sufficient reason for seeing claims (5) and (6) as the only true ones, nor therefore for denying an interest in how free people are in an overall sense. On the contrary, a clearer understanding of the ways in which freedom is valuable shows that the idea of freedom as such, and lesser or greater amounts of it, does a great deal of work in liberal political theorizing.

2.10 DEFINITIONS

Non-specific Value. A phenomenon, x, has non-specific value (is valuable as such) iff the value of x cannot be described wholly in terms of a good brought about or contributed to by a specific instance of x or set of specific instances of x.

Unconditional Value. A phenomenon, x, has unconditional value iff x is intrinsically valuable and more x is always better than less x both in terms of increasing quantities of x and in terms of the choice between x and other phenomena.

Intrinsic Value. A phenomenon, x, has intrinsic value iff x is an end in itself (that is, if x has a positive overall value which is not reducible to the value of any other phenomenon).

Non-specific Constitutive Value. A phenomenon, x, has non-specific constitutive value iff x, without regard to the nature of its specific instances, is a constitutive part of some other phenomenon, y, and y is intrinsically valuable.

Non-specific Instrumental Value. A phenomenon, x, has non-specific instrumental value iff x, without regard to the nature of its specific instances, is a means to some other valuable phenomenon, y.

Specific Constitutive Value. A phenomenon, x, has specific constitutive value iff a certain specific instance (or set of instances) of x is a constitutive part of some other phenomenon, y, and y is intrinsically valuable.

Specific Instrumental Value. A phenomenon, x, has specific instrumental value iff a certain specific instance (or set of instances) of x is a means to some other valuable phenomenon, y.

3

The Distribution of Freedom

IF freedom is a non-specifically valuable quantitative attribute, we ought to take an interest in how it is distributed in society. This is the basic thought that should now concern us, and the aim of the present chapter is to clarify its possible meanings and implications.

The non-specific value of freedom gives us an interest in knowing 'how free' people are in an overall sense, and thus in being able to measure overall freedom. In Parts II and III of this book we shall go on to see how far and in what ways overall freedom is indeed measurable. There, we shall be addressing what I have called the epistemic problems raised by defenders of the specific-freedom thesis (see s. 1.4). First, however, we need to see how the notion of overall freedom fits into the wider context of a liberal theory of distributive justice. This will be useful not only as a means of emphasizing the fundamental role played in such a theory by the notion of overall freedom, but also, more particularly, as a way of giving us a clearer idea of the demands made by theories of justice on our powers of measuring overall freedom. I shall begin by showing how the idea of the non-specific value of freedom gives rise to the need for a principle of justice for the distribution of freedom (section 1), and how different justifications of the normative version of the overall-freedom thesis can lead to the adoption of different distributive principles (section 2). In the third and final section, I shall look at the requirements made by different distributive principles on our powers of measurement.

3.1 FROM NON-SPECIFIC VALUE TO FREEDOM-BASED THEORIES OF JUSTICE

Those who accept the force of the arguments for the non-specific value of freedom presented in the previous chapter can be usefully described as *freedom-based* liberals. To be a freedom-based liberal is to endorse a freedom-based theory of distributive justice, which is to say, a theory of justice that assumes freedom to be one of the goods to be distributed in accordance with that theory among the people to whom that theory applies. If we hold that freedom is non-specifically valuable, then freedom itself ought to be one of the *distribuenda* of our theory of distributive justice: we should say that justice requires people to have an equal measure of freedom, or to have no less than a given measure of freedom, or something of the sort. This is because, quite simply, justice is about the distribution of benefits and burdens in society, and if we assume freedom to be non-specifically valuable, then we assume freedom as such to be one of the benefits to be distributed. The ideal of freedom need not of course be the *only* object of a freedom-based theory of justice. Such a theory must, however, be based on that ideal among others. Thus, a freedom-based theory of justice can also be, say, utility-based, as long as it contains some rule for weighing or ranking the competing claims of freedom on the one hand and utility on the other. Notice, too, that I use the expression 'ideal of freedom' in a weak sense. One need not see freedom as *intrinsically* valuable—as one of our ends—in order to appeal coherently to the *ideal* of freedom in the above sense; one need only see it as non-specifically valuable.

There are some self-described liberals who appear to endorse not a freedom-based theory of justice but, rather, what might be called a 'justice-based definition of freedom'. In the light of the above argument, these theorists get freedom and justice the wrong way round: rather than first discussing how far freedom should be seen as a valuable thing and then discussing the justice of various possible distributions of that valuable thing, they instead discuss the nature of justice without reference to freedom, and then go on to define freedom in terms of their favoured conception of justice. It is worth taking a closer look at these 'justice-based definitions of freedom'. In particular, it is worth asking what leads theorists to endorse them, as the answer to this question will further illustrate the ineradicability from liberal discourse of the idea of freedom as a quantitative attribute.

G. A. Cohen has detected an implicit reliance on a justice-based definition of freedom in the arguments employed by libertarians on the question of whether liberty and equality are necessarily conflicting ideals.[1] Cohen's particular target is Nozick, but the same flaw is to be found in the writings of a number of other anti-redistributionist libertarians.[2] According to Nozick, 'liberty upsets

---

[1] G. A. Cohen, *Self-Ownership, Freedom, and Equality* (Cambridge: Cambridge University Press, 1995), 55–7. See also: G. A. Cohen, 'Illusions about Private Property and Freedom', in J. Mepham and D. H. Ruben (eds.), *Issues in Marxist Philosophy*, iv (Hassocks: Harvester, 1981); id., 'Capitalism, Freedom and the Proletariat', in Ryan (ed.), *The Idea of Freedom*; C. C. Ryan, 'Yours, Mine, and Ours: Property Rights and Individual Liberty', in J. Paul (ed.), *Reading Nozick* (Oxford: Blackwell, 1982).

[2] See e.g. L. von Mises, *Human Action: A Treatise on Economics* (New Haven: Yale University Press, 1949), 283; B. Leoni, *Freedom and the Law* (Los Angeles: Nash, 1961), ch. 2; D. Den Uyl, 'Freedom and Virtue', in T. R. Machan (ed.), *The Libertarian Alternative* (Chicago: Nelson-Hall, 1974); M. N. Rothbard, *The Ethics of Liberty* (Atlantic Highlands, NJ: Humanities Press, 1982), part iv; R. Barnett, 'Pursuing Justice in a Free Society: Part One—Power vs. Liberty', *Criminal Justice Ethics* (1985), 64; J. Gray, 'Against Cohen on Proletarian Unfreedom', *Social Philosophy and Policy*, 6 (1988), 103–4. Moralized definitions of freedom go back at least as far as Locke, whose famous distinction between 'liberty' and 'licence' (*Two Treatises of Government*, ii, s. 6) may have had some influence on the above authors.

[distributional] patterns', such as equality of resources, since 'no end-state principle or distributional patterned principle of justice can be continuously realized without continuous interference with people's lives'.[3] Now it is clear that if this claim is to have any argumentative weight—if we are not to be able simply to answer that while patterns remove 'some specific liberties for some people' they also create 'other specific liberties for other people'[4]— then Nozick must be taken to be saying something like this: 'If you allow *more* liberty overall, your favourite pattern will be upset; if you want to keep your favourite pattern, you must allow *less* liberty overall.' And yet this more interesting and weighty claim will only be *obviously* true (that is, clearly true even in the absence of further investigation into what it is to be 'more' or 'less' free overall) if we accept as its justification a definition of freedom that is designed to bias the outcome of the argument from the start. According to this definition of freedom, the so-called 'freedoms' to which a pattern contributes are not really freedoms at all, because freedom is nothing more or less than the absence of constraints on the exercising of one's *property rights*. Imposing a pattern involves preventing actions which people have a right to perform, usually by taxing away some of their property. True, in taking from some, the pattern enforcer also gives to others. But those 'others' have no *right* to do as they wish with their immorally acquired taxed resources. Thus while the liberty of the taxed is decreased, the liberty of those receiving benefits is not increased. It is clear that on this definition of freedom, under a minimal state that respects and enforces people's rights, there will be complete freedom. Moreover, there will be no need for us to go out into the world and measure freedom in order to know this. The fact of there being complete freedom in such a situation follows *by definition*.

In light of the conceptual link it makes between the lack of freedom and the violation of moral rights, Cohen has called the above definition of freedom a 'moralized definition', or (more precisely) a 'rights definition'.[5] I shall use the expression 'justice-based definition of freedom' to refer to a moralized definition of freedom that is based on a conception of justice, regardless of the role of rights in that conception.

The Nozickian justice-based definition of freedom is seriously at odds with a number of basic liberal intuitions about freedom. According to most

[3] R. Nozick, *Anarchy, State and Utopia* (Oxford: Blackwell, 1974), 160–1.

[4] For a more developed version of this answer, see S. Lukes, 'Equality and Liberty: Must they Conflict?', in D. Held (ed.), *Political Theory Today* (Cambridge: Polity Press, 1991), 60.

[5] In the 1979 and 1991 versions, respectively, of Cohen's 'Capitalism, Freedom and the Proletariat'. As well as appealing implicitly to a moralized definition of freedom, Nozick also appeals explicitly to a moralized definition of voluntariness: cf. S. Olsaretti, 'Freedom, Force, and Choice: Against the Rights-Based Definition of Voluntariness', *Journal of Political Philosophy*, 6 (1998).

people's linguistic intuitions, there are just restrictions of liberty and unjust restrictions of liberty. If I am physically prevented from crossing your justly acquired land, do I not lack the freedom to do so? (People often disagree over whether physical prevention—say, for the sake of argument, *deliberate* physical prevention—is a necessary condition for being rendered unfree, but few dispute that it is a sufficient one.) Does the justly imprisoned thief in a high-security prison not lack the freedom to leave? And is he not 'less free' than the millionaire who is taxed one penny in the pound? On a Nozickian justice-based definition of freedom, we should have to answer all of these questions in the negative. We should have to say that the justly imprisoned thief suffers no unfreedom, and that he is indeed freer than the taxed millionaire. There is surely more intuitive appeal in Cohen's counter-assertion that 'private property is a distribution of freedom *and* unfreedom'.[6] My having and successfully exercising an exclusive right to a piece of land means that I am free to walk on that land *and* that others are *un*free to do so.

Even if we leave aside intuitions about the existence of specific freedoms, justice-based definitions of freedom are inconsistent with mainstream libertarian thinking, given that most libertarians ostensibly see freedom as non-specifically valuable. It is indeed only because we hold freedom to be non-specifically valuable that we see the claim that 'liberty upsets patterns' as interesting in the first place. For we have seen that such a claim is only interesting if interpreted as referring to the degrees of overall freedom implied by the enforcement of distributional patterns, and the only reason we have for being interested in degrees of overall freedom is, as we saw in the previous two chapters, a belief in freedom's non-specific value. Yet, if one endorses a justice-based definition of freedom, one cannot also say that freedom is non-specifically valuable. If one sees freedom as non-specifically valuable, then one virtue of one's theory of justice ought to be that it promotes freedom, or distributes it equally, or guarantees a fair amount of freedom to all, or something of the sort. But if freedom is simply defined *in terms of* what has *already* been labelled as just, such an appeal to freedom is not being made. By 'moralizing' the notion of freedom—by making the *meaning* of freedom depend wholly on that of another good—one indeed disposes completely of the need to talk about freedom in any literal sense. Freedom 'falls out of the picture':[7] it gets sacrificed as an ideal, and then defined in terms of another ideal merely to conceal the fact.

Notice, however, that these objections to justice-based definitions of freedom apply not only to libertarians, but also to the defender of distributional

[6] Cohen, 'Illusions about Private Property and Freedom', 227.
[7] G. A. Cohen, *History, Labour and Freedom* (Oxford: Clarendon Press, 1988), 296.

patterns who says that 'having freedom is not being prevented from doing what is possible within the constraints of this pattern', or, for that matter, to the Stalinist who says that 'having freedom is not being prevented from doing your duty on the collective farm'! It is therefore surprising to see the libertarians receiving all the limelight when redistributionists raise objections to the moralized definition of freedom, given that there is another freedom moralizer much closer to home, namely Ronald Dworkin, according to whom 'justice' consists in treating individuals with equal concern and respect, and 'freedom' consists in the power to do what one is able to do in an ideally egalitarian (i.e. just) society.[8] It is clear that Dworkin, no less than Nozick, relies at times on a justice-based definition of freedom.

Dworkin attempts to defend his recourse to a justice-based definition of freedom. But this defence can never convince us as long as we have clearly established in our minds the implications of freedom's non-specific value. Dworkin distinguishes between what he calls the empirical, or 'flat' meaning of liberty, and its 'normative' meaning (i.e. the above definition in terms of equality), and holds that when we say liberty has been sacrificed for equality, we really mean only liberty in the 'uninteresting', 'flat' sense, and that we do not thereby imply that any 'defensible *ideal of liberty*' has been compromised.[9] In fact, exactly the reverse of this is true. To be interested only in liberty in Dworkin's 'normative' sense is to imply that there is *no such thing* as a defensible ideal of liberty. It is to deny, rather than to affirm, that liberty has a 'distinct quality and value'.[10] Any defence of an ideal which involves *defining freedom in terms of that ideal* is not, whatever its other strengths, a defence by appeal to freedom. It is only by taking an interest in liberty in its empirical, 'flat', 'uninteresting' sense that we are able to accord liberty a 'distinct quality and value'.

Why is it that we find eminent political theorists like Nozick and Dworkin subscribing to such unconvincing definitions of freedom? I would suggest that they are led to these justice-based definitions less by any direct intuitive appeal

---

[8] This definition of liberty is implicit in R. Dworkin's 'What is Equality? Part 3: The Place of Liberty', *Iowa Law Review*, 73 (1987), 3–6. The definition was stated explicitly by Dworkin in a paper given at the Workshop on Ethics and Economics at the University of Siena in July 1991. Interestingly enough, Robert Nozick, who was present at the same workshop, objected to Dworkin's definition of liberty in exactly the same way as Cohen objects to the definition implicit in *Anarchy, State and Utopia*. Nozick pointed out that this was rather an easy way to show that liberty and equality were compatible, and that a Muslim fundamentalist could just as easily show liberty to be compatible with Muslim fundamentalism by defining liberty as 'the power to do what one is able to do in an ideally Muslim fundamentalist society'.

[9] 'What is Equality? Part 3: The Place of Liberty', 3, my emphasis. I am not suggesting here that there *is* a conflict between liberty and equality; only that such a conflict should not be excluded by definitional fiat (as it is by Dworkin).

[10] Ibid. 2.

of the definitions themselves than by a well-founded (albeit unconscious) reluctance to come out explicitly against the idea of a freedom-based theory of justice. If we deny freedom's non-specific value, freedom itself will not be one of our criteria for granting people certain freedoms rather than others; freedom will not itself be one of the *distribuenda* of our theory of justice, hence our theory of justice will not be freedom-based. A justice-based definition of freedom allows one to mask this fact by appearing to reconcile two incompatible commitments: the commitment to promoting 'freedom' (as such) on the one hand, and the commitment to denying its non-specific value on the other. In practice, the former commitment gets abandoned in favour of the latter, and this abandonment is what the justice-based definition serves to mask.

It is plausible to hypothesize that Nozick and Dworkin arrive at their respective justice-based definitions of freedom from different directions, Nozick starting out consciously with a commitment to promoting freedom as such, and Dworkin starting out consciously with a commitment to the normative version of the specific-freedom thesis. Nozick starts out with what appears to be an interest in freedom as such, but then realizes that he is really only interested in the specific freedom-type of doing what one likes with one's private property. *His* justice-based definition of freedom serves to *cover up* an implicit commitment to a particular normative version of the *specific-freedom thesis*, which is nevertheless incompatible with his explicit claim about the relationship between private property and *overall* freedom. Dworkin, on the other hand, starts out with a conscious commitment to protecting only certain specific freedoms, as we saw in the previous two chapters, but then finds himself unable to abandon the language of 'more' and 'less' freedom when theorizing about egalitarian justice, so demonstrating an implicit interest in freedom as such. We find such language creeping back into his theory, for example, in the form of a commitment to 'a substantial degree of liberty', or to 'ample' liberty.[11] *His* justice-based definition of freedom serves to *present the appearance* of desiring to promote *freedom as such*, which is nevertheless incompatible with his explicit endorsement of the *specific-freedom thesis*.

The source, then, of justice-based definitions of freedom is an unconscious desire for a kind of linguistic refuge from a more coherent but unpalatable scepticism over the possibility of appealing to the 'ideal of freedom'. A justice-based definition allows the specific-freedom theorist to appear to retain the idea that it is important whether one individual or society is freer than another, and that justice requires 'a substantial degree of liberty'. But if these last ideas are superfluous to the pursuit of the ideals of liberalism, why bother even to *appear* to retain them? Why not embrace the specific-freedom thesis openly

---

[11] Ibid. 3.

and wholeheartedly? The reason for this equivocation on the part of Nozick and Dworkin surely lies in the ineradicability from liberal discourse of the notion of freedom as a quantitative attribute, and the reason for that ineradicability, in the non-specific value of freedom.

3.2 FROM NON-SPECIFIC VALUE TO DISTRIBUTIVE PRINCIPLES

If we say that freedom is non-specifically valuable, freedom ought to be one of the *distribuenda* of our theory of justice, in which case we shall need a principle for the distribution of freedom. Various such principles now present themselves as candidates. Our *choice* of distributive principle will depend, among other things, on the *reasons* we have given for saying that freedom is non-specifically valuable, and—what is in part the same thing—on the *kind* of non-specific value we have attributed to freedom. Of the factors affecting the kind of value we attribute to freedom, those which in turn most constrain our choice of distributive principle are: first, the question of whether fulfilling people's interest in freedom is an insatiable principle; secondly, the question of whether freedom is good in the '*non-ceteris paribus*' sense (see s. 2.2); and thirdly, the question of whether freedom is seen as contributing to a good of individuals or to some overall social good.

My aim in this section is not to argue outright for one particular distributive principle, but simply to trace some of the links that can be made between distributive principles on the one hand and reasons for valuing freedom on the other. The acceptability of any one of these distributive principles will be sufficient to justify our continued interest in the overall-freedom thesis, so I need not commit myself to one such principle in particular. However, clarifying these links might also help the supporters of certain principles in defending themselves against certain ill-conceived objections that have been (or might be) levelled against them. This is, I think, particularly true of the principle of maximal freedom.

Let us begin, then, by looking at the principle of maximal freedom. This may be asserted as a purely aggregative principle ('maximize the total amount of freedom in society' or 'maximize the freedom of the average member'[12]—call these examples of the principle of 'maximal societal freedom'), or else it may be asserted in combination with some distributive principle in the strict sense, in which case we shall have a distributive principle that includes what might be called a 'maximizing element'. Examples are the principle of 'maximal equal freedom' or the principle of 'maximin freedom'.

---

[12] The application of these two aggregative principles will have different consequences only where the number of members of the relevant society is assumed to vary.

Clearly, if one believes that freedom should be maximized in some way (either in the purely aggregative sense or as an element of a distributive principle in the strict sense), one believes that fulfilling people's interest in freedom is an *insatiable* principle, which is to say that the fact of a society or individual having more freedom is always preferable to the fact of its having less. More precisely, it is to say that its having more freedom is always preferable regardless of the degree of freedom it already has, but not necessarily that its having more freedom is always preferable regardless of the implications for other goods (since one could still wish to maximize *ceteris paribus*). I shall return to this distinction shortly. Before doing so, I should make a couple of clarificatory points regarding the notion of 'satiability'.

First, one should bear in mind that to say that the *principle* of 'fulfilling an interest in freedom' is insatiable is not to say that freedom is itself a *non-satiating good*: we need to distinguish, in terms of satiability, between freedom as a good and the principle that our interest in freedom should be fulfilled. Here I shall follow Joseph Raz in referring only to the satiability of *principles*.[13] It is possible for a good to be non-satiating *even though* the principle prescribing the provision of that good is a satiable principle.[14] A satiating good, we may say, is a good of which it is conceptually true that it has a point of satiation. That is to say, it is a good the conditions for the existence of which can be wholly satisfied. The most obvious examples are physiological needs, such as the relief of hunger. A certain amount of food completely fulfils the condition of relieving hunger, after which the supply of further food therefore contributes nothing to that good. In other words, it is conceptually impossible to go on relieving hunger indefinitely by supplying ever increasing quantities of food. It is quite a different thing to say that a principle for the promotion or distribution of good x is satiable or insatiable. Here, we are referring to the question of whether the conditions for the fulfilment of the *principle* can be wholly satisfied. Some such principles are necessarily insatiable (such as 'maximize x'), and others are necessarily satiable (such as 'equalize x'), while the principle that our interest in x should be 'fulfilled' may be either satiable or insatiable. My present interest is in the satiability or otherwise of this last principle as applied to freedom— that is, the principle of 'fulfilling our interest in freedom'. Where one says that the principle of 'fulfilling an interest in x' is satiable, one may no longer be making a conceptual point either about the meaning of the principle itself (as in the case of distributing x equally), or about the meaning of x (as where

[13] Raz, *The Morality of Freedom*, ch. 9.

[14] Cf. T. Magri, 'Negative Freedom, Rational Deliberation, and Non Satiating Goods', *Topoi*, 17 (1998).

we say that x is a satiating good), but a value judgement about the relative worth of different degrees of x.[15]

There are many goods which, though not being satiating goods in the above sense, one might reasonably judge it wrong to pursue beyond a certain extent, thus rendering satiable the principle that one's interest in their possession should be fulfilled.[16] One example might be 'desire satisfaction'. One may always be capable of forming new desires that have not yet been satisfied, and so it would be wrong to see desire satisfaction as a satiating good. On the other hand, one might hold that a limitless supply of desire satisfaction would not be a good thing—say, because of its damaging effects on individuals' motivations. Another example might be the good of longevity. This is a non-satiating good, given that it is always possible in theory to increase the length of a life by adding more years to it. Yet the principle that we should fulfil people's interest in longevity might still not be an insatiable principle, for as Bernard Williams points out, living for ever might be unbearably tedious.[17] And freedom, too, might reasonably be seen in this light. It seems difficult to deny that in any circumstance in which one has new options added to those one already has, one's freedom increases. It seems difficult to deny, in other words, that freedom is a non-satiating good. But one might still not want to maximize freedom— say, for one of the reasons touched on in s. 2.6.

The second point about satiability is that we should distinguish between satiability in practice and satiability in theory. Those who endorse a principle with a maximizing element might believe that there is a theoretical point of satiation, but that this point is too high to be reachable in practice. Thus, I imagine that, within the constraints of current technology, even Bernard Williams favours the maximization of longevity. In the case of distributive principles like maximal equal freedom or maximin freedom, one might favour maximization because the point of individual satiation in terms of freedom is at a level to which no one could possibly have a right, given the low levels that would thereby be implied for others. In any case, we should bear in mind that the fulfilment of our interest in freedom only needs to be an insatiable principle *in practice* for a maximizing element to be sufficiently motivated.

[15] Given this reasoning, the logical relationship between the satiability of good x and of principles regarding the promotion or distribution of x is as follows: where the principle is necessarily satiable (e.g. 'equalize x' or 'reach a minimum of x'), x may be either a satiable or an insatiable good; where the principle is necessarily insatiable (e.g. 'maximize x'), then x is necessarily an insatiable good; where x is a satiable good, the principle of fulfilling an interest in x is necessarily satiable; where x is an insatiable good, the principle of fulfilling an interest in x may be either satiable or insatiable.

[16] This point is made particularly clear in Magri's 'Negative Freedom, Rational Deliberation, and Non Satiating Goods', from which I have taken the examples of desire satisfaction and longevity.

[17] See B. Williams, *Problems of the Self: Philosophical Papers 1956–1972* (Cambridge: Cambridge University Press, 1977), ch. 6.

We are now in a position to consider maximal freedom as a candidate-principle for a freedom-based theory of justice. First, as we have seen, there is the straightforward aggregative principle—that of maximal societal freedom. References to this principle abound in the freedom literature. Berlin apparently detects the principle, for example, in the writings of Mill and Constant.[18] Hayek also seems to have in mind maximal societal freedom when he says that 'we should accept only the prevention of more severe coercion as the justification for the use of coercion by the government',[19] as this suggests a comparison of the gains in freedom of one person (or group) with the losses in freedom of another person (or group) resulting from a given government policy. In any case, libertarians often explicitly claim that private property and markets 'maximize' freedom and that this fact counts in their favour.[20] And neither is the idea of maximal societal freedom exclusive to the libertarian literature. Both G. A. Cohen and David Miller apparently see as 'politically crucial'[21] the problem of assessing 'the overall amounts of freedom provided by particular *social systems*',[22] such as capitalism and socialism. They at least accept, therefore, that the freedom of some may be legitimately sacrificed in the name of overall societal freedom, even if they do not explicitly advocate *maximizing* societal freedom. To take one other example from the egalitarian left, according to Kai Nielsen, while both capitalism and socialism restrict certain specific liberties, 'the restrictions on liberty proferred by radical egalitarianism and socialism, . . . are justified for they, of the various alternatives, give us both the most extensive and the most abundant system of liberty possible in modern conditions'.[23] Again, this interest in overall 'systems of liberty' can reasonably be interpreted as implying trade-offs between the liberty of one group and the liberty of another so as to bring about net gains in liberty. Moreover, Nielsen seems to assume that, at least *ceteris paribus*, societal freedom should be as extensive as possible.

Now it might be that these references to maximal societal freedom are simply examples of sloppiness on the part of the theorists concerned, who should instead be taken to be referring implicitly to the principle of maximal equal freedom, or to some other combination of the purely aggregative principle and a distributive principle in the stricter sense. However, the principle of maximal societal freedom might also turn out to be the principle that is most consistent with a given account of the non-specific value of freedom. Where we find both the principle of societal maximization and the relevant

---

[18] Berlin, *Four Essays on Liberty*, 161.   [19] Hayek, *The Constitution of Liberty*, 44.
[20] See e.g. J. Buchanan, *Liberty, Market and the State* (Brighton: Wheatsheaf, 1986), 5.
[21] Cohen, 'Illusions about Private Property and Freedom', 232, cf. 232–42.
[22] D. Miller, 'Constraints on Freedom', *Ethics*, 94 (1983), 66, my emphasis.
[23] K. Nielsen, *Equality and Liberty: A Defence of Radical Egalitarianism* (Totowa, NJ: Rowman & Allanheld, 1985), 304.

account of freedom's non-specific value in the work of a single thinker, then the imputation of sloppiness seems unwarranted, regardless of the objections that might be raised against the principle of societal maximization.

The question of whether aggregative concerns should have priority over distributive ones will depend on whether freedom is seen as good because it contributes directly to some good of individuals or only because it contributes to some *social goal*. If one accepts the argument of Hayek and Mill examined in the previous chapter, to the effect that freedom is the best means to achieving 'societal progress', or to fulfilling 'the permanent interests of man as a progressive being', then the policy of maximizing societal freedom will appear to be the most appropriate one: all that we have to go on, according to this argument, is the empirical generalization that the more freedom there is, the more progress there is likely to be. Of course, one might not accept *only* this argument for the non-specific value of freedom. Like Mill, one might also see freedom as non-specifically instrumentally valuable or as non-specifically constitutively valuable because it contributes to some aspect of individual well-being, such as 'personal growth'. But it is not *incoherent* to accept only the argument from a social goal. And it is surely no accident that the name of Hayek comes to mind both in connection with the idea of maximizing societal freedom and in connection with the idea of freedom as the means to a social goal like that of 'progress'.

It might be thought that if one favours the maximization of societal freedom then one must be assuming freedom to be unconditionally valuable. This would certainly constitute a blow for supporters of maximal societal freedom, since we saw in the previous chapter that such a view of the value of freedom is implausibly strong. However, the implication does not follow: we need not see freedom as unconditionally valuable in order to favour its societal maximization. This fact will become clearer if we recall how the notion of unconditional value can be broken down into two component parts, namely, the idea that more freedom is always better than less in the 'insatiable sense', and the idea that more freedom is always better than less in the 'non-*ceteris paribus*' sense (see s. 2.2). If more freedom is always better than less in the first sense, then it is always better to have an additional unit of freedom, however much freedom one already has. If more freedom is always better than less in the second sense, then freedom always outweighs other values when it comes into conflict with them. Freedom is unconditionally valuable, we said, if more freedom is always better than less in both of these senses.

Bearing in mind this analysis, there are two ways in which one can avoid attaching unconditional value to freedom while still retaining the principle of societal maximization. The first way is by pointing out that even where freedom is seen as only non-specifically instrumentally valuable (and not unconditionally valuable), it can nevertheless be legitimate to treat freedom *as if* it were uncondi-tionally valuable. If freedom is non-specifically instrumentally valuable, it may well be reasonable to see the fulfilment of our interest in freedom as (at least in practice) an *insatiable* principle. If freedom is seen as a means to progress on the basis of the argument presented in the previous chapter, then the very lack of knowledge that makes freedom valuable in this way would appear to prevent us from specifying a point of satiation. Furthermore, although, on the basis of such an argument, freedom's value must be seen as conditional on that of progress, the conclusion of the argument was nevertheless that progress is in practice pursuable only through the pursuit of freedom. Now, if we say in addition that progress is good in the non-*ceteris paribus* sense (admittedly, something which is highly debatable), then we shall also be able to claim that freedom is in practice good in the non-*ceteris paribus* sense. The idea is that while freedom will not be unconditionally valuable, since it will not be the case that it is more valuable than any other thing regardless of its consequences, we shall nevertheless be warranted in treating freedom as if it were uncondi-tionally valuable, since *in practice* more freedom will always be better than less in both the 'insatiable' and the 'non-*ceteris paribus*' sense.

The second way of retaining the principle of maximal societal freedom while nevertheless rejecting the idea of its unconditional value is, quite simply, by abandoning the non-*ceteris paribus* clause: we can maximize societal freedom *ceteris paribus*. All that is required for the justification of this weaker pre-scription is that fulfilling our interest in freedom be (at least in practice) an insatiable principle—an idea which, as we have just seen, might be defensible on the basis of freedom's non-specific instrumental value. When we abandon the non-*ceteris paribus* clause, what we do is subordinate the societal maxim-ization of freedom to some other principle, or at least see the two principles as competing with one another. Thus, we might plausibly combine the principle of maximal societal freedom—indeed, we might combine *any* principle for the distribution of freedom—with the principle that each person should be guar-anteed a certain minimum of welfare, where the second principle has priority over the first. We might even decide to combine the principle of maximal societal freedom with another principle for the distribution of freedom, such as the principle that each person should have at least a certain minimum of freedom, again giving priority to the latter principle.

None of this is to deny that for many liberals the principle of maximal societal freedom is seriously flawed from the point of view of justice. It remains, after all, what Rawls would call a 'teleological' principle of justice—one which 'does not take seriously the distinction between persons'.[24] It treats

---

[24] Rawls, *A Theory of Justice*, 27.

'society' as if it were a single maximizing individual, so allowing us to sacrifice the freedom of some people in favour of a greater sum total of freedom. Kymlicka has indeed suggested that the principle of maximal societal freedom is incompatible with libertarianism, since the goal of that principle 'is not to respect people, . . . but to respect liberty, for which certain people may or may not be useful contributors', whereas libertarianism 'respects people first, and respects liberty as one component of respect for people'.[25] To the extent that libertarians do indeed favour freedom as a constitutive part of the ideal of respect for individuals (rather than for the reasons we have associated with the name of Hayek) this argument is certainly valid. It must surely have a hold on those who are persuaded by Nozick's claim that 'there is no *social entity* with a good that undergoes some sacrifice for its own good', that using one person to benefit others simply 'uses him and benefits the others', and that 'talk of an overall social goal covers this up'.[26] If one finds this a forceful argument when applied to income or resources or welfare, it is difficult to see why one should not also find it so when applied to freedom, *if*, as I have said, one values freedom (at least in part) for its direct effect on individual well-being. Some have gone as far as to suggest that the maximization of societal freedom could lead to grossly counter-intuitive distributions of freedom, perhaps even implying slavery—for example, in a situation where the slave owners outnumber the slaves.[27] No evidence has been provided to justify this extreme conclusion, and the societal freedom maximizer might yet disprove it, in particular if she can show that there is a law of 'diminishing marginal freedom', analogous to that of 'diminishing marginal utility'—the law to which some utilitarians have appealed in answer to the objection that they endorse anti-egalitarian distributions of utility. But in any case, such an answer is clearly of an *ad hoc* nature. The societal freedom maximizer cannot escape the fact that, on her theory of justice, sacrificing the freedom of some in the name of a social goal is not in itself unjust.

Rejecting maximal societal freedom for the above reason does not of course imply rejecting the idea of freedom maximization altogether. What it does imply is that freedom may only be maximized within the framework of an individualist theory of justice. On this view, we should never pursue the *societal* maximization of freedom, even *ceteris paribus*; at most we should aim to maximize, say, 'the freedom of each and every individual'. In the language of welfare economics, considerations of efficiency must be constrained by considerations of equity. We should therefore endorse a principle like that of maximal equal freedom or maximin or leximin freedom.

---

[25] Kymlicka, *Contemporary Political Philosophy*, 136.
[26] Nozick, *Anarchy, State and Utopia*, 32–3.   [27] Cited in Gray, *Freedom*, 145.

Perhaps the most famous expression of the principle of maximal equal freedom is to be found in the first principle of John Rawls's theory of justice,
although the principle gets qualified there so as to refer only to 'basic liberty'
or to 'the basic liberties'.[28] Statements of the principle in its unqualified form
go back at least to the early Herbert Spencer, who similarly called 'a first
principle' his idea that 'every man may claim the fullest liberty to exercise
his faculties compatible with the possession of like liberty by every other
man'.[29] In contemporary debates among political philosophers, the principle
is appealed to by both egalitarians and libertarians. To take two examples,
the egalitarian Richard Norman has appealed to the principle of equal freedom, and has then gone on to qualify it more precisely as 'the principle that,
other things being equal, we should aim at the promotion of the maximum
amount of freedom compatible with an equal distribution of freedom'.[30] And,
from the libertarian side, Jan Narveson sees his dispute with the egalitarians
in the following terms: 'Just as the equalitarian also wishes his equal distribution to be at the highest possible level, so one would suppose that the
libertarian would want liberty to be equally distributed at the highest possible
equal level. "Maximize equal welfare/income/wealth", says one; "Maximize
equal liberty", says the other.'[31]

Some philosophers have gone a step further than those who endorse maximal equal freedom, and have preferred to interpret the dictum 'maximize the
freedom of each and every individual' as implying the principle of *maximin*
freedom ('maximize the freedom of whoever has the least freedom'). Why,
after all, should we insist on equal freedom or maximal equal freedom, if
equal freedom (even *maximal* equal freedom) might leave everyone less free
than some *un*equal distribution of freedom? The idea of maximin freedom
can be plausibly attributed to Rawls, at least as far as the distribution of the
'non-basic' liberties is concerned.[32] Furthermore, it is possible to make out a
case for attributing the principle of maximin freedom to Rawls even regarding the distribution of liberty as such. The reason for this lies in Rawls's distinction between 'liberty' on the one hand and 'the worth of liberty' on the
other. According to Rawls, the first principle of justice, which states that individuals have an equal right to the 'same' basic liberties, does not imply any
rights to particular social or economic goods. The social and economic benefits

[28] Rawls, *A Theory of Justice*, respectively, 60 and 302.
[29] H. Spencer, *Social Statics* (London: Williams & Norgate, 1892), 35.
[30] R. Norman, *Free and Equal* (Oxford: Oxford University Press, 1987), 55.
[31] J. Narveson, 'Equality vs. Liberty: Advantage, Liberty', in E. Frankel Paul, F. D. Miller,
Jr., and J. Paul (eds.), *Liberty and Equality* (Oxford: Blackwell, 1985), 48.
[32] Unlike in Rawls in his theory of justice, I here use the terms 'maximin' and 'leximin' to
refer to distributions, and not merely to refer to principles of individual rational choice.

enjoyed by an individual determine, by their quantity or quality, the *value* of her liberty. Liberty can exist without them, but they are necessary in order for liberty to be enjoyed to the full. Thus, only 'the worth of liberty', and not liberty itself, is reduced by 'the inability to take advantage of one's rights and opportunities as a result of poverty and ignorance, and a lack of means generally'.[33] This is not to say, on the other hand, that Rawls is indifferent to the distribution of the 'worth of liberty', which, determined as this is by the distribution of the other primary goods, ought for the most part to be 'maximinned'. Now many philosophers have taken issue with Rawls's distinction between liberty and the worth of liberty,[34] holding as they do that if I lack the means to do *x*—most especially if you forcibly withhold from me the means to doing *x*—then I lack the freedom to do *x*. (For more on this, see s. 8.5.) In this case, what Rawls calls 'the worth of liberty' is exactly what many would call 'liberty', while what Rawls calls 'basic liberties' is what might be more felicitously termed 'formal rights' or, in Rawls's own words, 'constitutional safeguards' (where one's possession of the formal right to do *x*—'*x*' usually being an act-type—does not imply one's possession of the concrete, or what is often called the 'substantive', freedom to perform any tokens of *x*, and is therefore only a necessary and not a sufficient condition of 'liberty').[35] If these points are accepted—as they appear to be by a number of commentators—then to all intents and purposes one of Rawls's principles of justice is that of maximin freedom.

At a yet more sophisticated level, we find Philippe Van Parijs, an egalitarian and self-described 'real libertarian', arguing in favour of the principle of 'leximin freedom'. The leximin criterion of distributive justice is a variant on Rawls's maximin criterion. Maximin freedom represents a departure from strictly equal freedom in that it calls for the maximization of the freedom of the least free. The 'leximin' (or 'lexicographic maximin') criterion for the distribution of freedom seems to represent an improvement on the maximin criterion, by calling for the maximization of the freedom of the least free, of the next least free, of the next least free again, and so on, with the maximization of the freedom of the less free always having priority over that of the freedom of the more free. The motive behind this criterion is, plausibly enough, 'to express [as accurately as possible] the idea that the members of a (maximally) free society are *all as* free *as possible*'.[36]

[33] Rawls, *A Theory of Justice*, 204.

[34] See especially Norman Daniels, 'Equal Liberty and Unequal Worth of Liberty', in N. Daniels (ed.), *Reading Rawls* (Oxford: Blackwell, 1975).

[35] As Rawls himself admits, the 'distinction between liberty and the worth of liberty is . . . merely a definition and settles no substantive question' (*Political Liberalism*, 326).

[36] P. Van Parijs, *Real Freedom for All: What (If Anything) can Justify Capitalism?* (Oxford: Oxford University Press, 1995), 25.

Like the principle of maximal societal freedom, those of maximal equal freedom, maximin freedom, and leximin freedom follow in part from certain reasons for freedom's non-specific value. As we have seen, where the maximization of societal freedom is completely ruled out, as it is in these last cases, this will be because the goods which freedom is taken to promote are individual rather than social goals. In addition, since all of these principles incorporate a maximizing element, it seems reasonable to assume that those who endorse them see the fulfilment of our interest in freedom as (at least in practice) an insatiable principle. Given these constraints, the most likely implicit source of these principles is the view that freedom is non-specifically instrumentally valuable as a means to some aspect of individual well-being. This is certainly arguably the case for Rawls. Ignorance about the uses to which freedom might best be put plays an important part in Rawls's theory, not only in the original position, where rational persons in a state of ignorance about their own conception of the good will always prefer more primary goods to fewer, but also outside the original position, where individuals' conceptions of the good are expected to develop over time.

If on the other hand we assume freedom's value to be exclusively of a *non*-instrumental non-specific kind, it will be less plausible to say that fulfilling our interest in freedom is an insatiable principle. This is because in such a case, unlike where we assume freedom to have non-specific instrumental value, ignorance does not play an essential role in the justification of freedom's non-specific value. We have seen that where freedom is held to be non-specifically valuable as a means to progress, it seems reasonable to say that fulfilling our interest in freedom is (at least in practice) an insatiable principle, because the very ignorance which makes freedom valuable in this way makes it impossible for us to say how much freedom will lead to what kind or degree of progress. Neither the intrinsic value of freedom nor the constitutive value of freedom rests in a similar way on a premiss about our ignorance of the future. For example, where we say that freedom is non-specifically valuable as a constitutive part of self-respect, it need not be implied that we are ignorant of the empirical relations between amounts of freedom on the one hand and amounts of self-respect on the other. It seems reasonable, indeed, to say that our desire for self-respect is satisfied by a certain *degree* of freedom —in either absolute or relative terms—(together with the other necessary conditions of self-respect), and that having more freedom than this is not valuable as such (as far as providing a basis for self-respect is concerned).

If one believes that fulfilling our interest in freedom is (in practice) a satiable principle, then one should endorse a distributive principle with no maximizing element. The most obvious example of such a principle is that which specifies a guaranteed minimum of freedom for all. This principle, like the others we have examined so far, has found ample expression in liberal writings. It is implicit, for example, in the Millian idea that every individual is surrounded by some sort of a metaphorical 'boundary', which should not be 'crossed' by the actions of others without that individual's permission, where the size of the 'area' enclosed by the boundary is, however vague, to be understood as finite and as something we are capable in practice of respecting.

This is not to say, on the other hand, that the guaranteed minimum of freedom can *only* be endorsed by those who see increasing freedom as a satiable principle. It is possible to defend the guaranteed minimum on other grounds. What matters is that the language one uses to defend freedom is no longer one of maximization but, rather, one which expresses the more defensive strategy of not letting individuals' degrees of freedom fall below a certain level. For example, one might favour guaranteeing a certain minimum of freedom simply because one wishes to allow for the pursuit of other social goals with which further individual freedom is incompatible. This is consistent with seeing more freedom as being better than less in the non-satiable sense (but not in the non-*ceteris paribus* sense). Thus, one might see freedom as non-specifically instrumentally valuable and, while therefore seeing the fulfilment of the interest in freedom as an insatiable principle, see certain other goods as overriding the good of having an especially large degree of freedom. A guaranteed minimum of freedom might be defended in such a case on the grounds that the other goods with which freedom competes would nevertheless be worthless in the absence of a minimum of freedom. Along these lines, Isaiah Berlin approvingly cites Locke, Mill, Constant, and Tocqueville as supporters of a guaranteed minimum of freedom as a means to a minimum of individual autonomy or growth. These classical liberals believed 'that there ought to exist a certain minimum area of personal freedom which must on no account be violated; for if it is over-stepped, the individual will find himself in an area too narrow for even that minimum development of his natural faculties which alone makes it possible to pursue, and even to conceive, the various ends which men hold good or right or sacred'.[37]

The guaranteed minimum of freedom might be thought to be a rather weak principle by those who champion freedom as an 'ideal'. Two points are worth making to counter this thought. First, nothing in the principle itself implies that the guaranteed minimum should be particularly low; the relevant 'minimum' need not be merely the '*tolerable bare* minimum of liberty' advocated, for example, by Joel Feinberg.[38] Second, unlike in the case of the other principles

---

[37] Berlin, *Four Essays on Liberty*, 124. Cf. 126–7, and p. lxi.

[38] J. Feinberg, 'The Interest in Liberty on the Scales', in A. I. Goldman and J. Kim (eds.), *Values and Morals* (Dordrecht: Reidel, 1978), 31, my emphasis.

examined so far, it does not make sense to support a guaranteed minimum of freedom *ceteris paribus*. The idea of a guaranteed minimum of freedom has its own lexical priority built into it. To support the principle of a guaranteed minimum of freedom is to give a minimum of freedom lexical priority over the pursuit of other goals, be these freedom-maximizing goals or goals of any other kind.

There is one other widely mentioned distributive principle which does not incorporate a maximizing element, and that is the principle of equal freedom —a principle we find defended, for example, in the writings of Hillel Steiner.[39] Having already examined the principles of maximal equal freedom and of a guaranteed minimum of freedom, an endorsement of this principle might be found rather puzzling. Why should we say that the principle of equal freedom is superior to (or even as good as) that of maximal equal freedom? Should we be indifferent between a situation in which everyone has very little freedom and a situation in which everyone has a great deal? And if, on the other hand, we do not favour the incorporation of a maximizing element, why not be content with a guaranteed minimum of freedom for all? For Steiner, the answer to this objection lies in a conceptual claim he makes about societal freedom, namely that it cannot be increased or decreased, but only redistributed. The universal quest for individual freedom is, in Steiner's view, a zero-sum game.[40] Given this zero-sum thesis, the idea of maximizing freedom can have no place in a theory of justice; it is unjust to maximize the freedom of any one individual or group (since this can only be done at the expense of a departure from equal freedom), and it is conceptually impossible to increase the freedom of all individuals. I shall challenge the zero-sum thesis in Chapter 9.

The variety of libertarianism advocated by Steiner has sometimes been called 'the starting-gate theory' of justice,[41] and, being a freedom-based theory of justice, compares favourably with the Nozickian variety of libertarianism discussed in the previous section. Both are 'historical entitlement' theories of justice. However, only Steiner's theory combines the principles of historical entitlement with a particular interpretation of the Lockean 'proviso'—the proviso which specifies our original rights in unowned natural resources—such that each individual has a right to a measure of freedom. (For Steiner, the principle determining that measure of freedom is, as I have said, the principle

[39] See especially H. Steiner, 'The Natural Right to Equal Freedom', *Mind*, 83 (1974); id., 'Capitalism, Justice and Equal Starts', *Social Philosophy and Policy*, 5 (1987); id., *An Essay on Rights* (Oxford: Blackwell, 1994), ch. 6; and id., 'Choice and Circumstance', *Ratio*, NS 10 (1997), 310–12.

[40] See *An Essay on Rights*, 52–4, where Steiner calls this zero-sum thesis the 'Law of Conservation of Liberty'.

[41] Cf. R. Dworkin, 'What is Equality? Part II: Equality of Resources', *Philosophy and Public Affairs*, 10 (1981), 309.

of equal freedom, though my argument against the zero-sum thesis (s. 9.4) will suggest that a better candidate is that of maximal equal freedom.) As long as property-based libertarianism is seen as combining a commitment to the principles of historical entitlement with a commitment to a freedom-based theory of justice, 'starting-gate' libertarianism is the only coherent form of property-based libertarianism.

3.3 FROM DISTRIBUTIVE PRINCIPLES TO POWERS OF MEASUREMENT

Dworkin's claim that freedom cannot be 'even roughly' measured is certainly an extreme one. For there are many different possible scales of measurement, some more precise and demanding than others, and it would be surprising if freedom were not measurable on any of them. As S. S. Stevens writes, 'measurement is a relative matter. It varies in kind and degree, in type and precision.'[42] In attempting to address the problem of freedom measurement, then, we would do well to follow the advice of James Griffin: 'Our powers of measurement may be limited. But our demand on measurement may also be limited. In the end, what we need to know is rather, Do our powers match our demands?'[43] What demands do we make on our powers of measuring freedom? This will depend in part on *the choice of distributive principle* discussed in the previous section.

Following Griffin's advice involves steering a course between two equally erroneous tendencies regarding the demands we make on our powers of measurement. The first tendency involves assuming unnecessarily strong demands. Those who immediately give up the quest for a freedom metric having only taken a sideways glance at the problem are perhaps guilty of this first tendency, and I would class Dworkin as among them. The second tendency involves going too far in the other direction, and demanding too little. This latter tendency often appears to characterize those theorists who approach the problem of freedom measurement from the perspective of a welfare economist rather than of a political philosopher. My aim here is to counter both tendencies by making explicit the demands on our powers of measuring freedom normally made by freedom-based theories of justice. There are some respects in which the demands of a freedom-based theory of justice may not be especially strong, at least as long as we disregard the question of how to assess

---

[42] S. S. Stevens, 'Mathematics, Measurement and Psychophysics', in S. S. Stevens (ed.), *Handbook of Experimental Psychology* (New York: Wiley, 1951), 1.

[43] J. Griffin, *Well Being: Its Meaning, Measurement and Moral Importance* (Oxford: Clarendon Press, 1986), 76.

degrees of injustice (a point to which I shall turn at the end of this section). Perhaps the achievement of justice only requires ordinal comparisons of degrees of freedom, rather than cardinal measurements or measurements on a ratio scale with an absolute zero. (By 'absolute zero' I mean, in the case of freedom, the point on a scale which denotes 'no freedom', or 'complete unfreedom', two expressions which I assume to mean the same thing.) There are other respects, however, in which our demands on our powers of measurement can be fairly strong, notably in terms of interpersonal comparability, precision, and unidimensionality.

In what follows, I shall first explain why these three demands of interpersonal comparability, precision, and unidimensionality are made by all plausible candidate-principles for the distribution of freedom. I shall then go on to analyse the first of the three demands, by distinguishing between the different kinds of interpersonal comparisons required by the different distributive principles. Such differences will appear straightforward enough to the average welfare economist, but they are nevertheless worth spelling out, if only because this has never been done in the case of overall freedom.

The distributive principles examined in the previous section were those of *maximal societal freedom* (favoured, among others, by Hayek and Nielsen), *equal freedom* (favoured by Steiner), *maximal equal freedom* (favoured, among others, by Narveson and Norman), *maximin freedom* (favoured, arguably, by the earlier Rawls), *leximin freedom* (favoured by Van Parijs), and a *guaranteed minimum of freedom* (favoured, among others, by Berlin and Feinberg).

Now it might be suggested that we should add to this list the principle of 'Pareto optimal freedom'. This would be the principle that one should always prefer social state *a* to social state *b* if there is at least one person who has more freedom in *a* than in *b*, and no person who has less freedom in *a* than in *b*. Pareto optimality is the measurer's solution to a recognized impossibility of interpersonal comparisons: Pareto optimal freedom does not require any interpersonal comparisons of degrees of freedom; it only requires intrapersonal comparisons.

I did not mention the principle of Pareto optimal freedom in the previous section, for the simple reason that no liberal theorist of justice has ever proposed it. Why is this so? A possible explanation lies in their neglect of questions relating to the measurement of overall freedom. If those who favour maximal societal freedom were to conclude, from a belated investigation of such questions, that degrees of overall freedom could not be compared interpersonally, then the principle of Pareto optimal freedom might seem a natural second best. But I think that an explanation is also to be found in the fact that the concept of freedom has until recently been the preserve of political philosophers, rather than of welfare economists. It was the latter's experience of the problem of making interpersonal comparisons of *utility* that led to the solution of Pareto optimality, and the initial reaction of welfare economists to the idea of measuring overall freedom usually reflects this experience.[44] They point out that we should be sceptical about the possibility of interpersonal comparisons, not to speak of the possibility of cardinal measurements, or of the possibility of 'adding' and 'subtracting' different 'amounts' of freedom. Surely we should content ourselves with intrapersonal rankings. After all, they say, these are sufficient to produce judgements of Pareto superiority.

Now there is certainly much to be learnt about measurement problems in general from the work of welfare economists on the problems involved in measuring utility. But freedom is not utility. And there is no reason to assume, from the start, that the measurement of freedom should be subject to the same limitations as the measurement of utility. Utility is a subjective, intensive quality, and its measurement is hampered by the problem of knowledge of other minds. Overall freedom, on the other hand, is a non-subjective, extensive quality (a point to which I shall return in Chapters 5 and 7—above all at s. 7.3). It is, as we saw in Chapter 1, a complex relation between an agent, certain preventing conditions, and certain possible actions. What problems of measurement we do encounter are therefore likely to be quite different from those encountered in the case of utility. There is indeed no reason to suppose that intrapersonal comparisons of freedom will be any less problematic than interpersonal ones.

Those who approach the problem of freedom measurement from the perspective of a political philosopher tend to be more aware of the demands made by mainstream liberal theories of justice. From the point of view of such theories, Pareto optimalizing freedom may be wholly unjust, above all given the arbitrary nature of the distribution from which one starts. Justice, on such theories, necessarily requires interpersonal comparisons of some sort.

A second requirement of the above-mentioned principles of justice is that there be a minimum degree of *precision* in our comparisons, and thus a limit to the degree to which vague comparisons are acceptable. An important example of vagueness in comparisons is the occurrence of 'rough', rather than 'strict', equality; in pursuing equal freedom, we may find ourselves able to say no more than that two individuals are 'roughly equally free'. The acceptability of the occurrence of such rough equality will depend both on how endemic it is and on how rough it is. If vagueness in measurements can be kept within certain bounds, we may bring ourselves to accept it. However, the opposite extreme, whereby we are able to say little more than that most members of

---

[44] I refer here to the initial reaction of a number of economists in audiences to whom I have presented papers on this topic.

society are 'roughly equally free', clearly turns justice as equal freedom into an unacceptably weak requirement, and is thus itself highly unlikely to be acceptable. Precision can of course be a practical problem as well as a theoretical one. As I have already said, the problem of precision in *practical* terms lies outside the scope of this book, though in Chapter 10 I shall turn briefly to the problem of finding a more approximate metric of freedom.

The last of the three general requirements to be dealt with here is that of unidimensionality. It might be suggested that a suitably modest approach to the measurement of freedom would consist in attempting to make interpersonal comparisons of certain specific 'kinds' or 'dimensions' of freedom, such as 'freedom of movement' and 'freedom of association'. This would require no more than multidimensional measurements of freedom. Where one person had more freedom measured on one dimension and another person more freedom measured on another dimension, we would not necessarily attempt to say who had more freedom in an overall sense.

Each of the distributive principles examined in the previous section is at variance with the above proposal: each refers to the distribution of freedom conceived of as a *unidimensional* attribute. And this is no accident. As we have seen, freedom-based theories of justice presuppose the non-specific value of freedom (see s. 3.1). And it should be recalled from the arguments of the previous chapter that since the non-specific value of freedom is by definition independent of the value of the specific things freedom lets us do, it implies an interest in measuring freedom *tout court*, rather than in providing separate measurements of certain 'freedoms', such as 'freedom of movement', 'freedom of worship', 'freedom of association', and so on, and treating these as separate 'dimensions' of freedom (see s. 2.7). It implies, in other words, what Dworkin and Kymlicka pejoratively refer to as the 'single commodity' view of freedom.

To avoid a possible misunderstanding, we should distinguish between 'dimensions of freedom' in the above sense, which we can call 'freedom-type' dimensions, and 'dimensions of freedom' in the sense of the different ways freedom may be *constrained* (that is, the dimensions of prevention, punishment, threats, and so on), which we may call 'constraint-type' dimensions. The term 'dimensions of freedom' is sometimes used to refer exclusively to constraint-type dimensions, or at least so as to include them.[45] The question of the commensurability (in terms of overall freedom) of these constraint-type dimensions is one that we can legitimately put off until later in this book (see Chapter 8), though the distributive principles examined in the previous section clearly require their commensurability too. As far as freedom-type

---

[45] See e.g. Oppenheim, *Dimensions of Freedom*, and *Political Concepts*.

dimensions are concerned, on the other hand, I do not think that it makes sense to say that these are incommensurable *in terms of overall freedom*. Perhaps the different freedom-type dimensions *are* incommensurable *in terms of their overall values*. If they are, however, this will be because of the incommensurability of certain goods other than freedom, rather than because of some kind of incommensurability within the notion of freedom itself. Any incommensurability within the notion of freedom itself must instead have its source in an incommensurability between constraint-type dimensions. To the extent that constraint-type dimensions can be commensurated in terms of overall freedom, then, there will be something that freedom of association and freedom of worship have in common, in terms of which we are able to compare them. This will not stop us from saying that different kinds of freedom are incommensurable when evaluated in an overall sense, or indeed that one kind of freedom—say, freedom of religion—is more valuable than another kind of freedom—say, freedom of movement—because choosing to pursue a religion is more valuable than choosing to move in a certain direction.

I now turn to the differences between the main distributive principles in terms of the kinds of interpersonal comparisons of freedom they require. In terms of the kind of *scale* required, the differences are as follows. If we favour maximizing societal freedom, we shall need to make cardinal measurements of freedom, though not necessarily on a scale with an absolute zero: what we shall need here is cardinal comparisons of changes in individual freedom. We shall also require a cardinal scale if a minimum of freedom is to be guaranteed to all, though, as it stands, that principle is ambiguous between requiring and not requiring a ratio scale, as we need to know in addition whether the 'minimum' in question is to be fixed in relative or in absolute terms. The principle of equal freedom requires only that we be able to compare people's freedom ordinally, as does that of maximal equal freedom, according to which we are not allowed to depart from an equal distribution even if this means that the loss in freedom of one individual is smaller than the gain in freedom of another. The same requirement is made by the principles of maximin and leximin freedom, which only call on us to identify the least free individual and to increase her freedom as much as possible (or, in the case of leximin freedom, the least free, and the next least free, and so on).

The principles also differ in terms of the *extensiveness* of interpersonal comparability required: each is more or less tolerant of incompleteness in our orderings of individuals or social states. The principle allowing the highest degree of incompleteness appears to be that of maximin freedom. We can always maximin freedom if the *least free* person can be unambiguously identified. Even here, however, the freedom of the least free person needs to be comparable with that of every other, and the least free person might of course be a different person in different social states. The room for incompleteness may diminish further if one favours leximin freedom, and where we are dealing with the comparisons within states required by the principles of equal or maximal equal freedom, it disappears altogether. (I am here assuming the transitivity of interpersonal comparisons, which means, among other things, that if *a* and *b* are equally free, and *b* and *c* are equally free, then *a* and *c* are equally free. This assumption may not be reasonable in the case of 'rough equality'.)

Finally, it is important to note that the powers of measurement set out above only describe what is required in order to realize justice *perfectly*. What if we are instead interested in knowing *how closely* a particular society or situation *approximates* a just one? In that case, cardinal measurements would appear to be required even where we adopt one of the less demanding of the above principles. Although we only require ordinal comparisons in order to know whether or not equal freedom obtains, if we are to measure *degrees of inequality* of freedom, we may well need to know, for example, 'how much more free' is the freest than the least free.[46] And in assessing approximations to maximal equal freedom, we may be interested, further, in how much less freedom there is in a realized state of equal freedom than in another feasible state of equal freedom. Again, in assessing approximations to maximin freedom, we may wish to know how much less free is the least free person than might feasibly have been the case.

There are at least three reasons for being interested in assessing the degree, in cardinal terms, to which a distributive principle for freedom gets respected. The first reason is that instead of imposing a lexical ordering on our different principles of justice, we might instead favour 'weighing up' the importance of one against that of another. We might want to allow for 'trade-offs' between, say, maximal equal freedom on the one hand and, say, stability or development or equality of welfare on the other. A pluralistic theory of value such as that defended by Isaiah Berlin, according to which many of our ideals necessarily conflict with one another, might well be thought to imply such a position.[47] Even if such ideals are held to be incomparable, thus ruling out trade-offs, estimating approximations to an ideal distribution of freedom in the absence of the attainment of that ideal might still be held to be worthwhile.

---

[46] This may not be exactly what we shall need to know, or may not be all we shall need to know. On the different ways of measuring inequality, see A. Sen, *On Economic Inequality* (Oxford: Clarendon Press, 1972), and L. Temkin, *Inequality* (Oxford: Oxford University Press, 1993).

[47] Cf. I. Berlin, *The Crooked Timber of Humanity* (London: HarperCollins, 1991), 17–18, 79–80; id., *Four Essays on Liberty*, 167–72.

The second reason for wanting to measure approximations to ideal distributions of freedom may simply be that doing so provides the means of condemning unjust regimes with the appropriate degree of severity. Moreover, if one wishes to *improve* the distribution or overall degree of freedom in the real world (where freedom is as a matter of fact distributed unjustly or is at unsatisfactorily low levels) it will be helpful, in practical terms, to know how much needs to be done by means of remedy.

The third reason is that one may be interested in assessing degrees of injustice not only in order to be able to condemn the injustice of others with the appropriate degree of severity, but also as a condition for the active pursuit of justice on one's own part. Here, we enter the realm of what John Rawls has called 'non-ideal theory'.[48] For present purposes, the reason for constructing a 'non-ideal theory' lies in the propensity of a certain number of people to place unjust restrictions, come what may, on other people's freedom. A regime that aims to be just does its best to prevent this, but laws are invariably imperfectly enforced, and perfect redress after the event may not be possible.[49] If our theory of justice is freedom-based, and an ideal distribution of freedom is not practically feasible (assuming the above-mentioned propensity), then the degree of approximation to an ideal distribution of freedom ought to be one of the criteria we appeal to when assessing different possible systems of incentives, threats of punishment, actual prevention, and so on.

3.4 CONCEPTUAL AND REALISTIC THEORY, IDEAL AND NON-IDEAL THEORY

Measurements of approximations to ideal distributions are of course not to be confused with *approximate measurements of freedom*. These two things involve approximations to different things—the first to the achievement of perfect justice, the second to the achievement of precise measurements of degrees of freedom. The need for approximate measurements of freedom arises above all out of the existence of practical difficulties involved in achieving precise measurements. Though it complicates matters, there is in principle no reason why measurements of approximations to ideal distributions should not themselves be more or less approximate measurements.

Following Rawls, I call 'non-ideal' the kind of theory that deals with approximations to justice in a world in which injustices are assumed to occur, and

---

[48] Rawls, *A Theory of Justice*, 245–6.
[49] O'Neill talks in this context of the need for 'a measure of justice'. See *Towards Justice and Virtue*, ch. 6.

'ideal' the kind of theory that assumes no injustices to occur, so telling us, among other things, the nature of a perfect distribution of freedom. The conclusion of the previous section was that even if an ideal theory of justice does not require cardinal measurements of freedom, a non-ideal theory of justice is likely to do so. The distinction just mentioned, between precise and approximate measurements, has instead to do with the question of how 'realistic' our theory is, in so far as it compromises the requirement of precision in the face of practical difficulties, such as those having to do with the availability of information. An ideal theory can itself be more or less realistic. Rawls, for example, sees his own ideal theory of justice as more realistic than Sen's, because he thinks that the measurement of 'primary goods' is more feasible, in practice, than that of 'capabilities' (a point to which I shall return in s. 10.1). We can call the level of theorizing at which we ignore practical difficulties of measurement (in order to concentrate on conceptual issues) that of 'purely conceptual theory'. This contrasts with the level of 'realistic theory', at which those practical difficulties are taken into account. Most of Part III of this book will be concerned with developing a purely conceptual theory of overall freedom, and it is only in the final chapter that I shall look at the problem of how approximate measurements are to be made.

3.5 SUMMARY

The aim of this chapter has been to make three general claims: first, that to accept the arguments of the previous chapter, to the effect that freedom is non-specifically valuable, is to commit oneself to a freedom-based theory of justice; second, that our principle for the distribution of freedom, which forms a necessary part of our freedom-based theory of justice, will be affected by our reasons for seeing freedom as non-specifically valuable; and third, that the demands made by our theory of justice on our powers of measuring freedom will be affected by our choice of principle for the distribution of freedom. In addition, we have seen that these demands include the requirement of interpersonal comparability and unidimensionality, and, if only because of an interest in the approximate realization of a given distributive principle, the requirement of at least rough cardinality. If we trace our thoughts back to the beginning of this chapter, we can see that there are indeed clear connections between the arguments used in favour of freedom's non-specific value and the various demands made on the concept of freedom in terms of its overall measurability.

Later on, we shall see that while the demands we make on our powers of measurement are indeed quite strong, it is nevertheless possible, at least at the purely conceptual level, to meet such demands. This claim will be defended in Part III. The method I shall employ in those later chapters is that of seeking 'reflective equilibrium' between our intuitions about freedom, our definition of overall freedom, and the demands made by our theory of justice. The next chapter, which concludes Part I of this book, is devoted to setting out and defending the relevance of this 'reflective equilibrium' method to the problem of measuring freedom.

4

Reflective Equilibrium

WE are nearly ready to tackle the question of how far and in what ways over-all freedom can be measured. First, however, we should try to be as clear as possible about *how we should go about* tackling that question. What is it to measure something? How are the measurement and definition of freedom related? Is there anything wrong with simply taking the 'best' definition of freedom and then asking how freedom might be measured? Before proceeding further, we need to address these and other methodological questions. As will become clear in this chapter, I favour a coherentist approach which involves seeking a 'reflective equilibrium' between intuitions, definition, and measurements. I shall first defend this approach as a way of making sense of the notion of overall freedom (section 1) and then as a way of reconstructing its role in a freedom-based theory of justice (sections 2–4). At the end of the chapter (sections 5 and 6), I shall add some more general remarks in defence of the approach.

4.1 MEASUREMENT AND DEFINITION

What exactly do we mean when we ask if we can 'measure' freedom? What exactly *should* we be asking ourselves? Measurement theorists often cite S. S. Stevens, according to whom, 'in its broadest sense, measurement is the assignment of numerals to objects or events according to rules'.[1] This, how-ever, leaves open the nature of the rules. As F. N. Kerlinger writes, measure-ment is 'a game we play with objects and numerals. Games have rules. It is of course important for other reasons that the rules be "good" rules, but whether the rules are "good" or "bad", the procedure is still measurement.'[2] What then makes such rules 'good'? The answer to this question lies in the test of isomorphism.

Isomorphism is said to obtain when 'an empirical relational system' and 'a numerical relational system' are mutually representative. That is, if, in an empirical relational system A, R is a certain relation (for example, 'is

---

[1] Stevens, 'Mathematics, Measurement and Psychophysics', 1.
[2] F. N. Kerlinger, *Foundations of Behavioural Research* (Austin, Tex.: Holt, Rinehart & Winston, 1964), 427.

heavier than') obtaining between the objects or events in a given set, and in
a numerical relational system B, S is a certain relation obtaining between the
numerals in a given set, systems A and B are isomorphic if there exists a
function, f, such that for any x and y in the set of objects or events, x R y
implies $f(x)$ S $f(y)$.[3] C. H. Coombs and company put this point more access-
ibly in the following way: 'intuitively, A is represented by [is isomorphic
with] B if anything that "happens" in A is "reflected" in B.' Our rules will
be 'good', then, if they produce measurements isomorphic with the 'reality'
(as Kerlinger puts it) of the empirical relational system we are interested in.[4]
When our measurements are isomorphic with the empirical relational system
we are interested in, they are said to be *valid* measurements. A valid measurement is one which really measures the phenomenon we intend it to measure,
and not some other phenomenon.[5]

It seems clear that the test of isomorphism should be applied in some way
to the measurement of freedom. But how exactly are we to apply that test?
Against *what* should we check our rules for measuring freedom? The 'reality'
on which we are to base our measurements must surely be the empirical
relational system implied by a certain conception of overall freedom. But this
fact alone does not appear to take us very far, since there is no settled agreement over the definition of specific freedoms (at the level of conceptions),
and so there is unlikely to be any over that of overall freedom. Above all,
if we take a closer look at the *reasons* people give for preferring one conception of freedom (in the specific *or* the overall sense) to another—reasons
we can discover through examination of their *arguments* over the definition
of freedom—we shall see that such reasons often consist in the *extents of
overall freedom* of certain people, or types of people, that the conceptions of
freedom in question are taken to imply, and their compatibility or incompatibility with the extent-of-freedom assessments which we intuitively feel to
be correct. In other words, in arguing about the definition of freedom (at the
level of conceptions), people often appeal to what I have called their 'common-
sense comparisons' of freedom (see s. 1.3), which in turn presuppose the correctness of certain measurements.

It is worth illustrating this point with a simple example. Isaiah Berlin has
rejected the definition of freedom as 'being able to do (or not being prevented
from doing) what one *desires* to do' on the following grounds. If this is how
freedom is to be defined, then a contented slave (i.e. one who has—and is

    [3] C. H. Coombs, R. M. Dawes, and A. Tversky, *Mathematical Psychology: An Elementary
Introduction* (Englewood Cliffs, NJ: Prentice Hall, 1970), 10–11.

    [4] Kerlinger, *Foundations of Behavioural Research*, 431.

    [5] On this point, see also H. E. Kyburg, *Theory and Measurement* (Cambridge: Cambridge
University Press, 1984), 248.

therefore unconstrained from having—all of her desires fulfilled) enjoys a great deal of freedom (or is even completely free). And yet our considered judgement is that slaves enjoy very little freedom (or are even completely unfree).[6] Moreover, this judgement need not be based purely on the linguistic convention according to which slavery and freedom are in some sense or to some degree opposites; if we reflect on the structure of opportunities open to a slave, and on the various constraints to which she is subject, we find it difficult to call her 'very free', independently of the appropriateness of other descriptions. In the light of this, it seems wrong to say that a necessary condition for one's lacking the freedom to do x is that one desire to do it. Here, a particular point is being made about the definition of *a specific freedom*, but by appeal to an intuition about *overall freedom*.

When people argue for rival conceptions of freedom (in the overall *or* the specific sense), they appeal to premises which very often presuppose *measurements* of freedom. To be sure, Berlin's argument, like many others, appeals only to an obvious case, where crude and impressionistic measurements suffice to demonstrate his point. But why should more refined measurements, if we could make them, not play a similar role in arguments for conceptions of freedom? If I could provide measurements of freedom which I could show to follow from your conception of a specific freedom, and which you had originally thought yourself unable to make, and if those measurements were to conflict with certain of your firmly held convictions about who is freer than whom, might you not at least be torn between revising your conception of a specific freedom and relinquishing your convictions?

This interdependence of measurement and definition is not peculiar to the concept of freedom, and can at least be said to apply uncontroversially to other quantitative attributes in the social sciences. In attempting to supply an acceptable definition of power, for example, theorists commonly appear to assume that such a definition should reflect the comparisons we normally make of *degrees* of power. Alvin Goldman makes this assumption quite explicit: 'a theory of power', he says, 'must enable us to account for the fact that Nelson Rockefeller is, on the whole, an extremely powerful person.'[7]

In the foregoing discussion, I have made two separate points which can now be drawn together. The first point was that our measurements of freedom must be isomorphic with the relations between individuals implied by our conception of freedom. The second point was that when we come to define freedom (at the level of a conception), and to argue over the definition of

---

[6] This is at least the implicit form of Berlin's argument. See his *Four Essays on Liberty*, 139–40.

[7] A. I. Goldman, 'Toward a Theory of Social Power', in S. Lukes (ed.), *Power* (New York: New York University Press, 1986), 156–7.

freedom, we appeal in part to the measurements of freedom which certain definitions are taken to imply. These two points lead us respectively to two conclusions. The first conclusion is that we cannot know what it is to measure freedom without first having a conception of freedom; the second, that we cannot arrive at a conception of freedom without knowing what it is to measure freedom. The conjunction of these two conclusions may appear circular. If there is a circle here, however, it is not a vicious one. Rather, it is a complicating factor, which makes the subject of freedom measurement more far-reaching than it might at first have appeared to be. The circle would only be a vicious one if we were to find ourselves starting with nothing; with neither a conception nor any intuitions. Were that so, we would indeed not know *where* to start. But the fact is that most of us already have both, and all of us have at least a set of intuitions about freedom (where a moment's reflection will suffice to construct at least a crude and debatable definition of freedom out of those intuitions). We can therefore start our investigation either by considering certain intuitions about freedom or by considering a conception of freedom. As long as we do not treat either of these as in some sense foundational or final—as long as we do not give one automatic priority over the other —we are perfectly able to reason from our intuitions about freedom to our conception of freedom and back again, and to attempt to resolve conflicts between them according to the strength of our commitments to one or the other. Our train of reasoning should progress in both directions. Any attempt to resolve the question of how freedom is to be measured must itself be part of this wider process of seeking a coherent conception of freedom, whereby our definition and intuitions are brought into line. On the one hand we may feel the need to revise our conception of freedom in the light of certain measurements, given the common-sense comparisons of freedom with which those measurements have been shown to conflict. On the other hand we may feel compelled to reject certain previously held convictions about extents of freedom, given that they conflict with measurements which have been shown to follow from an otherwise convincing conception of freedom.

It should be clear by now that there is a marked similarity between the style of reasoning which I have advocated here in relation to *freedom* and that defended by John Rawls, and Norman Daniels after him, as the most fruitful way to proceed in arguing for a particular conception of *justice*—that is to say, by seeking a 'reflective equilibrium'.[8] According to Rawls, the role

[8] Cf. J. Rawls, 'Outline of a Decision Procedure for Ethics', *Philosophical Review*, 60 (1951); id., *A Theory of Justice*, 46–53; id., 'The Independence of Moral Theory', *Proceedings and Addresses of the American Philosophical Association*, 47 (1974–5); N. Daniels, 'Wide Reflective Equilibrium and Theory Acceptance in Ethics', *Journal of Philosophy*, 76 (1979); id., 'Reflective Equilibrium and Archimedean Points', *Canadian Journal of Philosophy*, 10 (1980).

of a theory of justice is to give the best possible account of our 'sense of justice', which comprises our 'considered moral judgements'. This is not to say, however, that we are simply to start with certain considered moral judgements and then choose the principles of justice which best 'fit' those judgements. For it may be that as a result of this search for principles of justice, and the attempt to arrive at a coherent theory, we become persuaded that certain of our original considered judgements were mistaken, given that they conflict with certain judgements implied by our principles of justice. Thus the theory which best captures our sense of justice is not simply a reflection of our pre-theoretical moral judgements, but is one which is also *reflected in* those moral judgements. To arrive at a theory of this kind is to achieve a state of reflective equilibrium. Reflective equilibrium is, in Rawls's words, the state reached 'after a person has weighed various proposed conceptions [of justice] and he has either revised his judgements to accord with one of them or held fast to his initial convictions (and the corresponding conception)'.[9]

To return then to our initial question—against what 'reality' should we check the isomorphism of our measurements of freedom?—it seems that the correct answer is to be found by seeking a conception of freedom in reflective equilibrium. As far as justice is concerned, Rawls's preferred style of reasoning, at least as I have described it, may be said to consist in progressing back and forth between the following three levels:

1. a set of considered moral judgements;
2. a set of principles of justice (which form a conception of justice);
3. the judgements implied by the principles of justice.

Respectively analogous to these three levels are what I have called

1. a set of intuitions about particular freedoms and a set of common-sense comparisons of overall freedom;
2. a conception of freedom (in the specific and the overall sense);
3. the judgements about specific freedoms and the measurements of overall freedom implied by the conception of freedom.

When our measurements of freedom are made within a theoretical context characterized by coherence between these three levels, such measurements may be said to be isomorphic in reflective equilibrium with our intuitions about freedom. In such a case, we can say that our conception of freedom is no longer merely an 'initial' conception in the sense mentioned above.

Our common-sense comparisons of freedom clearly play an important part in achieving this isomorphism in reflective equilibrium. Indeed, what little space

[9] Rawls, *A Theory of Justice*, 48.

theorists have already devoted to arguments for conceptions of overall freedom has generally been taken up, at least implicitly, by appeals to such common-sense comparisons, on the basis of which objections to rival conceptions are constructed. Like the argument of Berlin cited above, these objections from common-sense comparisons take the classic form of counter-examples: 'but if that were how freedom should be measured, then in such-and-such a situation A would wind up much freer than B, and you surely don't want to say that.' We shall therefore have to pay special attention to counter-examples of this sort in the remainder of this book. On the other hand, we should also remember that while they may certainly carry a hefty blow, such counter-examples will not always be decisive. In this connection, we should again heed the words of Rawls: 'objections by way of counterexamples are to be made with care, since these may tell us only what we know already, namely that our theory is wrong somewhere.'[10] Hillel Steiner makes a similar point more specifically about the concept of freedom: we must resign ourselves to the fact that ordinary language 'stubbornly persists in licensing . . . inconsistencies', and that the several inconsistent uses of the word 'free' probably 'each reflect some entrenched intuition we have about a kind of circumstance in which a person is describable as free'. In the name of consistency, 'we have to expel some of these reflections from our usage, to silence the intuitions they express'.[11]

The link between the task of fixing on a conception of freedom (at the level of a conception) and that of constructing a theory of justice does not of course stop at the analogy drawn above. In reality, as we saw in the previous chapter, as long as our theory of justice is freedom-based, our conception of freedom will form a *part* of that theory. I shall examine this part–whole relationship in s. 4.3. Before I can do so, however, there is an additional complication to be noted.

4.2 POWERS AND DEMANDS

The additional complication is this: that so far, I have only applied the concept of reflective equilibrium to the definition of overall freedom and its implied measurements, and have thus not yet taken into account the problem of how far, and on what kind of scale, freedom might be thought to be measurable. We need, in other words, to take into account the problems discussed in the previous chapter (at s. 3.3), regarding the *demands* we make on our powers of measurement. As I suggested there, in attempting to address such problems, we should be guided by Griffin's question, 'Do our powers

---

[10] Rawls, *A Theory of Justice*, 52.   [11] Steiner, *An Essay on Rights*, 7.

match our demands?' In my view, the reflective equilibrium method is no less relevant to Griffin's question than it is to the relationship between definition and measurement discussed above. The only difference is that the desired equilibrium here is no longer between a conception and considered judgements, but between a conception and demands on powers of measurement.

In order to see this, I think it will be helpful to consider the case of a particular quantitative attribute in relation to which problems of measurement have already been fairly widely discussed: that of welfare. Amartya Sen has criticized a number of welfare economists for assuming without sufficient argument that it is possible to provide complete and consistent measurements of welfare. It has often been the case that an overeagerness to produce 'results' has brought with it unacceptable distortions of what we commonly conceive welfare to be.[12] We should not rule out the possibility that, according to the way in which we commonly conceive of welfare, some people's welfare simply cannot be compared with that of others. 'Incompleteness is not an embarrassment,' Sen says.[13] If, when attempting to measure a certain phenomenon, we find that our powers of measurement are severely restricted, this should not automatically represent a hurdle to be overcome, but a fact which we should learn to live with.

Now Sen is surely right to point out that we should not simply ignore the measurement problems posed by the possibility of incommensurabilities. Otherwise, we may violate the all-important test of validity. That is to say, we may come up with what we believe to be an attractive way of measuring, and then discover that we are not in fact measuring anything like what we intended to measure. Certainly, then, a discovered weakness in powers of measurement must lead us to revise the demands we make on such powers. However, it should not be forgotten that the demands we make on our powers of measurement fall into two categories. What we demand is that a certain thing be distributed in a certain way. This reveals a commitment, first, to a certain distributive principle (for example, equality), and second, to a certain *distribuendum* defined in a certain way. What Sen has pointed out is that our distributive principle can conflict with our definition of the *distribuendum*, such that the powers of measurement demanded by the distributive principle are not available given the definition of the *distribuendum*, and that certain welfare economists have wrongly tried to mask that conflict by inventing imaginary powers of measurement.

[12] A. Sen, *Commodities and Capabilities* (Amsterdam: North Holland, 1985), 52–3. This is not to deny that Sen has also criticized economists who are too resigned over the weakness of their powers of measurement.

[13] Sen, 'Well-Being, Agency and Freedom', 200; id., *On Ethics and Economics* (Oxford: Blackwell, 1987), 67.

Does a perceived weakness in powers of measurement necessarily mean that we must modify our distributive principle? Sen appears to answer in the affirmative. This, however, is not the only way we have of revising the demands we make on our powers of measurement. For we might instead revise our commitment to distributing a certain thing rather than another. The question of which aspects of our theory are most subject to revision should surely depend on *the degree to which we are committed to them*, rather than on whether they constitute a distributive principle on the one hand or a certain way of defining the *distribuendum* on the other. There seems to be no reason for saying that the definition of the *distribuendum* should be taken as *foundational*, and as constraining the nature of our distributive demands *absolutely*. For there is nothing to stop those with an abstract ethical commitment to 'equality', or to 'maximin', or whatever other principle which implies completeness (or consistency or cardinality), from replying to Sen in the following way:

You are right that on my original definition of welfare, my powers of measuring do not live up to my demands. And I certainly do not propose to ignore this problem by simply inventing new imaginary powers of measurement without further ado. But incompleteness *is* an embarrassment for those of us who have initial distributive commitments which presuppose completeness! What I propose to do, therefore, is to reconsider my definition of welfare in the light of this inconsistency, and to see which course of action would involve the greater sacrifice *in terms of my present ethical commitments*; a revision of my ethically preferred distributive principle, or a revision of my conception of welfare.

We have here another reason for not simply taking the 'best' definition of freedom and then asking about its measurement. Sometimes, considerations about the feasibility of measuring something may affect the way we define that thing. James Griffin suggests as much in relation to the measurement of well-being. We cannot, he says 'first fix on the best account of "well-being" and independently ask about its measurement. One proper ground for choosing between conceptions of well-being would be that one lends itself to the deliberation that we must do and another does not.'[14]

Rather than only letting our definition of the *distribuendum* (and the powers of measurement which it allows) influence our distributive principle, then, or vice versa, we ought to aim, where possible, to bring into line our *distribuendum* and our distributive principle in *reflective equilibrium*. We cannot *make* our powers of measurement match our demands. We must revise our demands until they match our powers. But there are two ways, not one, in which this may be done. The correct 'mix' of these two alternatives is that obtained on achieving reflective equilibrium between the two.

[14] Griffin, *Well Being*, 1.

To illustrate the above point, it is worth noting that in welfare economics we find examples of both of these alternative paths of reasoning. A prime example of a curtailing of distributional demands, so as to accommodate a perceived weakness of powers of measuring a given *distribuendum*, is the principle of Pareto optimality. As we saw in the previous chapter, Pareto optimality is seen as a solution to the problem posed by an inability to make interpersonal comparisons of quantities of welfare. The solution is to demand no more than that we be able to compare social states in terms of the number of people who are made better off (where none are made worse off). As we also saw in the previous chapter, however, it is possible to attack the principle of Pareto optimality on the grounds that it presupposes too weak a commitment to *distributive justice*, and this method of attack has indeed often been employed. How, after all, are we to go about constructing a theory of justice, if we are to admit that 'the idea of equality in allocation has no strict *meaning*'?[15] And what kind of distribution (what degree of 'inequality', we might have asked, if that word had made any sense) are we to *start* from, before attempting to make 'at least some better off and none worse off'? To attack the principle of Pareto optimality in this way is, I submit, to say that its endorsement (in the place of a more demanding principle) requires too great a sacrifice, in terms of one's commitment to certain distributive principles, in favour of one's commitment to defining the relevant *distribuendum* in a certain way. In this case, the attack is an example of the second path of reasoning outlined above.

I should not be taken here to be saying that our *prescriptive* intuitions can somehow have sway over our *descriptive* intuitions. Our urge to give meaning to the prescription, say, that 'people should have equal welfare' cannot lead us to change our perception of the way the world *is*, for that would imply some sort of inferral of facts from values. What I do mean to suggest is that the urge to give meaning to that prescription might lead us to modify the way in which the terms in that prescription are defined. Now there are certainly limits to such modifications. Where we say 'distribute *x*-ness equally', our commitment to the promotion of '*x*-ness', and our commitment to equality as a distributive principle, are, within certain bounds, interdependent. If '*x*-ness' cannot be satisfactorily measured, we cannot opt arbitrarily for something which can, and distribute *that* equally. Neither, however, can it be inferred from the unfeasibility of distributing '*x*-ness' equally that we must totally abandon our commitment to equality. What might be said to be possible are certain revisions of our *initial conception* of *x*-ness, *given* that we also value *x*-ness when

[15] D. Rae, 'Maximin Justice and an Alternative Principle of General Advantage', *American Political Science Review*, 69 (1975), 633.

defined at the level of the *concept*. Suppose that a small revision of my initial conception of welfare would allow for the required powers of measurement, and would therefore make my commitment to 'equal welfare' coherent. In this case, might I not at least be torn between relinquishing my commitment to equality and revising my initial conception of welfare?

There is no reason why this point should not apply as much to the concept of freedom as it does to that of welfare. We must recognize the limits, should there be any, on our powers of measuring freedom imposed by our conception of freedom. We cannot simply invent greater powers where to do so would be to ignore the test of validity; we cannot pretend that the world is other than the way it is simply because this clashes with our moral or political prescriptions. Nevertheless, such a recognition need not necessarily lead us to weaken our principle for the distribution of freedom. For we may have a strong ethical commitment to a particular distribution of freedom, defined at the level of the concept of freedom, with which such a weakened distributive principle conflicts. Clearly, neither of these conflicting premises can simply be discarded. What we shall need to do, in attempting to resolve inconsistencies of this kind, is to examine *both* the extent of the powers of measuring freedom which may or may not be available to us given certain conceptions of freedom, *and* the strength of the distributive demands made by our theory of justice. It may be that *one* argument in favour of a certain conception of overall freedom consists in an appeal to our commitment to distributing freedom in a certain way. I should emphasize that I am not arguing that in any one case it should be one's initial conception of freedom that gets revised, rather than one's principle for the distribution of freedom; my point is simply that there may be issues of this kind which need settling, and to which no general rule (working in favour of either initial conceptions or distributive principles) can be applied.

4.3 FREEDOM AND JUSTICE

We can now bring together the factors identified so far into an overall scheme representing the process by which we should search for a conception of justice in reflective equilibrium in so far as that process affects and is affected by the search for a conception of overall freedom.

John Rawls and Norman Daniels have pointed out that there is a distinction to be made between 'narrow reflective equilibrium' and 'wide reflective equilibrium', and that Rawls's theory of justice should be interpreted as an example of the latter. Seeking narrow reflective equilibrium involves constructing principles of justice on the basis of one's considered judgements and

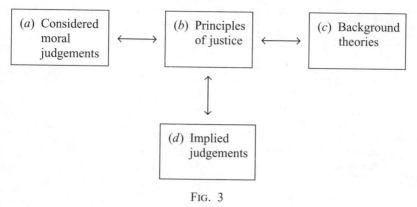

FIG. 3

attempting to resolve contradictions in the light of the judgements resulting from one's principles of justice by revising either those principles or one's considered judgements (the process described in s. 4.1). Seeking wide reflective equilibrium, on the other hand, involves taking into account different possible narrow reflective equilibriums, in the light of a set of relevant 'background moral theories', which might include 'a theory of the person', 'general social theory', and 'a theory of the role of morality in society (including the ideal of the well-ordered society)'.[16] In keeping with the spirit of Rawls's method, however, achieving wide reflective equilibrium does not simply imply revising one's considered judgements and one's principles of justice in order that they best fit one's background theories. For there is no reason why one's commitment to certain background theories might not itself become outweighed by one's commitment to certain considered judgements or to certain principles of justice. Thus, we should 'imagine the agent moving back and forth, making adjustments to his considered judgements, his moral principles, and his background theories'.[17]

Simplifying somewhat,[18] the search for a theory of justice in wide reflective equilibrium might therefore be depicted diagrammatically as in Fig. 3. How exactly does freedom fit into this picture? Four factors must be taken into account: three of these, discussed in s. 4.1, are our intuitions about freedom (including our common-sense comparisons), our conception of freedom, and our implied judgements about freedom (including measurements of overall freedom); a fourth factor, identified in the previous section, is that of our principle for the distribution of freedom (and the consequent demands we

[16] Daniels, 'Wide Reflective Equilibrium and Theory Acceptance in Ethics', 280.
[17] Ibid. 258–9; id., 'Reflective Equilibrium and Archimedean Points', 85.
[18] The diagram presented by Daniels is considerably more complex than Fig. 3. See 'Reflective Equilibrium and Archimedean Points', 88.

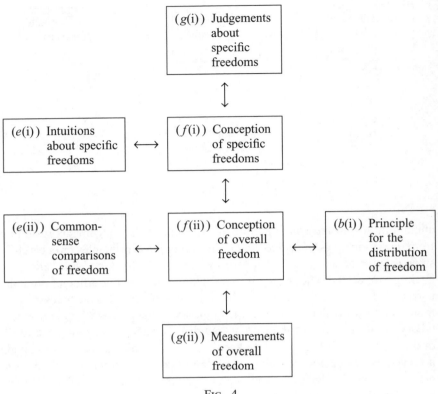

FIG. 4

make on our powers of measurement). It is clearly through this last factor that the connection is to be made with Fig. 3: our principle for the distribution of freedom supplies part of the content of (*b*) in Fig. 3. The other three factors affect the meaning of that principle, and in turn may be revised in the light of it. Let us think of (*b*) in Fig. 3 as being divided into the various principles of justice, where (*b*(i)) is the principle governing the distribution of freedom. Adding our intuitions about freedom, our conception of freedom, and our implied judgements about freedom (call these (*e*), (*f*), and (*g*) respectively), we can depict the search for a conception of freedom in reflective equilibrium, and its role in the search for a theory of justice, as shown in Fig. 4.

As I suggested in the previous section, each of our principles of distributive justice ((*b*) in Fig. 3) reveal two commitments—one to a particular *distribuendum*, the other to a particular distribution. In so far as the *distribuendum* is freedom, the role of (*f*(ii)) in Fig. 4 is to provide a precise definition of that *distribuendum.* (f(ii)), then, in part determines the meaning of (b(i)). On the other hand, the natures of both (f(i)) and (f(ii)) may themselves be affected by our demands on our powers of measurement, which are an outcome of (b(i)). The process of searching for reflective equilibrium between a theory of justice and a conception of overall freedom must therefore involve reasoning in this circle, from a principle of justice (b(i)), to the demand for certain implied powers of measuring freedom, to a conception of overall freedom (f(ii)) (consistent with an intuitively acceptable conception of specific freedoms ((e(i)), (f(i)), and (g(i))) and trying where possible to achieve isomorphism between implied measurements (g(ii)) and common-sense comparisons (e(ii))), back to the principle of justice (b(i)), and indeed to its relationship with the other principles of justice ((b(ii)), (b(iii)) ... (b(n))), and so on.

Our freedom-based theory of justice (including the idea of freedom's nonspecific value) might be said to perform a role in Fig. 4 analogous to that played by the 'background theories' in the models of Rawls and Daniels. The input provided by (b(i)) in Fig. 4, in other words, might be seen as analogous to the input provided by (c) in Fig. 3. In this sense, the content of Chapters 1 to 3 of this book can be called the 'background theory' as far as the search for a conception of *freedom* in reflective equilibrium is concerned. The idea is that having worked out alternative conceptions of freedom (f(i)), each of which has a certain degree of internal coherence, in terms both of the relationship between overall freedom and specific freedoms and of the relationship between conceptions and intuitions about freedom, our choice among such conceptions should be made not only on the basis of those degrees of internal coherence, but also in the light of our ideas about how and why freedom is valuable and about the nature of a just distribution of freedom.

It might be objected that this model of the relationship between freedom and justice risks letting a 'justice-based definition of freedom' in through the back door. Does Fig. 4 not specify that our theory of justice is to have some effect (via (b(i))) on the way we are to define freedom? And did our argument in the previous chapter against justice-based definitions of freedom not specify that freedom should be defined independently of justice? While this objection might at first appear a serious one, it is in fact based on a misunderstanding of the role played in Fig. 4 by our theory of justice. Such a role is different from the role played by a theory of justice in constructing a justice-based definition of freedom. A justice-based definition of freedom specifies that having freedom consists in being able to perform (or not being prevented from performing) *actions which are just* (see s. 3.1). Our conception of freedom in reflective equilibrium (as represented by Fig. 4), on the other hand, is only affected by our theory of justice in so far as such a theory of justice makes demands on our *powers of measuring freedom*, by requiring measurement on a certain type of scale, with a certain degree of completeness, and so on. What is more, the process by which one seeks a definition of freedom in reflective equilibrium involves reasoning in two or more directions, whereas the process by which one seeks a justice-based definition of freedom involves reasoning in one direction only (i.e. from a definition of justice to a definition of freedom). Above all, to endorse a justice-based definition of freedom is to abandon the view of freedom as non-specifically valuable, whereas the method of defining freedom set out in Fig. 4 *arises out of* the idea of freedom's non-specific value: our principle for the distribution of freedom is a necessary part of a freedom-based theory of justice, and the need for a freedom-based theory of justice is occasioned by freedom's non-specific value. Fig. 4 simply represents the process by which we should try to render these ideas coherent with our conception of freedom. It is one thing to say that when one aims at a precise conception of freedom one has a *purpose* in mind (here, that of arriving at a coherent theory of justice); it is another thing to define freedom *in terms of* that purpose (i.e. to define it in terms of justice), so robbing freedom of any independent supportive weight it might lend to that purpose, and with that the possibility of one's theory of justice being a *freedom-based* one.

4.4 SWANTON ON OVERALL FREEDOM AND REFLECTIVE EQUILIBRIUM

Christine Swanton's theory of freedom makes extensive use both of the notion of overall freedom and of the notion of reflective equilibrium, and therefore deserves some attention at this stage.[19] In particular, it will be useful to consider why, despite an apparent agreement on method, Swanton's conclusions about the nature of overall freedom are so different from mine. I think that this difference can be traced to a difference in the way we understand the nature of the search for a conception of freedom in reflective equilibrium.

Swanton suggests that the best approach to defining freedom is that provided by Rawls's idea of wide reflective equilibrium. Her reflective equilibrium is 'wide' because it includes a background theory, analogous to the background theory in Rawls's theory of justice, the purpose of which, in the case of freedom, is to explain why we should be interested in the first place in classifying a heterogeneous set of phenomena as 'freedom'. The answer, for Swanton, lies in the value freedom has as a means to realizing 'individual human potential

---

[19] C. Swanton, *Freedom: A Coherence Theory* (Indianapolis: Hackett, 1992).

in agency' given that this contributes to 'individual flourishing'.[20] This claim about the value of freedom leads to the construction of a 'formal property' of freedom, which is that of 'the absence of certain types of limitations in human practical activity, namely, those which limit individual potential in agency'.[21] My own theory, too, can be said to be one of freedom in wide reflective equilibrium, in as much as it too assumes a background theory. As I have said, it is reasonable to see this background theory as represented by the content of the first three chapters of this book. However, an important difference with Swanton here is that my background theory takes into account liberal views of *justice*. It is a theory not only about the value of freedom (Chapter 2), but also about just distributions of freedom (Chapter 3).

Another difference with Swanton's theory, which is no doubt linked to the above difference, concerns the set of intuitions about freedom to be taken into account. Swanton uses the Aristotelian term *endoxa* to refer to these intuitions, but she seems to have in mind exactly what I have referred to as our intuitions about specific freedoms and our common-sense comparisons of freedom. Swanton's *endoxa* are the claims about freedom made by 'the many or the wise': for example, that 'the man who hands over his money, having yielded to credible threat at gun point, does not perform a free act', that 'those in prison are not free regardless of their desires, goals, or choices', and that 'the individuals in *Brave New World* are not free'.[22] However, Swanton appears to neglect those *endoxa* which involve or assume the meaningfulness of on-balance comparisons of agents' overall freedom, such as Berlin's claim that in 1969 the Swedish were 'on the whole' more free than the Albanians, or Hobbes's claim that the citizens of Lucca were no freer than those of Constantinople, or the normative claim that people have a right to be 'equally free', and so on and so forth.

Swanton brings in the notion of overall freedom as a solution to the problem of accommodating prima facie incompatible *endoxa*. Her account of freedom is a 'liberal' one,[23] not in the political sense of the term, but in the sense of being ecumenical, thus including a wide range of apparently divergent claims about the nature of freedom. It is exactly Swanton's conception of overall freedom that allows her to render these different claims mutually consistent. The solution lies in producing a series of assertions about the conditions of overall freedom, each of which not only accommodates one of the apparently divergent claims, but also includes an all-important *ceteris paribus* clause. In this way, each assertion can accommodate a particular *endoxon* without contradicting any other. For example, on the one hand we have the *endoxon*

---

[20] Ibid. 38.   [21] Ibid. 49.
[22] Ibid., respectively, 68, 74, and 71.   [23] Ibid. 191.

'those in prison are not free regardless of their desires, goals, or choices', and on the other hand we have the *endoxon* 'those who can achieve their goals without interference are free'. The first appears to imply that valuational magnitudes such as those indicated by desires or goals are irrelevant to questions of freedom, while the second appears to imply that they are relevant after all. Swanton's theory accommodates the first *endoxon* by saying that 'an agent is freer overall, *ceteris paribus*, the fewer options are unavailable due to freedom-limiting factors', and it accommodates the second by saying that 'an agent is the freer overall, *ceteris paribus*, the less significant are the actions with respect to which practical activity is limited'.[24] One's overall freedom can therefore be limited either by a straightforward reduction in one's options or by a reduction in the significance of one's options, and the two *endoxa* can be seen as compatible after all. In the same way, we can accommodate the *endoxon* that 'the man who hands over his money, having yielded to credible threat at gun point, does not perform a free act', by saying that 'an agent is the freer overall, *ceteris paribus*, the less are his available options rendered ineligible [i.e. difficult or costly], due to freedom-limiting factors'.[25] Proceeding in this way, Swanton constructs five dimensions of overall freedom: (1) the availability of actions, (2) the eligibility of actions, (3) the absence of heteronomy, (4) the absence of 'executive failure', such as weakness of the will, and (5) the significance of actions. An increase in freedom in terms of any one of these dimensions makes one more free overall, *ceteris paribus*.

The *ceteris paribus* clauses in the above claims about overall freedom certainly allow for the accommodation of a wide range of conceptions of freedom that might otherwise appear to be incompatible. All that is required is the 'pruning and adjusting' of the various *endoxa*, the basic spirit of which can still be preserved. We can say, for example, that the more 'eligible' my options are, the more freedom I have, *all other dimensions being equal*. But this advantage of Swanton's theory of overall freedom brings with it a huge cost: in most cases, the possibility of making interpersonal comparisons of overall freedom will be ruled out. Where one individual is not at least as well off as another in terms of *all* of the dimensions of freedom, the five *ceteris paribus* clauses will not be satisfied, and we shall not be able to make a comparison of degrees of overall freedom. Each time a new 'dimension of freedom' is added to the theory, so widening and (some might say) 'enriching' the notion of overall freedom, that same notion becomes more indeterminate and its purpose less clear.[26]

[24] Swanton, *Freedom*, respectively, 79 and 80.   [25] Ibid. 79.

[26] Swanton herself suggests that her background theory could be widened so as to include a conception of the good which might allow us to 'weight' the various dimensions of freedom (ibid. 182). However, the suggestion is not explored at any length, and seems in any case to lead in the direction either of a moralized definition of freedom (see s. 3.1) or of what I call the 'value-based approach' to measuring freedom (see 5).

Rather than enriching our notion of freedom, I think it more appropriate to characterize Swanton's notion of overall freedom as playing the role of a metaphorical sponge, the usefulness of which lies almost exclusively in its ability to absorb the various inconsistencies we find among the *endoxa* listed by Swanton. The more inconsistencies the sponge soaks up, the more bloated and amorphous it becomes, and the less we are able to satisfy the very demands which made us interested in people's overall freedom in the first place: for example, that they have more than a certain minimum of freedom, or that they be as free as possible subject to the condition that others have (at least roughly) the same degree of freedom.

What is lacking in Swanton's theory is the constraint imposed on our conception of overall freedom by our theory of justice (in particular, by (b(i)) in Fig. 4). In addition, and probably as a result of this, Swanton neglects those *endoxa*, both about on-balance overall freedom (part of (e(ii)) in Fig. 4) and about justice (part of (a) in Fig. 3), which are likely to conflict with her multi-dimensional conception of overall freedom: *endoxa* like 'the average Iranian woman is on balance less free than the average Italian woman', or 'people have a right to maximal equal freedom'. These are the gaps in Swanton's theory which leave the profile of overall freedom unchecked, so allowing it to become bloated and amorphous. Perhaps a *wider* background theory—one which takes into account not only the value of freedom but also its proper role in a liberal theory of justice—will lead to a *narrower* conception of overall freedom, on the basis of which interpersonal comparisons will be more feasible. This would be a less liberal theory in terms of its ability to accommodate various rival conceptions of freedom, but perhaps a more liberal theory in the sense in which the term is used by political philosophers—more liberal, that is, in terms of its ability to accommodate philosophically and politically liberal *endoxa* about the just distribution of freedom, and therefore in terms of its ability to give meaning, in reflective equilibrium, to a freedom-based theory of justice.

4.5 FURTHER REMARKS ON REFLECTIVE EQUILIBRIUM

The core arguments of this chapter are now complete. But before bringing the chapter to a close, I should like to make some additional clarifying remarks about the nature of reflective equilibrium as such, in order to anticipate certain objections which might be raised at a more fundamental level. It is my view that the method of seeking reflective equilibrium not only represents the way we should proceed in reconstructing the meaning and rules of measurement of freedom, but is in any case unavoidable in moral and political philosophy in general.

This view gains plausibility once it is accepted that the idea of reflective equilibrium also gives a correct account of what goes on in the natural sciences. It was indeed in the philosophy of science that the idea of reflective equilibrium first emerged. Having refuted 'two dogmas of empiricism'—the analytic-synthetic distinction and the 'reductionist' idea that any single statement can admit of empirical confirmation or denial in isolation—Quine had pointed out that for an empiricism 'without dogmas', the 'unit' that is subject to empirical confirmation or denial must be 'the whole of science'. Any single statement might be held to be true even in the face of 'recalcitrant experience' (in extreme cases, by 'pleading hallucination') and, conversely, 'no statement is immune to revision'.[27] It follows that 'our statements about the external world face the tribunal of sense experience not individually but as a corporate body',[28] and are brought into agreement with one another (and with more abstract statements) 'through considerations of equilibrium'.[29] Nelson Goodman had applied this same idea to the question of the validity of rules of inference. The validity of such rules depends, according to Goodman, not on 'some self-evident axiom', but on 'accordance with the particular deductive inferences we actually make and sanction'. The appearance of circularity here is benign, for the circle is pragmatic rather than logical. It is simply a fact that we have such rules on the one hand and that we favour particular inferences on the other, and that we justify each in terms of its agreement with the other. Here too, the aim is overall coherence: 'a rule is amended if it yields an inference we are unwilling to accept; an inference is rejected if it violates a rule we are unwilling to amend.'[30] Rawls's insight consisted in recognizing that this model applies equally to the way we justify and argue about prescriptive rules in moral and political philosophy.

We should therefore reject the view, held by some critics as well as some defenders of reflective equilibrium, that Rawls's method *contrasts* with scientific method in terms of the implied process of theory acceptance. According to Ronald Dworkin, for instance, moral and political philosophers have, in seeking reflective equilibrium, a certain freedom to choose between intuitions (and to choose simply to discard those that conflict with their theories), whereas scientists lack a similar freedom, since they are not free to choose between sets of observational data (and are not free simply to discard those data that conflict with their theories). This view has led to the accusation that reflective equilibria in moral philosophy will be too arbitrary to have any moral authority. Why, after all, should the theorist choose one equilibrium rather than another?

[27] Quine, *From a Logical Point of View*, 42–3.   [28] Ibid. 41.   [29] Ibid. 43.

[30] N. Goodman, *Fact, Fiction and Forecast* (3rd edn., Hassocks: Harvester Press, 1979), 63–4.

The basic idea behind Dworkin's view seems to be that the philosopher is not 'stuck' with her intuitions in the same way as the natural scientist is 'stuck' with a piece of empirical evidence which does not conform to her theory. According to Dworkin, the difference between equilibria in science and equilibria in moral theory is that scientists are forced by contradictory evidence to provide new theories, whereas, in the case of moral theory, 'some of the phenomena, in the form of moral convictions, *may simply be ignored* the better to serve some particular theory'.[31] But this surely provides an inaccurate picture both of natural science and of moral and political philosophy. On the one hand, the natural scientist does not always revise her theory in the light of evidence that contradicts it; if her theory continues to be plausible *overall*, she might put the disturbing evidence down to misperception, or she might simply leave some questions open. On the other hand, as W. E. Cooper points out, the acceptance of moral or political beliefs in reflective equilibrium is not a matter of 'choice': we do not *choose* to believe or not to believe that a situation is a just one; we simply have a conviction that this is so. Such a conviction may be *overturned*, but only if there is a certain weight of intuitive evidence against it. In moral and political philosophy, just as in the natural sciences, we are *impelled* either to continue believing in our original theory, or to give credence to that which contradicts it.[32] The moral or political philosopher *is* 'stuck' with her linguistic and moral intuitions, just as much as the scientist is 'stuck' with disturbing data.

The process of theory acceptance in moral and political philosophy need not therefore be seen as any more arbitrary than that of theory acceptance in the natural sciences. To be sure, conflicting moral and political theories may be more *numerous* than conflicting scientific theories, and the intuitions and theories of a particular moral or political philosopher may be revised more *frequently* than the empirical beliefs and theories of a particular natural scientist. The beliefs we are dealing with in these two cases are of very different kinds. But this is not to deny that the process by which they are revised is the same in structure.

The above account of reflective equilibrium allows us to steer an acceptable course between the unrealistic extremes of foundationalism and antifoundationalism. A plausible account of Rawls's view consists in saying that the moral or political philosopher cannot allow herself any surer foundations than those of the kind that Quine and Goodman concede to the natural scientist, but, at the same time, that the process of theory acceptance in moral and political philosophy need not be seen as any *more* arbitrary than it is

---

[31] Dworkin, *Taking Rights Seriously*, 165.
[32] W. E. Cooper, 'Taking Reflective Equilibrium Seriously', *Dialogue* (Canada), 20 (1981), 554.

generally thought to be in the natural sciences. 'Absolute foundations' are certainly alien to the idea of reflective equilibrium, as they contradict the idea that no premiss is immune to revision. On the other hand, this does not leave us with the total subjectivism which is often taken to follow from an anti-foundationalist position. Adopting the method of seeking reflective equilibrium does not give us the freedom to choose arbitrarily between consistent sets of beliefs. It does not imply that our allegiance to a particular conception of justice will be 'no more arbitrary than choices of friends or heroes'.[33] What it does leave room for is the possibility of argument in the Socratic style:[34] it allows us to oppose principles or intuitions with contradictory evidence, which, if weighty enough, will impel others to agree with us.

Moral and political philosophy involves movement towards reflective equilibrium, however well or badly individual moral and political philosophers may carry this out.[35] Thus, even works which appear to be based on unquestionable premises and to proceed unremittingly to their logical conclusions are best thought of as a part of this more general equilibrium process. To see this, one has only to think of the number of authors of works of this last kind who have subsequently questioned their 'unquestionable' premises, given their subsequent dissatisfaction with the logical conclusions arrived at.[36] The original premises were not, after all, unquestionable, even if the strength of the theorist's commitments might in the end compel him to hold onto them. That any single linguistic or moral intuition can have some kind of absolute validity is a dogma analogous to the two exposed by Quine. On the other hand, our theorizing is constrained by the linguistic and moral intuitions we do have, just as natural science is constrained by 'the tribunal of sense experience'. Anyone who accepts these two points accepts that moral and political theorizing involves movement towards reflective equilibrium.

4.6 REFLECTIVE EQUILIBRIUM AND CONSENSUS

Far from producing the limitless variety of opinions over the definition of freedom presumably made possible by extreme anti-foundationalism, there may be reason for thinking that the Rawlsian-Socratic method outlined above

[33] R. Rorty, *Contingency, Irony and Solidarity* (Cambridge: Cambridge University Press, 1989), 54.

[34] Cf. Rawls, *A Theory of Justice*, 49; K. Nielsen, 'Rawls and the Socratic Ideal', *Analyse & Kritik*, 13 (1991).

[35] For a similar view of analytic philosophy in general, see D. Føllesdal, 'Analytic Philosophy: What Is It and Why Should One Engage in It?', *Ratio*, NS 9 (1996), 202–4.

[36] A clear example is Robert Nozick's change of heart between *Anarchy, State and Utopia* and ch. 25 of *The Examined Life* (New York: Simon & Schuster, 1989).

will, when applied to questions relating to the measurement of freedom, lead to an increase in *consensus*.

I do not mean to imply by this last claim—as Joseph Raz seems to believe some writers on reflective equilibrium have suggested—that an argument is strengthened by its tendency to produce consensus *as such*. Raz writes that 'many would agree that it is valuable to secure agreement based on moral truths', but adds that 'it is a long and hazardous way from here to the view which Rawls may hold, namely, that the fact that consensus can be achieved concerning a set of moral principles is a reason for holding them to state moral truths'.[37]

The implication of the arguments of this chapter, however, is that we do not have a straight choice between the highly demanding project of seeking 'moral truth' and the undemanding project of seeking mere agreement. As Raz himself points out, *mere* agreement might be achieved simply because one person's deliberations are 'arrived at by a series of logical howlers such as affirming the consequent'.[38] Furthermore, even allowing that all of the parties concerned have grasped the basics of logic, their mere agreement may not imply that each has achieved a state of reflective equilibrium, because it may be that some or all of them have failed to consider, or have yet to be confronted with, certain conceptual or empirical arguments. Reflective equilibrium is only achieved after the weight of all available evidence has been taken into account. It is indeed for this reason that the acceptance of 'received opinion' is neither a necessary nor a sufficient condition for the achievement of reflective equilibrium.

One of the aims of the rest of this book is to exemplify a Rawlsian-Socratic concern to seek consensus, through the confrontation of certain beliefs—here, people's beliefs about the nature and value of freedom—with certain arguments —here, arguments over the question of whether and how freedom can be measured. As Rawls says in reference to the concept of justice, a person will be especially likely to revise his initial judgements to accord with his principles of justice 'if he can find an explanation for the deviations which undermines his confidence in his original judgements and if the conception presented yields a judgement which he finds he can now accept'.[39] The same point will hold, I believe, in the case of freedom, once we come to examine the compatibility of given conceptions of freedom with given common-sense comparisons of overall freedom. Might we not sometimes come to see that we have been mistaken to some degree, through our neglect of questions relating to the measurement of freedom, over the supposed incorrectness of a

[37] J. Raz, 'The Claims of Reflective Equilibrium', *Inquiry*, 25 (1982), 312.
[38] Ibid. 309.   [39] Rawls, *A Theory of Justice*, 48.

conception of freedom proposed by a political adversary? Is there really the need for such a plethora of conflicting opinions as those which are currently held, for example, on the question of what does and does not constitute a constraint on a specific freedom? How essential are such conflicts to the conflicts between different people's common-sense comparisons of freedom? These are some of the questions which we must bear in mind as we now shift our attention away from the general theoretical framework set out here, and towards the more fine-grained problems encountered in actually attempting, within that framework, to make sense of the idea of measuring overall freedom.

PART II

Value-Based Freedom

5

The Value-Based Approach

IN this chapter I shall examine a particular answer to the question of how overall freedom should be measured. That answer consists in saying that the extent of freedom provided by a set of available actions depends on *how valuable* that set of actions is. Put as simply as possible (and in merely ordinal terms), if the things I am free to do are more valuable than the things you are free to do, then I am 'freer' than you. The idea here is that we should appeal to values other than freedom in order to attach weights to a person's available actions, and that those weights should be seen as determining or at least in some way affecting the person's degree of overall freedom. I shall therefore call this answer the 'value-based approach' to measuring freedom.

It should be emphasized that the value-based approach represents not so much a thesis about the *value* of freedom as an attempt to make sense of attributions of *degrees* of freedom. It is one thing to say that different specific freedoms should be assigned different weights in terms of their values. This idea does not take us beyond the normative version of the specific-freedom thesis examined in Chapters 1 and 2. It is another thing to say that those weights tell us something about a person's *extent of overall freedom*. This idea apparently *contrasts* with the normative version of the specific-freedom thesis.

Advocates of the value-based approach often take their lead from Isaiah Berlin, on whose suggestion

the extent of my freedom seems to depend [in part] on . . . how important in my plan of life, given my character and circumstances [the possibilities open to me] are when compared with each other,[1] . . . [and] what value not merely the agent, but the general sentiment of the society in which he lives puts on the various possibilities.[2]

The meaning of 'how valuable an option is' can of course be interpreted in many different ways. For example, it might be taken to mean 'how valuable an option is given the agent's preferences' (as it is, for example, in Amartya

---

[1] Presumably, Berlin does not mean *merely* 'when compared with *each other*', because this kind of comparison alone would not be sufficient to allow for interpersonal comparisons of degrees of freedom.
[2] Berlin, *Four Essays on Liberty*, 130.

Sen's interpretation of the value-based approach[3]), 'how valuable it is in an objective sense' (as in Charles Taylor's interpretation), or even, as Berlin suggests, 'how valuable it is according to the general sentiment of the agent's society'. But I shall leave aside these differences here, since what I aim to discuss in this chapter is the value-based approach as such, rather than any particular interpretation of it. Therefore, except where otherwise stated, my remarks should be seen as referring to the value-based approach on any interpretation. What is important for present purposes is that the values being referred to must be values other than freedom. Otherwise, all that we would be saying is that the extent of a person's freedom is a function of the value of her available actions in terms of freedom, in which case the value-based approach would amount to no more than a tautology.

The subject of the second part of this book (comprising the present chapter and the next) is the idea of 'value-based freedom', where this expression should be understood to mean overall freedom as measured in accordance with the value-based approach. The present chapter is concerned, as I have said, with value-based freedom as such. In the next chapter, we shall look at a *special case* of value-based freedom, namely, freedom as the absence of a certain kind of 'internal' preventing condition, or freedom as 'self-mastery'. Contemporary theorists of freedom most commonly associate this last conception with the work of Charles Taylor. My overall aim in Part II of this book is to show that the idea of value-based freedom is mistaken. My argumentative strategy will be the same in both chapters: it will consist in showing first of all that the conception of freedom under examination cannot help us in making *literal* sense of judgements about overall freedom, and secondly that, from a liberal standpoint, such a conception of freedom does not even serve any useful rhetorical purpose.

The most important argument of the present chapter, put forward in section 2, is that the value-based approach is incompatible with the idea of freedom's non-specific value. This point is of some consequence, given that it was the idea of freedom's non-specific value that justified our interest in measuring overall freedom in the first place (see Chapter 2). Those who adopt the value-based approach are, I shall suggest, no more than normative specific-freedom theorists in disguise. In order to preserve the coherence of the value-based approach, we shall therefore have to say that judgements about extents of freedom are merely elliptical for claims about degrees of goods other than freedom. But even here, as we shall see in sections 3 and 4, such elliptical judgements will encounter problems of isomorphism with 'common-sense

---

[3] Thus, Sen's approach to measuring freedom often gets called (by him and others) the 'preference-based approach'.

comparisons of freedom' (see ss. 1.3 and 4.1), including the common-sense comparisons of those who adopt the value-based approach. Section 5 of this chapter will also refer in an important way to common-sense comparisons of freedom: while sections 3 and 4 appeal to common-sense comparisons of freedom in such a way as to challenge the internal coherence of the value-based approach (where degree-of-freedom judgements are interpreted as elliptical), section 5 provides what seems to me to be the most plausible account of the place of common-sense comparisons of freedom in a liberal system of values. Such an account contradicts the value-based approach, as well as pointing to an alternative approach—an 'empirical' approach—which will be explored to the full in Part III of this book.

5.1 WHY THE VALUE-BASED APPROACH? AN ARGUMENT FROM COMMON-SENSE COMPARISONS

What is it that initially makes the value-based approach so attractive as a way of interpreting judgements about overall freedom? The answer is that it appears to lead to measurements that are isomorphic with our common-sense comparisons of freedom. Thus, according to Sen, 'a set of three alternatives that we see as "bad", "awful" and "dismal" cannot, we think, give as much real freedom as a set of three alternatives that we prefer a great deal more and see as "great", "terrific" and "wonderful" '. This is because 'we find it absurd to dissociate the extent of our freedom from our preferences over alternatives'.[4] Consider the following two option sets: 'travelling by (a stiff tricycle; hopping on one leg; rolling in the dust)' and 'travelling by (an efficient bicycle; a smart car; walking on two legs normally)'.[5] We have a clear sense that the second option set offers us more freedom than the first, and this is surely because the second option set is preferable to the first.

Making a similar appeal to our common-sense comparisons, Richard Arneson asks us to consider the following example involving two unfortunate individuals called Jones and Smith. Jones is a prisoner in a straitjacket, who has only been left free to twiddle his thumbs, while Smith is an ex-prisoner suffering from the disabling effects of thumbscrew torture. (Notice that in this case Jones's freedoms are not a subset of Smith's.) Given the fact that available actions can always be broken up into their component parts, and that this process can in theory be carried on indefinitely, it does not seem possible to find

---

[4] A. Sen, 'Welfare, Freedom and Social Choice: A Reply', *Recherches Économiques de Louvain*, 56 (1990), 470. Cf. id., 'Welfare, Preference, and Freedom', *Journal of Econometrics*, 50 (1991), 21–2.

[5] Sen, 'Welfare, Freedom and Social Choice', 470.

any 'value-neutral' grounds for saying, as we should like to, that Jones has fewer options than Smith. Both seem, in fact, to have an 'indefinite' number of options, despite the fact that Jones is in a straitjacket and Smith has walked free; if we simply 'count' the actions Smith and Jones are restrained and unrestrained from performing, their degrees of overall freedom will appear to be 'on a par'.[6] Therefore, our reason for intuitively seeing Smith as freer than Jones must be our implicit assumption that both Smith's and Jones's *desires* would be better satisfied by Smith's set of freedoms than by Jones's set of freedoms.

Unlike Arneson, Charles Taylor does not assume that the number of actions available to us is indefinite, but his view is still that the neutral counting of actions fails to provide measurements that fit our common-sense comparisons, whereas the value-based approach succeeds in doing so. Taylor points out that many more actions are prevented by traffic lights than by restrictions on religious worship. Why then, he asks, do we have the clear intuition that Londoners, who are subject to many traffic lights but to virtually no restraints on worship, are 'freer' than Albanians, who suffer restrictions on worship but encounter far fewer traffic lights?[7] Given the vast quantity of actions that traffic lights prevent, if we assess the actions available to the average Albanian and the average Londoner 'in sheer quantitative terms', the Albanian will probably come out on top. But this would amount to a 'diabolical defence of Albania as a free country'.[8] The reason we make the common-sense comparisons we do, Taylor suggests, is that 'freedom is important to us because we are pur- posive beings'. And some purposes matter more than others. Therefore, variations in degrees of freedom must be affected by variations in the degree of significance of different purposes. The free circulation of traffic is less significant than freedom of worship, and this must be what accounts for our view that Londoners are freer than Albanians.

An anticipation of Taylor's argument can be found in the work of the Italian philosopher Uberto Scarpelli, who was moved to object to Felix Oppenheim's sceptical position on the freedom of democracies and dictatorships.[9] As we have seen, according to Oppenheim, the claim that there is 'more freedom' in a democracy than in a dictatorship is meaningless (see s. 1.4): we might say that certain specific freedoms are differently distributed in a dictatorship and in a democracy, but we cannot say that one system is 'freer' than another. This claim was seen as deeply counter-intuitive by those Italians who had fought against the Fascist regime in the name of freedom. How are we to make sense of their view in the face of Oppenheim's sceptical objection? The answer, according

---

[6] Arneson, 'Freedom and Desire', 427.
[7] Writing in 1979, Taylor is referring to communist Albania.
[8] Taylor, 'What's Wrong with Negative Liberty', 182–3.
[9] U. Scarpelli, 'La dimensione normativa della libertà', *Rivista ai Filosofia*, 55 (1964).

to Scarpelli, must lie in the rejection of Oppenheim's 'value neutral' analysis of freedom. The specific freedoms guaranteed by democracies are of greater normative importance than those guaranteed by dictatorships. Comparative judgements about normative importance *are* possible, and these must be what give meaning to the claim that democratic Italy is 'freer' than Fascist Italy.

Sen, Arneson, Taylor, and Scarpelli apparently enjoy the company of a great many other political theorists. These other theorists agree that 'choices which matter' contribute more to our freedom than choices which do not matter, or matter less,[10] and that while measuring freedom may involve 'counting' available actions, 'the counting cannot be done without judging what counts'.[11] After all, some actions are simply trivial from the point of view of our freedom, like my moving of certain air molecules as I write these words, or my eating green ice cream.[12] Since some available actions matter to the agent more than others in terms of his freedom, it follows that when he is prevented from pursuing some course of action, 'the degree to which his liberty is thereby curtailed depends . . . on how important the course of action in question is to him'.[13] We feel intuitively 'that some liberties are more important than others', and that 'the restriction of the *more important liberties* is a *greater restriction of liberty* than that of the less important ones'.[14] 'Standards independent of the notion of liberty' are therefore required not only in order to know 'whether' liberty is restricted, but also '*in what degree*'.[15] Answering questions about 'net aggregate freedom' requires 'judgements about the *most important* freedoms and the *best* states of affairs'.[16] And this means that 'any assessment of *degrees of liberty* depends on the importance of various actions for the protection and promotion of *values other than freedom*'.[17] We could go on *ad infinitum*, but I think the reader gets the idea.[18] And I think that Sen is

[10] R. Norman, 'Liberty, Equality, Property', *Proceedings of the Aristotelian Society*, Suppl. Vol. 55 (1981), 198–202.

[11] Lukes, 'Equality and Liberty', 57.   [12] Cf. Raz, *The Morality of Freedom*, 246.

[13] E. Loevinsohn, 'Liberty and the Redistribution of Property', *Philosophy and Public Affairs*, 6 (1976–7), 232.

[14] Raz, *The Morality of Freedom*, 13, my emphasis.

[15] Gray, *Liberalisms*, 145, my emphasis.   [16] Kristjánsson, *Social Freedom*, 165.

[17] Raz, *The Morality of Freedom*, 16, my emphasis.

[18] Yet other important advocates of the value-based approach are: Feinberg, *Social Philosophy*, 18; Crocker, *Positive Liberty*, 54; J. Christman, 'Liberalism and Individual Positive Freedom', *Ethics*, 101 (1991), 353; Swanton, *Freedom*, 75; R. Bellamy, *Liberalism and Modern Society: An Historical Argument* (Cambridge: Polity Press, 1992), 255; Van Parijs, *Real Freedom for All*, 50; K. J. Arrow, 'A Note on Freedom and Flexibility', in K. Basu, P. K. Pattanaik, and K. Suzumura (eds.), *Choice, Welfare and Development* (Oxford: Oxford University Press, 1995); C. Puppe, 'An Axiomatic Approach to "Preference for Freedom of Choice"', *Journal of Economic Theory*, 68 (1996), 174–99; D. M. Hausman and M. McPherson, *Economic Analysis and Moral Philosophy* (Cambridge: Cambridge University Press, 1996), 122–3; P. K. Pattanaik and Y. Xu, 'On Preference and Freedom', *Theory and Decision*, forthcoming.

simply mistaken when he suggests that the value-based approach 'goes against some common presumptions about assessing freedom'.[19]

Notice that if one adopts the value-based approach, one should not look in isolation at the single actions available to a person in order to fix their weights, since the way in which specific options are combined may well be relevant to their values. For example, certain freedoms may constitute complementary goods, such as the freedom to drive a car and the freedom to buy petrol; and other freedoms, when all of the same kind, may have diminishing marginal value. Many of the authors cited above see this as a strength of their position, since it suggests another way in which the value-based approach accords with our common-sense comparisons of freedom. We feel that some increases in choice add very little to our freedom, even where those increases involve the addition of a large number of options each of which, when viewed in isolation, may be of considerable value. For example, we feel intuitively that the freedom to use one of ten Ford Escorts does not give us ten times more freedom than the freedom to use a single Ford Escort,[20] and that the choice between twenty-one brands of soap powder in a supermarket does not give us three times more freedom than the choice between seven such brands.[21] Given these last examples, it would seem that in order to make a difference to an agent's overall freedom, a new option must be *significantly different* from the options the agent already has.

I shall put to one side for now the question of the fit between our common-sense comparisons of overall freedom and the degree to which options are, in some value-based sense, 'significantly different'. In this chapter, my task is to deal with the very idea of weighting actions in accordance with their values. I shall return to the question of 'significant difference' in Chapter 7 (in particular at ss. 7.6–7.8), where we shall be better placed to compare the above approach to the car and soap powder examples with the alternative approach defended in Part III.

5.2 THE VALUE-BASED APPROACH AND THE SPECIFIC-FREEDOM THESIS

As a way of making *literal* sense of judgements of overall freedom, the value-based approach is a 'non-starter'.[22] For, on closer examination, the

---

[19] Sen, 'Welfare, Preference, and Freedom', 15.

[20] Cf. W. E. Connolly, *The Terms of Political Discourse* (2nd edn., Princeton: Princeton University Press, 1983), 171; P. K. Pattanaik and Y. Xu, 'On Ranking Opportunity Sets in Terms of Freedom of Choice', *Recherches Economiques de Louvain*, 56 (1990), 389–90.

[21] Norman, 'Liberty, Equality, Property', 201.

[22] This is how Charles Taylor describes the approach defended in Part III of this book ('What's Wrong with Negative Liberty', 182).

approach can be seen to reduce to the position of Dworkin and Kymlicka on the question of how and why freedom is valuable. This is my central reason for rejecting the value-based approach. A concise statement of my argument is as follows. In terms of its implications for the *value* of freedom, the value-based approach is ultimately indistinguishable from the normative version of the *specific-freedom thesis*. But according to the normative version of the specific-freedom thesis, attributions of degrees of overall freedom are normatively redundant. It follows that attributions of degrees of freedom on the value-based approach are normatively redundant. Why then bother with the value-based approach at all?

Let me expand on this argument by taking a look at Kymlicka's own discussion of the value-based approach. The Dworkin–Kymlicka view is, as we have seen, that the idea of 'greater and lesser amounts' of freedom does no serious work in political argument. Dworkin and Kymlicka endorse what I have called the normative version of the specific-freedom thesis. Now, since the many authors cited in the previous section ostensibly disagree with this view, Kymlicka obviously sees their approach as a challenge that needs to be dealt with. He also clearly believes the value-based approach to be the only approach to measuring freedom that has any chance of being feasible (that is, of refuting what in s. 1.4 I called the 'epistemic version' of the specific-freedom thesis). His answer (translated into my terms) is that the value-based approach to measuring freedom renders the measurement of overall freedom normatively redundant in the way just mentioned, and that this confirms his specific-freedom thesis.

Kymlicka's discussion contains a comparison of two possible justifications for giving people a certain specific freedom or set of freedoms, which he calls 'the liberty to *x*': on the one hand, we have the justification that we would expect to see put forward by an advocate of the value-based approach who happens to favour the principle of maximal equal freedom; and on the other hand, there is his own justification, which he calls 'Rawlsian' (although in my view it represents only one possible interpretation of Rawls's position[23]). The first justification is as follows:

(1) Each person's interests matter and matter equally
(2) People have an interest in the greatest amount of freedom
(3) Therefore, people should have the greatest amount of freedom, consistent with the equal freedom of others
(4) The liberty to *x* is important, given our interests
(5) Therefore, the liberty to *x* increases our freedom
(6) Therefore, each person ought (*ceteris paribus*) to have the right to *x*, consistent with everyone else's right to *x*.

---

[23] See s. 1.4 for Kymlicka's interpretation, and s. 3.2 for an alternative interpretation that is more consistent with freedom's non-specific value.

Kymlicka then contrasts this with his 'Rawlsian' argument:

(1) Each person's interests matter and matter equally
(4) The liberty to x is important, given our interests
(6) Therefore, each person ought (*ceteris paribus*) to have the right to x, consistent with everyone else's right to x.[24]

As Kymlicka himself points out, 'the step from (4) to (5)' (i.e. the step which inserts the value-based approach) adds nothing, 'and, as a result, . . . (2) and (3) also add nothing'. Therefore, the second argument for the 'right to x' will do just as well as the first, and the additional stages in the first argument are superfluous. According to advocates of the value-based approach,[25] 'because a particular liberty is important, . . . it increases our freedom, and we should have as much freedom as possible. But, in fact, the argument for the liberty is completed with its importance [i.e. the assertion of its specific value].'[26]

So far, I think that Kymlicka is right. The value-based approach is indeed reducible to the normative version of the specific-freedom thesis. However, it should be recalled from Chapter 2 that the normative version of the specific-freedom thesis does not accord with certain strongly held liberal beliefs about the value of freedom. This leaves us looking for an alternative approach to the measurement of freedom.

Now, as Kymlicka himself appears to recognize, (2) and (3) *need* not be redundant. Their redundancy depends on the deduction of (5) from (4) (i.e. on the value-based approach) together with a Kymlickian interpretation of (4). As I see it, if we can find a basis other than the value-based approach on which to make sense of (2) and (3), these premises might themselves play an important part in determining the truth of (4). In this case, we shall be departing from Kymlicka's interpretation of (4) in the way suggested in Chapter 2: one of the reasons for the 'liberty to x' being 'important' lies in the contribution it makes to our overall degree of freedom. Kymlicka is right in saying that value-based measurements of freedom add nothing to his *own* view about which are the most important liberties and why. However, once (5) has been eliminated from the first of the above arguments, and an alternative meaning is given to (2) and (3), then our having a certain measure of freedom can be seen as a non-redundant factor after all: it can be seen as one of the *interests* referred to in (4) in a sense that is *independent* of our interest in doing x, given the *non-specific* value of freedom argued for in Chapter 2.

---

[24] Kymlicka, *Contemporary Political Philosophy*, 143.

[25] In Kymlicka's text these are called 'libertarians'. Recall that, in Kymlicka's view, to see freedom as a quantitative attribute is to play into the hands of the libertarians. I refuted this view in s. 2.2.

[26] Kymlicka, *Contemporary Political Philosophy*, 143.

My central reason for rejecting the value-based approach to measuring freedom can therefore be reiterated in the following way. The value-based approach to measuring overall freedom fails to capture that part of freedom's value which I have called 'non-specific' value, and which motivates us in the first place to measure overall freedom. What it does capture is freedom's specific value. Yet freedom's specific value is already captured by the (normative) specific-freedom thesis. The value-based approach is incompatible with the non-specific value of freedom because it *reduces* the value of having a certain measure of freedom to the values of the *specific things* that one is free to do, when in fact our having a certain measure of freedom is valuable independently of the values of those specific things. If one sees freedom as non-specifically valuable, then one must reject the value-based approach.

Amartya Sen has recently challenged my claim that his 'preference-based' approach to measuring freedom is incompatible with freedom having non-specific value.[27] (Sen himself refers mostly to freedom's 'intrinsic' value, but if his approach is incompatible with freedom having non-specific value then it is, *a fortiori*, incompatible with it having intrinsic value.) Sen's defence consists in arguing that I have underestimated 'the *reach* of a preference-dependent view of freedom'.[28] In saying this, Sen means to point out that on his approach a great many more options will count as 'freedoms' (and a great many more preventions as 'unfreedoms') than might at first appear in the light of my critique. This, above all, because in his view the preference-based approach should take into account not only straightforward preferences over options, but also second-order preferences, or 'meta-preferences'—i.e. preferences over preferences. For example, the fact that I do not have a first-order preference for visiting an art gallery tomorrow morning does not imply that my being prevented from going to the art gallery tomorrow morning brings about no reduction in my overall freedom. For my overall freedom will still be reduced by such a prevention if, despite not having a preference for going to the art gallery, I nevertheless have a meta-preference for the preference for going to the art gallery.

This argument may indeed extend the 'reach' of the preference-based approach, but it does not remove that approach from the category in which I have placed it: that of value-based approaches, according to which we should

---

[27] A. Sen, 'Freedom, Capabilities and Public Action: A Response', *Notizie di Politeia*, 43–4 (1996), s. 1. In part, Sen is responding to the claims I made in 'The Concept of Freedom in the Work of Amartya Sen'. I should repeat that I now prefer the expression 'non-specific value' to 'independent value', though the two expressions mean the same thing. A similar criticism of Sen is to be found in M. van Hees and M. Wissenburg, 'Freedom and Opportunity', *Political Studies*, forthcoming.

[28] Sen, 'Freedom, Capabilities and Public Action', 108.

assess degrees of overall freedom in terms of the value of the specific things the agent is free to do—approaches which are therefore ultimately reducible to the normative version of the specific-freedom thesis. The preference-based approach rules out the non-specific value of freedom, regardless of how many of our specific freedoms it attributes specific value to, and for what reasons. The only way to extend the 'reach' of the preference-based approach far enough to accommodate the non-specific value of freedom is by admitting a preference that covers all options indiscriminately. For to say that freedom is non-specifically valuable is to express a preference for the presence of options *tout court* (while not of course denying that some options are also preferable to others for *specific* reasons).

Sen does at times appear to admit such a preference; hence my claim, in s. 2.5, that his own point of view on the value of freedom is rather ambiguous. He does claim, for example, that we can see the loss of an option as 'an impoverishment of the process of choice'.[29] Does this point not apply to disvalued options as well as to valued ones (whether evaluated by reference to first-order or to second-order preferences)? If the *process* of choice between options—rejecting less valuable ones and choosing more valuable ones—is itself valuable, should we not say, as I suggested in s. 2.5, that freedom has non-specific constitutive value? Should we not say that freedom has non-specific value as a constitutive part of agency?

Perhaps we should interpret Sen's view in the following way. Freedom, we should say, is non-specifically constitutively valuable because it is a necessary part of the process of choosing. But freedom is not intrinsically valuable, in the sense of being a good thing in isolation from other good things (see ss. 2.3 and 2.5). Rather, our exercising of choice among a minimally extensive range of options is itself a constitutive part of some wider good—perhaps the 'autonomy complex' mentioned in s. 2.5—where the latter also includes the *specific* value of freedom—that is, the availability of valuable options. This would explain Sen's concentration on valuable options consistently with a commitment to freedom's non-specific value. I argued against this view in s. 2.7. But, as I also noted in s. 2.7, such a view does not in any case contradict the arguments of Parts II and III of this book about how freedom should be measured. For even if the view is correct, we should still be careful not to confuse freedom's non-specific value with its specific value. We should be careful not to confuse our interest in the measurement of overall freedom with our interest in the other components of the autonomy complex, such as the fact of having specific valuable options, where the latter goods are measured by reference to first or second-order preferences over options, or by reference

---

[29] Sen, 'Freedom, Capabilities and Public Action', 110.

to objective values, or by reference to the values of our society, or whatever. We may be *tempted* to identify overall freedom with freedom's specific value if we believe that the former has no value in isolation from the latter. Nevertheless, to say that *a* has no value in isolation from *b* is not to say that *a* should be measured in terms of *b*. Even on such a view, *a* and *b* remain distinct goods (albeit complementary ones).

If my central argument against the value-based approach stands—as I think it does even in the face of Sen's defence—then those who were initially attracted to that approach must now follow one of three paths. First, they may simply admit their mistake, reject the value-based approach in the light of freedom's non-specific value, and, given their commitment to freedom's non-specific value, begin the search for an acceptable alternative approach. Second, they may reject the value-based approach for the opposite reason—that is, because they are persuaded by the normative version of the specific-freedom thesis and therefore agree with Dworkin and Kymlicka that judgements of overall freedom are normatively redundant. Third, they may accept the normative version of the specific-freedom thesis, but still hold on to the value-based approach for merely rhetorical purposes. According to this third alternative, one should admit that value-based judgements of degrees of overall freedom have no literal meaning—that they are really just *elliptical* for claims about the specific value of the alternatives open to the agent—but one should still see such judgements as meaningful in a rhetorical sense, given that it is more persuasive as well as more succinct to say, for example, that 'society A is freer than society B', than that 'the specific freedoms that most people have in society A do more to promote their interests than the specific freedoms that most people have in society B do to promote theirs'.

My hope is that in the light of the arguments of Chapter 2, most erstwhile supporters of the value-based approach will feel constrained to follow the first path rather than the second. And it should be emphasized that the first path is incompatible not only with the second path but also with the third, inasmuch as the first forces us to look for an alternative way of measuring freedom. This alternative way of measuring freedom must not reduce propositions about a person's extent of freedom to propositions about the specific value of that person's specific freedoms, which is exactly what the third path does.

In Chapter 7 I shall embark on the first path, and in s. 5.5 I shall provide some further arguments for doing so. The next two sections, on the other hand, are directed at those who are nevertheless tempted by the third path. My aim is to undermine their position by means of some counter-arguments from common-sense comparisons. The usefulness even of merely rhetorical claims referring to extents of freedom will be damaged if it turns out that those claims are less isomorphic with our common-sense comparisons than the authors cited in s. 5.1 appear to believe. The arguments of s. 5.3 suggest that there is indeed such a lack of isomorphism. They suggest that either the value-based approach leads to counter-intuitive measurements of freedom, or else, as we shall see in s. 5.4, the approach must be watered down in such a way as to make it largely redundant even as a rhetorical device.

5.3 THE RHETORICAL INTERPRETATION: SOME COUNTER-ARGUMENTS FROM COMMON-SENSE COMPARISONS

In this section and the next I shall deal with three possible interpretations of the value-based approach as a way of making rhetorical sense of the concept of overall freedom. On the first interpretation, we take it that the value-based approach involves assigning a positive value to some available actions and a negative value to others; on the second interpretation, we take it that a positive value is to be assigned to some actions and zero value to all others; and on the third interpretation (to be dealt with in the next section) we water down the value-based approach so as to say that the value of one's available actions is not the *only* factor determining how free one is. By examining each of these interpretations in turn, we shall see how the problems connected with the first give rise, logically speaking, to the second, and how the problems connected with the second give rise, in turn, to the third. We shall also see that the third interpretation removes what reasons there were in the first place for supporting the value-based approach.

The first interpretation is motivated by the following consideration. Assume that we are to weight freedoms and unfreedoms according to the degree to which they are desired by the agent (in either a first-order or a second-order sense). On what sort of *scale* are we to measure this kind of value?[30] It seems plausible to say that subjective value should be measured on a 'bipolar' scale. For are there not *aversions* as well as desires? In the words of W. E. Armstrong, 'there seem to be pleasant situations that are intrinsically desirable and painful situations that are intrinsically repugnant . . . [and] it does not seem unreasonable to postulate that welfare is +ve in the former case and −ve in the latter'.[31] Moreover, this point surely applies not only to welfare, but to 'value' on most interpretations of that term. If saving a life is valuable in an objective sense, what kind of objective value is to be attributed to murder?

---

[30] I leave aside problems of interpersonal comparability of welfare. Such problems—to the extent that they are genuine—can only strengthen the case against the value-based approach. But since they are controversial, I should not like to rest my case on them.

[31] W. E. Armstrong, 'Utility and the Theory of Welfare', *Oxford Economic Papers*, 3 (1951), 269; cf. Y. R. Ng, *Welfare Economics* (London: Macmillan, 1979), 14.

The existence of negative values creates problems for the value-based approach. Surely we cannot assign negative numerals to actions, for this would imply that whenever the summed negative values of one's available actions outweigh their summed positive values, one has a negative degree of overall freedom, and this is counter-intuitive. As long as we have at least one specific freedom, common-sense tells us, then we have 'some freedom'; and if we have no freedoms at all, then we have 'no freedom'. It is difficult to grasp under what conditions we could reasonably be thought to have 'less than zero' freedom.

Another, perhaps even more strikingly counter-intuitive implication, pointed out by Hillel Steiner, is that it would be possible as a result of this discrepancy to *decrease* a person's freedom by *increasing* the number of her available actions (that is, where the newly available actions have an on-balance negative value).[32] Notice, moreover, that it will not do to suggest as a solution to this problem that a disvalued action should simply be assigned a positive value that is lower than the value assigned to a positively valued action. Whether or not this would avoid counter-intuitive measurements, it would surely lead to an absence of isomorphism between the weights we attach to actions (for the purpose of measuring freedom) and the values we assign to them. As Steiner says, assigning a low positive numeral to a disvalued action, such as a murder, 'would have the utterly absurd consequence that a sufficiently large number of life-taking actions would be equal or greater in value than one life-saving act'.[33]

Perhaps we can avoid this absurd consequence by abandoning the idea of measuring freedom on a ratio scale, thus seeing the weights assigned to actions in terms of their values as merely relative (if still cardinal). This solution, suggested by Keith Dowding, would allow us to assign a low positive numeral to the least valued (that is, the most disvalued) action in terms of *freedom*, but not in terms of its *absolute value*.[34] In other words, each numeral representing the *value* we attach to actions is (for the purpose of measuring *freedom*) to be added to a positive constant, in such a way as to render all assigned numerals positive. By admitting that these numerals represent only the *relative* values of the actions in question, and that resultant measurements of freedom are themselves only relative, it seems that we are able to avoid assigning positive values to what are in reality disvalued actions.

However, this solution still seems to involve abandoning many of the common-sense comparisons of freedom which motivate people to favour the value-based approach in the first place. Taylor, at least, would certainly not

---

[32] H. Steiner, 'How Free: Computing Personal Liberty', in A. Phillips-Griffiths (ed.), *Of Liberty* (London: Cambridge University Press, 1983), 81.

[33] Ibid.

[34] K. Dowding, 'Negative Liberty and its Value', unpublished paper, London School of Economics.

wish to say that the availability of a morally despicable action does anything to increase one's freedom. This is because the valuational magnitude according to which Taylor proposes that we weight available actions is a function of the degree to which those actions would contribute to an agent's 'fundamental purposes'. Murder does not, on Taylor's account, contribute anything to anyone's fundamental purposes, let alone a sufficient number of murders more than a single life-saving act.

Furthermore, Dowding's solution is simply not open to some supporters of the value-based approach. Arneson's position, for example, cannot be interpreted in this way, because he explicitly states that actions should be weighted according to what he calls their 'vitality'. An option is 'vital' for a person 'to the extent that its very availability will bring it about that the person acquires an increased basic desire either for having the option or exercising it or both', and an option is 'inert' if it is not desired by the person and its availability would have no effect on the degree to which he desired it. The availability of such an inert option '*does not increase his freedom*'.[35] Arneson only mentions 'in passing' the existence of 'morbid options, whose very availability lessens people's basic desire for them'.[36] But it is of crucial importance that if 'inert' options are to be given the value zero (solely *in virtue* of their being inert), 'morbid' options must be given a negative weight. Arneson therefore appears committed by implication to the assignment of negative numerals to actions, despite the fact that, for him, 'the idea that one can diminish a person's freedom by expanding his options is worse than paradoxical'.[37]

Perhaps, then, we should admit only ordinal comparisons of the values of actions. This will not allow us to aggregate action values, but it may still permit the comparison of whole sets of available actions in different situations. Even here, however, if the availability of disvaluable actions really constitutes *freedom*, it is difficult to see how the continual addition of a sufficient number of disvalued options to an option set originally judged to offer 'less freedom' than another should not in some circumstances eventually reverse our judgement, so turning it into the option set that offers more freedom. And this is not the kind of judgement that most advocates of the value-based approach appear to find intuitively acceptable. A mere shift from cardinality to ordinality does not appear to be sufficient to remove the problem of isomorphism with common-sense comparisons created by the existence of disvalued options.

It seems that the only way to avoid the counter-intuitive measurements implied by the existence of disvalued options is by saying, as Taylor appears to, that such options *do not contribute to our freedom at all*. But *can* we say

---

[35] Arneson, 'Freedom and Desire', 437–8.   [36] Ibid. 437.   [37] Ibid. 443.

that disvaluable options do not contribute anything to our overall freedom? Would *that* be intuitively acceptable? There are two ways of arriving at such a conclusion, neither of which will be very palatable even for the majority of the authors cited in s. 5.1. The first says that the availability of a disvalued action *is not a specific freedom at all*. The second says that the availability of a disvalued action *is* a *specific* freedom, but that it nevertheless contributes nothing to one's *overall* freedom.

Take the first horn of the dilemma. The arguments against defining freedom as 'not being prevented from doing what one wants' have already been well rehearsed. As Berlin has pointed out, if the definition of 'specific freedoms' were 'the lack of constraints on the satisfaction of one's desires'—if, that is, a necessary condition for 'being rendered unfree to do x' were 'wanting to do x'—then it would be possible to remove an agent's unfreedom to do x by removing her desire to do x. It would also be possible for an agent to remove that unfreedom herself, by convincing herself that she did not desire to do x.[38] An example of the first kind of desire removal is brainwashing. An example of the second is the formation of 'adaptive preferences' on the part of the poor or underprivileged—a phenomenon to which Sen has been particularly sensitive and which partly motivates his critique of welfarism.[39] If we accept this implication, we shall have to say that a person need not suffer any unfreedoms at all, as long as she is content with her lot. To say that a perfectly contented person suffers no unfreedoms is to confuse 'being unfree' with 'feeling unfree'. If I am prevented from doing x, although I may not 'feel' the unfreedom to do x (because x is, for me, a worthless option), this is not to deny that I *am* unfree to do x.[40] A prison inmate who places no value whatever on going to the theatre is nevertheless unfree to go to the theatre.[41] In the face of arguments like these, a great many political philosophers now agree that 'freedom' should be taken to mean the lack of constraints not merely on doing what one wants to do (as might, prima facie, appear to be the case), but rather, on doing what one *might conceivably* want to do.[42] Furthermore, this point is clearly intended to establish a distinction not only between one's freedoms and their desirability, but, more generally (if less dramatically), between one's freedoms and their value, whatever meaning 'value' is taken to have. The general intention is to establish that the question of *whether or*

---

[38] Berlin, *Four Essays on Liberty*, 139–40.

[39] Sen, 'Well-Being, Agency and Freedom', 191.

[40] Cf. Oppenheim, *Dimensions of Freedom*, ch. 7, s. I, B; J. P. Day, 'On Liberty and the Real Will', *Philosophy*, 45 (1970), 180.

[41] H. Steiner, 'Individual Liberty', *Proceedings of the Aristotelian Society*, 75 (1974–5), 34.

[42] Cf. Gray, *Freedom*, 62–73; J. Feinberg, *Rights, Justice and the Bounds of Liberty* (Princeton: Princeton University Press, 1980), 39–40; Van Parijs, *Real Freedom for All*, 19.

not one is free to do something is quite independent of the question of the value of that thing (regardless of whether the definition of freedom must be value-laden for other reasons[43]). Many of the authors cited in s. 5.1 appear to agree on this point.[44]

The other horn of the dilemma has been grasped explicitly by G. A. Cohen. 'Reference to a man's desires' is, he says, 'irrelevant to the question "what is he free to do?"' But it is, he believes, 'relevant to the question "how much freedom (comprehensively) does he have?"'[45] Along similar lines, Lawrence Crocker has suggested that 'while . . . the negative account [of freedom] could do perfectly well without mentioning desire in the case of freedom to perform particular actions, desire may not be so easily dispensed with from an account of the *total freedom* of a person'.[46] But this second alternative seems to be equally unattractive. What it implies is that disvalued *freedoms* contribute nothing to a person's *overall freedom*. As Van Parijs explicitly states, 'the measure of the added freedoms [in terms of overall freedom] is zero'.[47] In this case, a person whose only available actions are disvalued must be seen as 'completely unfree' (i.e. as 'having no freedom at all'), while at the same time (given the argument of the previous paragraph) having 'the freedom to do certain things'. Such a disalignment between the definition of 'a specific freedom' and the definition of 'overall freedom' is surely too great for ordinary language usage to accommodate. Saying that a person can have 'a freedom' without having 'any freedom' is formally analogous to saying that you can eat 'a slice of cake' without eating 'any cake'. This would be, quite literally, 'having your cake and eating it'. Neither will abandoning the idea of an absolute zero (complete unfreedom) do much to get around this problem, since we shall still have to acknowledge the point made earlier about the effect of the continual addition of disvalued freedoms to a given option set. Assigning the numeral zero to a disvalued freedom does not remove the fact that the disvalued freedom *is a freedom*. To see this, consider the problem of assessing departures from 'equal freedom'. Take any two 'equally free' people. Give one of them an additional (disvalued) freedom (not just an additional 'option', but an additional 'freedom'). Are these two people not now 'unequally free'? Even if it is answered that one can never say more than that people are 'roughly equally free', one would still expect there to be a sufficient number of disvalued

---

[43] For example, because the notion of a constraint on freedom is taken to depend on that of moral responsibility (see s. 8.1, below).

[44] Those who explicitly say so include Van Parijs, Swanton, Feinberg, and (although not cited in s. 5.1) G. A. Cohen (see below).

[45] Cohen, 'Illusions about Private Property and Freedom', 231.

[46] Crocker, *Positive Liberty*, 45, my emphasis.

[47] Van Parijs, *Real Freedom for All*, 238 n. 39.

'freedoms' (which, on the present suggestion, count for 'no freedom' in the overall sense), the granting of which to one of the two people ought to be seen as sufficient to render them 'unequally free'.

The existence of disvalued options therefore remains a genuine stumbling block for the value-based approach. It will not do either to say that the presence of those options reduces overall freedom, or to say that their presence neither reduces nor increases overall freedom. As far as I can see, the only remaining alternative is to say that their presence increases overall freedom for some *non*-value-based reason.

5.4 THE HYBRID APPROACH

In order to arrive at intuitively acceptable judgements of freedom (both specific and overall), the value-based approach must be watered down so as to produce what we might call a 'hybrid approach'. On this hybrid approach, we should follow Cohen and Crocker in grasping the second horn of the above dilemma, but we should also avoid the unwanted consequence of 'having our cake and eating it', by admitting that the value of the things we are free to do is not *all* that affects how free we are. We should admit, in other words, that a *quantitative* assessment of our available actions is relevant too. As the preceding arguments already suggest, this hybrid approach may be unacceptable to some of the less compromising advocates of the value-based approach, such as Taylor. But the approach is nevertheless worth investigating further, not only because it has been explicitly proposed by some other advocates of the value-based approach, but also because such an investigation will conveniently see the emergence of an intuitively plausible alternative approach which will be investigated further in the next section and in Part III of this book.

Cohen himself arrives at the hybrid approach by a line of reasoning similar to that set out above. As Cohen writes, 'unless we deny that if you have one more thing you are free to do you have more freedom, the amount of freedom you have is determined not only by the value but also by the sheer number of significantly different choices open to you'.[48] Other advocates of the hybrid approach include Christine Swanton, as we saw in the previous chapter (s. 4.4), and Berlin, whose suggestion in its complete form (as opposed to the edited version of it quoted earlier) is that the extent of my freedom depends *both* on the value of the possibilities open to me *and* on 'how many possibilities' are open to me.[49] Arneson, too, concedes that 'we had better add

---

[48] Quoted with Cohen's permission from an unpublished paper on 'measuring freedom'.
[49] Berlin, *Four Essays on Liberty*, 130; pp. xxxix–xl; p. xlviii.

an "other things being equal" rider to the desire thesis [i.e. his version of the value-based approach], and admit that when neutral counting unequivocally finds in one situation more freedom than in another, then so far as the desire thesis is concerned, other things are not equal'.[50]

According to the hybrid approach, then, the extent of a person's freedom is a function of two variables; first, the importance (in terms of variables other than freedom) of her available actions, and second, the sheer number of those actions. As the above quote indicates, Cohen sees the quantitative assessment of available actions as involving an enumeration of 'significantly different' possible actions. Cohen uses the term '*significantly* different' here, because he believes that actions can only be individuated, and therefore enumerated (for the purpose of measuring freedom) by reference to certain values. As I have said, I shall leave aside the question of 'significant difference' here. The important point to bear in mind is that there is clearly a quantitative notion of action at work behind his use of the phrase 'sheer number of significantly different choices'. The extent to which choices are 'significantly different' is no guide to the extent to which they are 'significant' in Taylor's sense (see s. 5.1); two options which are utterly 'insignificant' in Taylor's sense can still be significantly different in Cohen's sense. Indeed, this must be possible if 'the sheer number of significantly different choices' open to an agent is to be distinguishable from 'the significance of the choices open to an agent', which, *ex hypothesi*, it is. This said, the idea of measuring available actions in purely quantitative terms clearly needs examining in some detail. I shall turn to this task in Chapter 7. For now, let us assume that we can make sense of the idea of quantifying over actions in terms of their *physical dimensions*. Cohen clearly assumes this to be possible, and, as I shall shortly argue, so do a number of other supporters of the value-based approach, even in spite of explicit denials.

A problem with the hybrid approach (on the rhetorical interpretation of degree-of-freedom judgements) is posed by the indeterminacy of the relative weights of the quantitative and qualitative assessments of a person's available actions when it comes to producing overall measurements of freedom. Who is freer, on the hybrid approach, when one person has ten options each of which is of moderate, little, or no value, and another has two options each of which is of great value? It seems that we will only be warranted in attributing 'more freedom' (on the rhetorical interpretation) to individual A than to individual B in cases of 'Pareto superiority'—that is, where A has more freedom than B in terms of one variable and at least as much as B in terms of the other variable. No other attributions of 'more', 'less', or 'equal' freedom will

---

[50] Arneson, 'Freedom and Desire', 443–4.

be adequately grounded, because the overall freedom of A will be incomparable with the overall freedom of B. There is surely no well-grounded, non-arbitrary basis for specifying whether *any given number of actions* is less than, equals, or outweighs *any given action value* in terms of freedom (on the hybrid approach to the rhetorical interpretation). Neither will it do to suggest that one of these two dimensions should have lexical priority over the other, such that if A has more freedom on one particular dimension, A has more freedom overall regardless of how much freedom B has on the other dimension. Lexical priority is simply one among the many possible ways of combining the two variables—like the claim that one variable should count for, say, 40 per cent of a person's overall freedom. What seems to be lacking in our ordinary notion of freedom, including in the ordinary notion of freedom of those who support the value-based approach, is a *reason* for assigning lexical priority to one particular dimension, or for saying that it counts for 40 per cent, or 60 per cent, or 10 per cent.

It might be objected that I am being overzealous in my search for cases of incomparability, and that such cases need not be nearly so widespread on the hybrid approach. This might be thought to be demonstrable by appeal to examples of other multidimensional quantitative attributes, in terms of which we are frequently able to produce rankings even in the absence of 'Pareto superiority'. A can be a 'better restaurant' than B even though B has better service. A can be a 'healthier person' than B even though B suffers less from bronchitis. In both of these cases A is judged to have more x-ness overall, even though A does not have more in terms of every dimension of x-ness, and even though the person judging feels unable to specify exactly how much x-ness in terms of one dimension is equal to a given degree of x-ness in terms of another. Why should 'freedom' be any different?[51]

The answer is that the comparisons made in the above counter-examples are not strictly analogous to comparisons of overall freedom. In any one of the counter-examples which might be given in support of the objection—like those of the quality of restaurants, of health, and so on—the problem raised by the apparent incomparability of different quantities of x-ness is avoided in a way in which it cannot be in the case of overall freedom (on the hybrid approach). Thus, we need not deny comparability in the case of these counter-examples in order to assert incomparability in the case of overall freedom (on the hybrid approach).

The problem of incomparability is found to be superable in the above counter-examples because in such cases a claim apparently referring to an objectively standardized quantitative attribute can in fact be shown to be a veiled reference

---

[51] This objection was suggested to me by Cohen (in personal correspondence).

to an overall *individual preference*, the components of which are themselves combinable. There is indeed no *standard* way of combining the variables which affect the quality of a restaurant. 'Restaurant A is better than restaurant B' is really just elliptical for 'I prefer A (overall) to B' (or 'a writer for the *Good Food Guide* prefers A (overall) to B'). The case of freedom is different, because we expect more of the definition of overall freedom than we do of the definition of a good restaurant. While we do not expect it to be part of the definition of a good restaurant that the relative weights of its various criteria be specified, we do expect a definition of overall freedom to reflect our common-sense comparisons of freedom and to imply measurements of freedom that are isomorphic with those common-sense comparisons in reflective equilibrium. We should be surprised if we were to discover that after a person has committed herself to a particular *definition* of overall freedom, she nevertheless has to express a *further* commitment (i.e. to a certain way of combining the variables) before she can make judgements about who is freer than whom. If this were so, then judgements about overall freedom would be hotly contested by different individuals *who nevertheless agreed over the definition of overall freedom*. It is not clear that we can tolerate such differences in judgement in the way in which we tolerate similar subjective differences in judgements about restaurants.

What is wrong with the incomparability implied by the hybrid approach? Why can it not simply be tolerated? After all, as we saw in s. 5.2, once we support the value-based approach, we shall in any case be giving up any commitment we had in the first place to a freedom-based theory of justice, and therefore to the demands on our powers of measurement set out in s. 3.3. My point of criticism, however, has not to do with the demands of a freedom-based theory of justice, but with the common-sense comparisons that motivate the value-based approach in the first place. What the above cases of incomparability rule out is the possibility of making extent-of-freedom judgements in exactly those cases where the value-based approach is put to the test in terms of isomorphism with common-sense comparisons. These are the cases in which, of the individuals or groups being compared, the one with the fewer actions is the one thought to have more freedom. Cases in which the individual has more freedom on *both* dimensions do not put the value-based approach to the test, for our common-sense comparisons in those cases are also reflected by the ordering that results from a *non*-value-based approach. This renders the value-based approach redundant, even on the rhetorical interpretation being assumed here.

An example where the value-based approach is put to the test is that discussed by Arneson, involving Smith and Jones. Recall that Smith can do most of the things that a normal person can do, except twiddle his thumbs, whereas Jones can only twiddle his thumbs. In order to show that it is the relevance of Smith's and Jones's *desires* that sways our judgement about their relative degrees of freedom, Arneson asks us to imagine a reversal of Smith's and Jones's preference orderings, such that 'both Smith and Jones are fanatical adherents of an obscure religion which places overwhelming value on the performance each day of a great array of devotional exercises performed with the thumbs'.[52] Here my own common-sense comparison is at odds with that of Arneson. I should still want to say that Smith is freer than Jones. And perhaps many erstwhile supporters of the value-based approach will feel less sure of themselves in agreeing with Arneson in connection with this second version of his example. But this fact is not relevant for present purposes. The point, rather, is that Arneson's own common-sense comparison in this second version of his example will *not* be reflected by our measurements of freedom if we accept the watered-down version of the value-based approach (i.e. the hybrid approach). Instead, it will not be clear who has more freedom. The overall freedom of Smith and Jones will be incomparable, or will at least depend unacceptably on a subjective judgement of the freedom measurer in the way mentioned above.

Most of the other examples used by advocates of the value-based approach are examples where the actions available to the individual or group that we intuitively feel to be more free are not only actions that are more valuable, but are also actions that we intuitively feel to be more *extensive*. Several of these examples will be discussed in the next section. They include the *first* version of Arneson's example.

The upshot of the above argument is that the hybrid approach does not do the work it is apparently intended to do: that of helping us to make sense of and to verify judgements of overall freedom. In those cases where we can compare the overall freedom of different individuals, the value-based element of our comparative judgement will add nothing to the non-value-based element (i.e. the empirical, or 'neutral counting', element). And in those cases where the value-based element does make a difference (like the second version of Arneson's Smith–Jones example or Taylor's Londoner–Albanian comparison), it nevertheless fails to lead to an unequivocal overall-freedom judgement. As before, the question which naturally comes to mind at this point is, why then bother with the value-based approach at all?

My general conclusion regarding the rhetorical interpretation of the value-based approach is therefore as follows: that if on such an interpretation the approach is not to produce the kind of counter-intuitive measurements mentioned in the previous section, it must avoid producing measurements at all in exactly those cases where it might serve some purpose—i.e. those cases where

---

[52] Arneson, 'Freedom and Desire', 427.

the agent whom theorists like Arneson and Taylor see as having more freedom also has a smaller extent of available action in terms of 'neutral counting'. The 'third path' mentioned at the end of s. 5.2 is therefore either unattractive or redundant. It is unattractive if it is taken to imply that a person's 'extent of freedom' (in the elliptical sense) is *no more than* a function of the value of her available actions, as it will lead in this case to counter-intuitive measurements. And it is redundant if it is taken to imply only that a person's 'extent of freedom' (in the elliptical sense) is *partly* a function of the value of her available actions, as it will fail in this case to confirm exactly those measurements that would make it worth defending. There is no good reason for preserving the value-based approach to the measurement of overall freedom, even where 'overall freedom' is interpreted as a mere ellipsis.

As an addendum, I should point out that disagreeing with Arneson's comparison of the freedom of Smith and Jones in the second version of his example does not necessarily commit one to saying that Albanians are freer than Londoners in Taylor's example. This last example is taken from a complex real-life situation, and is open to a number of factual objections. For example, is it true that traffic lights reduce the overall quantity of action available to motorists? Were traffic lights not in fact designed to produce an increase in that quantity?[53] And what about the overall quantity of action available to motorists and pedestrians combined? Even disregarding this, is it true that Albanians in 1979 (that is, when Taylor was writing) had more freedom of movement in an overall sense than Londoners? Complex factual examples like these do not seem to be very helpful in *isolating* the factors which best explain our common-sense comparisons of freedom. That is why analytical philosophers rightly prefer to construct abstract, de-contextualized examples for such purposes.

5.5 THE VALUE-BASED APPROACH VERSUS THE EMPIRICAL APPROACH

Having rejected the hybrid approach, I now invite the reader to consider the value-based approach on the one hand and the 'purely quantitative' or 'empirical' approach on the other as mutually exclusive alternatives, and to ask two questions. First, which approach fits best with our common-sense comparisons of freedom? Secondly, which approach provides the best account of the place of those comparisons in a liberal system of values? As Arneson recognizes, in answering the first question, an important test consists in reversing

---

[53] On related questions about group freedom, see Ch. 9.

the imagined preferences of the individuals or groups whose freedom is being compared, although, as we have seen, this test may prove more decisive for some readers than for others. Regarding the second question, the test consists in seeing how well the two approaches fit in with our conception of the logical relation between freedom and other values in practical reasoning. The two questions are in fact very closely related, and I shall therefore try to deal with them in tandem. The empirical approach proves superior on both counts, and I think that this is no accident, the reason lying in the non-specific value we attach to freedom.

Let us begin by returning to one of Sen's examples. We asked earlier which of the following two option sets offers the most freedom: 'travelling by (a stiff tricycle; hopping on one leg; rolling in the dust)', or 'travelling by (an efficient bicycle; a smart car; walking on two legs normally)'.[54] Most of us would judge that the second set provides more freedom. And because most of us would also greatly *prefer* the second set to the first, Sen believes that examples such as this demonstrate the 'abiding relevance of preference' for the measurement of freedom.[55]

Does Sen's conclusion reflect our view of the logical relation between 'freedom' and 'preference' in this example? It is true that most of us would prefer the second set of freedoms, and that most of us would also see it as providing more freedom. But do we really think that the second set provides more freedom because we prefer it, or do we prefer it (at least in part) because we think it offers us more freedom? The former point of view is Sen's; the latter, mine. Is either point of view incoherent? The only way Sen can have of denying the coherence of my point of view is by showing that in his example, the magnitude of our *desires* (expressed in terms of our preferences) with regard to the two sets of options is the *only* magnitude isomorphic with that of the relative overall freedom which we commonsensically see the two sets as providing. In other words, for Sen's argument to be conclusive, it must be the case that our preference over the two sets is the only possible determinant of our common-sense comparison of the amounts of freedom they provide. Surely, however, this is not in fact the case. If we compare the possession of 'a stiff tricycle' with that of 'an efficient bicycle', 'hopping on one leg' with 'walking on two legs normally', and 'rolling in the dust' with possession of 'a smart car', we can see that, in *all three* cases, the options differ in respect of a magnitude *other* than that of the degrees to which we normally desire them: that of the 'physical extension' of the actions which the options make available. Could it be that the persuasive power of Sen's example really rests

---

[54] Sen, 'Welfare, Freedom and Social Choice', 470.
[55] Sen, 'Welfare, Preference, and Freedom', 26.

on the difference in this other, unacknowledged magnitude? The test regarding this issue is where the agent expresses an authentic preference for 'hopping on one leg' over 'walking on two legs normally', or for a stiff tricycle over an efficient bicycle. Perhaps in such cases it would be *better*, on balance, to give the agent the stiff tricycle than to give her the efficient bicycle, or to cut off one of her legs than to prevent her from hopping. But would this really be what makes her *freer*?

Consider the unlikely event in which we find ourselves trying to persuade such a person that she would be better off not having one of her legs cut off. What *reasons* would we present to her? We might say that it would be painful, or that it would make her less attractive. Equally, however, we might use freedom-related reasons. We might point out that she would be *much less free* with only one leg. On Sen's account of the logical relation between preference and freedom, this last reason is denied us. We cannot prefer being left with two legs to having one of our legs cut off on the grounds that we are freer in the first case than in the second. For according to Sen our freedom judgements are determined by our preferences, and not the other way round.

If we look at other examples given by Sen, we can see that the same points apply. Thus, according to Sen, 'It is absurd to say that we have *as much unfreedom* if we are forced to live in a world in which we cannot have smallpox, as in a world in which we cannot escape it. We do have more "freedom to live as we would like", if smallpox is eliminated, since we would choose not to have it if we do have that choice.'[56] But while it is certainly absurd to deny that we have more freedom in a world in which we are prevented from having smallpox than in a world in which we are forced to have it, this is surely not because we would choose not to have smallpox were we to have that choice. Rather, it is because we perceive that the extent of action available to us in the first world will be vastly greater than that available to us in the second. The point is not that we have more freedom in the absence of smallpox '*since* we would choose not to have it', but rather, that we have more freedom in the absence of smallpox, '*and therefore* we would choose not to have it'. One of the *reasons* we would choose a world without smallpox is that in the absence of smallpox we would have more freedom. On Sen's analysis, this *cannot* be one of our reasons. To many, this implication will appear just as absurd as the claim that we can increase people's freedom by giving them smallpox— something, moreover, which we *would* be doing, on Sen's account, in the unlikely event that they preferred smallpox.

One further example: Richard Norman defends the value-based approach by pointing out that the choice between a certain number of different careers

---

[56] Sen, 'Welfare, Preference, and Freedom', 25.

clearly provides more freedom than the choice between the same number of washing powders.[57] However, the comparison of the choice between different careers and the choice between different washing powders can be made by reference not only to degrees of importance but also to extents of action. Therefore, we must once again ask ourselves *why* the choice of careers 'matters' so much more than that of washing powder. Might this not be, *in part* (though of course not *only*), because choosing between two different careers involves choosing between two enormous sets of actions ranging over whole lifespans, whereas the choice between two brands of washing powder does not? As in the case of Sen, what is disputable is not the common-sense comparison of freedom made by Norman, but the explanation he gives of its *basis*. In my view, the best explanation lies in the extents of action the two choice sets make available. As before, an important test for this view consists in reversing the imagined preference ordering of the agent. Imagine, then, an individual similar to the housewives we see in washing powder commercials, who cares about nothing other than the whiteness of her washing (and imagine, if you can, that that individual is wholly rational). In such a case, it *might* conceivably be *better* on balance to give that individual the choice between the washing powders rather than the choice between the careers. But would that really be to make her *freer*?

It might be answered that such a person could *not* be wholly rational, and that the choice between the careers, like the fact of not having smallpox, matters more in some *objective* sense. But this answer does not contradict my central point, that one of the *reasons* the choice between the careers matters more is that it is the choice which offers us more freedom—a reason which an objectivist version of the value-based approach, no less than Sen's version, excludes. The only difference is that, in the case of the objectivist version, it is more difficult for us to conduct an analogous thought experiment whereby the overall values of the two choice sets are reversed.

There remains of course the objection that we cannot make sense of the purely quantitative notion of 'extents of action'. As I have said, I shall turn to this objection in Chapter 7. However, it is worth pointing out here that such a notion is implicitly assumed even by some of those who explicitly deny its meaningfulness. This seems to me to be particularly clear in the case of Arneson, as the following line of reasoning shows. In spite of my own doubts, Arneson himself must believe that the second version of his Smith–Jones example,

---

[57] Norman, 'Liberty, Equality, Property', 201. This is of course to be distinguished from Norman's example comparing the choice between seven brands of washing powder and the choice between twenty-one brands of washing powder, which I cited at the end of s. 5.1, and which concerns the question of the degree to which options are 'significantly different' (see ss. 7.6–7.8).

in which Smith's and Jones's preferences over their respective option sets are reversed, adds some intuitive weight to his argument for the value-based approach. Otherwise, he would not have taken the trouble to introduce the second version. What makes the second version different from the first? The only difference in the extent to which the agents' desires are satisfiable in the two versions is that in the first Smith's are more satisfiable and in the second Jones's are more satisfiable. But this difference is not sufficient on its own to motivate the introduction of the second version of the example, since the coincidence between freedom and potential desire satisfaction is already well illustrated by the first version. The difference that motivates the introduction of the second version must therefore be that, in the second version, the agent whose desires are the *more* satisfiable is also the agent who has '*less* available action'. From this it follows that in supposing the introduction of the second version of his example to strengthen the intuitive case for the value-based approach (contrary to my own view that it does not), Arneson is assuming that we have a clear intuitive grasp of the notion of 'extents of action'. Arneson and I *agree* that in both versions of his example Smith has available a greater extent of action than Jones, *despite* the fact that in the second version our common-sense comparisons of their degrees of freedom do not coincide.

Intuitively, what I hope to have provided in the notion of 'extents of action' is something that captures what we have in mind when we talk of the magnitude of *capability*, at least on Cohen's interpretation of Sen's use of that term. According to Cohen, 'capability' properly refers to a person 'being able to *do* certain . . . things'.[58] It is an *active* notion; 'Sen intends capability to have an *athletic* character.'[59] My only difference with Sen here (on Cohen's interpretation) is that we must reject his identification of freedom with '*evaluated* capabilities'.[60] As far as comparisons of freedom are concerned, what is needed is not an index for the evaluation of capabilities, but, as we saw in s. 2.5, an index for the measurement of capabilities themselves.

5.6 EVALUATION AND MEASUREMENT

Given the foregoing account of the logical relation between freedom and other goods, it should be clear that the measurement of overall freedom is a part, and only a part, of the overall *evaluation* of a set of specific freedoms. On

[58] Cf. A. Sen, 'Equality of What?', *Tanner Lectures in Human Values*, 1 (1980), 218.

[59] G. A. Cohen, 'Equality of What? On Welfare, Goods and Capabilities', *Recherches Économiques de Louvain*, 56 (1990), 375, my emphasis.

[60] Sen, 'Welfare, Freedom and Social Choice', 460, my emphasis.

the other hand, this is not to belittle the importance of freedom as a distinct and independent ideal. On the contrary, it is the very importance of freedom that has led people mistakenly to identify it with all good things—something Berlin himself has warned us against[61]—and thus to suppose that the evaluation of freedom is identical to the measurement of freedom. This, in my view, is the mistake responsible for the idea that the empirical approach to measuring freedom lacks 'ethical appeal'.[62] It is indeed telling that there are times at which Sen uses the expression 'evaluation of freedom' to mean 'measurement of freedom'.[63] Advocates of the value-based approach mistake the part for the whole. 'Measuring one's freedom' is to 'evaluating one's freedom' as the javelin is to the decathlon. The javelin is a *part* of the decathlon; you need to throw the javelin in order to complete the decathlon. Likewise, when we evaluate a thing, we need to measure certain variables. When we evaluate a set of freedoms, one of the variables we need to measure is 'freedom' itself. The reason we need to measure this variable is, as we saw in Chapter 2, that freedom is *non-specifically valuable*. And freedom's non-specific value is by definition independent of the value of the specific things one is free to do.

The absurdity of the identification of evaluation and measurement is at its clearest in the case of the hybrid approach examined in s. 5.3. For, once we have perceived the mistake made by supporters of the value-based approach regarding the distinction between measurement and evaluation, we can see that the hybrid approach has the following rather startling implication: that the degree of one's freedom is a function both of the degree of one's freedom and of the importance of that freedom in terms of other goods. No doubt it is important to provide overall evaluations of freedom in such a way as to combine these two variables. What certainly cannot be the case is that the measurement of these two variables in combination is identical to the measurement of one of them.

It should now be clear exactly what was wrong with the idea, mentioned at the end of s. 5.3, that one could 'have one's cake and eat it'—that is, the idea that one could eat 'a piece of cake' without eating 'any cake', or that, analogously, one could have 'an additional freedom' without having 'any more freedom'. There is nothing to stop us from *stipulating* that 'varying quantities of cake' are a function, say, of 'the varying degrees to which cake is flavoursome',

---

[61] Berlin, *Four Essays on Liberty*, 125, 167–72.

[62] Van Parijs, *Real Freedom for All*, 51.

[63] See e.g. Sen, 'Welfare, Preference, and Freedom', 26, and 'Freedom, Capabilities and Public Action', 110–11. In the latter passage, the term 'valuation' is used instead of 'measurement' in an argument against my idea that freedom has 'independent' (i.e. non-specific) value. Here Sen seems to assume that the measurement of freedom's independent (i.e. non-specific) value is, on my view, the measurement of the whole of freedom's value.

and thus that the question 'How much cake do I have?' is simply elliptical for the question 'How flavoursome is my cake?' In this case it would not be *logically* contradictory to say that I can eat 'a piece of cake' (if a flavourless one) without eating 'any cake'. Nevertheless, to define 'quantities of cake' in this way would be to deny the difference between what are in fact two plainly distinguishable magnitudes, namely, the size of a piece of cake, and how flavoursome it is. Perhaps we are not very interested in the size of a flavourless piece of cake (although one suspects that it is only people with full bellies who would see the size of a cake as irrelevant to its overall evaluation). But this point does not contradict the distinction just made. And neither does it hold analogously in the case of freedom. For it is clear that liberals set great store not only on the worth of people's freedom in terms of certain other goods, but also on their freedom as a distinct good, and hence on their having a measure of freedom.

5.7 SUMMARY

I have said that Part II of this book concerns value-based conceptions of overall freedom, by which I mean those conceptions of freedom which adopt the value-based approach to measuring freedom. In the present chapter, I have examined the value-based approach as such. In the next chapter, I shall turn to a particular conception of value-based freedom: that of freedom as self-mastery. The reason for considering self-mastery a form of value-based freedom will be argued in s. 6.2. Ranged against the conception of freedom as self-mastery will be a series of objections comprising those of a general nature already presented in the present chapter and those concerning that conception in particular.

Among the general objections to value-based conceptions of overall freedom, the most important is that they are incompatible with freedom having non-specific value: they fail to capture anything about the value of freedom that is not already captured by the normative version of the specific-freedom thesis—a thesis which implies *dispensing* with judgements of overall freedom. In addition, even if judgements about degrees of overall freedom are treated as merely rhetorical (rather than as motivated by the non-specific value of freedom), the value-based approach to the measurement of overall freedom has the counter-intuitive feature of either contradicting many of our common-sense comparisons of overall freedom or else failing in too many cases to produce determinate measurements. In the latter case—where we have already moved towards a combination of the value-based approach and the empirical approach—those common-sense comparisons of freedom that do get confirmed are in any case also confirmed by the purely empirical approach.

What leads theorists to endorse the value-based approach is probably a tendency to confuse the measurement of a quantitative attribute with its evaluation. This confusion is most likely to occur when the attribute in question is especially valuable, as in the case of freedom. *Despite* freedom being especially valuable, the measurement of freedom is a part, and only a part, of its overall evaluation. To measure freedom is to measure that part of freedom's overall value which consists in freedom's non-specific value, and which the empirical approach alone is capable of capturing.

6

Self-Mastery

WE can now turn our attention to the idea of freedom as the absence of 'internal' constraints—that is, to the idea that freedom consists in some form of 'self-mastery' or 'autonomy'.[1] The agent that achieves self-mastery is said to be in control of her own actions, in the sense that her deeds do not result from desires with which she does not really identify, or from irrational dispositions, or vicious instincts, or something of the sort. From this perspective, such inauthentic desires, irrational dispositions, and so on are thought to qualify as 'preventing conditions'. They are obstacles to action that count as constraints on the agent's freedom.

To be more precise, I shall use the term 'self-mastery'—and, at times, 'autonomy'—to single out a particular way of conceiving of freedom as the absence of internal constraints. Now the conception of freedom defended in this book does not rule out *all* ways of conceiving of freedom as the absence of internal as well as external constraints. We need not deny that an agent's overall empirical freedom can sometimes reasonably be described as being reduced by physical obstacles that are located 'inside' the agent, in particular where another agent can be held responsible for such obstacles (the most obvious example being brainwashing), and I shall indeed touch briefly on such a possibility in the next two chapters (at ss. 7.9, 8.1, and 8.2). My aim here, however, is to argue against the incorporation in our conception of overall freedom of the more common idea of internal freedom that is captured by the idea of self-mastery, and my use of the expression 'internal freedom' in this chapter should therefore be interpreted in this way.

I shall clarify the idea of self-mastery in section 1. Freedom as self-mastery is, as we shall see, necessarily a species of value-based freedom—hence its place in Part II of this book. In a way that parallels the arguments of the previous chapter, I shall first show how the defence of freedom as self-mastery is inseparable from the specific-freedom thesis (section 2), and then point to the counter-intuitive measurements of freedom that would be implied by integrating internal constraints (conceived of as lack of self-mastery) into our

[1] As I stated in the Introduction to this book, I have decided where possible to avoid the term 'positive freedom', since this has been used in the literature to refer to many different conceptions of freedom, including conceptions not examined in this chapter.

measurements of overall freedom even where 'overall freedom' is given a rhetorical interpretation (section 3). The critique of freedom as self-mastery put forward in section 3 is not new—the basic point can be found in the writings of a number of liberal philosophers since and including Berlin—except perhaps in so far as that critique is worked out from the point of view of a theorist interested in measuring overall freedom.

6.1 THE IDEA OF SELF-MASTERY

As Joel Feinberg points out, the question of what, exactly, is to count as an 'internal' rather than an 'external' constraint on freedom will depend on where we set the boundaries of the 'self' (i.e. the agent) that is being constrained.[2] Feinberg's own suggestion is that an agent's body should be seen as a part of her 'self' for the purpose of distinguishing between internal and external constraints on freedom.[3] For my part, I find it more in keeping with the literature on internal freedom to say that if I lose the use of my legs, I suffer an *external* obstacle to action. I shall therefore assume that the 'self' in question consists in a bundle of beliefs, character traits, dispositions, and so on, and that an internal constraint on freedom is one that can be described in terms of such *mental* phenomena.

Clearly, however, we cannot say that *any* parts of the agent—any character traits or dispositions—can constitute internal constraints on freedom, for in this case we should have to say that agents are unfree to do all of the things they are externally free to do but decide not to do. Determinists will point out that our character traits and dispositions always force us into doing the things we in fact do (given a particular set of external conditions). But this is not the kind of 'force' with which 'unfreedom as the absence of self-mastery' is to be equated.

We therefore need a criterion that will distinguish those action-determining characteristics of the agent that count as 'constraints on freedom' from those that do not. The idea of freedom as self-mastery provides one such criterion. According to this criterion, the agent is to be separated into those characteristics that are in some sense 'authentic', and those that merely belong to her in an empirical sense, so that authentic agency 'is something to be achieved rather than a merely empirical phenomenon'.[4] On this view, internal constraints on freedom are character traits or dispositions that count as obstacles for the authentic agent. While they are a part of the empirical agent, they are also considered (by her or perhaps by others) as in some sense *alien* to her—a

[2] Feinberg, *Social Philosophy*, 12–13. [3] Ibid., ch. 1.
[4] A. J. M. Milne, *Freedom and Rights* (London: George Allen & Unwin, 1968), 146.

fact which implies that they could be removed from the empirical agent without in any way affecting the nature of the authentic agent—without the authentic agent feeling any 'loss'. Such constraints might be said to consist in phenomena like compulsions, phobias, obsessions, illusions, ignorance, and irrational fears.

Perhaps the most influential contemporary defence of the idea of freedom as self-mastery is that of Charles Taylor,[5] who contrasts such an idea with what he calls the 'negative' view of freedom normally identified with Hobbes and Bentham—the view that freedom is the straightforward absence of *external* impediments. Sometimes Taylor calls this last view the 'quantitative' notion of freedom.[6] But one should not be misled by this into thinking that he does not conceive of freedom as a quantitative attribute. Taylor's rejection of the Hobbesian 'quantitative' notion of freedom is really just a rejection of what I have called the 'empirical approach' to measuring freedom. To see this, one need only note his frequent use, in expounding his own conception of freedom, of expressions like 'more free', 'less free', 'freer' and 'judgements of degrees of freedom'.

It will be helpful to examine Taylor's argument in some detail. The argument contains three main points, which I shall call (1) the validity of the value-based approach, (2) the existence of subjectively identifiable internal constraints, and (3) the existence of objectively identifiable internal constraints. These three points can be summarized in the following way.

1. *The validity of the value-based approach.* Freedom consists not merely in the availability of actions, but in the availability of *significant* actions, and the more significant an action is, the more its availability increases an agent's freedom.[7] The empirical approach to measuring freedom is therefore mistaken.

2. *The argument for subjectively identifiable internal constraints.* A person's freedom may be diminished not only by an external constraint on an option, but also by an internal constraint, which leads her to forgo the pursuit of a more significant option in favour of the pursuit of a less significant (or wholly insignificant) option. In such a situation the agent recognizes that she is mistaken in pursuing the less significant option; she has a second-order desire not to pursue it,[8] or as Taylor would put it, she 'strongly evaluates' its pursuit as

---

[5] Taylor, 'What's Wrong with Negative Liberty'; id., *Hegel and Modern Society* (Cambridge: Cambridge University Press, 1979). But see also B. Gibbs, *Freedom and Liberation* (London: Chatto & Windus, 1976); Milne, *Freedom and Rights*; J. Charvet, *A Critique of Freedom and Equality* (Cambridge: Cambridge University Press, 1981); Christman, 'Liberalism and Individual Positive Freedom'.

[6] Taylor, 'What's Wrong with Negative Liberty', 183.   [7] Ibid.

[8] The language of first-order and second-order desires comes not from Taylor, but from Harry Frankfurt. See his 'Freedom of the Will and the Concept of a Person', *Journal of Philosophy*, 68 (1971).

not being among her 'fundamental purposes';[9] she identifies with the significant option and not with the insignificant option, but she still has a propensity
to pursue the insignificant option. Such internal constraints might be caused by
fears, compulsions, obsessions, or limited aspirations. Even if I am externally
unprevented from going on an expedition over the Andes (which I judge to be
significant), I am still just as unfree to do so if my attachment to comforts
(which I judge to be insignificant) is somehow holding me back and preventing
me from doing so.[10]

3. *The argument for objectively identifiable internal constraints.* Internal
obstacles need not be 'just confined to those that the subject identifies as
such'. While a person may be internally constrained because she is mistaken
regarding the course of action best suited to the fulfilling of what she regards
as her fundamental purposes, she may also be internally constrained because
she is mistaken about what her fundamental purposes really *are*. Charles Manson
and Andreas Baader are obvious examples. And 'once we recognize such
extreme cases, how avoid admitting that many of the rest of mankind can
suffer to a lesser degree from the same difficulties?'[11]

In line with a classification of conceptions of autonomy proposed by Onora
O'Neill, we can say that points (2) and (3) belong respectively to the 'empiricist'
and 'Kantian' philosophical traditions. (2) identifies an authentic self by reference to second-order desires, and to this extent rests on a 'preference-based'
account of action. Here, autonomous action is simply action that is empirically
determined by *a particular kind of desire* (or preference), namely, a second-
order desire (or preference). (3), on the other hand, appears to rest on the idea
that the authentic self is in some sense rational, where 'rationality' is defined
non-instrumentally—either in purely formal terms, or else more substantively,
by reference to the norms of a particular culture or tradition. To this extent, (3)
rests on an account of actions as the expression of maxims, or principles, rather
than as mere natural, empirically determined events.[12] O'Neill points out that
because (2) and (3) rest on radically different accounts of action, they also imply
radically different accounts of autonomy. She also provides some forceful reasons
for rejecting the empiricist account of autonomy expressed in point (2).[13]

---

[9] I assume that a person's 'strongly evaluated' fundamental purposes have been worked
out rationally so as not to conflict with each other, or at least, that if they have not been, or
cannot be (given that moral dilemmas may be inevitable), then the fact of a person having to
forgo the pursuit of fundamental purposes *as a result of a conflict between fundamental purposes* does not constitute an internal constraint on her freedom.

[10] Taylor, 'What's Wrong with Negative Liberty', 185. Cf. id., *Hegel and Modern Society*, 157.

[11] Taylor, 'What's Wrong with Negative Liberty', 191–3.

[12] O'Neill, *Constructions of Reason*, ch. 4. See s. 7.11, below.

[13] O. O'Neill, 'Autonomy, Coherence and Independence', in D. Mulligan and W. Watts Miller
(eds.), *Liberalism, Citizenship and Autonomy* (Aldershot: Avebury, 1992), 205–10.

Taylor does not explicitly recognize the radical nature of the shift from (2) to (3). However, interpretative charity suggests that he in fact sees (3) as superseding (2) as his argument progresses, and that (2), in Taylor's eyes, should therefore be seen as no more than a stepping stone in what is essentially an argument for objectively identifiable internal constraints.

For present purposes, we may remain agnostic about whether a coherent conception of freedom as self-mastery necessarily requires acceptance of (3) (as Taylor and O'Neill appear to believe), or whether it might still be plausible to retain an empiricist, subjectivist conception of internal constraints by accepting (1) and (2) but rejecting (3). The main object of this chapter is to criticize the idea that a coherent conception of overall freedom can incorporate the idea of freedom as self-mastery, regardless of whether that idea is defined subjectively or objectively (and of whether, if defined objectively, it is to be understood in purely formal or more substantive terms).

Before moving on to the problem of integrating internal unfreedoms thus conceived into our measurements of overall freedom, we should note that *specific* internal freedoms may very often themselves be seen as a matter of degree. This fact does not itself present problems for aggregation, but it is important to be aware of the reason that lies behind it.

When talking of external freedoms, it is normal to distinguish between the probability of an agent being restrained from doing x and the probability of the agent actually *doing x*. This is because, as we saw in s. 5.3, it is normal to say that an agent's own desires, and hence also her own dispositions to act in certain ways, are irrelevant to the question of whether she is externally unconstrained from doing a certain thing (see also s. 8.4). When we come to examine internal constraints, on the other hand, we find that there is a strong link between the presence of such constraints and the fact of there being some probability of the agent's acting in a certain way. What makes me internally constrained is my propensity—arising from certain irrational desires, fears, weaknesses, or whatever—to take options which exclude the possibility of my acting in certain other ways, or, as Taylor would put it, which exclude the possibility of my acting in accordance with my 'fundamental purposes' (be they the dictates of my second-order desires, of the test of universalizability, or of some more substantive objective morality). In Taylor's terms, freedom as self-mastery is an 'exercise concept' rather than an 'opportunity concept'—it involves actually doing something rather than the mere existence of open doors. Thus, according to Taylor, we are less free than we might be '*when we find ourselves carried away* by a less significant goal to overrule a highly significant one', or '*when we are led to act* out of a motive we consider bad or despicable'. It is this '*acting* out of some motivations, for example, irrational fear or spite', which 'is not freedom, is even a *negation* of freedom'.[14] Clearly, then, an internal constraint does not consist *simply* in an 'irrational fear' or a 'phobia', or whatever other mental state; in order for there to be a real *constraint* on my doing x, that irrational fear or phobia must *lead me to do not-x*. In other words, my being more or less internally constrained against doing x (while not externally constrained against doing x) simply *is* the greater or lesser probability of my frustrating some purpose (for Taylor, one of my 'fundamental' purposes), as the result of an irrational fear, phobia or whatever, by doing not-x. It therefore seems reasonable to measure the internal unfreedom of an agent to do x in terms of her propensity to do some other thing (any one thing) that entails her doing not-x. Were we to integrate internal constraints into our measurements of *overall* freedom, then, we would assign a number between 0 and 1 to each externally unconstrained action according to the degree to which it is internally constrained, where '0' represents the complete internal unfreedom to perform it and '1' the complete internal freedom to perform it.[15]

As a means of assessing degrees of internal constraint, we might borrow from Richard Flathman's categorization of their various possible strengths. These different strengths of constraint would appear to correspond to the 'strength of will' that is required to overcome them. Flathman suggests the following continuum, starting with the least free kinds of behaviour: '(a) psychotic [behaviour] . . . (b) obsessions, phobias, and compulsions . . . (c) habits in the at least mildly perjorative sense in which we say that smoking and pot-taking are habits (d) a wide variety of so-called akratic behaviours'.[16] Flathman's continuum goes beyond these categories to include increasingly faultless rational behaviour, and ending with the god-like philosopher. But we need not discuss this continuum any further here; I shall leave it to the reader to decide whether it is only philosophers who can reasonably be described as wholly internally unconstrained.

6.2 SELF-MASTERY AND THE SPECIFIC-FREEDOM THESIS

I now turn to the most important of my objections to the idea of incorporating internal freedoms (as self-mastery) into our conception of overall freedom. This objection is neatly illustrated by the fact that each of Taylor's points

[14] Taylor, 'What's Wrong with Negative Liberty', 185–6, my emphasis.
[15] This proposal would be complicated somewhat by the existence of degrees of *external* freedom to perform single actions. However, I argue against the idea that external constraints are a matter of degree, in Ch. 8 (in particular, at s. 8.2).
[16] R. E. Flathman, *The Philosophy and Politics of Freedom* (Chicago: Chicago University Press, 1987), 93–4.

(2) and (3), which affirm the existence of internal constraints, depends for its meaning on point (1), which states his adherence to the value-based approach to measuring freedom. As we saw in the previous chapter, the value-based approach to measuring freedom entails that freedom really only has specific value; as a way of making *literal* sense of judgements of degrees of overall freedom, it is self-refuting.

Are all advocates of the idea of self-mastery forced to follow Taylor in endorsing the value-based approach? I think that the answer must be 'yes'. We have seen that advocates of freedom as self-mastery must employ some criterion for distinguishing between actions that the agent simply chooses not to perform and actions that the agent is 'internally unfree' to perform; otherwise, it will follow that the agent is prevented from doing everything she in fact chooses not to do. Some way must be found of distinguishing between desires that constrain (internally) and desires that do not. And the only adequate way to do so is by recourse to Taylor's notion of 'significance'.

To see this, consider an example of a 'compulsive' desire. Smith has what most would call a 'compulsive' desire to attend church, and as a result he attends church at 7 a.m. and 7 p.m. every day. Now it might at first be thought that we can simply single out this compulsion as a particular psychological phenomenon, and say on this purely empirical, psychological basis that Smith's freedom to do any number of other things at 7 a.m. and 7 p.m. is curtailed. And it might then appear that a judgement about self-mastery has been made without reference to the values (either subjective or objective) of going to church or of doing these various other things, but instead by reference to a neutral psychological fact about Smith. It is a trivial fact, however, that such a judgement about Smith's unfreedom will not be possible without some means of distinguishing between compulsive and non-compulsive desires. What is it, then, that makes Smith's desire to attend church a compulsive one? Is it merely the fact that his desire to do so is especially strong and occurs especially frequently? Is it merely the fact that his desire to do so tends generally to override any other desires he might have? This is surely not sufficient, for it would not allow us to distinguish Smith's case from that of Jones, an extremely religious individual whose one fundamental purpose is to praise God. It is part of Jones's plan of life to attend church twice a day, and the praise of God is lexically prime in his personal hierarchy of values. Given this, we should not like to call Jones's behaviour compulsive. If we see Smith's behaviour as compulsive, it is exactly because we see him as differing in this respect from Jones. It is because the desire to attend church so frequently is not *authentic* in his case, and because other important purposes with which he identifies could be pursued in the place of his church attendance without him undergoing any loss. If we do not describe his compulsion in this way, as subverting other valuable purposes, we shall be forced to describe anyone with desires similar to Smith's as internally constrained, and this we should not like to do in the case of Jones. Compulsions and obsessions are not simply strong, frequently occurring desires; similarly, phobias are not simply strong, consistent aversions. Such psychological phenomena cannot be identified without discriminating between purposes in the way suggested by Taylor. Compulsions and obsessions are *over*-strong, *over*-frequently occurring desires, where the meaning of 'over' in this context depends not on some empirical human average, but on a background of relative values.

The idea of freedom as self-mastery is therefore logically inseparable from the value-based approach to measuring freedom: freedom as self-mastery is necessarily a form of value-based freedom. This, as I have said, brings us right back to the normative version of the specific-freedom thesis. As far as the idea of freedom as self-mastery is concerned, the normative version of the specific-freedom thesis is correct. Self-mastery just is the freedom to realize specific purposes singled out by means of some value-based criterion. This means that self-mastery cannot be non-specifically valuable in the way I have argued overall freedom to be.

It might be objected that self-mastery can be seen as non-specifically valuable if the criterion one uses for distinguishing between desires that constrain and desires that do not constrain refers to the process by which those desires come about rather than to their content. This criterion provides an alternative defence of point (2), and is based on what John Christman has called a 'content-neutral' conception of freedom as self-mastery.[17] According to Christman, what makes a person free is not her acting on certain desires as such but, rather, her acting on desires that have *come about* in a certain way. A person can be a self-master whatever her desires—even, in principle, if they include the desire to act subserviently towards others—as long as those desires were formed in a way that involved reflection on her part about the change in her own desires (or would have involved such reflection had she turned her attention to the change), and were not 'oppressively imposed upon her',[18] say, by keeping her ignorant about all her options.

The problem, however, is that in order to know whether the process of desire change has come about autonomously, we must know what the change is a change *from*. This is because the presence of a freedom-reducing factor in the process of desire-change depends on the truth of a counterfactual conditional affirming that the change *would not* have taken place in the *absence*

---

[17] Christman, 'Liberalism and Individual Positive Freedom', esp. 358–9, and id., 'Autonomy and Personal History', *Canadian Journal of Philosophy*, 20 (1991), esp. 22–3.
[18] Christman, 'Liberalism and Individual Positive Freedom', 345.

of that factor.[19] Consider the example of ignorance. Clearly not all cases of ignorance are to be seen as creating internal unfreedoms. What we must say, on Christman's conception of self-mastery, is that A's desire for p constitutes an internal constraint on A's freedom if and only if A is ignorant of a certain fact, x, and A starts to desire p while ignorant of x, and A would not have started to desire p had A not been ignorant of x. The counterfactual conditional is necessary in order to see the ignorance of x as having created an internal constraint. But in order to verify this counterfactual conditional, we shall need information about A's *prior* set of desires, which must be taken as authentic (or else themselves assessed in terms of their process of formation, and so on back to some original set of authentic desires).

So even on Christman's conception of self-mastery, we still need to refer to the content of the agent's desires to see if she is a self-master. This is not to deny that Christman's conception is 'content-neutral' in the way in which any subjectivist interpretation of internal constraints is content-neutral; it is content-neutral in the sense that all desires, including morally bad or self-demeaning desires, can in principle qualify as desires of self-masters. But this is not enough to make freedom as self-mastery non-specifically valuable, since self-mastery remains, even in this content-neutral sense, the freedom to realize purposes that the authentic agent actually desires to realize. What would be needed in order to make self-mastery non-specifically valuable would be a content-*less* conception of self-mastery, and that is impossible.

6.3 THE RHETORICAL INTERPRETATION: SOME FURTHER COUNTER-ARGUMENTS FROM COMMON-SENSE COMPARISONS

Let us then consider the view that attributions of degrees of overall freedom are really elliptical for degrees of other goods (and are thus compatible with the specific-freedom thesis), in a way that parallels the discussion in the previous chapter. As in s. 5.3, having accepted the normative redundancy of value-based judgements about overall freedom, we should now turn to an examination of their fruitfulness in purely rhetorical terms.

In this section, I shall consider a rhetorical interpretation that simply *extends* the rhetorical interpretation examined in Chapter 5, so as to *include* the notion of self-mastery: I shall consider the suggestion that a person's degree of overall freedom (interpreted rhetorically) is a function of the degree to which her possible actions are unconstrained both externally and internally, where those actions are weighted in accordance with the value-based approach. The

---

[19] Cf. Christman, 'Autonomy and Personal History', 11.

idea, here, is to combine the absence of external constraints on action and the absence of internal constraints on action into a single quantitative attribute. As we shall see, the inclusion of internal constraints within the value-based conception of freedom examined in the previous chapter only serves to increase the counter-intuitivity of that conception. Not only do value-based measurements of overall freedom that combine internal and external freedoms fail the test of isomorphism with our common-sense comparisons in the way in which, more generally, value-based measurements were seen to in the previous chapter; such measurements also often have strongly illiberal implications.

The alternative to the above interpretation is to confine the purely rhetorical interpretation of 'degrees of freedom' to the notion of freedom as self-mastery. I have no objection to this position, which I touch on in the next section. The important thing is that this last interpretation of 'degrees of freedom' not be confused with the literal, empirical interpretation which emerged in the course of the previous chapter, and which must be seen as *excluding* the notion of self-mastery.

Let us begin by considering the combination of Taylor's points (1) and (2). We can bring in point (3), and with it Taylor's own objectivist account of internal constraints, once we have seen the implications of these first two points. Consider then the combined effect of (1) and (2) in connection with one of Taylor's own examples of an internally constrained agent—that of the agent whose 'attachment to comforts' prevents her from 'going on an expedition over the Andes'. Here, the agent (call her A) has a choice between the two options 'crossing the Andes' and, say, 'sitting in her favourite armchair'.[20] These options provide differing amounts of freedom. For Taylor, as an advocate of the value-based approach, the amount of freedom they provide will be determined by their qualitative significance.

Let us say that, in terms of their degrees of significance, the Andes option in the above example is worth ten units of freedom, and that the armchair option is worth one unit of freedom. Remember that on the present interpretation, in *all* cases of internal unfreedom, the constrained option is necessarily more significant than the option which the constrained agent chooses instead to take. The numbers '10' and '1' need not be interpreted as anything other than crude numerical representations of this fact. Neither is the assumption of cardinality essential to my argument; it merely serves to make the point clearer. (An alternative assumption would be that the value of the Andes option is 'incommensurably higher' than that of the armchair option.[21]) Let us further

[20] The term 'option' should not be confused with Taylor's term 'opportunity'. The latter can be taken to mean 'externally unconstrained option'.

[21] Cf. C. Taylor, 'The Diversity of Goods', in A. Sen and B. Williams (eds.), *Utilitarianism and Beyond* (Cambridge: Cambridge University Press, 1982).

assume, for simplicity's sake, that A is *wholly* internally constrained (by her attachment to comforts) from taking the Andes option. Given these assumptions, we can picture four possible situations in terms of the amounts of freedom they allow:

(*a*) A is free to take either option   (11 units)
(*b*) A is free to take only the Andes option   (10 units)
(*c*) A is free to take only the armchair option   (1 unit)
(*d*) A is unfree to take either option   (0 units)

In Taylor's example, A is in situation (*c*): although externally unconstrained from taking either option, she is internally constrained from taking the Andes option by her propensity to take the armchair option. Considering the fact that it is A's propensity to take the armchair option which reduces her freedom here—i.e. that her attachment to comforts only constitutes an internal constraint on her freedom (and indeed, is only an *over*-attachment) as long as she has that propensity—how are we to go about increasing her freedom? The answer is, by removing her propensity to take the armchair option. But say that we are unable to remove A's 'over'-attachment to comforts, thus achieving situation (*a*)? In this case, we should aim for situation (*b*), by imposing an external constraint on the armchair option. This will prevent A from exercising her freedom-constraining tendency, so opening up to her the option which that tendency was closing off. The introduction of an insignificant external constraint will have removed a significant internal constraint, and A's overall freedom will thereby have been increased from one unit to ten. We have thus arrived at a freedom measurer's version of the classic critique of many so-called 'positive' definitions of freedom: the objection that on the basis of such definitions it is paradoxically possible to force a person to be free.[22]

I have left aside here the possibility of re-educating A and have assumed, as has in fact been assumed in the historical examples I shall refer to later on, that achieving situation (*a*) will sometimes be impossible or at least impracticable. Notice, however, that even where this assumption is incorrect, we will still be *increasing* A's freedom if we move A up the freedom scale from situation (*c*) to situation (*b*), and that governments which take analogous measures are apparently to be applauded for doing so (from the point of view of overall freedom on the rhetorical interpretation under consideration), albeit not as much as those which are able, at little cost in terms of other freedoms, to implement policies with effects analogous to that of moving A up the scale as far as situation (*a*).

[22] Cf. Berlin, *Four Essays on Liberty*, 132–4.

Taylor must hold to the above conclusion, because he endorses exactly the conception of overall freedom that we are here assuming—i.e. the view that external and internal freedoms are just individual instances of that single quant-itative attribute we call 'freedom'. An internal constraint on doing x is, for Taylor, sufficient to remove the freedom to do x, and leaves us indifferent (from the point of view of assessing overall freedom) to the question of whether or not x is constrained externally. The man who is 'driven by spite' or 'prevented by unreasoning fear' from pursuing his most fundamental purposes '*is not really made more free if one lifts the external obstacles* to his venting his spite or his acting on his fear'.[23] And, most importantly, when we consider the relative degrees of significance attached to these options (degrees of significance on which the notion of internal constraints itself depends), we can see that such a man is in fact made *less free* if one removes such external obstacles, because to constrain externally in such cases is to remove constraints on significant actions; it is to *impose* obstacles *on* the agent's 'venting his spite or his acting on his fear'. *Because* the agent is externally constrained, he has a higher degree of freedom *overall*.

What are the implications of this analysis for our attempt to square measurements of overall freedom (here, elliptically interpreted) with liberal common-sense comparisons of overall freedom (elliptically interpreted)? One of Taylor's expressed intuitions—and one which will surely be shared by most liberals who take an interest in overall freedom in either the literal *or* the elliptical sense—is that if we compare the average Albanian with the average inhabitant of London (at least in 1979, when Taylor was writing), the latter should turn out to be more free than the former. As we saw in the previous chapter, Taylor appeals to this intuition in order to justify the value-based approach. But are the final implications of his analysis in tune with this intuition? A brief consideration of the facts shows that they are not.

Taylor's comparison of religious unfreedom with the constraints imposed by traffic lights backfires when we come to consider the relationship between external and internal religious freedom: external religious freedoms may also be an important source of internal religious unfreedoms. The guilt feelings imposed by Christian notions of sin, for example, may easily be said to con-strain an individual from realizing her most fundamental purposes. These guilt feelings may be merely the result of childhood indoctrination, and therefore feelings with which the individual no longer identifies, but which nevertheless induce in her a propensity to act in a way which frustrates her most funda-mental purposes. Consider the following first-hand account of the effects of 'growing up Catholic':

---

[23] Taylor, 'What's Wrong with Negative Liberty', 191–2, my emphasis.

It is still unthinkable that one could pass Christmas or Easter without going to church, passionately devoted to a ritual that no longer holds the same transcendent meaning for you. . . . At home, at work, in relationships, in arguments, some nagging sense of wrong-doing *trips you up*. It is *a disabling hangover* from those early years, perhaps the thing that leaves you most embittered about your Catholic past.[24]

Or again,

I left my convent at seventeen with *inhibitions impenetrable*, a *deep fear of life*, an armory of draconian laws to govern my every action, and no sense at all of a loving God. It was only because *I dared not do otherwise* that I continued to call myself a Catholic.[25]

An erstwhile Christian may indeed be 'prevented from taking up a career she truly wants'[26] which involves working on Sundays, or 'driven . . . to jeopardize her most important relationships'[27] through her refusal of sex before marriage, or her over-attachment to monogamy. It is a consequence of Taylor's analysis that in such a case, if we are interested above all in the freedom of that individual, and if the guilt feelings cannot be removed, we should prevent that individual externally from acting in such guilt-induced ways. It is difficult to work out the exact practical implications of such a policy, but what we can at least see is that, given the existence of such examples, the Albanian abolition of religion must have increased the overall freedom (elliptically interpreted) of at least *some* individuals. Of course, the opposite of this example may be the case. It may be that an individual is prevented from pursuing her fundamental religious purposes by her propensity to fornicate and to work double time on Sundays. But then, it is a consequence of Taylor's analysis that *that* individual's freedom might well be increased (overall) by our externally preventing her from fornicating and from working on Sundays. Again, this implication fails to square with liberal commonsense comparisons of freedom.

It might be objected that it can never in practice be said of a person who is constrained against doing *x* by her propensity to do not-*x*, that we can increase her overall freedom by preventing her from doing not-*x*. This is because, the objection goes, the prevention of not-*x* will entail the prevention of all actions other than *x*, which must, when combined, be of greater significance than *x* taken on its own. However, it is simply not true that the prevention of not-*x* must involve preventing a great many actions in combination. Consider, for

---

[24] J. Walsh, *Growing up Catholic* (London: Macmillan, 1989), 160–2. The emphasis is mine, and is meant to point to the similarity between the kinds of terms used by Walsh and those used by Taylor to describe examples of internal constraints.
[25] Mary Craig, cited ibid. 159, my emphasis.
[26] Taylor, 'What's Wrong with Negative Liberty', 191.   [27] Ibid.

example, a case where x is 'staying away from church'. Here, to prevent not-x is to prevent the person from going to church, whereas to prevent x is to *force* her to go to church (that is, to prevent her at a specific time from doing *anything else*). Perhaps it should be admitted that this example is more analogous (in terms of the quantities of action which x and not-x consist in) to cases of 'compulsion' (which imply an appetite for a specific thing) than to cases of 'fear', 'phobia', or 'ignorance' (which tend, rather, to eliminate certain specific things from one's range of choices). Nevertheless, there is no reason why the example should not *sometimes* be analogous to these last three kinds of cases. There is no reason, for example, why a person should not correctly describe herself as going to church merely out of an irrational fear of hell (with the consequence that in the meantime certain of her fundamental purposes get frustrated), nor therefore why, given Taylor's points (1) and (2), this person's overall freedom cannot be said to be increased by our preventing her from going to church.

So far, authoritarianism can nevertheless be kept within certain limits by stipulating the condition, contained in any subjectivist conception of internal constraints, that in order to qualify as internally constrained, an individual must *consciously identify* with the fundamental purpose being frustrated (and not with the purpose which is frustrating it). With the introduction of Taylor's point (3), even these limits are removed. Point (3) supersedes the above condition, implying as it does that an agent can be internally constrained against pursuing a certain course of action *despite* the fact that she acts on fundamental purposes with which she consciously identifies, for the simple reason that her choice of fundamental purposes in life is erroneous. Charles Manson and Andreas Baader were mistaken not because they tended to pursue courses of action which frustrated what they believed to be their fundamental purposes. They were unfree not because they were mistaken in their choice of the means to pursuing their chosen ends in life. Rather, according to Taylor, they were mistaken because those supposed fundamental purposes were themselves 'largely shaped by confusion, illusion and distorted perspective'. They were unfree because they were mistaken in their very choice of ends in life.[28]

Taylor draws no conceptual line between the cases of Manson and Baader and those of the rest of us, and the drawing of such a line seems indeed to be unwarranted. If there exist criteria for saying whether or not Manson's fundamental purposes (his chosen *ends* in life) are mistaken, then those same criteria must apply equally to my fundamental purposes and to yours. For, unlike an assessment of Manson's choice of means, Taylor's assessment of Manson's ends cannot appeal in any way to Manson's own subjectively identified values (given

---

[28] Ibid. 192.

Manson's subjective disagreement with Taylor's assessment). It therefore follows that the criteria for individuating and assigning degrees of significance to an individual's fundamental purposes must be values that are objectively valid, rather than any of the subjective values of that particular individual.

The way in which Taylor moves from (2) to (3)—that is, from an instrumental conception of rationality to a conception of rationality that applies to ends—is, as I have said, not at all transparent. And yet the consequences of this move are far from trivial. For the difference between the implications of (1)+(2) and of (1)+(3) appears to amount to the difference between paternalism and unlimited authoritarianism. On the basis of (3), it becomes possible for us to ask not merely whether a Christian has the propensity to choose courses of action that frustrate her fundamental religious purposes but, further, whether those fundamental religious purposes are themselves mistaken. And because the answer to the latter question must appeal to an objective good (rather than to the good of that particular Christian), it must apply equally to all other Christians, as well as to non-Christians. Stalinists believe that they have indeed been able to answer this question. Religious purposes are mistaken because they lead to the reification of existing orders, because they stunt human potential, and because, like those of Manson, they are 'largely shaped by confusion, illusion and distorted perspective'.[29] Since such mistaken purposes 'partake . . . so much of the nature of spite and unreasoning fear in the other cases',[30] the propensity to act on them is an internal constraint on freedom. Where such a propensity widely exists, it follows that the universal prevention of such action will increase societal freedom.

Taylor will no doubt feel that my critique of his conception of overall freedom goes too far. To assume that his theory presupposes the objectivity of such *specific* fundamental purposes as 'being a Catholic' or 'being a communist' is, he might say, mistaken: as the Albanian–Londoner example suggested, what is significant in the relevant sense is not anything as specific as 'being a Catholic', but rather, 'being free to pursue whatever religious purpose—or even non-religious purpose—one feels called to pursue'. But if this is Taylor's position, then it starts to look very much like my own position on the value of freedom. It is my view that 'being free' (to a certain extent), and not just 'being a Catholic' or 'being a communist', is *itself* one of our 'fundamental purposes'. If this is how Taylor's position is to be interpreted, then he ought to accept at least some of the reasons set out in Chapter 2 for seeing freedom as non-specifically valuable. These reasons need to be followed through to their logical conclusion. But if Taylor does *that*, then he will have to reject the value-based approach on which his conception of overall freedom has been shown to rest.

---

[29] Taylor, 'What's Wrong with Negative Liberty', 192.   [30] Ibid.

6.4 THE PRIORITY OF EMPIRICAL FREEDOM

This leaves us with the second alternative mentioned at the beginning of the previous section: that of confining the rhetorical interpretation of 'degrees of freedom' to the notion of self-mastery. What must be rejected is Taylor's view of *overall* freedom as *including* the notion of self-mastery. This does not prevent us from talking about degrees of self-mastery in the elliptical sense, nor indeed from valuing self-mastery. Such talk must be supplemented, however, by a recognition of the distinctness of that attribute the independent value of which was affirmed in Chapter 2, and the proper method of measuring which was deduced in Chapter 5. It must be supplemented, in other words, by a recognition of the distinct value of overall freedom interpreted empirically.

Taylor's all-inclusive conception of overall freedom contradicts what many will see as the most important reasons given in Chapter 2 for seeing freedom as valuable: that individuals need to be given the *space* to determine and develop their own ends in life (what Hobhouse called the conditions under which the human personality can be allowed to 'grow'), that being allowed to make mistakes is a necessary means to economic, social, and cultural progress (given human fallibility and ignorance), and that freedom is (non-specifically) a component of the 'autonomy complex', or of 'self-respect'. If we treat overall freedom as the combined absence of external *and internal* constraints, as measured in accordance with the value-based approach, then we need not accord individuals the space to grow or the above-mentioned basis for progress or autonomy or self respect. Concluding the argument for his conception of freedom, Taylor says that the question of whether or not such a conception implies totalitarianism is one which 'must now be addressed'.[31] In the absence of such a discussion on his part, however, it is not clear what element of his conception of freedom he sees as standing in the way of such an implication. What *would* stand in its way, but is not present in Taylor's theory, is a commitment to guaranteeing a measure of the empirical kind of freedom that Taylor shuns as 'philistine'.

This leads me to conclude that the most liberals can permit themselves is an interest in the promotion of certain specific instances of self-mastery (or—what amounts to the same thing—an interest in increasing or maximizing overall self-mastery in the elliptical sense implied by the value-based approach), subject to the lexical priority of an interest in overall freedom in the empirical (i.e. *non*-elliptical) sense. If and only if lexical priority is accorded to giving individuals a measure of freedom in the empirical sense, such a concern for self-mastery may not have illiberal implications, and indeed might

[31] Ibid. 193.

coherently be seen as another necessary part of a liberal's concern for individual well-being.

In connection with the priority of empirical freedom, it is worth citing the example of Kant. Though often seen as one of the fathers of the modern ideal of 'freedom as self-mastery', Kant himself recognized the need to accord priority to securing a just distribution of empirical freedom for all. This was partly because, like many of the other authors cited in Chapter 2, he recognized that the ideal he held to be supremely important was nevertheless not one that any individual or group could pursue *directly* on behalf of others. Indeed, Kant went further, and suggested that being a wholly rational agent in his intended sense (being a self-master on *his* interpretation of that term) itself implied respecting the principle of equal empirical freedom.[32] It implied respecting human beings as ends in themselves, or, in the words of Taylor, as 'the points of origin of ends'. And 'to respect a being as an originator of ends is above all to respect his freedom of action'.[33] (Note that we are indeed talking here of 'freedom of action', and not of 'acting freely', on which point see s. 7.11.)

A community of individuals who act rationally by respecting others as the originators of ends is thus a community in which 'each may seek his happiness in whatever way he sees fit, so long as he does not infringe upon the [empirical] freedom of others to pursue a similar end which can be reconciled with the [empirical] freedom of everyone else'.[34] As Hilary Putnam puts it, 'Kant's ideal community is a community of beings who think for themselves without knowing what the "human essence" is, without knowing what "Eudaimonia" is, and who respect one another for doing that. *That* is Kant's "Kingdom of Ends".'[35] It seems, then, that Kant, at least on Putnam's interpretation, recognized the non-specific value of freedom in a way in which many subsequent defenders of the ideal of 'freedom as self-mastery' have not. Perhaps it is their tendency to want to 'fill in' Kant's formal notion of self-mastery with more substantive claims about what constitutes a rational end (e.g. attending church, or pursuing the interests of a particular nation or class) that has blinded so many non-liberal philosophers to the non-specific value which only empirical freedom possesses, so allowing them to roll together empirical freedom and self-mastery into a unidimensional quantitative attribute.

---

[32] Steiner denies this implication, believing that 'there is no logical necessity to adopt the equal freedom rule'. He does believe, however, that 'if you adopt it, it must be lexically prime' (*An Essay on Rights*, 220).

[33] C. Taylor, 'Kant's Theory of Freedom', in Z. Pelczynski and J. Gray (eds.), *Conceptions of Liberty in Political Philosophy* (London: Athlone Press, 1984), 114.

[34] I. Kant, 'On the Common Saying: "This May be True in Theory, but it does not Apply in Practice"', in his *Political Writings*, 74.

[35] H. Putnam, *The Many Faces of Realism* (La Salle, Ill.: Open Court, 1987), 51, emphasis in original.

6.5 SUMMARY

We have seen that freedom as self-mastery is by definition only 'specifically' valuable: it is the internal freedom to do what is valuable (be this realizing one's authentic self in accordance with one's second-order desires, acting rationally in a purely formal sense, or obeying more substantive objective moral principles). We therefore have no interest in making literal sense of the idea of 'degrees of overall self-mastery'. For as far as self-mastery is concerned, the normative version of the specific-freedom thesis is correct. When we talk about 'degrees of overall freedom' in a literal sense, and in a way that is in tune with the concerns set out in Part I of this book, we must be taken to be referring exclusively to degrees of empirical freedom. Moreover, as the above arguments from common-sense comparisons imply, it is difficult for liberals even to find any rhetorical use for value-based measurements of freedom as self-mastery—at least where this is seen as a dimension of overall freedom. On the contrary, most liberals will see such implied measurements as having strongly illiberal consequences. As far as the pursuit of justice is concerned, any value that liberals do attach to self-mastery should be considered lexically subordinate to the non-specific value they attach to empirical freedom.

PART III

Empirical Freedom

7

Individual Freedom: Actions

> Henry had become angry when the twins were voicing moral objections at the idea of killing Bunny. 'Don't be ridiculous', he snapped.
>
> 'But how', said Charles, who was close to tears, 'how can you *possibly justify* cold-blooded murder?'
>
> Henry lit a cigarette. 'I prefer to think of it', he had said, 'as redistribution of matter'.[1]

THERE is *something* in what Henry says, however morally reprehensible we might consider his position on cold-blooded murder. It is normal *not* to 'prefer to think of it as redistribution of matter'. Yet Henry's killing Bunny clearly *is*, among other things, a redistribution of matter. So what is it that puts Henry in the wrong? The answer is that, despite being true, his description of the action of killing Bunny is inappropriate to the context in which it is given. What puts him in the wrong is his declared preference for that description in that context. The context in this case is given by the nature of Charles's question, which has to do with the *morality* of killing Bunny. The point, then, is that in this case we do not consider the description of Henry's action 'as redistribution of matter' to be relevant to its moral worth.

There are many different kinds of act-description. Each description serves a different purpose. Donald Davidson gives some examples: a particular act-description may help to 'supply the motive ("I was getting my revenge"), place the action in the context of a rule ("I am castling"), give the outcome ("I killed him") or provide evaluation ("I did the right thing")'.[2] The idea motivating this chapter is that while a description of an action as 'redistribution of matter' may not be pertinent to the subject matter of the conversation between Henry and Charles, it nevertheless is the appropriate kind of description when it comes to making judgements about degrees of overall freedom, that kind of description being the only one on which we can base an approach to the measurement of freedom that is consistent with freedom's non-specific value. Henry's answer would have lost its immoral character, and would indeed have been correct, had Charles instead asked (no doubt *not* close to tears), 'How

---

[1] From the novel by Donna Tartt, *The Secret History* (Harmondsworth: Penguin, 1992), 355.

[2] D. Davidson, *Essays on Actions and Events* (Oxford: Clarendon Press, 1980), 110.

are we to go about measuring the extent to which your being unprevented from killing Bunny contributes to your overall freedom?'

The conversation between Charles and Henry brings out the importance of the relevance of an act-description to the purpose at hand. The assessment of degrees of overall freedom is just one purpose among many, and not necessarily the most important purpose. It is simply that purpose which arises out of a belief in freedom's non-specific value. It should therefore be clear that what I have called the 'empirical approach' to measuring freedom in no way implies what is often referred to as a 'reductionist' theory of action. The empirical approach to measuring freedom does not rest on the 'physicalist' claim that human action is 'nothing more than', or is 'fundamentally', the redistribution of matter. Rather, it rests on the uncontroversial assumption that any act (unless a purely 'mental act') can be described in terms of the redistribution of matter, together with the claim that such a description happens to be the appropriate one in contexts in which our concern is the measurement of overall freedom. I shall expand on this defence against the charge of 'reductionism' in the final section of this chapter. There is much ground to be covered before that final section, and in the meantime there are likely to be those who for some reason come to believe that the empirical approach to measuring freedom (or at least, my interpretation of it) rests on a fallacious theory of human action. I must ask these potential opponents to content themselves for now with the opening thought set out above. Only if we first provide a full clarification of the empirical approach will we really be qualified to engage in a satisfactory discussion about its fundamental presuppositions regarding the nature of human action.

Since the subject matter of this chapter is primarily the *actions* that one is free or unfree to perform, it should not be expected that all of the conceptual problems confronting the freedom measurer will get solved here. My aim in this chapter is to set out the essentials of the empirical approach to measuring freedom (according to which the extent of my freedom is a function of the extent of action available to me, in 'sheer quantitative terms'), in so far as this contrasts with the rival 'value-based' approach. The present discussion should therefore be seen as a parallel to the discussion in Chapter 5. Both the value-based and the empirical approach to measuring overall freedom encounter further problems when it is realized that there may be different and incommensurable kinds of 'preventing conditions'—in other words, that it may be difficult to combine different 'constraint-type dimensions of freedom' (see s. 3.3) so as to produce overall measurements. This problem will be discussed in the next chapter, where I shall suggest an analysis of 'constraints on freedom' which should put us in a position to assert both the feasibility and the intuitive plausibility (at the purely conceptual level) of measurements of overall individual freedom. The analysis contained in the next chapter is most in tune with the spirit of the empirical approach, but it is not logically incompatible with the value-based approach. I say that that analysis puts us in a position to assert the measurability of *individual* freedom, because this and the next chapter deal exclusively with the measurement of the freedom of a single person. Only in Chapter 9 will we turn to the implications of this discussion for degrees of group freedom.

As well as asking those already armed with action-theoretic objections to hold their fire for now, I also crave the indulgence of those whose first inclination is to reject as unrealistic or pedantic the kind of fine-grained theoretical analysis of action on which we are about to embark. Since the claims of this chapter (as well as those of Chapters 8 and 9) are all pitched at the level of purely conceptual theory, they are not themselves necessarily adequate as instructions for those wishing to go out into the world and measure overall freedom. Enumerating possible actions might be unfeasible for practical reasons, and might even be seen as counter-productive in terms of freedom—that is, as itself involving unacceptable levels of interference on the part of the information-gathering freedom measurer (although it would be foolish to jump to conclusions on this last question). In order to arrive at practical instructions for the freedom measurer, it is necessary to descend to the level of 'realistic' theory, and consider the feasibility and validity of approximate metrics (see s. 3.4). I take a tentative look at some such metrics in Chapter 10. The important point to bear in mind here is that a purely conceptual account of the empirical approach is necessary exactly in order to make sense of such realistic, approximate metrics. This is because the choice between such metrics will be arbitrary unless we have a standard on the basis of which such a choice is to be made. Any 'second-best' metric will be flawed from the start if we do not succeed in refuting the widely raised objection that the quantification of possible actions is a theoretical non-starter. Approximate measurements are, after all, approximations to *something*.

7.1 STEINER'S FORMULA

As a starting point for a fuller elaboration of the empirical approach, it is useful to consider a formula suggested by Hillel Steiner. According to Steiner, the extent of an agent's overall freedom can be represented in the following way. Where 'Red' is an agent, for any given list of actions, Red's freedom is equal to the value of

$$F_r/(F_r+U_r)$$

where F_r and U_r stand for the numbers of actions Red is free and unfree to perform respectively.[3] It is clear that the measurements resulting from this formula will depend on the nature and extent of the 'given list of actions' referred to above. It is equally clear, however, that if we are interested in measuring the *overall* freedom of Red, in the sense implied in Chapters 1 and 2, then that 'given list of actions' must be a list of *all* the actions which Red can reasonably be described as either free or unfree to perform.

Steiner represents a person's overall freedom as a fraction, rather than a straightforward numeral, because he believes that a person's overall freedom must be a function not only of the number of her specific freedoms, but also of the number of her specific *unfreedoms*, that function consisting in the *ratio* of the number of actions that she is free to perform (F_r) to the number of actions that she is either free or unfree to perform ($F_r + U_r$). Why should a person's overall freedom not simply be represented by the value of F_r—that is, by a straightforward sum of her specific freedoms? The answer, Steiner says, is that we do not want to ignore increases in the number of a person's unfreedoms which might accompany increases in the number of her freedoms. It is not sufficient to conclude from the fact that one person has more specific freedoms than another that he has more freedom overall, because 'there [may also be] many more actions which he is *unfree* to do. Simply to ignore them in estimating the extent of a person's liberty, is to misconstrue the object of such an enterprise.'[4]

Is the set of actions which one is 'either free or unfree to perform' ($F_r + U_r$) not the same for any two individuals whose freedom we are comparing? If so, is the above point not thereby invalidated? If $F_r + U_r$ is the same for all individuals, surely their comparative degrees of freedom *are* accurately represented by their comparative numbers of freedoms. This objection may hold in the case of two individuals at any one time. But if we are to compare my freedom with that of my former self—if, that is, we are to measure *changes* in overall freedom—we shall have to take into account technological advancements. Such advancements may add new actions to the 'given list', and these actions may be available to some people and not to others (depending on their degree of access to the benefits of technology). In Steiner's view, this point also applies to intersocietal comparisons within the same time-slice. Whether or not this is true, the important point to bear in mind is that in his view technological advancements should not in themselves be thought to guarantee increases in freedom, for 'it is not to physicists, doctors or engineers whom we turn in seeking answers to the question "How free?" '[5]

---

[3] Steiner, 'How Free', 74.   [4] Ibid. 75; cf. id., *An Essay on Rights*, 43.
[5] Steiner, 'How Free', 75.

This last claim of Steiner's is based on an intuition about the meaning of 'a specific freedom' the validity of which has usually been acknowledged by liberals and the implications of which have been much discussed in the freedom literature (see s. 8.1). The intuition is that in order for an obstacle to count as a constraint on the freedom of a human agent to do a particular thing, that obstacle must have been created by some other human agent (or group of human agents). The idea, in other words, is that freedom is a *social* concept—that 'freedom' expresses a relation between *persons*—so that mere natural obstacles do not as such constrain a person's freedom. The creation, through technological innovation, of the means by which obstacles can be overcome does affect freedom, but only in the sense that we must ask ourselves, *once* such means have been created, whether and how far certain agents withhold those means from others.

Henceforth, I shall assume that Steiner is right in this respect, and that a person's freedom should indeed be represented by a fraction rather than simply by a number of freedoms. It seems reasonable to say that the denominator of the fraction should represent the list of all technologically feasible actions (at the time at which the agent has the degree of freedom under investigation).[6] This suggestion is not wholly unproblematic. For one thing, it is not clear where we should draw the line between actual technological feasibility and potential technological feasibility. (Do governments restrict freedom to the extent that they refrain from financing technological research?) Another suggestion for the value of the denominator, which Steiner appears to endorse, is that it should represent all *logically* possible actions. This suggestion is less problematic at a purely conceptual level, despite being more problematic in practical terms, given the resultant proliferation of actions the agent is free or unfree to perform. A third candidate is 'nomic' possibility (i.e. possibility given the laws of nature),[7] which implies a larger denominator than in the case of technological possibility and a smaller denominator than in the case of logical possibility. But the exact interpretation of the denominator is not a question that need concern us any further here, since it does not in itself raise any 'action counting' problems that are significantly different from those to be investigated below.

Moreover, none of what I have said so far should be taken to imply that the analysis of empirical freedom contained in this and the next two chapters must *of necessity* distinguish between natural and human obstacles. On the contrary, as we shall see in s. 8.1, the question of the *source* of constraints

---

[6] Cf. M. van Hees, 'On the Analysis of Negative Freedom', *Theory and Decision*, forthcoming, s. 1.

[7] Cf. N. Rescher, *A Theory of Possibility: A Constructivistic and Conceptualistic Account of Possible Individuals and Possible Worlds* (Oxford: Blackwell, 1975), 80.

on freedom is in fact largely irrelevant to the question of whether or how far overall freedom can be measured. Its only relevance lies in its implication for the question just discussed—that is, whether or not F_r+U_r in Steiner's formula will always be the same for all individuals.

Steiner has subsequently expressed dissatisfaction with his formula,[8] and this is presumably because it does not itself provide us with an answer to the objection, neatly expressed by Berlin, that 'possibilities of action are not discrete entities like apples, which can be exhaustively enumerated'.[9] It is certainly not immediately clear what 'counting' available actions amounts to, or whether it is indeed possible. Is the 'number' of actions I might perform not infinite, or at least indeterminate? This consideration constitutes one of the most frequently posed 'epistemic' objections to the idea of measuring freedom (see s. 1.4).

The basic intuition behind Berlin's objection can be unpacked, and so clarified, by pointing to three particular problems to do with the 'counting' of actions. I think that it will be sensible to deal with each of these three problems separately. The first may be called the problem of *indefinite numbers of descriptions*. This is the problem that will first spring to the minds of those philosophers of action who hold that every different description of an action is a description of a different action, and therefore that there are as many actions as there are descriptions of actions.[10] On this view, 'extending my arm' will count for one action, 'signalling for a turn' will count for another, 'following the highway code' will count for yet another, and so on indefinitely. Steiner notes this problem, and the worry that it seems to force us into 'either arbitrary omissions or numerous instances of double counting' in the compilation of our list of actions (F_r+U_r), but suggests, in answer to it, that 'there is no reason why *all* these descriptions cannot be entered in our list'.[11] But this is surely not sufficient to overcome the problem of indefinite numbers of descriptions. After all, if there is an indefinite number of act-descriptions available, and each consitutes a potential entrant on our list of actions, then it will always be possible to reverse a judgement to the effect that A is freer than B by including a sufficient number of descriptions of the actions that A is unfree to perform and B free to perform. As a result, all measurements will appear arbitrary. More recently, Steiner has suggested that the arbitrariness of the number of descriptions we provide will not be a problem as long as we count freedoms and unfreedoms symmetrically, so that if what is intuitively seen as a single freedom (the freedom to do x) were to count for, say, ten (because ten alternative

---

[8] Steiner, *An Essay on Rights*, 42.   [9] Berlin, *Four Essays on Liberty*, 130.
[10] See e.g. A. B. Cody, 'Can a Single Action Have Many Different Descriptions?', *Inquiry*, 10 (1967).
[11] Steiner, 'How Free', 75.

descriptions of *x* are entered onto the list), the removal of that 'single freedom' (the *un*freedom to do *x*) would similarly count for ten. But it is not true that the mere symmetrical counting of freedoms and unfreedoms means that the problem of indefinite numbers of descriptions 'poses no danger of deforming our resultant calculation'.[12] For it remains the case that for Steiner an agent's overall freedom is to be calculated in terms of the *proportion* of the actions on our list that she is free to perform. The value of any given fraction expressing that proportion (as well as the ratio of one such fraction to another) will *vary* with the value of a given constant that is added to both the numerator and the denominator.

The second problem is what we might call that of *indefinite subdivision*. Even leaving aside the problem posed by the number of descriptions of actions, if we take any one action, we can see that that action can be subdivided in spatio-temporal terms. For example, should we think of my raising my arm two feet as a single action, or should we think of it as two actions (my raising my arm one foot, and then my raising it another foot)? Or should we think of it as eight actions (my raising my arm three inches, then three more inches...)? Similarly, my spending an evening at the theatre 'can be subdivided into my attending Act I, scene i, my attending Act I, scene ii, and so forth, with each of these being further and indefinitely subdivisible'.[13] It seems, as Onora O'Neill has suggested, that 'it would always be possible to show that any given set of liberties was as numerous as any other merely by listing the component liberties more specifically'.[14]

The third problem may be called the problem of *indefinite causal chains*. I move my arm, I operate a pump, I replenish the water supply, I poison the inhabitants of a house...[15] As the events in this causal chain unfold, we feel that the bringing about of each thing that happens is something that I *do*. When should we stop adding to the list of actions that are the bringing about of consequences of my bodily movements? We cannot allow that the addition may go on indefinitely, otherwise we will find ourselves up against the same problem of arbitrary measurements implied by the other two problems. Once again, it seems difficult to fix on a definite number of available actions.

7.2 THE PROBLEM OF INDEFINITE NUMBERS OF DESCRIPTIONS

In order to deal with the problem of indefinite numbers of descriptions, we need to be able to make sense of the idea of *re*describing an action. The idea

---

[12] Steiner, *An Essay on Rights*, 49.   [13] Ibid. 50. Cf. Gray, *Freedom*, 125–6.
[14] O'Neill, 'The Most Extensive Liberty', 50.
[15] This example comes from Elizabeth Anscombe, *Intention* (Oxford: Blackwell, 1957), 45.

that the problem at hand *is* a problem depends on the idea that we have no non-arbitrary basis on which to stop adding new act-descriptions to our list of all the actions that Red can be described as either free or unfree to perform ($F_r + U_r$). It depends, in other words, on the idea that every distinct act-description is a description of a distinct action. If, on the other hand, we can make sense of the idea of *re*describing an action, then we will have made sense of the idea that a single action can have many descriptions, and it will no longer be true that every different act-description is a description of a different action. This will allow us to fix on one particular description of each possible action, and to enter only that description on our list. It will also allow us both to make sense of, and to avoid, what appears to be the 'double counting' of actions, where to 'double count' an action is, we intuitively feel, to list it twice under alternative descriptions.[16] Just as 'Cary Grant' is a redescription of 'Archie Leach', so 'signalling for a turn' might simply be a redescription of 'raising one's arm'. If so, seeing these two act-descriptions as describing *two* actions would be akin to counting both Archie Leach and Cary Grant in a head-count of Hollywood actors. Once we have applied the strategy of listing each action under only one description, then we can safely assume that if we are still left with an indefinitely long list, this will not be because of the problem of indefinite numbers of descriptions but, rather, because of one of the other two problems mentioned above—that of indefinite subdivision or that of indefinite causal chains.

The key to being able to redescribe actions lies in conceiving of them, along with Donald Davidson, as spatio-temporally located particulars.[17] This conception of actions provides us with a criterion of act-identity—a criterion which allows us to say when two act-descriptions are descriptions of the *same* action—which fits nicely with the answer provided by the empirical approach to the question of which act-descriptions are relevant to the measurement of freedom. It is an action's physical location (say, raising my arm at the crossroads outside my house at time *t*) which allows us to say that another act-description (say, signalling for a turn) is simply a redescription of that same action (once, that is, we have established that that particular act of signalling takes place outside my house at time *t*). And it is exactly this physical location of an action (which implies, *inter alia*, its physical dimensions) that provides the relevant kind of act-description that we should include in our list.

Davidson's theory of action includes what is often referred to as the 'unifier thesis' of act-individuation, which is said to contrast with the 'multiplier thesis'. It will clarify matters somewhat if we now take a brief look at these two rival theses.[18]

---

[16] Cf. Steiner, *An Essay on Rights*, 49.   [17] Davidson, *Essays on Actions and Events*.

[18] Other proponents of the unifier thesis include Anscombe, *Intention*; J. Hornsby, *Actions* (London: Routledge & Kegan Paul, 1980); and K. Pfeifer, *Actions and Other Events: The Unifier–Multiplier Controversy* (New York: Peter Lang, 1989).

Analytical philosophers of action tend to refer to actions as being either 'basic' or 'non-basic'. A basic action is an action that we do not perform *by* performing another action.[19] A non-basic action is an action that we perform by performing a basic action. The concept of basic action arises out of the following consideration: 'if there are human actions at all, and at least some actions are actions we perform by performing other actions, then there must be basic actions.'[20] If this were not the case, then the 'by-relation' could be traced back *ad infinitum*, which it cannot, if agents are to be seen as intervening at certain points in the causal chains which link the events of the world. One's basic actions can, for our purposes, be identified with one's bringing about of one's own bodily movements, and one's non-basic actions with one's bringing about of events as a result of one's bodily movements.[21] The unifier–multiplier controversy turns on the relationship between basic and non-basic actions. According to Davidson, any non-basic action is *identical* to the basic action by means of which it is performed. To take a well-known example, if I flip a switch, turn on the light, illuminate the room, and alert a prowler, 'I need not have done four things, but only one, of which four descriptions have been given', in which case we can say that my illuminating the room *is* my flipping of the switch.[22] Davidson's view, then, is that 'we never do more than move our bodies',[23] the reason for this being that the only thing the agent can truly be said to have 'done' in bringing about a chain of events is the bodily movement which initiates that chain. Once begun, the events that make up an action chain are out of the agent's hands. To take another example, where the queen kills the sleeping king by pouring poison into his ear, 'is it not absurd to suppose that, after the queen has moved her hand in such a way as to cause the king's death, any deed remains for her to do or complete? She has done her work; it only remains for the poison to do its.'[24]

This contrasts with the view of Alvin Goldman, the leading proponent of the multiplier thesis, according to whom two act-tokens represent numerically distinct actions if they are tokens of different act-types. An act-type 'is simply an act-property, a property such as moving one's arm' and an act-token 'consists in the exemplifying of an act-property by an agent at a particular time'.[25] This

[19] The performance of a basic action is therefore direct and unmediated, in the same way as is the knowledge acquired through a basic cognition (see A. C. Danto, *Analytical Philosophy of Action* (Cambridge: Cambridge University Press, 1973)).

[20] J. Annas, 'How Basic are Basic Actions?', *Proceedings of the Aristotelian Society*, 78 (1977–8), 195.

[21] Not all philosophers of action agree on this point. For Hornsby, for example, basic actions take place inside the body, and consist in 'trying' to do things (see her *Actions*). But this difference does not affect my present analysis, as long as it is admitted that basic actions involve *some* kind of movement, be these movements inside the body or movements of the body itself.

[22] Davidson, *Essays on Actions and Events*, 4.   [23] Ibid. 59.

[24] Ibid. 57–8.

[25] A. I. Goldman, *A Theory of Human Action* (Englewood Cliffs, NJ: Prentice Hall, 1970), 10.

means that for Goldman my flipping the switch and my illuminating the room are two different actions. Goldman does not deny that there is a distinctive relationship between actions like these. However, rather than identifying them, he prefers to see one action as 'level-generating' the other, and goes on to distinguish between four kinds of 'level-generation': causal generation (such as when a shooting generates a killing), conventional generation (such as when 'John's extending his arm' generates 'John's signalling for a turn'), augmentation generation (such as when 'John's extending his arm' generates 'John's extending his arm out of the window'), and simple generation (such as when 'John's jumping 6 feet 3 inches' generates 'John's outjumping George').[26]

There may appear to be a problem here, in that while the multiplier thesis clearly allows for too many actions for our purposes, the unifier thesis appears to exclude too many. That the multiplier thesis allows for too many actions is clear from the fact that according to that thesis, every act-description is a description of a different action. This leads us straight into the problem of indefinite numbers of descriptions. On the other hand, in terms of degrees of freedom, the unifier thesis seems intuitively to go too far in the other direction, by identifying *all* level-generated actions with basic actions. It is not clear that we should like to say that freedom consists in the absence of constraints on basic actions alone. If my available bodily movements have counterfactual consequences which yours are prevented from having, we should like to say that I have more freedom than you in this respect. And yet, if the counterfactual consequences of my available bodily movements are, as actions, to be identified with my bodily movements themselves, those counterfactual consequences will not confer on me any *additional* available actions. Davidson's theory of act-individuation is often praised for its ontological parsimony, and ontological parsimony is certainly what is needed in order to overcome the problem of indefinite numbers of descriptions. For it is only on Davidson's theory that we shall be able to say that there is a definite number of available actions (subject to our solving the other two problems of act-individuation) despite there being an indefinite number of act-descriptions. But might that theory not turn out to be *too* parsimonious to allow for isomorphism with our common-sense comparisons of overall freedom? Should we really say that the set of available actions is no larger than the set of available basic actions?

There are two possible solutions to this problem. The first is to say that the freedom measurer should take account of causal generation, but not of the other three kinds of level-generation identified by Goldman—in other words, that only an action generated by 'convention', by 'augmentation', or

---

[26] Goldman, *A Theory of Human Action*, 24–8.

'simply', is identical, for the purpose of measuring freedom, to the action which generates it. According to this solution, 'John's signalling for a turn', when spatio-temporally specified, will be seen as a redescription of 'John's extending his arm', but a shooting and a killing, even if they are the bringing about of causally related events, will be seen as two different actions.[27] What appears to be distinctive about causal generation is that an action generated in this way always has further physical components, in addition to the physical components of the action which generates it, and to be in possession of the physical components of actions is, on the empirical approach, to have freedom.[28] The freedom to kill, for example, as opposed to the freedom to shoot, requires access to physical things such as the space between the gun and the victim's body, and the victim's body itself.

The problem with this first solution is that it is difficult to think of the shooting and the killing as distinct actions once it has been admitted that actions are spatio-temporally located particulars. For at this point, the unifiers will raise familiar objections regarding the temporal location of actions. They will point out that non-basic actions do not take place *after* the basic actions that level-generate them: if John killed George by shooting him (i.e. if John's shooting George level-generated John's killing George), then John's action of killing George took place when John shot George, and indeed when he squeezed the trigger. This will be so even if George did not die until a day after the shooting. For how can John be said to be still 'killing George' a day later, when George dies? This makes him 'sound like a fiendish torturer rather than a poor shot'.[29] And what if *John* were to die immediately after the shooting (and before George dies)? Dead people cannot perform actions.[30] Even some multipliers admit that level-generated actions take place at the same time as the actions that level-generate them.[31] Assuming that these arguments are correct—that the killing (as distinct from the death) took place when John shot George—*and* that actions are spatio-temporally located particulars, how can the shooting and the killing not be identical? Goldman can say that a causally generated action takes place at the same time as the action which generates it *and* that the two actions are numerically distinct, because he conceives of

[27] This solution appears to be endorsed by Gorr in *Coercion, Freedom and Exploitation*, 114 n. 27.
[28] Steiner, 'Individual Liberty', 48; id., *An Essay on Rights*, ch. 2.
[29] N. Richards, '*E Pluribus Unum*: A Defense of Davidson's Individuation of Action', *Philosophical Studies*, 29 (1976), 195.
[30] Cf. J. Hornsby, 'Actions and Identities', *Analysis*, 39 (1979), 198.
[31] See, in particular, Goldman, *A Theory of Human Action*, 21. For a dissenting view, see J. J. Thomson, 'The Time of a Killing', *Journal of Philosophy*, 68 (1971). For counter-arguments, see L. B. Lombard, 'Actions, Results and the Time of a Killing', *Philosophia* (Israel), 8 (1978).

actions as exemplifications of act-properties, rather than as spatio-temporally specified particulars. But we cannot say both of these things if we instead conceive of actions as spatio-temporally specified particulars—as we must, if we are to overcome the problem of indefinite numbers of descriptions.

A second solution, which is more coherent with the unifier thesis, consists in rejecting the notion of causal generation along with the other kinds of level-generation, but also thinking of a longer action chain as constituting a single action that should be assigned a greater *weight* for the purpose of measuring freedom, where that weight is a function of the physical dimensions of the events caused by the agent's relevant bodily movement. This solution accommodates the common-sense view that the extent of my freedom is not just a function of the extent of my available bodily movements—the view on the basis of which Davidson's theory was called over-parsimonious—by saying that different available basic actions contribute in differing degrees to my overall freedom in virtue of the extensiveness of the events of which those basic actions are the 'bringing about'.

Now, despite this second solution being theoretically superior in terms of coherence with the unifier thesis, it is important to notice that in practical terms (that is, as far as the measurement of freedom is concerned) it makes no difference whether one endorses the second solution or the first, since the resultant measurements will always be identical in the two cases. To see this, we have to bring in a further consideration about the way in which the actions available to an agent should be aggregated. That consideration has to do with the *compossibility* of those actions.

For two things to be compossible, they must both be members of a single possible world, which is to say that they must be possible in combination. Steiner has already done much to show the importance of the notion of compossibility for political philosophy, above all through his work on the compossibility of rights as a necessary requirement of any acceptable theory of justice.[32] His specification of the conditions under which two or more rights are compossible itself rests on a theory about the conditions under which two or more *actions* (of different people) are compossible.[33] However, he does not appear to take advantage of the applicability of the idea of the compossibility of actions (here, of the same person) to the assessment of degrees of overall freedom.

If a set of actions is compossible, then there is a possible world in which they all occur. For any set of compossible actions, we can ask whether that

---

[32] H. Steiner, 'The Structure of a Set of Compossible Rights', *Journal of Philosophy*, 74 (1977); id., *An Essay on Rights*, ch. 3; M. Kramer et al., *A Debate over Rights: Philosophical Enquiries* (Oxford: Oxford University Press, 1998).

[33] Steiner, *An Essay on Rights*, 33.

set of actions is prevented or unprevented for (unavailable or available to) a given individual. We can say that the individual is free to perform that set of compossible actions if she is not restrained by the relevant 'preventing conditions' from bringing it about that the actual world is one of the possible worlds that contains that set. The conditions under which two actions should, for our purposes, be seen as compossible are a matter of debate on which I need not pronounce here. That two actions are compossible might be taken to mean that they are logically compossible, or that they are nomically compossible, or that they are technologically compossible. This will depend on how we interpret the denominator of Steiner's formula (as discussed in the previous section).

To see the relevance of the compossibility of a single agent's available actions to her extent of overall freedom, consider the following three actions: (*a*) walking down the street at time *t*; (*b*) stealing a beer from the shop at *t*+1, (*c*) walking away from the shop at *t*+2. Assume that I am free to perform all three of these actions in combination, whereas you are not, because you are being followed by a policeman who would arrest you if you performed (*b*), so preventing you from performing (*c*). Assume, also, that there is nothing stopping you from performing (*c*) if you refrain from performing (*b*). Each of us is free to perform (*a*), free to perform (*b*), and free to perform (*c*). Yet intuitively, it is clear that I am freer than you (in a purely empirical sense) in terms of the availability of these actions. The reason for this is that we feel that freedom judgements should take account not only of the single actions available to an individual agent, but also of the *act combinations* available to her. Some possible act combinations are 'and/or' options; we can perform either one or the other or both (or neither). Others are 'or only' options; we can perform only one or the other (or neither). Others still are 'and only' options; we can only choose to perform both actions (or neither). The way in which we can take account of this fact in our measurements of freedom is by saying that a person's freedom is a function not simply of the number of actions she is constrained and unconstrained from performing, but rather, of the number and size of the *sets of compossible actions* she is constrained and unconstrained from performing. Thus, in the above example, assuming neither of us is free to perform (*b*) or (*c*) without first performing (*a*), I have available the sets of compossible actions (*a*), (*a b*), (*a c*), (*a b c*), whereas you only have available the sets of compossible actions (*a*), (*a b*), (*a c*). Aggregating over sets of compossible actions instead of over single actions allows us to accommodate the basic common-sense comparison according to which, in the above example, *ceteris paribus*, I am freer than you.

This point about compossibility, which is of considerable importance for the analysis of unfreedom proposed in the next chapter, suggests that we should revise Steiner's formula as follows. The extent of Red's freedom, we should say, is equal to the value of

$$\sum_{i=1}^{n} F_{r,i} \bigg/ \left(\sum_{i=1}^{n} F_{r,i} + \sum_{i=1}^{n} U_{r,i} \right)$$

where $F_{r,i}$ stands for the number of sets of compossible actions available to Red of which a specific action, i, is a member, and $U_{r,i}$ stands for the number of sets of compossible actions unavailable to Red, of which i is a member.

We can now return to the unifier–multiplier controversy, and to the two solutions, proposed above, to the problem posed by the fact that the unifier thesis appears to exclude too many act-descriptions. The first solution was to see causally generated actions (but not actions generated in other ways) as being distinct from the basic actions that generate them. The second solution was to admit that Davidson is right in seeing each and every action as identical with some basic action, but to add that basic actions can differ in terms of the extent of freedom their availability provides, in virtue of the extensiveness of the events of which they are the 'bringing about'. The second solution is the one that is strictly consistent with Davidson's theory of action. But the first solution will serve our purposes better, as we shall see later on, in particular in ss. 7.6 and 7.7.

In what sense can it be coherent for a unifier to adopt the first solution? The answer is that the first solution is adequate, to all intents and purposes, as far as the measurement of freedom is concerned. To see this, we need to bring in the above point about compossibility, and note that generationally related acts are only ever performable in combination. The separate elements of what Goldman would call a chain of causally generated actions are themselves components of a single Davidsonian action, and on the second solution, the number assigned to any single Davidsonian action will be equal to the sum of the numbers assigned to those separate components. Given this, if we count the separate components as distinct actions (in line with the first solution) we should not in theory produce measurements that differ in any way from those implied by the second solution. This is because *two generationally related actions must always be members of the same set of compossible actions.* Where x and y are generationally related actions, x's membership of any given set implies y's membership, and x's exclusion from any given set implies y's exclusion. As long as we recognize that the components of an action chain are not separately performable, we can count them as distinct actions purely for the purpose of measuring freedom, and without producing measurements that conflict with the unifier thesis. In adopting the second solution, what we shall be doing, strictly speaking, is counting spatio-temporally specific *events*.

But these will all be events that the agent is free or unfree to bring about in certain combinations and not in others. In effect, this is the same as counting sets of compossible (individually weighted) Davidsonian actions.

7.3 THE PROBLEM OF INDEFINITE SUBDIVISION

We have seen that the problem of adding indefinite numbers of act-descriptions to the list of actions that a person is free and unfree to perform can be overcome in a way that is in tune with the spirit of the empirical approach. This can be done by first of all restricting ourselves to spatio-temporally specified descriptions of actions (and calling all other descriptions of actions *re*descriptions), and then considering the list of actions the agent is free and unfree to perform as a list of sets of compossible actions, so as to produce measurements that are compatible with Davidson's 'unifier thesis' of act-individuation. Solving this first problem is, however, not sufficient to render either Steiner's formula or our revised version of it a feasible model for freedom measurement. We have said that we are to describe actions in terms of the spatio-temporally specified physical movements of which they are the 'bringing about'. But that means that we must now face up to the problem of space and time being indefinitely divisible, which suggests that the set of actions I am free to perform and the set of actions I am unfree to perform are each of an arbitrary size. On one account I might be very free, on another I might be very unfree, and we would seem to be left with no acceptable criterion for judging between these accounts. Steiner says that while the list of actions which a prisoner is prevented from doing is 'indefinitely long', it is also true 'that there is an indefinitely long list . . . of actions which this individual is not prevented from doing', and that this second list is 'not as long as the previous one'.[34] But we do not yet seem to have sufficient grounds for saying that the second list is 'not as long'.

In order to overcome this problem, we need to explore the idea of the 'physical dimensions' of actions referred to in Chapter 5. In this connection, it is useful to follow Morris Cohen and Ernest Nagel in classifying measurable qualities as either *intensive* or *extensive*. Where a quality is *extensive*, it is possible to *add* one instance of it to another. This possibility of an addition or 'concatenation' operation allows us to say *how much* of a certain quality an object possesses. Thus, for example, if using a balance we have found that object b is equal in weight to object c, and we also now find that $b+c$ (b concatenated with c) is equal in weight to object a, then the number we assign

---

[34] Steiner, 'Individual Liberty', 45.

to the weight of *a* should be twice that assigned to the weight of *b*.[35] The measurement of an extensive quality involves an *empirical counting procedure*. It is on the basis of the counting of individual units which have been demonstrated to be of equal size (by reference to certain physical dimensions) that we can say that one object possesses 'more of', or 'much more of', a certain extensive quality than another object. An *intensive* quality is one that cannot be measured by means of such an empirical counting procedure. Examples of intensive qualities are the hardness of rocks or the intelligence or pleasure of human beings. The measurement of intensive qualities is generally seen as more complex and problematic than that of extensive qualities, and this partly explains the difficulties involved in attempting to measure utility. Some have indeed suggested that cardinal measurements of intensive qualities are impossible, or even that in the case of intensive qualities one should not talk of 'measurement' at all.[36]

It seems to me that offhand scepticism about the idea of measuring freedom is often motivated by the vague, pre-theoretical belief that overall freedom is an intensive quality. The upshot of the foregoing Steinerian analysis, on the other hand, is that overall freedom is an extensive quality. The basic idea behind the empirical method that emerged from the discussion in Chapter 5—the basic idea that we are here trying to make sense of—is, after all, that the degree of a person's freedom depends on how 'extensive' the actions available to her are. The measurement of an extensive quality requires, as we have seen, the individuation of units of that quality that can, at least in theory, be concatenated. In order to provide measurements of extents of action, then, we need to divide space and time into equally sized units, and matter into equally sized units that are at least as small as the units of space. Depending on their size, physical objects will then consist in varying numbers of units of matter, and what we shall be interested in measuring is, for any particular unit of matter, the number of space-time units in which it might be located as a result of hypothetical (prevented or unprevented) actions on the part of the agent. In effect, we shall not be measuring possible motions as such (despite the fact that events are often thought to consist in motions); rather, we shall be counting possible 'occupyings'. Space and time must be thought of as an immobile *grid*, made up of a finite series of spatio-temporal *regions*. A physical object of a standard volume can then be seen as a potential occupant of one or another spatio-temporally fixed region.

[35] M. R. Cohen and E. Nagel, *An Introduction to Logic and Scientific Method* (New York: Harcourt Brace, 1934), 293–7; cf. Coombs et al., *Mathematical Psychology*, 10–11.

[36] This last view is expressed, for example, by N. R. Campbell, in *An Account of the Principles of Measurement and Calculation* (London: Longmans, Green, 1928). It is criticized by D. H. Krantz et al. in *Foundations of Measurement*, i (London: Academic Press, 1971).

This solution to the problem of the actual infinity of movements open to a person has been suggested by Jonathan Bennett, according to whom 'if space and time were *granular*, there would only be finitely many positions that a person's body could occupy'.[37] Bennett says that he would not like to bet on space and time really being granular, and neither should I. What I do mean to suggest is that we need to *think of* space and time *as* granular in order to produce measurements of the 'extensiveness of available action' that reflect our common-sense perceptions of that same phenomenon. In measuring 'extents of available action', we are not interested in getting to the heart of what physical movements 'really' consist in. We are not interested, for example, in the possible movements of protons or electrons. Rather, we are interested in producing mathematical representations of possible movements of matter as we commonly conceive of them.

While it is true that space and time can in theory be divided up indefinitely, then, the division of space and time into equal finite units allows us to represent what we do as a matter of fact see as the possibility of greater or lesser possibilities of movement. The fact that a finite quantity of space can be divided up indefinitely is not something that stops us from saying that it is greater or smaller than another finite quantity of space; if I can move my arm anywhere within a space of a given size, and you can move yours anywhere within a space twice as large (leaving aside the dimension of time), then we will want to say that you have twice as much available action as me in this respect, and the division of space into equal units is something that will allow us to say this.

I should add, in line with the discussion in the previous section, that we shall have to take into account the *compossibility* of the various locations of the various units of matter determinable by the agent's actions. Thus, for example, I may be free to determine the various spatio-temporal locations of a particular unit of matter which forms part of a door that I am free to open or shut, but I am free to determine those locations only in combination with the determining of certain specific locations of the other units of matter which make up the door. If I can only open or shut the door, then the number of combinations will be relatively low. If I am given an axe, with which to chop up the door, then that number will greatly increase. If the door is a Dutch door rather than a standard door, the number will be somewhere in between.

In order to anticipate the objection that I am being wildly optimistic about the feasibility of such intricate measurements and calculations (while also registering my suspicion that physicists and computing technologists will be less impressed by such an objection than the average moral or political philosopher

---

[37] J. Bennett, *The Act Itself* (Oxford: Clarendon Press, 1995), 93, my emphasis.

might be), it should also be said that nothing in the foregoing analysis fixes the *size* of the space-time units on the basis of which we are to make our comparisons. Clearly, the smaller the units we are working with, the more accurate our measurements will be in reflecting what is commonly meant by 'the extent of movement available to us'. Ideally, the units will be smaller than any of the distances of the movements (or differences in sizes of objects) that we are interested in measuring. They will be smaller, for instance, than Jones's thumbs in Arneson's Smith–Jones example (see ss. 5.1 and 5.4), if Jones is to be represented as having any freedom at all. But the only absolute requirement contained in what has been said so far is that the space-time units be of an equal size. This equal size might be increased for practical purposes, as long as one is aware that the measurements one is producing increase in roughness along with increases in the size of the units. An example of a judgement made on the basis of rather larger units than the size of Jones's thumbs is provided by Felix Oppenheim, who, despite his scepticism about the possibility of measuring *overall* freedom, nevertheless suggests that the freedom to visit a museum which is closed on Mondays (and thus open only six days out of seven) can be represented (by means of Steiner's formula) as $6/6+1=0.857$.[38] If the curator of the museum locks one of the rooms of the museum but leaves people free to visit the other rooms, or if he further limits museum visits to mornings only, then these additional constraints will not be reflected in measurements which assume as their units of time and space, respectively, 'the days' on which one is free to visit 'the museum'. Such additional constraints would, on the other hand, be reflected in measurements which counted 'the hours' in which one is free to visit 'this room' or 'that room' of the museum. So the degree of accuracy of our measurements, even at the level of purely conceptual theory, will clearly depend on the size of the units we adopt.

Finally, it should be borne in mind that in counting future possible actions we are necessarily counting future possible *act-types* rather than future possible *act-tokens*. This will be so whatever the size of the units we assume, given that those units must be finitely (not infinitely) small. It is implied, in other words, by the very fact that we are looking at events that occur *within* certain spatio-temporal *regions* rather than *at* certain spatio-temporal *points*. The boundaries of the act-types to be counted are set by the size and location of the various units of space-time and the particular units of matter that may occupy them. Counting (spatio-temporally bound) act-types rather than (spatio-temporally pinpointed) act-tokens is necessary if we are to make any sense at all of the basic intuition that different agents have available different

[38] F. Oppenheim, 'La libertà sociale ed i suoi parametri', *Sociologia del Diritto*, 22 (1995), 26.

'extents of action'. For the number of act-tokens available to us is nearly always infinite, given that each act-token occurs at an exact point in space-time, and the number of points in space-time is itself infinite.

Because they are described by reference to specific, equally sized units of space-time, the counting of act-types rather than act-tokens does not compromise the empirical approach to measuring freedom. We should only compromise the empirical approach if we were to count act-types as Goldman conceives of them. An act-type is, as Goldman says, simply an act-property. But the only kind of act-property *we* should be interested in is that of making a physical object, *x*, occupy or not occupy a fixed spatio-temporal region, *y*. This is the only sense of 'act-type' that is relevant to the concerns of the overall-freedom measurer. It remains an act-type, because it might still be exemplified by any number of act-tokens each of which is the moving of object *x* to cover a set of specific spatio-temporal points within region *y*. But it is not just any kind of act-type, because it is itself nevertheless described spatio-temporally. Thus, to return to the example of the museum visit, what we should do is count, say, the act-type of visiting room A in the museum next Tuesday morning, and ignore all of the possible tokens of visiting room A next Tuesday morning (each of which involves different possible movements, and their combinations, in room A next Tuesday morning); what we should *not* do is count the act-type of visiting room A in the museum next Tuesday morning, and the act-type of broadening our cultural knowledge next Tuesday morning, and the act-type of doing what is expected of us next Tuesday morning, and so on and so forth. For this would lead us back into the problem of indefinite numbers of descriptions dealt with in the previous section.

The method I have proposed here for making sense of the notion of extents of possible action is analogous to that employed in certain probabilistic calculations concerning the time or location of possible events. Consider the case of a clock face with a hand which can be spun and which will come to rest at a certain place. Given that the number of *points* at which the hand may come to rest is infinite, the probability of its landing on the figure '4' on the clock face is equal to $1/\infty = 0$. But this does not stop us laying bets on 'where' the hand will come to rest. For we are still able to assess the probability of the hand coming to rest between two points. We can still say, for example, that the probability of the hand coming to rest between the figures '4' and '5' is equal to $1/12 = 0.083$, and that the probability of its coming to rest between the figures '4' and '6' is equal to $1/6 = 0.167$. In the same way, we can avoid the conclusion that every person with at least a minimal range of possible action is infinitely free (because free to perform any of an infinite number of actions), by referring not to possible actions that are located at certain spatio-temporal points (i.e. to possible act-tokens), but to possible actions that are located within certain spatio-temporal regions (and which are, in *this* sense, act-types).[39]

7.4 THE PROBLEM OF INDEFINITE CAUSAL CHAINS

Finally, there is the problem that action chains might in theory continue for ever. No one lives for ever, but that does not stop an action chain continuing for ever, since, as we have seen, the time of a causally generated action is the time of the basic action that generates it, and this means that I can be free to perform an action now which is, among other things, the bringing about of a chain of events which in part occurs after my death.

It seems to me that resignation in the face of such a problem rests on a failure to see the acceptability and usefulness of assessing freedom in terms of the *foreseeable* consequences of given possible (or actual) actions, rather than in terms of what *would actually happen* (or does actually happen) as a consequence of the performance of such actions. If we try to look at what *would* happen (or does happen) as a result of our possible (or actual) basic actions, we shall indeed not solve the problem of indefinite causal chains, since it is true that what would happen (or does happen) might consist in never-ending chains of events. Notice, however, that the fact of our not knowing everything about what would happen as a result of the basic actions people are known to be free or unfree to perform does not prevent us from making *common-sense comparisons* of their degrees of overall freedom. And it would surely be bizarre to think that such common-sense comparisons are invalidated by this limitation in our knowledge. After all, as we saw in Chapter 2, this very kind of limitation in our knowledge contributes to making freedom valuable in such a way as to create an interest in making comparisons in the first place. A more sensible way to proceed is by taking a closer look at our common-sense comparisons and seeing why we make them even in the face of the problem of indefinite causal chains. And the answer to this question, it seems to me, is to be found in the fact that in making such comparisons we implicitly limit the list of consequences of possible basic actions to those that we *foresee* as occurring in the event of the basic actions being performed. If this is so, then the presence of indefinitely long causal chains will not be sufficient to invalidate assessments of overall freedom made with respect to a list of *known* available and unavailable actions. As Steiner says, 'a doctor

---

[39] Steiner appears to suggest that the measurement of overall freedom involves the counting of possible act-*tokens* (*An Essay on Rights*, 43–4). While the last three paragraphs contradict such a view, they do not represent a fundamental disagreement with Steiner, given that I favour the specification of the spatio-temporal dimensions of the act-types to be counted.

does not reserve judgement on whether a patient is healthy merely on the grounds that the latter may be afflicted with a disease as yet unknown to medical science. And one is correspondingly unwarranted in refraining from extent-of-freedom judgements because there may be some unknown actions which [agent] Red is free or unfree to do.'[40]

More precisely, it seems reasonable to limit the counting of causally generated actions, for the purpose of measuring freedom, to those that could in principle be foreseen *at the time at which the agent has the degree of freedom under investigation*. As well as the actions an agent is free to perform, the agent's freedom itself has a temporal location: an agent is free *at time t* to do *x* at *t*+1. Thus, when we say at *t* that an agent is free at *t* to do *x* at *t*+1, we should also (at *t*) list any actions that would be causally generated by *x* and are foreseeable at time *t*. I do not mean by this that we should limit ourselves to listing consequences which could in principle be foreseen by the agent herself at *t*; only that we should limit ourselves to listing consequences which could be foreseen by *some* person—the best-informed person—at *t*.

The reason for this condition, specifying the *time* at which consequences must be foreseeable in order to be included in our list, is that we may be interested in comparing the freedom of agents who themselves have different temporal locations. Where *t* is the present, the above restriction is one to which we are in any case subject, whether we like it or not. But where *t* is some time in the past, then in order to put such assessments of past degrees of freedom on all fours with assessments of present degrees of freedom (so as to allow for valid intertemporal comparisons of freedom), we should disregard any consequences of basic actions about which we have come to know only with hindsight. Powers of foresight may of course not be the same at different times. In particular, some of them have been improved over time by the advance of science. But this fact need not in itself create a problem for intertemporal comparisons of freedom. As we have already seen more generally in relation to technological advances (at s. 7.1), new inventions do not necessarily imply increases in freedom; as long as we see freedom as the absence of humanly imposed constraints, they simply imply that more actions get added to the list of things that the agent is either free *or un*free to do.

7.5 PROBABILITY

This last point, about the limits to our knowledge of the future, is one which should also be generalized to cover the question of *whether or not* we are free

---

[40] Steiner, 'How Free', 74.

to perform *known* possible actions. Not only is it the case that we are unable to foresee a great many of the counterfactual consequences of our possible basic actions, so that these consequences cannot be taken into account in our assessments of overall freedom; it is also the case that, for those counterfactual consequences that we *can* foresee, we can never be absolutely sure whether we are at present free or unfree to bring them about. This applies as much to known possible basic actions as to known possible causally generated actions. Now the extension of our limited knowledge of the future to cover the question of whether we are free or unfree to perform given actions is again not a sufficient reason for abstaining from making judgements about overall freedom. What it does imply is that our common-sense comparisons of freedom implicitly contain *probabilistic judgements*—i.e. judgements about the probability of being prevented from performing certain future actions—and that measurements of overall freedom should incorporate such probabilistic judgements too.

For the same reason as that given above in the previous section—in order to allow for intertemporal comparisons—such probabilistic judgements should be the best-informed judgements that could be made at the time at which the agent in question has (or had) the degree of freedom we are interested in measuring. Clearly, where possible the probabilistic judgements should be statistical in nature, although recourse might be had to judgements of so-called subjective probability where statistical judgements are impossible (as, for example, in the case of unique events). The latter alternative is still preferable to assuming that the agent is certainly free or certainly unfree to perform a given action. While it would inevitably involve compromising the supposed impersonal basis for degree-of-freedom judgements, we should bear in mind that the subjectivity of such judgements would be constrained by the relevant body of information.

Probabilities can be integrated into our revised version of Steiner's formula (see s. 7.2) by imitating the way utility theorists compare certain utility gains with probable ones. In assigning numbers to the symbols $F_{r,i}$ and $U_{r,i}$ in our formula, we should take account, for each known set of compossible actions of which i is a member, of the probability of that known set being available or unavailable (respectively) to the agent. This means multiplying the number assigned to a given set of compossible actions (that is, the number of equally sized spatio-temporally specific events of which it constitutes the 'bringing about' —see s. 7.3) by the probability of that set being prevented or unprevented. In formal terms, then, the value of $F_{r,i}$ (in our revised version of Steiner's formula) will be equal to

$$\sum_{s=1}^{n} sp$$

and the value of $U_{r,i}$ will be equal to

$$\sum_{s=1}^{n} s(1-p)$$

where s stands for a set of compossible actions of which i is a member, and p stands for the probability of the agent being unprevented from performing s.

The implications of incorporating probabilistic judgements in this way will become especially clear in the next chapter, where we come to look at different kinds of constraints on freedom, and in particular where we come to look at the so-called 'republican' conception of constraints (s. 8.6).

7.6 DIFFERENT WAYS OF DOING THE SAME THING

There is a further problem of act-individuation that has not been dealt with in the arguments between unifiers and multipliers. This is the question of whether or not there can be different ways of doing the same thing. Where I have the choice of doing x *either* by doing y *or* by doing z, is 'x' in each case a different action, or is it the same action? The gruesome metaphorical saying that 'there's more than one way to skin a cat' might be true on some definitions of 'an action' and false on others. It seems to me that those sympathetic to the empirical approach ought to want to defend the idea that there can be different ways of doing the same thing, given that to deny this would result, intuitively, in the double counting of available actions. If I am free to do x in one of two ways, would we not be engaging in double counting if we said that 'my freedom to do x' here counts for two freedoms rather than one? The fact that most of us would answer in the affirmative needs to be taken into account by the empirical approach. This, not only because of the importance of the basic intuition underlying such an answer, but also because our ability to accommodate it will have useful implications for our analysis of the idea of 'significant differences' between options (see ss. 5.1 and 7.8).

The truth of the metaphorical saying about cat-skinning will of course be uncontroversial if we assume that 'skin a cat' refers to an act-type in Goldman's sense, as indeed it does in many of the situations in which the saying is used. There can easily be different ways of performing the same act-type in Goldman's sense; all that one needs for this is to have available two alternative act-tokens of that act-type. What I have in mind, however, is the rather more precise claim that there can be different possible spatio-temporally specified causal chains each leading to the same possible spatio-temporally specified event (where, in line with the analysis proposed in s. 7.3, a 'spatio-temporally specified event' means an event that occurs somewhere within a given spatio-temporal *region*). What the empirical approach needs to accommodate is the idea that where two such possible spatio-temporally specified causal chains converge in this way, the freedom to bring about one or the other of them is in some sense a freedom that gives us different ways of doing the same thing.

Is it possible for unifiers to say that there are, in this last sense of the expression, 'different ways of doing the same thing'? This might be thought to be problematic, as a consideration of the following example will show. Imagine that I am in a position to fire a bullet from my gun by squeezing the trigger either with my right hand or with my left hand, and that in each of these two hypothetical scenarios, the movement of the bullet out of the gun and through the air occurs within the same (freedom-relevant) spatio-temporal region. The two hypothetical scenarios can be mapped out as follows:

(*b*) I fire a bullet   (*d*) I fire a bullet
  ↑   ↑
  | |
  | |
(*a*) I move my left index finger   (*c*) I move my right index finger

The basic intuition that we would like to see accommodated by the empirical approach is that (*b*) and (*d*) are identical, and therefore that to count (*b*) and (*d*) as two separate available actions would be to engage in double counting. However, we have seen that, for the unifer, (*a*) is identical to (*b*) and (*c*) is identical to (*d*). As Davidson would put it, there is nothing 'more' that I have to do, having once squeezed the trigger, in order to make the bullet fly through the air, and therefore no reason to see (*b*) as an action that is distinct from (*a*) (or to see (*c*) as an action that is distinct from (*d*)). It follows that if we say in addition that (*b*)=(*d*), then (assuming transitivity) we shall have to say that (*a*)=(*c*), which is absurd. Clearly the only way to deny that (*b*) and (*d*) are distinct is by denying that (*a*) and (*b*) are identical. However, to deny the identity of (*a*) and (*b*) would be to deny the unifier thesis. Therefore, the unifier thesis appears to be incompatible with the commonsensical idea, expressed above, that there can be different ways of doing the same thing.

It might be objected that, even from the point of view of the multiplier, the identity of (*b*) and (*d*) would be unacceptable, given that it would contradict Leibniz's Law, according to which if two things are identical then everything that can be predicated of one can be predicated of the other and vice versa. For it can be predicated of (*b*), but not of (*d*), that it is level-generated by (*a*). However, it is possible to accommodate Leibniz's Law by distinguishing between intrinsic and extrinsic properties—where the extrinsic properties of objects are irrelevant to their identity conditions. This is the way in which Saul Kripke establishes his distinction between 'rigid' and 'non-rigid' designators, where a rigid designator is 'a term that designates the same object in all possible worlds'.[41] Applying the distinction between intrinsic and extrinsic properties to the problem at hand, we can say that the fact of being level-generated by x is an extrinsic property of action y (where x level-generates y) and thus that $(b)=(d)$ consistently with a version of Leibniz's Law. This at least makes it possible for the multiplier (though not yet for the unifier) to say that $(b)=(d)$.

The only way for the unifier to agree that there can be different ways of doing the same thing (assuming that we are talking about actions and events as spatio-temporally located particulars) is by endorsing a particular interpretation of the expression 'doing the same thing'—one which, as we shall see, distinguishes between 'performing an action' and 'bringing about an event'. The basic idea behind this interpretation is that while the *actions* (b) and (d) are not identical, the *events* of which they denote the 'bringing about' *are* identical. Consider the following two sets of hypothetical *events*, where events (q) and (s) involve the same bullet and occur within the same spatio-temporally specified region:

(q) a bullet flies through the air	(s) a bullet flies through the air
$\uparrow$	$\uparrow$
(p) my left index finger squeezes the trigger	(r) my right index finger squeezes the trigger

We have seen that it is logically impossible for the unifier to assert the identity of (b) and (d). My point, however, is that it is possible for the unifier to make some sense of the claim that there can be different ways of doing the same thing, by asserting the identity of (q) and (s). In order to substantiate this point, a brief parenthesis on the problem of event-identity is called for.

How should we construct a criterion of event-identity consistent with the identity of (q) and (s)? Davidson's own work on event-identity will not help us here. For, according to his proposed criterion, 'events are identical if and only if they have exactly the same causes and effects'.[42] This will mean that (q) and (s) are distinct events, since they have different causes. There has been much controversy over the validity of Davidson's criterion, centred, above all,

---

[41] S. Kripke, 'Identity and Necessity', in S. P. Schwartz (ed.), *Naming, Necessity and Natural Kinds* (London: Cornell University Press, 1977), 78. I assume, with Kripke, and in opposition to David Lewis, that we can make sense of trans-world identity, i.e. the idea that the same object or event can occur in different possible worlds (cf. D. Lewis, 'Counterpart Theory and Quantified Modal Logic', *Journal of Philosophy*, 65 (1968), 114).

[42] Davidson, *Essays on Actions and Events*, 179.

on the question of whether or not it is ultimately circular.[43] I shall not concern myself here with that controversy; my aim is simply to emphasize what appears to be an independent reason for abandoning the criterion, namely that it implies the distinctness of the hypothetical events (q) and (s). The unifier has no logical reason—similar to that given in the case of (b) and (d)—for denying the identity of (q) and (s), given that she does not assert the identity of (p) and (q) or of (r) and (s). Moreover, the identity of (q) and (s) ought to be intuitively compelling on a Davidsonian conception of events as particulars. Davidson suggests that his own criterion of event-identity helps to explain why we often talk of and describe events in terms of their causes and effects. The causes and effects of events help to individuate them, he says, 'in the sense not only of telling them apart but also of telling them together'.[44] This may be true of *actual* events, but it is, I suggest, much less true of *possible* events, such as the events that we are free to bring about. For while we do often describe events in terms of their causes and effects, it is also true that we often talk about being free or able to bring about the same result by different means, and it is quite conceivable for a person who talks in this way to be using the term 'same result' to refer to a hypothetical event-type defined by reference to a spatio-temporal region (as outlined in s. 7.3). It is even possible in theory (if unlikely in practice) for them to be using the term to refer to a hypothetical Davidsonian event-token.

In order to accommodate the identity of (q) and (s), we need an identity criterion that refers to the spatio-temporal location of events. What is therefore implied by the above consideration is, I would suggest, a variant on the criterion endorsed by Quine and originally rejected by Davidson, according to which a necessary and sufficient condition for events x and y being identical is that x and y cover the same space-time coordinates, and involve the same physical object(s).[45] This criterion is not *exactly* the same as Quine's, according to which events are identical if 'they take up the same place-time'. I have added 'and involve the same physical object(s)', in order to allow for the difference between two hypothetical events in different possible worlds which involve changes in two different objects over exactly the same space-time coordinates. The reference to physical objects in this alternative criterion will mean that the identification of physical objects is prior to the identification of events, in which case we ought not to agree with Quine's further claim that

[43] See e.g. Monroe Beardsley, 'Actions and Events: The Problem of Individuation', *American Philosophical Quarterly*, 12 (1975), 271, where the criterion is criticized as circular, and Pfeifer, *Actions and Other Events*, ch. 8, where the criterion is defended against this charge.

[44] Davidson, *Essays on Actions and Events*, 179.

[45] See ibid. 178–9; W. V. O. Quine, 'Events and Reification', in E. Le Pore and B. McLaughlin (eds.), *Actions and Events* (Oxford: Blackwell, 1985), 167.

events simply *are* physical objects.[46] My own proposed criterion remains true to Davidson's intuition that, 'occupying the same portion of space-time, event and object differ. One is an object which remains the same through changes, the other a change in an object or objects.'[47] I should also add that, for the purpose of measuring freedom, in line with the analysis proposed in s. 7.3, we should modify the criterion further, and say that two events (strictly, two event-types) are identical if they take place within the same space-time *region* and involve the same physical object(s).

Establishing the identity of (q) and (s) is, as I say, sufficient to allow the unifier to make some sense of the claim that there can be different ways of doing the same thing. To do so, what he needs to point out is that 'doing the same thing' might be taken to mean 'performing the same action' or it might be taken to mean 'bringing about the same event'. While for the unifier it is not possible to say that there are different ways of *performing the same action*, it is both possible and plausible for him to say that there are different ways of *bringing about the same event*. The term 'different ways' here refers to different *actions*, and we have seen that for the unifier two different actions cannot each be a way of performing the same action (in this he differs from the multiplier). What the unifier *can* say, however, is that the same hypothetical *event* (e.g. (q/s)), can be the result of either of two different hypothetical *actions* (e.g. either (a/b) or (c/d)). According to the unifier thesis, to perform a single action is to bring about a *set* (i.e. a chain) of events. And the two actions (a/b) and (c/d) are *not* the bringing about of the same set of events; they are merely two 'bringings about' of two respective sets of events that have in common a certain *subset* of events (i.e. at least (q/s)). These two sets of events are not coextensive, but intersect, hence the two hypothetical actions (a/b) and (c/d) are not identical, even though to perform either is to bring about (q/s).

Thus, whereas for the multiplier two different hypothetical actions can each be a level-generator of the same hypothetical action, unifiers can say that two different hypothetical actions can each be the bringing about of the same hypothetical event. In so far as 'doing the same thing' can be plausibly interpreted as meaning 'bringing about the same event', the unifier is able to make as much sense as the multiplier of the intuitively plausible claim that there can be different ways of doing the same thing.

We must, however, bear in mind the unifier's reason for distinguishing in the first place between performing an action and bringing about an event. To say that action (a) is the bringing about of event (q) is only to provide one

---

[46] Quine, 'Events and Reification', 167.

[47] D. Davidson, 'Reply to Quine on Events', in Le Pore and McLaughlin (eds.), *Actions and Events*, 176.

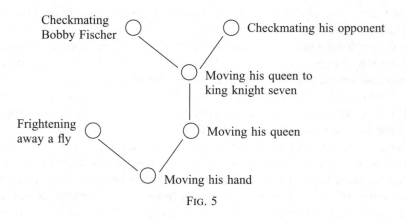

FIG. 5

among many possible descriptions of action (*a*). That is indeed how we are able to keep actions (*a*) and (*c*) distinct: (*a*) and (*c*) are the bringing about of one and the same particular event (*q/s*), but that only makes them identical under one description, whereas for (*a*) and (*c*) to be the *same action* they would have to be identical under *all* descriptions (at least, all those referring to their intrinsic properties). Any single action, for the unifier, is a 'bringing about' of a *set* of events, where to refer to the bringing about of any one member of that set is to provide a particular description of that single action. One might say, in the interests of clarity if not of elegance, that for the unifier two actions are identical if they are the same 'event-set bringing-about'.

7.7 ACT-TREES AND ACT-ROOTS

The discussion in the previous section shows that action possibilities are not in fact straightforward possibilities of bringing about single, isolated chains of events; typically, the chains of events we are free to bring about converge and diverge. In order to clarify this point further, we can make use of Goldman's notion of an 'act-tree', together with an additional notion, which I shall call that of an 'act-root'. In Goldman's terms, an act-tree maps out the various actions that are level-generated by a single basic action, where the 'trunk' of the tree represents the basic action and the 'branches' represent different examples of level-generation. Fig. 5 provides a simple example.[48] Here, the agent's moving his hand causally generates both his frightening away a fly and his moving his queen. (Recall that the actions in Fig. 5 which Goldman sees as in turn

[48] Fig. 5 is a simplified version of fig. 3 at p. 34 of Goldman's *A Theory of Human Action*.

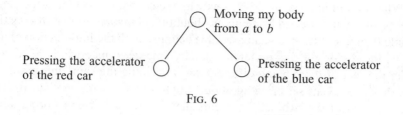

FIG. 6

level-generated by the moving of the queen should be disregarded by the freedom measurer, given that they are 'conventionally' rather than 'causally' generated.)

As a visual representation, an act-root looks rather like an inverted act-tree, and depicts what Goldman would call two or more possible ways of level-generating the same action. Fig. 6 gives an example, in which I am free to use either of two cars—a red car or a blue car—as a way of moving my body from *a* to *b*.

Act-roots, unlike act-trees, can only represent *hypothetical* sets of generational relations between actions (still assuming Goldman's conception of actions), and this perhaps explains their absence from Goldman's own analysis. Goldman's main concern is, after all, to provide an analysis upon which *explanations* of actions can be based, and, like most philosophers of action, he tends as a result to focus on actions that are actually performed. My focus, on the other hand, is on the actions that one is free to perform, which are necessarily actions that have not yet been performed. And it is clear that the structure of one's set of *future possible* actions is a structure that is normally made up of roots as well as trees.

Now on the Davidsonian account of action—which, we have seen, must be assumed in order to make sense of the empirical approach to measuring freedom—what Goldman calls a single act-tree is in fact a description of many facets of a single action. However, as we saw in s. 7.2, it is acceptable from a Davidsonian point of view to measure freedom by counting each of the distinct physical events of which an act-tree is the bringing about, as if the bringing about of each of these events were itself a distinct action. This amounts to counting causally generated actions *as if* they were distinct—for the purpose of measuring freedom—while admitting that such actions are, strictly speaking, identical. As we saw, the results of such a measurement strategy will not differ in any way from the measurements provided by a unifier who counts available act-trees but weights them according to the extensiveness of the events of which they are the bringing about. Those measurements will not differ, we saw, as long as we aggregate over sets of *compossible* actions, rather than simply over single actions.

What we did not see, in s. 7.2, was why the strategy of counting the single events an agent is free to bring about should be *preferable* to that of counting single (weighted) Davidsonian available actions. With the introduction of act-roots, the reason for this preference finally emerges. Once we come to consider the fact of there being different ways of doing the same thing, we can see that one 'event-set bringing-about' might *overlap* with another. In such a case, each of the two sets of events that the agent is free to bring about will have in common a particular subset of events, and we should like to avoid double counting the agent's freedom to bring about that subset. Therefore, the strategy of weighting single Davidsonian actions would in any case have to take account of this fact; even if we adopt this strategy, the weight deriving from the extensiveness of the above-mentioned subset of events ought not to be assigned to more than one Davidsonian action. And yet, it is not clear why two available Davidsonian actions, each of which is quite *distinct* from one another (despite an overlap in the event-sets of which they are the bringing about), and each of which is the bringing about of an *equally extensive* set of events, should be assigned *different weights*. We can circumvent this problem quite neatly by adopting the more straightforward solution of counting the separate events of which the agent's available actions are the bringing about.

7.8 THE VARIETY OF OPTIONS

We have now come far enough in our elaboration of the empirical approach to answer a number of possible objections from common-sense comparisons. These objections will form the subject matter of this section and the next. In dealing with them, I shall make extensive use of the analysis of action provided in the previous sections.

In this section, I shall deal with what might initially appear the most potent objection from common-sense comparisons: the objection which I raised and then immediately set aside at the end of s. 5.1, according to which the empirical approach fails to take account of the *variety* of the options available to an agent. The degree of variety of one's options is, the objection goes, a *qualitative* matter. It has to do with the degree to which one's options are *significantly different* from one another, and the notion of significant difference is a value-based notion.

To take an example, according to Richard Norman, an adherent of the value-based approach, an important reason for seeing a purely quantitative assessment of a person's options as an inadequate representation of her extent of freedom is the fact that some differences between options matter more than others. 'The person who has to choose between twenty-one brands of detergent is not to that extent freer', he says, 'than the person who has only seven brands to choose from, and this is because though the twenty-one brands may all be different in some respects, they are not likely to differ in ways which *matter*.'[49]

On this point, Norman has the support of G. A. Cohen. As we saw in Chapter 5, where Cohen comes down in favour of what I have called the 'hybrid approach', his claim is that the amount of one's freedom depends not only on the 'importance of one's choices', but also on 'the sheer number of significantly different choices' one has (see s. 5.4). Cohen clearly agrees with Norman that the *significance* of the differences between choices must come into play, even where we are assessing quantities rather than qualities of available actions.

In fact, the force of Cohen's claim is twofold, referring as it does both to the question of the feasibility of counting available actions and to that of isomorphism with common-sense comparisons. First, he is claiming that available actions can be neither individuated nor enumerated without taking into account the notion of significant difference. This claim is a consequence, above all, of the problems of indefinite numbers of descriptions and of indefinite subdivision—problems which, we have seen, the empirical approach can in fact overcome. Second, like Norman, he is claiming that even if we assume a non-arbitrary means of individuation of actions, counting the freedom to perform two actions that are not significantly different as 'two freedoms' amounts, intuitively, to double counting, or at least to an exaggeration of the agent's extent of freedom. It is this second claim that concerns us here.

Must we say, counter-intuitively, that the choice between twenty-one brands of washing powder provides more freedom than the choice between seven? Must we say that it provides *three times* as much? In fact, even on an empirical conception, the former choice may be seen as providing only very slightly more freedom than the latter. To see this, one needs to look not only at the agents' sets of available actions of which a box of washing powder is a physical component, but also at the actions that would be causally generated by them. Once we take these causally generated actions into account, it becomes clear that two sufficiently similar brands of washing powder provide us with *different means of doing the same thing*. If the analysis of 'act-roots' in the previous two sections is correct, this will mean that the acquisition of the freedom to use a second kind of washing powder adds much less to one's overall freedom than does the prior acquisition of the freedom to use *a* kind of washing powder. Most obviously (and not only), the new freedom to use the second kind of washing powder will not add to our option set the option of washing

[49] Norman, 'Liberty, Equality, Property', 201.

our clothes (with a certain degree of efficiency), in the way that the freedom to use the first kind of washing powder did. For this is an option that we already had when we were free only to use the first kind of washing powder. Indeed, if the two brands are identical in terms of what can be done with them, then the only additional action made available through the availability of the second brand (as an alternative to the first) will be that of taking it (rather than the first brand) off the supermarket shelf.

This same point applies to any number of other examples of so-called 'qualitative differences' between options, including that of the choice between the use of a red car and the use of a blue car referred to in the previous section. Prasanta Pattanaik and Yongsheng Xu use exactly this example in criticism of the empirical approach, suggesting that on such an approach the option set of travelling by (train, red car) provides no more freedom than the option set of travelling by (red car, blue car), and that this result is counter-intuitive.[50] The result would indeed be counter-intuitive, but it is not implied by the empirical approach, which takes account of the fact that the sets of events that the option of travelling in the red car and the option of travelling in the blue car respectively allow one to bring about intersect to a greater degree than do the sets of events that the option of travelling by train and the option of travelling in the red car respectively allow one to bring about.

Notice, furthermore, that the objection of Cohen and Norman can be answered not only by appeal to the case of qualitatively similar actions which *causally generate* other actions, but also by appeal to the case of qualitatively similar actions whose performance is a necessary precondition for the performance of *subsequent*, generationally distinct actions, where the performance of *any one* of the qualitatively similar actions is sufficient to provide such a precondition. An example of a set of qualitatively similar actions of the second kind might be that of riding a bicycle from *a* to *b* via many alternative routes. The acquisition of the freedom to ride the bicycle along a second route from *a* to *b* does not necessarily increase one's overall freedom as much as does the first-time acquisition of the freedom to ride the bicycle from *a* to *b*. It will not do so, for example, if there are things that one can do at *b* that one cannot do without getting there first on the bicycle from *a*. The extent to which the performance of an action is a precondition for the possibility of performing subsequent, generationally distinct actions, we may call, with Feinberg, the 'fecundity' of that action.[51] It is clear that the availability of a more fecund action increases one's freedom more than that of a less fecund action. It is equally clear, however, that where two available actions are fecund in the same

[50] Pattanaik and Xu, 'On Ranking Opportunity Sets in Terms of Freedom of Choice', 390.
[51] Feinberg, *Rights, Justice and the Bounds of Liberty*, ch. 1.

or a similar way (that is, where the two sets of actions for which their performance is a precondition are identical or intersect), the freedom to perform both actions contributes to one's overall freedom less than twice the amount contributed by the freedom to perform one of them.

What the notion of an act-root and Feinberg's notion of fecundity have in common is the fact that they each suggest a way in which the bringing about of one event may be a precondition for the bringing about of another. It seems to me that this fact can indeed often help to explain *why* two options appear to be 'qualitatively similar'. The fact that two alternative actions do not appear to be significantly different often results from the fact that their physical components are *similar in appearance* (as in the example of the brands of washing powder or of the riding of the bicycle or of the driving of the cars). And when two physical components appear similar, it is likely to be the case that many of the events they are a means to bringing about are identical. Indeed, the *less* significant the difference between them appears to be, the *greater* the set of actions they are both a means to performing is in practice likely to be. Thus, there would appear to be a law of 'diminishing marginal freedom' with respect to the acquisition of options which are not significantly different from those one already has—not because we should discount those additional options themselves (why should we do that, if they differ to *some* degree?), but simply because they provide us with diminishing marginal extents of available action.

If we look yet more closely at our reasons for perceiving qualitative similarities and differences between options, we can see that those reasons might in fact take one of two forms. The first kind of reason, which I have already mentioned, is that two similar options are necessary preconditions for bringing about a common set of events. A second reason—which appears to have been seen by Cohen, Norman, and Pattanaik and Xu among others as the *only* possible reason—is that two similar available actions provide different ways of increasing the quantity, in the world, of *the same particular value*. In our terms, the first kind of reason has an empirical basis, whereas the second is necessarily value-based. Only the first kind of reason is reflected in the empirical approach to measuring freedom. But this is already saying a great deal, since, as the above examples show, it is often the case that what is initially perceived as a reason of the second kind is in reality simply a reason of the first kind, or is at least independently supported by a reason of the first kind. It seems to me, then, that most of our perceptions of degrees of variety will be reflected in ideal measurements of empirical freedom, and that our search for a reflective equilibrium between such measurements on the one hand, and those common-sense comparisons apparently based on perceptions of variety on the other, will not warrant the abandonment of the empirical approach.

There will of course be *some* perceptions of variety of options that really are based wholly on a perception of differences between the values they allow us to increase. These perceptions of variety will not, as I say, be reflected in measurements of empirical freedom. Rather, they must be recognized for what they are: perceptions of differences in the *specific values* of different sets of available actions, where one set of available actions is seen as more specifically valuable than another on the grounds that there is less overlap between the specific values that can be increased through the performance of its individual member options. The best candidates for this category of perceptions of variety seem to be those that concern available actions the physical components of which are not *movable*. Consider another of Cohen's examples, which appeals to our perception of the similarities and differences between the options of holidaying in the Bahamas, in Clacton, or in Brighton. The choice menu (Brighton, Bahamas) offers more freedom than the choice menu (Brighton, Clacton), Cohen says, and this is because the difference between Brighton and the Bahamas is more significant than that between Brighton and Clacton.[52] Perhaps, on the empirical approach, each of the above two choice menus indeed offers roughly the same amount of freedom, except in so far as Brighton is further away from the Bahamas than it is from Clacton. Even here, however, doubts may be raised. Perhaps the relative distances between Brighton and the Bahamas and Brighton and Clacton are doing more work here (in determining our common-sense comparison) than Cohen leads us to believe. If it is really a purely value-based difference between Clacton and the Bahamas that lies behind the fact of the choice set (Brighton, Bahamas) giving us more freedom than the choice set (Brighton, Clacton), we must be prepared to say that this would be so even if the 'Clacton' referred to were really a town situated in, say, New Zealand (while being similar in quality to the Clacton situated in Great Britain). And we should not forget that there are things one can acquire in the Bahamas—various objects, and a suntan—that one cannot acquire in Brighton or Clacton, and that these will themselves be preconditions for further actions.

Although we doubtless sometimes see two options as similar simply because they are preconditions for increasing similar values, it is surely also the case that we sometimes see two options as similar because they are preconditions for *doing the same things* (either because they present us with act-roots or because they have diminishing marginal fecundity). It seems to me that a number of recent attempts to formalize degree-of-freedom judgements by reference to the variety of options suffer from a failure to distinguish between these two reasons that lie behind our perceptions of degrees of variety, and from

---

[52] The example comes from the same unpublished paper from which I quoted in s. 5.4.

a failure not only to recognize the exclusive validity of the empirical reason (as a consideration relating to *extents of overall freedom*), but also its potential in providing isomorphism with common-sense comparisons of freedom.[53]

Indeed, I would go further, and say that, in correctly recognizing the relevance of degrees of variety to degree-of-freedom assessments, theorists have often been mistakenly led into inverting the logical relation between the empirical reason and the value-based reason. Recall the general conclusion reached in Chapter 5, where we examined the reasons behind various common-sense comparisons that were purported to justify the value-based approach. As we saw there, adherents of the value-based approach mistakenly invert the true logical relation between (*a*) our reasons for valuing a set of freedoms, and (*b*) the extent of freedom provided by that set of freedoms. It is not that a set of freedoms provides a great deal of freedom because we place a great deal of value on that set of freedoms; rather, we often place a great deal of value on a set of freedoms (*in part*) because it provides a great deal of freedom. It cannot be the case that both of these accounts are correct, and the arguments of Chapter 2 suggest that we should go with the second account: (*b*) is logically prior to (*a*), in terms of reason-giving, and not the other way round, as adherents of the value-based approach mistakenly believe. A similar point can be made regarding those who see the *variety* of options as a value-based notion. Where option-set X has more qualitative variety than option-set Y, it is not that X offers us more freedom because we see it as a more varied set of options; rather, *one* of the reasons we see X as a more qualitatively varied set of options is that we perceive it as offering us more freedom (where this perception of greater freedom results from the fact that there is less perceived overlap between the sets of events that one is free to bring about as a result of having option-set X than there is between the sets of events that one is free to bring about as a result of having option-set Y).

Finally, it is worth noting a possible objection to my attempt to accommodate our perceptions of the variety of options. The objection is that my argument cannot apply to options that are located at the *end* of (what Goldman would call) a chain of causally generated actions, or to available actions that are located so far in the future that they have no perceivable fecundity value.[54] These options will themselves be qualitatively more or less similar, yet in their case we cannot take into account the greater or lesser intersection of the sets

[53] Among these recent formal attempts to take into account the variety of options are: M. Klemisch-Ahlert, 'Freedom of Choice: A Comparison of Different Rankings of Opportunity Sets', *Social Choice and Welfare*, 10 (1993) (where the expression '*range* of set of options' is used to refer to the same characteristic); E. F. Rosenbaum, 'On Measuring Freedom', unpublished paper, Darwin College, Cambridge; M. van Hees, 'An Axiomatic Analysis of Freedom', unpublished paper, University of Twente.

[54] I owe this objection to Martin van Hees.

of further actions for whose performance or availability they are necessary conditions. As we pointed out in s. 7.4, the chains of events we are free to bring about must be considered to be of a non-arbitrary, finite length; otherwise, we should be considered free to bring about arbitrary or infinite numbers of events. Yet this prevents us from saying that options located at the extremities of the branches of act-trees are themselves different possible ways of doing the same thing. A similar point applies to my appeal to the notion of fecundity: bringing about event a and bringing about event b may be alternative preconditions for bringing about event c, bringing about c and bringing about d may be alternative preconditions for bringing about e, and so on, but at a certain point the chain of reasoning must stop—say, at event m—in which case we shall not be able to say that bringing about m and bringing about n are alternative preconditions for doing the same thing, even if we perceive a qualitative similarity between m and n.

This objection is best dealt with by pointing out that it only affects a small proportion of the events we are free to bring about. This might appear something of an *ad hoc* answer, but it is not. To see this, one should recall the criterion suggested in s. 7.4 for seeing the lengths of causal chains as both finite and non-arbitrary. That criterion was not arbitrary, but consisted in limiting hypothetical chains of events to the *foreseeable* consequences of available basic actions. It follows from this that we cannot foresee the consequences of events at the extremities of the branches of possible act-trees, and therefore that any reason we do have for seeing such events as qualitatively similar *must* be of a *value-based* kind. And we have seen that this kind of reason must be disregarded by the freedom measurer. On the other hand, our reasons for seeing such events as qualitatively similar are, fortunately, *necessarily* value-based *only* when they concern events at the extremities of act-trees. A similar line of reasoning applies to actions to which we are unable to assign a fecundity value. If two such actions are perceived as qualitatively similar, then the reason for this perception can only be a value-based reason, and must therefore be disregarded by the freedom measurer. On the other hand, our reasons for seeing such actions as qualitatively similar are necessarily value-based *only* when we are unable to assign them a fecundity value. There is a limit to the frequency with which this can occur, given that such actions will normally stand at the end of a chain of (generationally distinct) actions that do have a fecundity value.

7.9 UNDER- AND OVER-REPRESENTED ACTIONS

I now turn to other possible objections from common-sense comparisons. These are generally aimed at showing that, intuitively speaking, on the empirical approach, certain kinds of actions will be 'under-represented' or 'over-represented' in terms of degrees of freedom. In other words, they are aimed at showing that, on the empirical approach, the availability of a particular action, x, will count for much less freedom, or for much more freedom, than our common-sense comparisons of freedom suggest, and that this fact indicates either the superiority of the value-based approach or the unfeasibility of measuring overall freedom in any acceptable way at all. Freedom of speech, for example, would appear to be represented by the empirical approach as contributing very little to our overall freedom, given that the exercising of one's freedom of speech involves only small movements of one's tongue and vocal chords.[55] And yet, we intuitively feel, freedom of speech contributes a great deal to our overall freedom. On the other hand, the freedom to start an avalanche might appear intuitively to be over-represented by the empirical approach in terms of the amount it contributes to one's overall freedom; the physical magnitude of an avalanche is very great, whereas some might feel intuitively that the freedom to start an avalanche counts for little in terms of overall freedom.

Let us turn first to the objection based on the example of freedom of speech. It seems to me that the force of this objection is greatly diminished once we take into account the way in which actions are generationally related. We have seen that all actions are (in Goldman's terms) either *basic* or *non-basic*, and require for their performance certain *physical components* (s. 7.2). The performance of a basic action requires some part of the agent's own body and the physical space within which it moves. The performance of a non-basic action requires the agent's causal power over additional matter (the matter the movement of which that action is the bringing about, plus the physical components of any generationally prior actions). Given this, it should be clear that a lack of possession of the physical components of one's doing x implies not only one's unfreedom to do x, but also one's unfreedom to perform any action which would have been (and could only have been) generated by x. Thus, as Steiner points out, in order to prevent an agent from performing any actions at all, we need only directly deprive her of possession of her own body, for to do so is to deprive her indirectly of possession of all other physical components.[56] The fact that most events are brought about *by* bringing about other events would therefore suggest a certain relationship between the 'generational status' of an action and the amount of freedom which its impossibility restricts: that the closer an unavailable physical component is to the agent's body (in the causal chains of events of which actions are the bringing about), the greater the quantity of action its unavailability is likely to prevent.

[55] Cf. Gray, *Freedom*, 127.   [56] Steiner, 'Individual Liberty', 49.

Empirical Freedom

Where agent A is rendered unfree to speak, then, there is very likely to be a great reduction in A's freedom *in an overall sense*. For A will as a result be unfree to perform certain bodily movements, or will at least be deprived of access to the physical space (through which the sound waves would have travelled) which would otherwise have been directly causally linked to A's body. And this will also imply A's unfreedom to bring about those events that would be consequent upon A's moving her body in those prevented ways (or upon A's use of the space or matter to which she has been deprived of access). Of course, laws against free speech do not usually involve such direct preventions in the first instance, but where they threaten arrests and imprisonment, the same argument is likely to apply to the set of compossible actions 'saying x at time t and walking down the street at $t+1$', and where they threaten fines, the point is likely to apply to the set of compossible actions 'saying x at time t and buying a new car at $t+1$'. (I shall have much more to say about this in the next chapter.) It should also be borne in mind that to prevent the act-set 'saying x at time t and walking down the street at $t+1$' is to prevent *all* of the act-sets which, however large, include these two actions among their members.

The above argument can also be applied, up to a point, to the case of 'freedom of thought'. Mental acts cannot themselves be members of the set of acts that are taken into account by measurements of overall empirical freedom: even where such acts are conceived in physical terms, their 'extensiveness' will be trivial. However, this is not to deny that there may be a considerable fit between measurements of overall freedom and those common-sense comparisons that are normally imagined to incorporate judgements about freedom of thought. Just as non-basic actions can be said (in Goldman's terms) to be level-generated by basic actions, so basic actions can in turn be said to be level-generated by thoughts. Therefore, just as basic actions are necessary for the performance of non-basic actions, so thoughts are necessary for the performance of basic actions. Given this fact, if I force you to think certain thoughts, then there are also likely to be many actions that I am preventing you from performing, so that it can at least be said that forcible hypnosis and brainwashing can entail great reductions in freedom on an empirical conception. Notice, moreover, that from the fact that you are free to avoid being brainwashed by me, either by physically escaping my clutches or by complying with my threats, it does not follow that the possibility of your being hypnotized implies no reduction in your freedom, given an analysis of unfreedom in terms of the unavailability of sets of compossible actions. Thus, while Winston Smith, in George Orwell's *1984*, was free not to read Goldstein's rebellious book, thus complying with the will of the Ministry of Love (which threatened to brainwash offenders), he nevertheless suffered a great deal of unfreedom even before reading Goldstein.

What of available actions that are seen as *over*-represented by the empirical approach in terms of the amounts of overall freedom they provide? Must the freedom to start an avalanche count for a great deal of freedom? Some, though not perhaps all, will find this counter-intuitive. The empirical approach does not appear to be able to accommodate a common-sense judgement to the effect that such a freedom contributes little to a person's overall freedom. However, a plausible attempt might be made to subvert that common-sense judgement: it may be that the option of destroying three Alpine villages at the flick of a finger can only be thought to contribute little towards one's overall freedom on value-based grounds (i.e. by appeal to the view that such an action is evil), in which case the objection is based on a common-sense comparison that must, in reflective equilibrium, be abandoned; or it might be hypothesized that such an action is a member of only a very small number of sets of compossible actions, assuming the likelihood of one's spending the rest of one's days in a Swiss prison as a result of its performance, in which case the common-sense comparison on which the objection is based would to some extent be accommodated by the empirical approach.

It is unlikely, however, that in conceptual terms we can answer the above counter-examples in a way that really hits the nail on the head: despite the above answers, some common-sense comparisons will continue to lack isomorphism with empirical measurements of freedom. Pointing out that an avalanche can, among other things, destroy three Alpine villages certainly might narrow the range of possible avalanches that appear to be over-represented in our measurements, but it does not eliminate such counter-examples. For the erstwhile adherent of the value-based approach might not be similarly persuaded to retract her counter-example (*despite* her now being persuaded that the value-based approach is mistaken) where we are sure that the avalanche in question will *not* destroy three Alpine villages. Again, in the case of under-represented actions, one can think of restrictions on freedom of speech that are not accompanied by the removal of other freedoms: some laws may restrict specific freedoms in a way analogous to so-called smart bombs, eliminating only certain specific targets while leaving all other freedoms intact.[57] An example might be the prevention of transmission on, or access to, certain radio frequencies, where this occurs without any interference with the agent's other bodily movements. Such counter-examples may be less serious than they first seem to be, given that they concentrate on very specific cases of freedom of expression: if the agent's other freedoms really are left intact, then she probably has many alternative ways of expressing herself, in which case we should not consider the reduction in her freedom such a drastic one; if on the other

---

[57] I owe this analogy to Simon Caney.

hand she has no such alternative ways of expressing herself—if what is reduced is her freedom of expression *per se*—then she is probably suffering a large degree of physical interference after all. However, the objector might still insist that the *specific* freedom eliminated by the 'government smart bomb' should *in itself* be felt to count for a great deal of freedom in our measurements, and that it is therefore under-represented by the empirical approach.

Another way of addressing these counter-examples might consist in hypo-thesizing an empirical rather than a conceptual link between there being certain specific freedoms and there being high degrees of overall freedom (a point to which I shall return in s. 8.6). For example, there might plausibly be claimed to be an empirical correlation between the presence of certain specific democratic freedoms, including freedom of speech, and maximal equal empir-ical freedom. This might explain the common-sense comparison on which the above objections rest, without accommodating it in conceptual terms.

Nevertheless, some discrepancies, for some people, will remain. There will inevitably be a limited number of common-sense comparisons of freedom that conflict, conceptually if not empirically, with the empirical approach to meas-uring freedom. These common-sense comparisons will therefore have to be revised or abandoned if one is to endorse the empirical approach in reflective equilibrium. Is this feasible?

7.10 DEALING WITH THE REMAINING COUNTER-EXAMPLES

We have seen that if we are honest in our account of the empirical approach to measuring freedom, we shall be left with a number of counter-examples that cannot be accommodated. These are examples of initial common-sense comparisons of freedom that appear, even after a careful construction and consideration of the empirical approach, to lack isomorphism with empirical measurements. They may include certain comparisons that refer to the 'under or over-represented' actions mentioned above, or certain comparisons that refer to the 'qualitative similarity' of options mentioned in s. 7.8.

As we saw in Chapter 4, the only way of facing up to such discrepancies is by working towards reflective equilibrium. The discrepancies confirm the prediction made in Chapter 4 that we would be unlikely to find a coherent definition of overall freedom that would prove *initially* intuitively appealing in *all* respects. For most people, in other words, the appeal to initial common-sense comparisons alone will not prove conclusive. A revision of some of our initial common-sense comparisons of freedom therefore has to be made if we are to progress towards reflective equilibrium in theorizing about the measurement of overall freedom. Which initial common-sense comparisons, then, should we go with, and which should we revise?

We should begin by recalling that if the arguments of Chapter 5 were correct, then any failure of empirical measurements of freedom to provide isomorphism with our common-sense comparisons can only mean one of two things:

1. those common-sense comparisons are really incorrect comparisons of freedom—i.e. our actual degrees of freedom are, in such cases, different from the degrees our common-sense comparisons say they are; or
2. those common-sense comparisons should not really be understood as comparisons of degrees of overall freedom at all, but as (elliptical for) comparisons of the specific values of specific freedoms.

Can the remaining counter-examples be sufficient to bring about an abandonment of the empirical approach? If we do abandon the empirical approach, then we must interpret not only the remaining counter-examples, but indeed *all* of our common-sense comparisons of freedom, in the way described by category (2), regardless of their degree of fit with the empirical approach. We must, in other words, embrace the normative version of the specific-freedom thesis (a position to which, as we saw in Chapter 5, the value-based approach reduces), and therefore the view that all attributions of degrees of overall freedom, be they common-sense comparisons or resultant measurements, are really elliptical for attributions of degrees of goods other than freedom. This would imply the abandonment, in reflective equilibrium, of a central element of our initial 'background theory': the idea of freedom's non-specific value, together with the endorsement of a freedom-based theory of justice. For most erstwhile adherents of the value-based approach—who, after all, share the initial intuition that freedom is a quantitative attribute—this conclusion ought to appear rather extreme. Why, in any case, should the counter-examples be seen as contradicting the empirical approach any *more* than they contradict the specific-freedom thesis, given that they are, if taken literally, examples of comparisons of degrees of overall freedom?

Even if all of the remaining counter-examples *are* to be seen on reflection as falling into category (2), we need not abandon the empirical approach to measuring freedom. For there will still be a great many common-sense comparisons of freedom that the empirical approach reflects, as shown in Chapter 5, as well as in the previous two sections of this chapter. In my view, the most likely result will be even more favourable to the empirical approach, namely that in reflective equilibrium, while some of those remaining counter-examples will be felt to fall into category (2), others will be felt to fall into category (1). In this case, the initial common-sense comparisons of the erstwhile adherent of the value-based approach should be categorized as follows:

(*a*) comparisons which are initially isomorphic with empirical measurements of freedom (in the ways shown in ss. 5.5, 7.8, and 7.9);

(*b*) comparisons which initially conflict with empirical measurements (in
the ways suggested above), but which, in reflective equilibrium, are
either:

    (i) revised, in the light of this conflict, to conform with empirical
    measurements of freedom, or

    (ii) recognized as elliptical for comparisons of goods other than
    freedom.

If I have shown enough of our common-sense comparisons of freedom to fit
into category (*a*), there ought to be sufficient pressure to revise at least some
others (category (*b*(i))). This will mean that some common-sense comparisons
can fit into the third category (*b*(ii)) without leading to an abandonment of the
empirical conception of freedom. For example, one might deal with certain
of the common-sense comparisons involving freedom of speech (mentioned
in the previous section) by saying that these are really elliptical for claims
about the *importance* of freedom of speech, and that the good of freedom
of speech can compete with the good of overall freedom. Erstwhile adherents of the value-based approach whose common-sense comparisons divide
into the above three categories are likely to recognize that while some of the
common-sense comparisons which they initially took to justify the value-based
approach are really elliptical for comparisons of goods other than freedom
(those in category (*b*(ii))), this is not to deny that many attributions of degrees
of freedom (i.e. those which correspond to the common-sense comparisons
in categories (*a*) and (*b*(i))) have both a literal meaning and, given the non-
specific value of freedom, considerable importance. The greater the number
of their common-sense comparisons that fit into category (*a*) (or the greater
their conviction about the correctness of such comparisons), the more likely
are their other common-sense comparisons to fall into category (*b*(i)) as well
as category (*b*(ii)).

It seems to me that the arguments presented in the previous two sections
(as well as in Chapters 5 and 6) *are* sufficient to sway many erstwhile supporters of the value-based approach towards acceptance of the empirical
approach. We have seen that no coherent account of overall freedom is without its counter-examples. And the remaining counter-examples to the empirical approach are surely not as strong as those that apply to the 'rhetorical'
version of the value-based approach (discussed in Chapters 5 and 6). Moreover, it should be clear from the arguments of Chapter 2 that while empirical
measurements of freedom are indeed insensitive to the significance of certain
features of given specific freedoms, there is nothing to say that judgements

about degrees of overall freedom need provide, or even can provide, a *sufficient* basis on which to decide who rightly gets which specific freedoms. My only claim in Chapter 2 was that such judgements are *indispensable* as a means to deciding who rightly gets which specific freedoms—a claim that is quite compatible with seeing *some* of the judgements people normally make about degrees of overall freedom as being really elliptical for judgements about the importance, in terms of other goods, of certain specific freedoms.

To be sure, for many, the adoption of this more coherent position will carry a price, in the form of a revision of certain common-sense comparisons of freedom. But this price may well be lower than that attached to the complete exclusion of alternative (1) in favour of alternative (2)—in other words, the price consisting in abandonment of the notion of freedom as a quantitative attribute in favour of the specific-freedom thesis. This, in any case, is where *my* reflective equilibrium lies, and I find that as a result I am sufficiently motivated to explore the empirical conception of freedom further, in particular in relation to the question of the commensurability or otherwise of the different ways of *constraining* overall freedom. That task, however, must be put off until the next chapter. First, we must return to the question raised at the very beginning of this chapter; namely, does the empirical approach to measuring freedom assume a theory of action that is somehow fallacious, or at least rather narrow in appeal?

7.11 PHYSICALIST, EMPIRICIST, AND KANTIAN CONCEPTIONS OF ACTION

I want to argue here that the analysis of empirical freedom presented in this chapter, and further explored in the next two, does not, despite possible first appearances, rest on any kind of reductionist claim about 'what action is'. I shall proceed in two stages, defending the empirical approach against (*a*) the possible charge of 'physicalism', and (*b*) the possible charge that it presupposes an empiricist (if not necessarily physicalist) account of action. The first objection might be made by non-physicalist empiricists as well as by anti-empiricists, whereas the second objection will be made exclusively by anti-empiricists. As usual, my strategy is that of casting my net as widely as possible; I do not think that either of the above groups of philosophers ought on reflection to be alienated by my analysis of empirical freedom.

(a) *The charge of physicalism*

In general, I use the term 'reductionist' to describe any view to the effect that 'X is nothing but Y' despite an initial appearance to the contrary—despite, that is, the initial appearance that X is something *more* than mere Y. An example given by Robert Nozick is the view that 'a performance of a violin sonata is nothing but the scraping of horsehair on catgut'.[58] But there is also a more specific meaning of 'reductionism', on which the first of the above-mentioned charges of reductionism is based. This more specific meaning is given in Antony Flew's *Dictionary of Philosophy*, according to which reductionism is 'the belief that human behaviour can be reduced to or interpreted in terms of that of lower animals . . . and . . . ultimately to the physical laws controlling the behaviour of inanimate matter'. Here, 'reductionism' is taken to imply a physicalist conception of human action—the Hobbesian view that 'life is but a motion of limbs'.[59]

The empirical approach to measuring freedom does not rest on such a physicalist conception of human action. Rather, it rests on the view that purely physical descriptions of actions are the relevant kinds of descriptions when it comes to measuring degrees of overall freedom. This last view does not imply that human actions are 'nothing but physical movements', and it certainly does not imply that human actions can be explained in terms of 'the physical laws controlling the behaviour of inanimate matter'. As we saw at the beginning of this chapter, there are many different ways of describing actions, and each description serves a particular purpose. To say that an act-description of type *x* serves some particular non-explanatory purpose is plainly not to say that descriptions of type *x* are in some sense more 'explanatorily basic' than other types of description.[60] There *is* something that marks off purely physical act-descriptions from other kinds of act-descriptions, and that is the fact that they apply to all (non-mental) acts. For all (non-mental) acts are, *inter alia*, the bringing about of some physical movement. But there is no reason why this fact alone should make it appropriate to call the employment of purely *physical* act-descriptions (for a particular non-explanatory purpose) 'physical*ist*'.

It might be objected that if I wish to remain agnostic about the validity of physicalism, I should not advocate measuring 'the freedom to perform *actions*' purely in terms of possible physical movements. For while it is true that all actions involve, *inter alia*, physical movement, it is not true that all

[58] R. Nozick, *Philosophical Explanations* (Oxford: Oxford University Press, 1981), 627.

[59] Hobbes, *Leviathan*, introd., 81. The charge of 'behaviourism' is levelled against Steiner by John Gray in 'On Negative and Positive Liberty' in his *Liberalisms*, and by Flathman in *The Philosophy and Politics of Freedom*, 31–3. The charge of 'physicalism' is levelled, in passing, by O'Neill, in *Constructions of Reason*, 227 n. 15. See also her *Towards Justice and Virtue*, 67 n. 2.

[60] I think Steven Lukes confuses 'basic' action with 'explanatorily basic' action in 'The Contradictory Aims of Action Theory', in G. Seebass and R. Tuomela (eds.), *Social Action* (Dordrecht: Reidel, 1985). Cf. my 'Is Analytical Action Theory Reductionist?', *Analyse & Kritik*, 8 (1991).

physical movements (even of human bodies) involve action. A classic example of a bodily movement that is not an action is the movement involved in 'falling over'. If I were to reject the physicalist account of action, then, would I not have to go back on my account of the way in which we should measure the extent of freedom agents have to act? This objection can be answered by pointing out that it confuses the criteria for identifying a set of *possible* actions with the criteria for identifying a set of *actual* actions. It is true that any number of *actual* bodily movements fail to qualify as actions, but it does not follow from this that an agent's *available* (*unprevented*) bodily movements do not all qualify as *available* (*unprevented*) actions. Actions are normally distinguished from 'mere behaviour' by saying that the former are carried out for some *reason*. For example, the piece of behaviour consisting in my falling over does not qualify as an action because it was not, under whatever description, done for a reason. However, as Steiner points out, all that is needed for an *available* piece of behaviour to count as an *available* action is that the agent *could conceivably* have a reason to carry it out (even though she might not *actually* have a reason to carry it out).[61] To say otherwise would be to say that an agent is free to the extent that she is unprevented from performing actions she actually has a reason to perform, and would therefore involve employing a value-based conception of freedom. I have been assuming, on the other hand, that freedom is a non-specifically valuable phenomenon, and as such includes the possibility of performing actions that one could conceivably (but does not actually) have a reason to perform. And that includes the action of throwing oneself to the floor over the same spatio-temporal coordinates as those that would be covered in falling over. As Steiner says, for any given piece of behaviour, we should be interested in the agent's 'freedom or unfreedom to do whichever actions that behaviour could be'. Rather than arising from a failure of the empirical approach to distinguish between behaviour and action, the commitment to physicalism is mistakenly inferred from the refusal of those who adopt the empirical approach 'to restrict freedom judgements to the subset of actions associated with only actually held reasons', and from their 'insistence on extending such judgements to the full set of actions associated with possibly held ones'.[62]

It is true that, in expounding the empirical approach to measuring freedom, I have taken a stand in favour of Davidson's claim that all actions can be *redescribed* as the bringing about of certain bodily movements. Will my reliance on this claim not at least alienate those action theorists who claim instead that

---

[61] Steiner, *An Essay on Rights*, 17–18.

[62] Ibid. 18. Unlike me, and despite this argument, Steiner does not apparently object to the label 'physicalist', at least as long as it remains in scare quotes. What he explicitly objects to is the label 'behaviourist'.

every act-description is a description of a different action? The answer, of course, is that it will. But this fact does not compromise my claim not to have pre-supposed any particular view of 'what action is', because the task of giving an account of 'what action is' is logically distinct from the task with which Davidson's thesis is concerned. Davidson's thesis is concerned with the *identity conditions* of actions. In asking about the identity conditions of actions, we ask questions of the form 'is action *a* the same as action *b*?' Thus, we join Elizabeth Anscombe in asking whether one's moving one's arm, one's oper-ating a pump, one's replenishing a water supply, and one's poisoning of the inhabitants of a nearby house amount to four actions or only one.[63] Anscombe, like Davidson, believes that the answer is 'one'. However, she explicitly states that she does not see this answer as implying that we should privilege one description over the others on the grounds that it somehow refers to the *essence* of the action in question. If we are asked, 'What is *the* action, which has all these descriptions?', we should answer, Anscombe says, simply by giving one of the descriptions—'any one, it does not matter which: or perhaps it would be best to offer a choice, saying "Take whichever you prefer." '[64] As Carl Ginet puts it, the identity/individuation question (that is, Anscombe's question) turns not on the nature of 'action-designators' (that is, on what action *is*), but on 'what metaphysical category of thing action-designators designate, what category of thing actions are'.[65] The question of 'what metaphysical category of thing action-designators designate' depends on whether they are abstract entities (i.e. exemplifications of act-properties), as Goldman has suggested, or whether, instead, they are concrete particulars, as Davidson has suggested. This is a question on which I do take a stand, but it does not imply an answer to the question of whether actions are 'nothing but' bodily movements. Actions can be *redescrib-able as* bodily movements without being *nothing but* bodily movements.

Carlos Moya has provided a useful explanation of 'the temptation to make of Davidson's ontological claims more than they are, namely a tool for *reducing* actions to bodily movements'.[66] Davidson's thesis, that a single action can have many descriptions, allows us to make identity statements about actions, like ' "A's extending his arm" *is* "A's signalling for a turn" '. This implication might be thought problematic, given that not all arm-extendings are in fact signallings. And from this 'there is only one step to thinking that the claim is reductionist'.[67] But this doubt rests on a confusion between sense and reference.

[63] Anscombe, *Intention*, 45.

[64] G. E. M. Anscombe, 'Under a Description', *Noûs*, 13 (1979), 220.

[65] C. Ginet, *On Action* (Cambridge: Cambridge University Press, 1991), 48.

[66] C. J. Moya, *The Philosophy of Action: An Introduction* (Cambridge: Polity, 1990), 41, my emphasis.

[67] Ibid. 42.

'That A's extending his arm (at t) is A's signalling for a turn (at t) means only that both descriptions *refer* to the same particular action, not that both descriptions mean the same or have the same *sense*. This latter claim is reductivistic; the former is not.'[68]

It should be clear, then, that the assertion that we should measure overall freedom in terms of possible physical movements does not prejudge the question of whether action is 'nothing but' physical movement. The question of 'what action is' is not one that I aim to answer in this book, beyond making the uncontroversial assumption that actions are the bringing about of events on the part of agents. The postion being defended here is, rather, that all events have physical dimensions, and that the degree of overall freedom provided by the availability of a set of actions is to be measured in terms of the physical dimensions of the events of which those actions are the bringing about. Even the ruthless and nihilistic Henry of the conversation that prefaces this chapter does not say that cold-blooded murder is 'nothing more than' the redistribution of matter. He just says that he 'prefers to think of it' as the redistribution of matter. And, as far as the measurement of overall freedom is concerned, so should we.

(b) *The charge of empiricism*

Having saved the empirical approach from the charge of physicalism, I could at this stage rest my case, contenting myself with a broad consensus among contemporary empiricist philosophers of action. But I think that I can also go further, and claim that the empirical approach to measuring freedom does not even presuppose an empiricist theory of action—not, at least, in so far as such a theory of action itself incorporates a reductionist claim about the nature of action.

What does an empiricist (but not necessarily physicalist) theory of action look like? Empiricist theories of action are what Onora O'Neill has called 'preference-based'. Such theories attempt to explain human actions by reference to agents' beliefs and desires (or preferences) and are supposed to provide a basis for rational choice theory, where rationality is understood as purely instrumental and preferences are treated as given (and therefore intrinsically arbitrary).[69] Whether or not this model of action is interpreted in physicalist terms, the important point is that it still involves seeing human action as a species of natural event and, as such, as something that in principle can be explained causally.

---

[68] Ibid.   [69] O'Neill, *Constructions of Reason*, 66.

The causal, 'preference-based' model of action becomes reductionist once those who employ it say in addition that this is *all* that action amounts to. Empiricists do generally make this claim; that is why we call their account of action empiric*ist*, and not merely empiric*al*. And such a reductionist claim clearly contradicts the 'dual' account of action that O'Neill, inspired by Kant, is herself keen to defend.[70] On the empiricist account of action, the causal model described above is seen as adequate both for *explaining* action and for *guiding* action (with the help of instrumental rationality). On a Kantian account of action, on the other hand, the causal model serves only to *explain* action, whereas in order to understand how action is *guided* we need to see actions as determined by maxims—that is, by practical *principles*. Truly autonomous action can then be understood as action guided by maxims that can be universalized. In O'Neill's view, this is probably the only coherent account of human autonomy, given that, whatever account empiricists try to give of autonomy (e.g. one that characterizes autonomous action as action in conformity with second-order desires), they must see autonomous actions as ultimately no less caused than non-autonomous actions, and therefore as lacking the 'independence' that 'autonomous action' is normally felt to signify.[71] In contrast to empiricists, then, Kant 'does not and cannot offer a single model of human action that can both serve for empirical explanation and guide choice'.[72] Instead, he offers two accounts of action, based on two 'distinct, indispensable, yet mutually irreducible frameworks of thought'.[73] Only a non-empirical (or 'intelligible') model of action is, in Kant's view, compatible with human autonomy. On this non-empirical account, action is not the causing of certain events by certain beliefs and desires; rather, it is the conscious following of a maxim.

Now it might be true that some of the views I criticized in Chapter 5 rest on a 'preference-based' conception of action. Perhaps this can be said of Amartya Sen's 'preference-based approach' to measuring freedom. The writings of Sen do not themselves seem to provide us with an answer to the question of whether or not he necessarily assumes such a conception of action.[74] But in any case, this is a question for Sen to answer. For my part, I have disavowed all reference to an agent's preferences in making judgements about her degree of overall freedom. The empirical approach to measuring freedom does not imply any

---

[70] O'Neill, *Constructions of Reason*, 69.

[71] Cf. O'Neill, 'Autonomy, Coherence and Independence'.

[72] O'Neill, *Constructions of Reason*, 70.   [73] Ibid. 68.

[74] O'Neill does not herself think that Sen relies on a preference-based conception of action. See her 'Justice, Capabilities and Vulnerabilities', in M. Nussbaum and J. Glover (eds.), *Women, Culture, and Development* (Oxford: Clarendon Press, 1995), 143–4. On the other hand, she does not take into account Sen's preference-based account of the measurement of freedom.

assumptions about how action is or should be guided, any more than it implies assumptions about how action should be explained. It makes no reference to motivational factors, such as preferences or intentions or the will. This, despite such motivational factors being relevant to the distinction between actual action and actual behaviour, in the way we have seen. The set of actual actions is a subset of the set of actual pieces of behaviour, and the question of how large that subset is will indeed depend, among other things, on whether we give an empiricist or a Kantian account of how action is guided. But the empirical approach to measuring freedom is neutral between such accounts. What the empirical approach does assume is the particular empirical account of action given in this chapter. According to that approach, a person's degree of freedom is to be measured in terms of purely empirical features of the hypothetical actions that she is prevented and unprevented from performing—in particular, in terms of their physical dimensions. However, to base our approach to measuring freedom on an *empirical* account of action is not to base it on an *empiricist* account; it is not to say that action from the empirical point of view is *all* that action amounts to. Given this, the empirical approach is compatible with a two-tiered Kantian theory of action.

In the language of contemporary analytical philosophers, we can say that an empirical account of action is necessary for the construction of a conception of 'freedom to act', whereas a non-empirical account is—for Kantians but not for empiricists—necessary for the construction of a conception of 'free action' (or 'acting freely'). These two kinds of conception ought not to be confused. When we talk of 'free action' we refer to freedom as a property of actions, whereas when we talk of 'freedom to act' we refer to freedom as a property of agents.

To construct a conception of 'free action' (or 'acting freely') is to construct a conception that is closer to the idea of *self-mastery*, examined in Chapter 6, than to the idea of 'overall freedom' as analysed in this book. As we saw in s. 6.4, there is nothing to stop us from endorsing a conception of freedom as self-mastery (one interpretation of which is as Kantian autonomy) in addition to our empirical conception of overall freedom. As we also saw there, however, empirical freedom and self-mastery are not simply different dimensions of a single attribute, and to roll them together into one (as, for example, Charles Taylor appears to) is surely no less reductionist than saying that action from the empirical point of view is all that action can ever amount to.

The non-empirical account of action which grounds the Kantian version of the ideal of self-mastery does not then conflict with—indeed, for Kantians, it is complemented by—the empirical account of action which grounds the empirical approach to measuring freedom. After all, while 'most of what Kant has to say about action is said from the standpoint of agency and freedom [i.e.

from the standpoint of autonomy, or 'acting freely'] . . . , the other standpoint [i.e. the empirical standpoint] is never denied'.[75] Furthermore, Kant explicitly adopts the empirical standpoint, in his discussion of how positive laws should govern our conduct.[76] Empirical freedom is the absence of preventing conditions on the performance of any action described in empirical terms and is (my arguments so far suggest) what liberals generally refer to when, in the context of a theory of justice, they make prescriptions about degrees of overall freedom. It is something that liberals see as non-specifically valuable, and it should as a result be one of the *distribuenda* of their theory of justice. Kantian autonomous action arises out of respect for, among other things, the moral side-constraints imposed by a freedom-based theory of justice. Moreover, it is specifically rather than non-specifically valuable, directed as it is towards particular, morally valuable ends (see s. 6.2). In Kantian terms, an account of action 'from the standpoint of the sensible world' serves to describe the content of our principle for the distribution of empirical freedom, while an account of action 'from the point of view of the intelligible world' serves to show how we can *act on* such a principle.

[75] O'Neill, *Constructions of Reason*, 68.
[76] Cf. I. Kant, *The Metaphysical Elements of Justice*, trans. J. Ladel (New York: Macmillan, 1965).

8

Individual Freedom: Constraints

A Czech and a Dutchman are talking about housing problems in their respective countries.

Dutchman: 'Housing problems we Dutch can understand, but what must be so terrible for you is not having freedom of speech to complain about them.'

Czech: 'But we do have freedom of speech!'

Dutchman: 'What do you mean?'

Czech: 'We are free to say absolutely anything we like. The only difference is that we don't have freedom after speech!'[1]

THE Czech, who, incidentally, is speaking before 1989, is assuming a definition of 'specific freedoms' which makes the *physical impossibility* of doing something a necessary condition for being unfree to do it. It is difficult to see how a liberal can deny that, at least under certain conditions, the physical impossibility of doing x constitutes the unfreedom to do x. But is this really all that can render an agent unfree to do x? It is often pointed out, in opposition to such a view, that a law making us unfree to do x may not make it impossible for us to do x, but may instead involve the threat to impose a sanction in the event of our doing x. In other words, it is often said that a *threat of punishment* renders one unfree to do x. And are there not yet more ways in which one can be rendered unfree to do x? What if doing x is simply rendered physically *difficult*? How strong must a threat be in order to make one unfree to do the thing that the threatener aims to deter? Or is the question one of degree, such that there can be different degrees of freedom to do a specific thing depending on the strength of the threat in question? How great must a difficulty be in order to make us unfree to do a difficult thing? Or is the question again one of degree, such that there can be different degrees of freedom to do a specific thing depending on how difficult it is? Can all these different ways of constraining freedom be combined so as to allow for measurements of overall freedom?

In the present chapter I aim to answer these questions in such a way as to respect two important commitments identified in Chapter 4: first, there is the

---

[1] S. Lukes and I. Galnoor, *No Laughing Matter: A Collection of Political Jokes* (Harmondsworth: Penguin, 1987), 126.

commitment to being able to make unidimensional measurements of overall freedom (where the dimensions are 'constraint-type dimensions'); and second, there is the commitment to being able to do so in a way that is more or less consistent both with our common-sense comparisons of freedom and with our intuitive judgements about specific freedoms. There is no logical reason why these two commitments need turn out to be even roughly consistent. Nevertheless, I believe that they *are* roughly consistent, and that this is no accident. As in the previous chapter, all that I shall really be doing here is attempting to trace the true sources of our common-sense comparisons of overall freedom, and attempting on that basis to construct a coherent account of overall freedom that explains how and why, intuitively and implicitly, we see those comparisons as making sense.

I shall argue in this chapter that, at the purely conceptual level, physical impossibility is the only kind of constraint that the freedom measurer should take into account. (In Chapter 10 we shall see that for practical purposes other kinds of constraint can be taken into account. But those practical purposes are not among our present concerns.) To many, this 'impossibility view' will seem to represent a very narrow account of what constitutes a constraint on freedom. However, I shall not argue for this view merely by pointing out that statements about specific freedoms will as a result have greater coherence (as is usually the case in defences of such a definition of 'constraints on freedom'), nor even merely by pointing out that, given such a restricted view, our powers of measurement are more likely to meet our demands. While these two factors will certainly weigh in favour of my conclusion, they would not show that the 'impossibility view' of constraints fits our intuitive judgements about specific freedoms and overall freedom. Instead, the main thrust of my argument will be to show that an analysis of overall freedom in terms of physical possibility is not, in any intuitive sense, 'restricted' or 'narrow' in the way its opponents often claim it to be, given that it implies a much greater degree of isomorphism with our common-sense comparisons than is often supposed. If one finds that an alternative to one's own initial definition of freedom is better able to meet one's demands on one's powers of measurement, a revision of that initial definition of freedom which calls for little or no corresponding revision of one's common-sense comparisons ought to have a great deal of appeal in reflective equilibrium.

8.1 CONSTRAINT VARIABLES AND THEIR SOURCES

The three constraint-types mentioned above—those of *physical impossibility*, *threats*, and *difficulty*—are what I shall call the possible *constraint variables* of overall freedom. In calling them the possible constraint variables, I mean that they are the constraint-types with which we should concern ourselves if we are to deal with the difficulties involved in making comparisons of overall freedom. They, and only they, are the candidates for being 'dimensions' of the quantitative attribute overall freedom.

There are certainly other conditions which liberals (in the broad sense) often suggest as necessary for the existence of a constraint on freedom. But the question of whether they are right about these other conditions for a constraint on freedom is not directly relevant to an enquiry into the measurability of overall freedom.

An important example of another condition for the existence of a constraint on freedom is the idea that, in order to count as freedom-reducing, an obstacle must have been imposed by a human being (or group of human beings), rather than by natural forces. The reason for this additional clause is, as we saw in s. 7.2, that freedom tends to be seen by liberals as a *social relation*— a relation between persons—and that we should therefore avoid confusing unfreedom with mere inability. For example, in the event of an earthquake destroying a bridge over a river, we should not say, according to most liberals, that I am rendered unfree to cross the river, but only that I am rendered unable to cross. On the other hand, not everyone accepts this limitation of the range of preventing conditions. Some—normally radical egalitarians—believe that natural obstacles restrict a person's freedom no less than humanly imposed obstacles.[2] Others still adopt an intermediate position, noting the importance of the distinction between social and non-social freedom without actually abandoning the latter notion.[3] And then, moving in the direction of the more restrictive wing, we find many liberals making the 'humanly imposed' clause even more narrow, so as to cover only constraints for which other agents can be held *morally responsible*,[4] or only constraints which have been *intentionally imposed*.[5]

This last group of liberals is often taken to be arguing about where, exactly, the line between the concepts of unfreedom and inability should be drawn

---

[2] See e.g. Crocker, *Positive Liberty*; Van Parijs, *Real Freedom for All*, ch. 1.

[3] See e.g. Sen, 'Freedom, Capabilities and Public Action', 113.

[4] Cf. Miller, 'Constraints on Freedom' and *Market, State and Community: Theoretical Foundations of Market Socialism* (Oxford: Clarendon Press, 1989), ch. 1; Kristjánsson, *Social Freedom*. For a debate on this point, see F. E. Oppenheim, 'Constraints on Freedom as a Descriptive Concept', *Ethics*, 95 (1985), and D. Miller, 'Reply to Oppenheim', *Ethics*, 95 (1985). To take the 'moral responsibility' view of 'constraints on freedom' is not to endorse a 'moralized' or 'justice-based' definition of freedom (see s. 3.1), for the former does not imply that obstacles preventing immoral (or rights-violating) actions are not constraints on freedom.

[5] Cf. Hayek, *The Constitution of Liberty*, ch. 1; W. A. Parent, 'Some Recent Work on the Concept of Liberty', *American Philosophical Quarterly*, 11 (1974).

—whether by reference to the causal responsibility of agents for the presence of obstacles, by reference to their moral responsibility, or by reference to their intentionality. This debate is of great importance, not only for ideological reasons, affecting as it does questions like that of whether or how far a government interested in the maximization or fair distribution of freedom should pursue certain welfarist policies, but also from the point of view of the internal coherence of one's definition of freedom itself. According to David Miller and Kristján Kristjánsson, the view that 'constraints on freedom' cover all obstacles for which humans are causally responsible—a view defended, for example, by Felix Oppenheim—is not consistent with a plausible distinction between unfreedom and inability, since, on the strictly causal view, the set of purely natural obstacles shrinks virtually to vanishing point. After all, it is usually possible to say of an obstacle that there is *some* piece of human behaviour, in the however distant past, in the absence of which that obstacle would not have occurred. It is also worth noting that restricting the relevant obstacles to those for which humans can be held morally responsible seems to be necessary if we wish to include obstacles that are located 'inside' the agent (such as those resulting from brainwashing) without at the same time going as far as endorsing a conception of freedom as self-mastery.[6]

Perhaps there is some criterion that lies in between moral responsibility and strict causal responsibility—a criterion that can somehow be found in conventional ideas about who is responsible for what in a non-moral sense, such that in this conventional sense, the set of actions for which one is non-morally responsible is greater than the set of actions for which one is morally responsible yet smaller than the set of actions for which one is strictly causally responsible. This appears to be the solution now favoured by Oppenheim.[7] But perhaps this idea is unavoidably mysterious, and Oppenheim should simply admit that the set of our unfreedoms is indeed much more coextensive with the set of our inabilities than many liberals have supposed.

As I have said, however, the above problems are not directly relevant to our present concerns. I mention them simply in order to underline their importance for any complete theory of freedom. Apart from a brief parenthesis at s. 8.5, I need not pursue them any further in this book. The reason for this is simple. We need to distinguish between a *constraint variable* on the one hand and its *source* on the other. The constraint-types identified by the phrases 'humanly imposed obstacles', 'obstacles for which humans are causally responsible', 'obstacles for which humans are morally responsible', and 'intentionally imposed obstacles' are not, in the above-mentioned sense, among

---

[6] Cf. Kristjánsson, *Social Freedom*, 100.
[7] Cf. Oppenheim, 'La libertà sociale ed i suoi parametri', 10–11.

the possible constraint variables the aggregation of which needs to be discussed in this chapter. Rather, they are constraint-types defined by reference to the *causal history* of obstacles—that is, by reference to the possible *sources* (human or natural causality, intention, responsibility) of particular instances of the possible constraint variables (physical impossibility, threats, difficulty). Thus, while the revised Steinerian formula presented in the previous chapter (at s. 7.2) assumes at least an interest in distinguishing between humanly imposed and naturally imposed obstacles, and with it the need for work on how best to make that distinction, neither the distinction nor the way in which it is made is directly relevant to the question of whether or how far different kinds of constraints on freedom can be commensurated in terms of overall freedom.

The question of the nature of the sources of constraints on freedom is, then, a question about the definition of 'a specific freedom' that affects the definition of overall freedom *unproblematically*. Rather than posing additional problems for aggregation, by increasing the set of variables to be commensurated, the function of a constraint-type defined by reference to the source of obstacles is simply that of specifying which instances of the already existing set of variables are to be taken into account. This means that we should be careful to distinguish between the following two questions: (1) that of whether one should side with Sen or Oppenheim or Miller or Hayek on the source an obstacle must have in order to count as a constraint on freedom, and (2) that of whether and how far overall freedom can be measured. The answers to these two questions are logically independent of one another. The only reason one could have for seeing them as interdependent would be that intentionality or causal or moral responsibility are themselves to be seen as matters of degree, and that the *degree* to which I am, say, morally responsible for your being unable to do x determines the *degree* to which you are free to do x. Such a point has never, to my knowledge, been made by the authors referred to above. On the contrary, it is normally assumed that as far as unfreedom is concerned, an obstacle should be seen as either intentionally or unintentionally imposed, and an agent as either bearing or not bearing causal or moral responsibility for its imposition.

Given the above distinction, it should be borne in mind that while the view that I shall defend here—that physical impossibility is the only real constraint variable—is sometimes claimed to be a 'narrow' one, it is by no means the narrowest view possible, even if such a claim is correct. For the 'breadth' of one's conception of constraints on freedom has at least two dimensions, the first having to do with the selection of possible constraint variables, and the second having to do with the selection of particular sources of obstacles. The view defended here concerns only the first dimension.

8.2 THREATS AND OFFERS

Let us begin by assuming a conception of 'specific freedoms' that admits both physical impossibility and threats as constraint variables. In this case, we shall be assuming that if you threaten me (at least, if you credibly threaten me) with the aim of deterring me from doing x, you render me unfree to do x. We shall be assuming that when a mafioso says to a shopkeeper, 'give me two million lire or I'll burn your shop down', the shopkeeper suffers a constraint on the freedom not to hand over the two million lire. The idea is that he has been coerced into handing over his money, and that there is therefore a sense in which he is unfree to keep it. *Ceteris paribus*, his overall freedom has been reduced. But by *how much*? Surely, he is not *as* unfree to keep his money in this case as in one in which the mafioso simply takes his money by force and makes off with it. Surely we should distinguish between these two cases in terms of degrees of freedom, given that there is always the possibility of ignoring a threat, whatever the cost of doing so.

Are we to say, then, that the degree of unfreedom incurred by a threat against doing x is equal to a particular *fraction* of the degree of unfreedom incurred by x's becoming physically impossible? If so, how are we to determine the value of that fraction? Suppose that we develop a scale from 0 to 1 on which to measure the strength of threats: say, by reference to the 'strength' of the threatened sanctions (on some non-value-based interpretation of 'strength'). And imagine that the fraction we obtain for the threat against doing x is 0.5. Will we have sufficient grounds for saying that the amount of unfreedom incurred is 'half' that incurred by physical impossibility? Would exactly two threats of this strength mean the same amount of unfreedom as is implied by one instance of physical impossibility? Surely, the 'half' in question refers to degrees of coercion of the will, not of physical impossibility. Even assuming that we have a workable scale for assessing the degree of unfreedom incurred by threats, then, we seem to lack a convincing way of commensurating those degrees of unfreedom with the degrees of unfreedom incurred by physical impossibility. All that we shall know of any particular threat is that it implies something more than 'no unfreedom' and something less than 'complete unfreedom' to do the particular thing that it is intended to deter.

We are also likely to be faced with the problem of commensurating threats with the physical *difficulty* of performing certain actions. Assume that if I make it more difficult for you to do x, your freedom to do x is reduced. How, in this case, are we to measure the degree of such a reduction? Presumably, once again on a scale ranging from 0 (maximal ease) to 1 (physical impossibility). But do we really want to say that 0.5 unfreedom in terms of physical difficulty is equal to 0.5 unfreedom in terms of a threat? How are we to judge how much coercion of the will is equal, in terms of freedom, to a given degree of physical difficulty? How, moreover, are we to integrate *probabilistic* judgements into measurements that combine the variables of threats and difficulty? We should not be surprised to find philosophers converging on the conclusion that 'these various dimensions are quite incommensurable' and 'cannot be aggregated into a single measure of an actor's overall freedom'.[8] 'How', after all, 'can we have such radically comprehensive judgements about freedom, given the internal diversities and ambiguities in the concept?'[9]

In my view, the problem of seemingly incommensurable constraint variables can be solved by distinguishing more frequently and more precisely between our intuitions about *specific* freedoms and our intuitions about *overall* freedom. Consider the following two propositions:

> When I am subjected to a threat against doing x, I remain as free as before. (P1)
>
> When I am subjected to a threat against doing x, my freedom is restricted. (P2)

P1 and P2 are usually taken to be incompatible, and most authors on the concept of freedom have therefore denied one or the other.[10] Each side in this debate backs its arguments up by appeal to strong intuitions which are taken to conflict with those of the other side. Hillel Steiner has presented a rigorous defence of P1. He begins by pointing out that the only way in which a threat constrains the range of actions available to its recipient is by altering the relative degrees to which those available actions are desirable. Before you say to me, 'Hand over your money or I'll shoot you', I prefer keeping my money to handing it over, whereas after you have said it (assuming that I find your threat credible), I prefer handing it over to keeping it. Threats simply reverse the preference ordering of the recipient with respect to bringing about and not bringing about the result desired by the threatener. David Miller recognizes that 'we must concede to Steiner that any account of freedom which extends constraint beyond impossibility makes some assumptions about human desires', such that if the agent's desires and aversions were to change radically enough,

---

[8] Oppenheim, *Political Concepts*, 78. Cf. id., 'Social Freedom and its Parameters'.

[9] Sen, 'Freedom, Capabilities and Public Action', 114.

[10] P2 is implicitly denied by Steiner in *An Essay on Rights*, ch. 2, s. B, where he argues for P1. P1 is also defended by M. Gorr in *Coercion, Freedom and Exploitation*, ch. 2 (as long as 'freedom' is interpreted to mean what Gorr calls 'freedom of action') and M. Taylor in *Community, Anarchy and Liberty*. P1 is denied (and P2 affirmed) in: S. I. Benn and W. L. Weinstein, 'Being Free to Act and Being a Free Man', *Mind*, 80 (1971); P. Jones and R. Sugden, 'Evaluating Choice', *International Review of Law and Economics*, 2 (1982); Miller, 'Constraints on Freedom'; Flathman, *The Philosophy and Politics of Freedom*; S. I. Benn, *A Theory of Freedom* (Cambridge: Cambridge University Press, 1988); Pettit, 'A Definition of Negative Liberty'; Swanton, *Freedom*; Kristjánsson, *Social Freedom*.

'what was formerly a constraint might no longer be so'.[11] But this means that a definition of freedom which includes threats as a form of constraint contradicts a basic, widely supported premiss about the relationship between freedom and desire. This premiss, first argued for explicitly by J. P. Day and Isaiah Berlin, is that the question of whether or not (or the degree to which) I *desire* to do something is *irrelevant* to the question of whether or not (or the degree to which) I am *free* to do it (see s. 5.3). We do not say that a wholly contented slave is wholly free simply on the grounds that she can give full rein to her desires. Neither would we deny that the inmate of a high-security prison is unfree to go to the theatre, even if she does not desire to go to the theatre. Steiner therefore concludes that since it is unacceptable to take an agent's desires into account in assessing her freedom, it cannot be acceptable to see threats as reducing freedom.

Steiner also argues that if threats restrict freedom then offers do too. For there is no difference between these two kinds of intervention in terms that are relevant to a discussion of the freedom of the agent to comply or not comply. Both threats and offers invert the preference ordering of the recipient with respect to performing and refraining from performing the action desired by the intervening agent. The fact that offers leave the recipient better off and threats worse off than before the intervention is not relevant to the question of how effective they are in modifying the agent's behaviour; the effectiveness of an intervention depends on nothing more or less than the degree to which complying with the intervention is made preferable to not complying.

On the other hand, many have found Steiner's conclusion counter-intuitive. Do we not commonly see threats of punishment as reducing freedom? Does a state which *physically prevents* me from eating green ice cream restrict my freedom more than a state which *threatens life imprisonment* for eating *any* colour of ice cream? Do we not feel, on the contrary, that I am rendered unfree to eat any kind of ice cream in the latter case, whereas in the former I am only rendered unfree to eat green ice cream? It is undeniable that many of us perceive some kind of reduction in the freedom of the recipients of threats. How are we to explain that perception?[12]

An answer can be found if we aim in every possible context to be more precise about whether we are referring to specific freedoms or to overall freedom. For the fact is that our statements about when 'freedom is reduced' are often ambiguous in this respect, and the wording in P1 and P2 is a case in

---

[11]　Miller, 'Constraints on Freedom', 76.

[12]　This question is asked by Gorr (*Coercion, Freedom and Exploitation*, chs. 2 and 3), and I agree with him that those who take the Hobbesian stance on threats need to address it. Unlike Gorr, however, I think the answer can be couched exclusively in terms of what he calls 'freedom of action'.

point. A coherent and plausible way of resolving the ambiguity is surely by interpreting P1 as referring to a specific freedom—the freedom to do *x*—and interpreting P2 as referring to overall freedom. These interpretations make P1 and P2 compatible: those who administer threats generally reduce the *overall* freedom of those whom they threaten, without removing the freedom to perform the specific action they aim to deter. Such interpretations of P1 and P2 also allow us to solve both of the main problems identified so far. First, they allow us to avoid the problem of commensurating degrees of freedom to perform a specific action with the complete freedom or unfreedom to perform an action implied by its physical possibility or impossibility. They do this by removing the need to speak of degrees of freedom to perform a specific action. Second, they allow us to say that a conception of 'specific freedoms' that admits physical impossibility as the only constraint variable can nevertheless accommodate the common-sense comparisons which most strongly motivate people to admit threats as a constraint variable.

In order to see how recipients of threats generally suffer reductions in overall freedom (*without* suffering the removal, on the part of the threatener, of any of their specific freedoms), we need to make use of our earlier analysis of overall freedom in terms of the availability of *sets* of actions.[13] As we saw in the previous chapter (at s. 7.2), some possible act combinations are 'and/or' options; we can perform either one or the other or both. Others are 'or only' combinations; we can perform only one or the other. Rather than isolated actions, then, what agents are more accurately described as free or unfree to perform are various *sets of compossible actions*. Hence our suggested revision of Steiner's formula for measuring freedom, such that Red's overall freedom is equal to the value of

$$\sum_{i=1}^{n} F_{r,i} \bigg/ \left(\sum_{i=1}^{n} F_{r,i} + \sum_{i=1}^{n} U_{r,i} \right)$$

where $F_{r,i}$ stands for the number of sets of compossible actions available to Red of which a specific action, i, is a member, and $U_{r,i}$ stands for the number of sets of compossible actions unavailable to Red, of which i is a member.

Goebbels said that 'anybody can write what he likes if he is not afraid of the concentration camp'.[14] There is an element of truth in this. Indeed, he

---

[13] This argument bears some resemblance to that of J. P. Day presented in his article 'Threats, Offers, Law, Opinion and Liberty', *American Philosophical Quarterly*, 14 (1977). But it also differs in an important respect: Day's analysis does not imply the denial that threats represent a constraint variable in their own right. The same point applies to H. Spector, *Autonomy and Rights* (Oxford: Clarendon Press, 1992), 17–18.

[14] Cited in D. Gabor and A. Gabor, 'An Essay on the Mathematical Theory of Freedom', *International Journal of Social Economics*, 6 (1979), 346.

should have gone further, adding that anybody can write what he likes even if he *is* afraid of the concentration camp. On the other hand, we do not supply the whole truth about the freedom of two agents, A and B, if we simply say, 'A in Nazi Germany can write what he likes and B in Britain can write what he likes.' 'Writing what he likes' is an act-type of which A should be seen as being unrestrained from performing a much greater quantity than B, once we look at the spatio-temporal regions within which that act-type can be performed. Unlike B, A is threatened with the concentration camp. As a consequence, *if* A writes what he likes at time *t*, and the threat is both sincere and practicable, he will not be unprevented from doing so at *t*+1. What is more, there are a great many other actions which A may be restrained from performing *if* he writes what he likes, given that there is not 'much' to be done in a concentration camp. In all likelihood, then, he suffers a great reduction in the number of sets of compossible actions available to him. Similarly, there is a sense in which the Czech, in the conversation that prefaces this chapter, is quite right to say that she enjoys freedom of speech, and is only denied 'freedom after speech'. What is misleading about her statement is her lack of reference either to the degree of her freedom of speech or to the degree of her overall freedom.

In my view, then, the belief that P2 contradicts P1 very often rests on mistaking an intuition about overall freedom for one about specific freedoms. The freedom to do *x* is not a matter of degree; one either is or is not free to do *x*. When we perceive a reduction in the freedom of an agent consequent upon her receiving a threat, what we have really spotted is a likely reduction in the degree of her overall freedom. Those who see a threat against doing *x* as removing the freedom to do *x* may well have wrongly interpreted P2 as arising out of an intuition about *specific* freedoms, and consequently as *referring* to a specific freedom. This, in my view, best explains the continued insistence that threats themselves reduce freedom, despite the rigour of Steiner's argument to the contrary. P2 is in fact an *empirical generalization* about the *overall* freedom of the recipients of threats.

Steiner claims that it is the execution of a threat that reduces freedom, and not the threat itself.[15] It must also be said, however, that, even *before* the threat is executed, if there is some probability that the threat *would* be executed in the event of the recipient not complying, then the agent's overall freedom is reduced by the threatener. Even while the agent is still pondering about whether or not to comply with the threat, it is already the case that she has suffered a reduction in the number of her available sets of compossible actions, given the truth of the counterfactual claim contained in the threat. In other words,

---

[15] Steiner, *An Essay on Rights*, 29.

if it is true now that I *would* execute my threat *should* you do *x*, it is also true now, *given* the truth of this counterfactual conditional, that I have already removed from your set of sets of available compossible actions a certain number of those sets of which *x* is a member. As Steiner himself says, freedom is not only the *actual* possession of physical objects, but also their *subjunctive* possession.[16] This means that an agent is rendered unfree to do a specific thing (here, a specific *set* of things) not only if another person is actually preventing her from doing it, but also if it is true that *were she to attempt* to do it, she *would* be prevented. If we apply this point to *sets* of actions, we can see that, *ceteris paribus*, being the recipient of a threat generally means being less free.

There are two kinds of situation in which, on the above analysis, a threatener does *not* reduce the recipient's freedom, and which explain why I have been careful up to now to say that threatened agents 'generally' suffer, or 'very likely' suffer reductions in overall freedom. The first kind of situation is one in which the threatener is bluffing or is in any case not able to execute the threat—in other words, where the threat would not in fact be carried out in the event of the recipient not complying. The second kind of situation is one in which the threatened sanction would not itself impose any costs on the recipient in terms of available actions.

With regard to the first kind of situation, it should be recalled that when freedom *is* reduced, it is reduced by threateners, and not by threats. The latter are generally *descriptions* of reductions in overall freedom—descriptions that are true or false depending on whether the threatener is sincere or insincere, as well as on the competence of the threatener in carrying out the sanction. It is useful, in this connection, to follow Oppenheim in distinguishing between threats and 'punishability', where threats are sincere or insincere statements about the punishability of specific actions or kinds of action, and punishability is an empirical generalization about the tendency of certain kinds of action to provoke sanctions. Only punishability itself constitutes a constraint on freedom (which in my terms, but not in Oppenheim's, means a constraint on *overall* freedom).[17] If the threatener is bluffing, then, she brings about no reduction in the overall freedom of the recipient, however skilfully she persuades the recipient that she is not bluffing, because she renders no actions punishable.

Is this implication counter-intuitive? It seems to me that in this matter, our intuitions regarding specific freedoms are not clear, or else are unhelpfully

---

[16] Ibid. 39.

[17] Oppenheim, *Dimensions of Freedom*, ch. 4, s. II; id., *Political Concepts*, 72–3; id., 'Social Freedom and its Parameters', s. I.4.

divergent from one person to another.[18] It is not obvious that many people have even the initial intuition that successful bluffers reduce freedom, quite apart from the fact that in practice it is in any case extremely difficult to sustain a successful bluffing campaign over time. Moreover, where it is felt, such an initial intuition cannot be as strong as the initial intuition that sincere and competent threateners reduce freedom. The former intuition ought therefore to be more easily abandoned in reflective equilibrium, above all in the face of the combined force of Steiner's argument and the fact of its compatibility with the claim that sincere and competent threateners reduce freedom.

The second kind of situation in which a threatener does not reduce the overall freedom of the recipient is one in which the sanction does not involve the removal of any of the agent's own options. One variant of this kind of sanction involves the punishment of someone other than the agent—presumably of someone about whom the agent cares. An example of the threat of such a sanction would be 'give me $1,000 or I'll kill your brother'. We can assume, to give this counter-example as much force as possible, that, despite the agent caring about his brother, the brother never does anything to enhance the agent's freedom—for example, by presenting him with gifts (for this would imply that a threat to kill the agent's brother would refer to at least something of a reduction in the agent's overall freedom). On the above analysis, the threatener does not in such cases reduce the overall freedom of the recipient. It is worth noting, however, that the threatener does reduce overall *group* freedom, as long as there is any chance at all of the recipient not complying (and as long as the threatener is sincere and competent). We shall see how this is so in the next chapter. Another variant of this second kind of threatened sanction is one that involves the imposition on the agent of costs that cannot be understood in terms of the availability of actions. It is not easy to think of concrete examples here—that is, of examples where the sanction really does not close off any options for anyone. Michael Taylor gives the (more or less convincing) example of a damaged reputation.[19] However, I follow him in finding the disqualification of such a case intuitively unproblematic (where it really does not imply the restriction of available actions), and in seeing it as more plausibly described in terms of some harm other than unfreedom. If it is ever possible for one person to exercise power over another without restricting their freedom (an idea which many find intuitively plausible, and which fits in with the above analysis of freedom), this is surely a case in point.

As for offers, these clearly generally describe *increases* in overall freedom on the above analysis, in a way that exactly mirrors the reductions in

---

[18] The claim that successful bluffs reduce freedom is made by Van Parijs in *Real Freedom for All*, 239 n. 40.

[19] Taylor, *Community, Anarchy and Liberty*, 144.

overall freedom described in threats. Just as a threat is (usually) a true or false description of a reduction in the number of the recipient's available sets of compossible actions, so an offer is (usually) a true or false description of an increase in the number (and sometimes also the size) of the recipient's available sets of compossible actions. Offers that are insincere, or for some reason cannot be understood as increasing the recipient's options (e.g. because they do not reward the recipient but, rather, someone she cares about) do not describe increases in the recipient's overall freedom. On the other hand, an offer to reward some person other than the recipient does increase *group* freedom if it is sincere and if it has some chance of being complied with.

Setting aside the counter-examples mentioned above, which do not seem to me to be anywhere near decisive, the above solution surely provides the neatest way of gauging the *strength* of an offer or a threat in terms of the degree to which, at least in the majority of cases, we commonsensically see it as increasing or decreasing freedom. We need not rely here on vague or contestable claims about how likely the 'normal' agent would be to comply with a threat,[20] or about how 'reasonable' it would be to comply.[21] Neither need we struggle to clarify judgements about whether certain borderline threats are 'strong' (a clear example being 'do x and I'll cut your legs off') or 'weak' (a clear example being 'do x and I'll pinch you'), so as to see whether or not they remove a specific freedom. Instead, we look at the act combinations that the sincere and competent threatener or offerer renders physically impossible or possible respectively. In the vast majority of cases, where we see a threat as describing a great restriction in freedom, the threatener is indeed imposing a great reduction in the number of sets of compossible actions available to the agent. And so on, down the scale ranging from 'strong' to 'weak' threats.

None of the arguments I have presented here imply that it is *logically* mistaken to include coercion of the will as a constraint variable in our conception of freedom. The more popular view that a threat (and, more generally, coercion of the will) can itself constitute a restriction of freedom is logically compatible with what has been said so far, as long as one adds some other criterion that halts the slide towards a conception of freedom as self-mastery. (An example of such a criterion is provided by Kristjánsson, who claims that obstacles 'internal' to the agent—such as those brought about through coercion of the will—only count as constraints on freedom if some other agent can be held morally responsible for their presence—see s. 8.1.) Nevertheless, the advantages of my alternative analysis of the relationship between

---

[20] Cf. Pettit, 'A Definition of Negative Liberty', 157; id., 'The Freedom of the City: A Republican Ideal', in P. Pettit and A. Hamlin (eds.), *The Good Polity* (Oxford: Blackwell, 1989), 144.

[21] Benn, *A Theory of Freedom*, 148.

freedom and threats are, as far as I can see, decisive. If we say that coercion of the will itself restricts freedom, we shall encounter the problems of incommeasurability mentioned at the beginning of this section. And we shall also have to say that offers as well as threats restrict freedom, for the only way to distinguish between them, *in terms of the way they affect the agent's deliberation process*, is by reference to the value of their compliance-consequences and their non-compliance-consequences, and that *is* ruled out logically, by the arguments of Chapter 5. My own analysis, on the other hand, does not run into problems of measurement (at the conceptual level), and at the same time allows us to make empirical generalizations that accommodate the common-sense view that agents suffer decreases in freedom when they are subject to threats and increases in freedom when they receive offers.

8.3 DIFFICULTY

So far, we have only looked at the constraint variables of threats and physical impossibility. How does our revised Steinerian formula fare when we are faced with a conception of freedom which also recognizes as constraints on freedom the physical difficulty of performing actions?

Assume that A has a few easy-to-perform options and that B has many difficult-to-perform options. Tim Gray asks, 'How can we trade off a gain in range against a loss in difficulty, in order to be able to arrive at a comparative judgement of their overall liberty?' Moreover, he asks, how can we measure difficulty in the first place?[22] As we noted in s. 8.1, the second question might be answered by assigning numbers ranging from 0 to 1 to given actions, where 0 represents impossibility and 1 represents maximal ease, and where the numbers in between somehow represent the degree of difficulty the agent would experience should she try to perform the action. However, it is not clear on what basis, exactly, such degrees of difficulty are to be gauged. Will they depend on the subjective judgement of the agent herself? Even having solved this problem, we might still find it difficult to answer the first question, about the comparison of difficulty and range.

Our revised Steinerian formula, on the other hand, provides a neat answer to both questions. The difficulty of performing an action, x, can be measured in terms of the *cost* of doing x. By this I do not of course mean its cost in terms of utility—for that would imply a value-based conception of freedom— but, rather, its cost in terms of the sets of other actions which are unperformable in combination with x. If the performance of x is made more difficult for me,

---

[22] I quote from an early, unpublished draft of Gray's *Freedom*, ch. 4. Cf. pp. 133–4.

its performance will consume more of my resources, and we can expect that this will be reflected by a reduction in the number of my available sets of compossible actions. As in the case of threats, our formula does two things: first, it accommodates the intuition that a person who finds x difficult is less free, *ceteris paribus*, than a person who finds x easy; second, it does away with the problem of commensurating measurements of difficulty with those of the range of physically possible actions. As before, it does these two things by denying the claim that specific freedoms are a matter of degree (i.e. that one can be more or less free *to do x*), while nevertheless accommodating the intuition behind that claim: those who see the difficulty of doing x as reducing the agent's freedom *to do x* have very likely mistaken an intuition about degrees of overall freedom for an intuition about degrees of a specific freedom.

8.4 PROBABILITY AGAIN

Sometimes, it might be objected, when we say that action x is 'difficult' we mean not only that the performance of x uses up a great deal of my resources, but also (or simply rather) that I may or may not succeed in performing x if I try. This is the meaning of 'difficulty' which Steiner has in mind when he suggests that claims to the effect that Red is less free to perform x are often really elliptical for claims to the effect that Red is 'less probably free' to perform x. An example given by Steiner is that of the difference between a British passport holder and a Canadian passport holder, where the former but not the latter requires a visa to enter the United States. The former is not in fact less free to enter the United States, as might at first be supposed; rather, she is *less probably* free to do so (assuming that there is some chance of the British being refused a visa).[23]

The accommodation of this meaning of 'difficulty' does not present any problems for my analysis of overall freedom. Taking into account the probability of constraints would only represent a potential problem if we were to say that specific freedoms can be a matter of degree. In that case, we should have to take into account the fact that each conceivable degree of freedom to do a specific thing is itself realized with a certain degree of probability. The probability of a constraint on the freedom to do x and the degree of a constraint on the freedom to do x do indeed seem to be difficult to combine. But in any case, I have already denied that the freedom to do x is a matter of degree. Therefore, we need only concern ourselves with judging the probability of given actions being *physically impossible*. More precisely, as we saw

---

[23] Steiner, 'How Free', 78–9.

in s. 7.5, what we need to take into account is, for any set of compossible actions, the probability of the agent finding it physically possible or impossible to perform that set. By multiplying the number assigned to the set by the probability of its availability (in the case of $F_{r,i}$) and the probability of its unavailability (in the case of $U_{r,i}$), our revised formula is able to accommodate the idea that, *ceteris paribus*, a person who is less probably free to do x has less freedom overall.

Why, if probabilities can be integrated into our calculations in this way, was it not suggested earlier, in relation to threats, that the freedom-reducing effect of a threat can be measured in terms of the probability that the agent (whose freedom is being reduced) will comply, and thus be deterred from acting in a certain way? The reason for this—quite apart from its failure to show us why threats reduce freedom if offers do not—is that to have done so would have been to confuse *the freedom to act* with *the probability of acting*. We do not normally suppose that because a person always chooses (and will always be certain to choose) in the same way, she is unfree to choose otherwise.[24] And yet, if we measure an agent's freedom not to comply with a threat in terms of the *probability* that she will not do so, we appear to be making exactly this kind of inference. My own analysis does not confuse the freedom to act with the probability of acting; while it implies that the probability of my choosing to do x (and of my doing it) may directly affect the freedom of *others*, it certainly does not imply that that probability directly affects my own freedom.

8.5 'SOCIALIST' VERSUS 'LIBERTARIAN' CONCEPTIONS OF CONSTRAINTS

It is worth noting an implication of the above analysis that has to do with the distinction between unfreedom and inability, mentioned in s. 8.1 (see also s. 7.1). This implication will turn out to be useful later on we come to look at possible 'indicators' of degrees of overall freedom (see s. 10.3). It is sometimes said, usually by libertarians, that to lack money is not to be unfree but, rather, to be unable.[25] This means, as some socialist critics of libertarianism

---

[24] The failure to distinguish between the freedom to act and the probability of acting represents a central flaw in the method of measuring freedom proposed by Dennis and André Gabor. See e.g. A. Gabor, 'The Measurement of Freedom', *International Journal of Social Economics*, 6 (1979); Gabor and Gabor, 'An Essay on the Mathematical Theory of Freedom'.

[25] An exception to this generalization is Steiner. The libertarians who make the above claim are for the most part the same as those who adopt a moralized definition of freedom (see s. 3.1, and the references therein). They also include Hayek. See *The Constitution of Liberty*, ch. 1, s. 5.

have ironically pointed out, that the penniless tramp is completely free (only unable) to dine at the Ritz. Many socialists have assumed that they must deny the distinction between unfreedom and inability if they are to counter this claim, and thus reach their desired conclusion that poverty is a form of unfreedom.

I confess that I have never understood either of these positions. Libertarians are simply wrong when they make the above claim about the relationship between money and social freedom, and it is not necessary to embrace a more 'positive' notion of freedom (by rejecting the distinction between unfreedom and inability) in order to challenge them on this point. The fact is that the money in one's possession partly determines whether or not others will physically prevent one from performing certain sets of actions. Thus, the tramp is physically prevented, not by his lack of money, but *because* of his lack of money, and *by other people*, from eating at the Ritz and then walking away unimpeded (assuming he is not thrown out first for bad dress). Cohen has put this point nicely: 'the assimilation of money to mental and bodily resources [so as to classify the lack of money as a lack of ability rather than of freedom] is a piece of unthinking fetishism, in the good old Marxist sense that it misrepresents *social relations of constraint* as *things* that people lack. In a word: money is no object.'[26] As Cohen says, money is best thought of as 'a [highly generalized] license to perform a disjunction of conjunctions of actions—actions, like, for example, visiting one's sister in Bristol, or taking home, and wearing, the sweater on the counter at Selfridges'.[27] Thus, the total exchange value of the resources at my disposal implies, given certain market prices, the availability to me of a particular set of sets of compossible actions. Any gift of money (including welfare benefits) increases that available set of sets of compossible actions, and any confiscation of money (including taxation) reduces it. Remember that as long as we endorse a freedom-based theory of justice, rather than a justice-based definition of freedom, the question of the *justice* of a proposed tax is a question to which we can turn only after having ascertained how far that tax reduces people's freedom, and not *in order to* ascertain it (see s. 3.1).

It might be objected that the above argument assumes a particular view of the sources of constraints on freedom—namely a 'causal responsibility view' —and that the libertarian can avoid the conclusion that the poor are less free than the rich by recourse to the 'moral responsibility view' of the sources of constraints on freedom (see s. 8.1). On the latter view, it might be said, the rich, with the help of the state, do not restrict the freedom of the poor when they forcibly withhold resources from them, because, given a libertarian

---

[26] Cohen, *Self-Ownership, Freedom and Equality*, 58–9.   [27] Ibid. 58.

account of their moral obligations, neither the rich nor the state should be held morally responsible for the plight of the poor. But this objection confuses moral responsibility with moral culpability, and so leads us straight back to the moralized definition of freedom just alluded to. The 'moral responsibility view' of the sources of constraints on freedom does not say that the only freedom-restricting obstacles are those which are morally *wrong*—i.e. those which someone has an obligation to remove—for this would amount to a moralized definition of freedom. Rather, it says that the only freedom-restricting obstacles are those for which an agent or group of agents can be held morally responsible, regardless of whether those obstacles are themselves morally justified.[28] I doubt that the rich (with the help of the state) can in most cases be said to lack the moral *obligation* to help the poor, even given a libertarian account of obligations, which typically includes obligations other than those involving the respecting of property rights.[29] But in any case, what cannot be denied is that, be the rich in the right or in the wrong in withholding their resources from the poor, they remain morally *responsible* for their decision. So it is not true that my claim that the poor are generally less free than the rich rests on a 'causal responsibility view' of the sources of constraints.

The fact that exchange values in a free market provide useful indicators of the size and number of sets of compossible actions available to agents can also be employed in gauging the strength of certain threats: those which describe the counterfactual *fining* of certain activities. *Ceteris paribus*, the strength of such threats, in terms of the degree of reduction in overall freedom they describe, is roughly proportional to the extent of the fine. Thus, for example, we can safely say that a fully enforced threat to fine motorists £50 for speeding in a certain country reduces their freedom by roughly half as much as a fully enforced threat to fine them £100 for speeding in that country. This is because the way in which the threatener reduces the freedom of the recipient in these cases is by rendering unavailable to the recipient any set of compossible actions that includes both speeding on the motorway and performing actions the physical components of which would have to be bought (in part) with the fine money. I have reasons for saying that the reduction in freedom is only 'roughly', and not precisely, proportional to the strength of the fine, but those reasons need not be dealt with until we turn to the discussion of exchange values as an indicator of overall freedom (s. 10.3).

---

[28] Cf. Kristjánsson, *Social Freedom*, 19–20.

[29] Those political philosophers who most frequently miss *this* point are *non*-libertarians. They, as a result, wrongly accuse libertarians of not *caring* about the plight of the poor. Particularly clear examples are to be found in a number of the reviews of Nozick's *Anarchy, State and Utopia*.

8.6 'LIBERAL' VERSUS 'REPUBLICAN' CONCEPTIONS OF CONSTRAINTS

The analysis of constraints on freedom provided in this chapter can also help us to clarify the debate between supporters of the so-called 'liberal' and 'republican' conceptions of liberty. The most influential 'republican' critics of liberal conceptions of freedom are Quentin Skinner and Philip Pettit,[30] according to whom liberals mistakenly conceive of freedom as the straightforward absence of the kind of interference talked of so far in this chapter —interference like the erection of physical barriers or the issuing of threats— and ignore an essential further ingredient of freedom: the presence of certain factors which *guarantee* this absence of interference, such as constitutional safeguards and the exercise of republican virtues, where the latter include a sense of civic duty, vigilance against corruption in politics, and active democratic participation. It is also the view of Skinner and Pettit that liberals have been wrong to classify this rival view of liberty as 'positive', and to see it as leading to the kind of paradox identified in Chapter 6. Republicans, they say, are sometimes wrongly interpreted as defining freedom in terms of self-mastery or self-determination, and therefore as implying that one can be 'forced to be free', when in fact they define freedom 'negatively', as the absence of constraint; the difference between republicans and liberals lies in their interpretations of the notion of a 'constraint on freedom'.

Thus, according to Skinner, republican (or what he also calls 'neo-roman') theorists of freedom 'have no quarrel . . . with the liberal . . . tenet that the concept of liberty "is merely a negative one" '; what they do dispute is 'the key assumption of classical liberalism to the effect that force or the coercive threat of it constitute the only forms of constraint that interfere with individual liberty'. For neo-roman theorists, 'to live in a condition of dependence is itself a source and a form of constraint', for such a condition implies 'a diminution not merely of security for your liberty but of liberty itself'.[31]

An interesting conceptual clarification of this negative republican ideal is to be found in Pettit's defence of freedom as 'resilient non-interference'. The liberal, Pettit says, favours non-interference with individuals' actions 'no

---

[30] See e.g. Q. Skinner, 'The Paradoxes of Political Liberty', *Tanner Lectures on Human Values*, 5 (1984); id., 'The Republican Ideal of Political Liberty', in G. Bock, Q. Skinner, and M. Viroli (eds.), *Machiavelli and Republicanism* (Cambridge: Cambridge University Press, 1990); id., *Liberty before Liberalism* (Cambridge: Cambridge University Press, 1998); Pettit, 'The Freedom of the City'; id., 'Negative Liberty, Liberal and Republican', *European Journal of Philosophy*, 1 (1993): id., *Republicanism: A Theory of Freedom and Government* (Oxford: Oxford University Press, 1997).

[31] Skinner, *Liberty before Liberalism*, 82–4.

matter how' that non-interference is realized, whereas the republican favours '*resiliently* realized' non-interference. Non-interference is 'resilient' to the extent that conditions are in place which safeguard non-interference. Those conditions can be specified by reference to certain institutional arrangements, which are suitable both for 'maintaining the continued presence' of non-interference, and for 'restoring it in the event of disturbance'.[32] Liberals see freedom simply as an attribute of individuals without reference to institutionally entrenched rules. Republicans, on the other hand, see liberty as inseparable from such entrenched rules, since these guarantee the resilience of non-interference.

Pettit has recently suggested a further refinement of the republican conception of constraints. He now says that freedom consists in 'non-domination', which means the resilient absence of that form of interference which consists in an exercising of arbitrary power (i.e. of interference which, among other things, occurs 'without reference to the interests or the opinions of those affected').[33] In other words, he now says that for non-interference to count as freedom it must satisfy two conditions. The first qualifies the 'non' in 'non-interference': the non-interference in question must be realized resiliently. The second condition specifies the relevant meaning of 'interference': for interference to count as unfreedom it must be interference that is not 'forced to track the interests and ideas of the person suffering the interference'.[34] The upshot of this refinement is that 'I may . . . undergo interference without being dominated' (i.e. without being unfree) if 'the interference promises to further my interests and promises to do so according to opinions of a kind that I share'.[35]

I shall say no more here about this further refinement of the republican notion of constraints, as it has already been rejected in Part II of this book. To say, as the second of the above conditions does, that one is free (at least in part) to the extent that one's interests are fulfilled is to endorse (at least in part) a value-based conception of freedom, and I have argued against such a conception for independent reasons, the most important of which is its incompatibility with freedom's non-specific value. Since Pettit is clearly interested in the concept of overall freedom in a literal sense, I shall assume that his move from conceiving of freedom as resilient non-interference to conceiving of it as non-domination is an invalid one. I shall assume, that is, that republican freedom is simply resilient non-interference.

If this is what republican freedom consists in, then in my view the most that can be attributed to Skinner and Pettit is a useful set of empirical hypotheses

---

[32] Pettit, 'Negative Liberty, Liberal and Republican', 17. Cf. id., *Republicanism*, 24.
[33] Pettit, *Republicanism*, 55.   [34] Ibid.   [35] Ibid. 23.

(which point to certain sets of institutional arrangements) about how liberty is best to be maximized (or maximally equalized, or perhaps even maximinned). If I am right about this, then the difference between republicans and liberals is an empirical rather than a conceptual one, and the supposed difference over the meaning of 'constraints on freedom' is an illusion.

My reason for holding this view ought to become clear once it is recalled that any calculation of overall freedom must take account (among other things) of two factors: the number of available *sets of compossible actions* (ss. 7.2, 8.2, and 8.3) and the *probability* of the availability of those sets (ss. 7.5 and 8.4). Once we take account of the compossibility of actions and of the probability of their prevention, we shall in any case reach the conclusion that the kind of institutional arrangements favoured by Skinner and Pettit tend to maximize liberty (or maximally equalize it, or maximin it)—assuming their empirical hypotheses to be correct—and there will be no cause for challenging the liberal conception of liberty. It may indeed be empirically demonstrable that in a state in which citizens exercise the 'republican virtues', or even in a state where citizens are coerced into performing certain services to the state, there is an especially high probability of high degrees of non-interference being maintained over time. Certainly we should say that democratic systems of government usually imply a greater extent of freedom for most people than do dictatorial ones, given that the probability of being subjected to future interference in the latter systems is much higher. It is also true that some liberal theorists have ignored this fact, and have been content to note the conceptual truth that dictatorships are compatible with high degrees of freedom and democracies with low degrees of freedom.[36] Limiting oneself to this conceptual truth can blind one to another: that an increase in the probability of future constraints implies, *ceteris paribus*, a decrease in one's freedom here and now, and that it would therefore be wrong to say, for example, that the subjects of a given dictatorship enjoy a great deal of freedom but are very likely to lose it in the near future. However, it is one thing to say that certain liberals, in comparing democracies and dictatorships in terms of freedom, have neglected the dimension of probability that they would (as shown in ss. 7.5 and 8.4) normally and commonsensically integrate into their comparative extent-of-freedom judgements; it is quite another thing to say that if we do take account of the 'resilience' of non-interference we shall be employing an *alternative conception* of liberty—a 'republican', as opposed to a 'liberal' one.

---

[36] Here, the culprit that republicans normally cite is the not-so-liberal Hobbes, who claimed that the inhabitants of republican Lucca were not necessarily more free than those of Constantinople (*Leviathan*, ch. 21). But see also Hayek, *The Constitution of Liberty*, ch. 1, s. 2, and Berlin, *Four Essays on Liberty*, 129.

Consider some of the reasons Skinner and Pettit give for saying that two individuals can enjoy equal degrees of non-interference (in the liberal sense), but with differing degrees of resilience. Pettit points out that the individual enjoying only 'fragile' (i.e. non-resilient) non-interference may be able to enjoy non-interference only 'through currying favour with the powerful, toadying to them in a way that wins their tolerance'.[37] If she were to become 'less likeable, less lucky, or less cunning', interference would immediately follow.[38] The fact of her being subject to the arbitrary powers of such rulers means that she is 'at all times dependent on their good will', and this 'is equivalent to living in a condition of servitude'.[39] However, such an individual clearly enjoys less freedom in terms of the number of her available sets of compossible actions, since each of those sets whose performance does not result in a considerable diminution of her future options must include actions which curry favour with the powerful. Although she is free not to curry favour with the powerful, she is unfree to perform a large number of *sets* of actions which *include* not currying favour with the powerful. She is therefore less free in the *liberal* sense. Whatever Hobbes might have said, the liberal has little reason for believing that in 'arrangements that make people fearful and deferential . . . short of *actual* interference, those people will still enjoy perfect liberty'.[40]

Pettit also claims that the individual enjoying only fragile non-interference may be enjoying non-interference at the whim of a potential interferer (the clearest example of which would be a Hobbesian sovereign). There is 'no guarantee', for such a person, that she will not be interfered with. She leads, as Skinner rightly says, a life of 'extreme precariousness' given that the ruler's goodwill could be 'withdrawn at any time'.[41] But that person clearly enjoys less freedom in the liberal sense inasmuch as our probability calculations tell us that she is much more likely to be interfered with in the future. This remains true even if, as it turns out, she does not get interfered with. In assessing the degree of a person's freedom *at any one time*, one has to take into account the probability, *at that time*, of her being subject to constraints (see ss. 7.4 and 7.5), and the 'precariousness' of a state of non-interference must surely come into play here. No liberal has any reason to deny this much. And yet, once we see that this is the case, we can have no reason for seeing the republican conception of liberty as distinct from a liberal one.

Even if this argument is accepted, however, Pettit might still claim that there is a significant difference between 'liberal freedom' and 'republican freedom'.

---

[37] Pettit, 'Negative Liberty, Liberal and Republican', 19.

[38] Pettit, *Republicanism*, 24.   [39] Skinner, *Liberty before Liberalism*, 70.

[40] Pettit, 'Negative Liberty, Liberal and Republican', 33, my emphasis.

[41] Skinner, *Liberty before Liberalism*, 86 and 70.

For he does appear to concede that overall freedom judgements, for liberals, ought to consist in what he calls judgements of '*expected* non-interference' (i.e. judgements that incorporate assessments of the probability of future instances of non-interference), but also argues that the concept of resilient non-interference is *distinct* from that of expected non-interference. This would indeed make republicanism something more than just a wise insurance scheme for liberals interested in maximizing expected non-interference.

If the proponent of resilient non-interference is not simply interested in expected non-interference, what *is* she interested in? Pettit's answer is that favouring resilient non-interference implies risk aversion: the proponent of resilient non-interference prefers a smaller number of instances of non-interference that are highly probable to a larger number of such instances that are less probable. This, despite the fact that the expected non-interference (i.e. what liberals but not republicans would call the extent of freedom) may be the same in the two cases, or even higher in the second case. The republican favours institutional safeguards against the erosion of certain instances of non-interference, however improbable those erosions might be. Where there is a threat of interference, T, which can be successfully and certainly met by an institutional safeguard, P (though P would itself involve a degree of certain interference), the 'devotee of non-interference as such' will favour P if, and *only* if, the interference implied by T multiplied by its probability is greater than the interference certainly associated with P. Republicans, in contrast, will incorporate an extra bias in favour of P into their freedom-judgements, because 'what matters to them is that however far they enjoy non-interference, they enjoy it with minimal risk of invasion'.[42] This is why we say that republicans favour *resilient* non-interference.

I do not think that the above argument successfully shows the republican to be operating with an alternative conception of overall freedom. In order to see why it does not, we shall need to go back a step in Pettit's argument, and take a look at a particular characterization he gives of the notion of resilient non-interference. I think that this characterization is correct, but that it backfires when we consider the supposed distinction between resilient non-interference and expected non-interference.

Pettit asks whether resilient non-interference is a 'composite' value or a 'simple' one. He considers the objection that resilient non-interference is a composite value, in the sense that it combines 'two distinct values: on the one hand, non-interference as such, and on the other, the enjoyment of a certain security'. This, Pettit admits, would undermine his claim to have provided 'a genuinely alternative explication of negative liberty: an equally primitive

---

[42] Pettit, 'Negative Liberty, Liberal and Republican', 27, and, more generally, 25–8.

articulation of the value of being free from interference'. Were the objection to go through, his observations would have to be taken, instead, as 'arguments for the value, in addition to negative liberty, of a certain security'.[43] Pettit answers the objection by showing how non-interference and its resilience are not two distinct properties. To specify degrees of resilience is simply to provide 'a more determinate version' of non-interference, in the same way as to specify that something is blue is to provide a more determinate version of the idea that it is coloured and to specify that something is triangular is to provide a more determinate version of the idea that it has a regular shape. Resilient non-interference is therefore a 'simple' value. Its pursuit 'does not involve realizing a certain amount of non-interference on the one hand, as if that were one sort of thing, and a certain amount of security on the other, as if that were a thing of a distinct kind. Whenever non-interference is realized, it is always realized with some degree of resilience or non-resilience.'[44]

As I see it, there is a tension between the two claims set out above—that is, between the claim that (*a*) resilient non-interference is distinct from expected non-interference, and the claim that (*b*) resilient non-interference is a simple rather than a composite value. I think that (*b*) is true, and that as a result (*a*) must be false.

Consider another simple value analogous to resilient non-interference. Imagine that you and I each have a number of glasses of water. Inasmuch as each is a glass of water, we can say that each glass contains *some* quantity of water. The simple value I would propose as analogous to resilient non-interference is that of having 'water-in-one's-glasses'. (I prefer this alternative example to that of blueness or triangularity, because 'water-in-one's glasses', though stranger sounding, is more easily characterized as being a matter of degree.) Suppose now that I have eleven half-full glasses of water, and you have five full ones. Assuming that the glasses are identically sized, I clearly have more 'water in my glasses' than you have in yours. Perhaps you do not mind about this, because you have a strong preference for full glasses over half-full glasses. But you cannot deduce from this fact that you have *more* of the simple value 'water in your glasses'. All that is indicated by such a fact is that you prefer to trade off 'water in your glasses' against having full glasses of water.

Analogous to the fact that each glass of water contains a certain amount of water is the fact, admitted by Pettit, that 'whenever non-interference is realized, it is always realized with some degree of resilience or non-resilience'. We should therefore also say, analogously, that if I have eleven instances of

---

[43] Pettit, 'Negative Liberty, Liberal and Republican', 23.
[44] Ibid.

non-interference with a degree of resilience of 0.5, and you have five such instances which are certain (i.e. wholly resilient), I possess more of the simple value 'resilient non-interference' than you. Perhaps you do not mind about this, because you have a preference for wholly or highly resilient instances of non-interference over less resilient ones. But you cannot deduce from this fact that you have *more* of the simple value 'resilient non-interference'. All that is indic- ated by such a fact is that you prefer to trade off resilient non-interference (i.e. overall freedom) against having instances of non-interference that are highly resilient (i.e. security and predictability, in the form of certain specific freedoms with a high degree of probability).

The risk aversion that Pettit claims to be characteristic of republicanism certainly need not be irrational. It would only be irrational if freedom were unconditionally valuable (see s. 2.2). Risk aversion, at the cost of achiev- ing sub-maximal overall freedom, will be rational if one also values some relevant competing value, such as security or predictability (assuming, with Pettit, that security and predictability *do* conflict with maximal expected non- interference). What is undeniable, however, is that when described in these terms, the difference between republicans and liberals will not turn on how they interpret the concept of freedom. It will turn, instead, on the relative values they assign to freedom on the one hand and security or predictability on the other (assuming, again, that liberals really do value security less in relation to freedom than do republicans).

One further argument might be appealed to by Pettit in attempting to dis- tinguish between resilient and expected non-interference. His most recent suggestion is that the difference is not even one of risk aversion versus maximization but, rather, one of impossibility versus zero probability. What matters to the republican, he says, is not that there be zero probability, or a very low probability, of the powerful exercising their arbitrary power, but that this simply be impossible for them—i.e. that their arbitrary power be removed. A's interfering with B may be possible, in the sense that A is free to interfere with B, and yet have a probability of zero or near to zero, given A's particular preferences or character. In this case, Pettit now believes, B will still lack resilient non-interference, despite her not lacking expected non-interference:[45] one can still be unfree to do *x* because that freedom is subject to the whims of a tyrant, even if the tyrant's character is such that there is zero probability, or an extremely low probability, of his ever prevent- ing one from doing *x*. But this argument is flawed in a more straightforward way by a failure to take into account the degree of compossibility of B's avail- able actions in the way I suggested earlier. For if A really *will not* intervene

---

[45] Pettit, *Republicanism*, 73–4, 86–8.

whatever B does (and B knows this), then B will simply *not* have to practise the 'strategic deference and anticipation', the 'currying' and 'toadying' which, *ex hypothesi*, characterize the unfree subject. B will only be strategically deferent if she believes that there is some probability of her being prevented from performing a set of compossible actions that includes (i) actions that are non-deferent with respect to A and (ii) other actions that A's possible interference would prevent. B will only curry and toady if she believes there to be some probability of A preventing this set of compossible actions. So it is simply implausible, even on Pettit's own characterization of unfreedom, to say that B suffers unfreedom at A's hands despite there being a zero probability of A's interfering with B and despite B being aware of this. (It is, of course, also highly implausible to suppose that the probability of interference by A (not to speak of A's possible successors) really is zero.)

The supposed difference between resilient non-interference and expected non-interference therefore dissolves into nothing. Given this, we should also reject the widely held idea that there is a difference between liberal and republican attitudes to the relationship between freedom and *law*. In typical republican mode, Pettit contrasts the view of law as 'inimical to liberty' (supposedly the liberal view) with the view of law 'as inherently fitted . . . for the promotion of liberty' (supposedly the republican view).[46] If there is a difference here, it is that the republican sees law as good because it promotes security and predictability as well as freedom (though much more would need to be said to establish even this difference). As far as the relationship specifically between law and *freedom* is concerned, the differences between the republican and liberal views are, as expressed by Skinner and Pettit, purely rhetorical. Liberals see many laws as partly justified by the fact that they lead to a net gain in freedom or a just distribution of freedom: justified laws imply limitations of freedom to a certain extent and with a certain degree of probability, but are also often instrumental in promoting freedom or distributing it fairly, because their enforcement prevents certain cases of interference which would otherwise be realized, or more probably realized. It is difficult to see how the rule of law can be indispensable to freedom in any more intimate a sense than this, unless one assumes either (i) that laws made in the public interest simply do not constrain freedom[47]—a view I earlier rejected for independent reasons—or (ii) the more 'positive' view of freedom whereby obedience to the rule of law is seen as a *constitutive part of* (rather than merely a means to) the possession of liberty. On the second assumption, liberty is not the non-interference, resilient or otherwise, which the maintenance of certain

[46] Pettit, 'Negative Liberty, Liberal and Republican', s. 5.

[47] Pettit, *Republicanism*, 35–7, 66.

institutions and the exercise of the republican virtues tend, causally speaking, to increase or safeguard; it is simply the maintenance of those institutions and the exercise of the republican virtues themselves. In this case, liberty on the republican view will certainly be distinct from liberty on the liberal view. But it will only have been made so at the cost of a move in the direction of a conception of freedom as collective self-mastery or self-determination—a cost which neither Pettit nor Skinner is willing to pay, and, given the arguments of Chapter 6, wisely so.

8.7 CONCLUSION

We have now reached the end of our analysis of constraints on freedom—at least, that is, of constraints on the freedom of *individuals*. In the next chapter, I shall turn to the question of how to measure group freedom, and this will involve asking, among other things, whether the overall freedom of a group can be constrained without the freedom of any of its individual members being constrained. So far, my conclusion is that there is a great deal of appeal to be found, in reflective equilibrium, in an analysis of overall freedom in terms of the physical possibility of sets of actions, and that the reason for this lies not only in the ability of such an analysis to meet a number of sceptical objections regarding the possibility of overall measurements, but also in its ability to accommodate many of the common-sense comparisons of freedom that might at first be thought to conflict with it. The foregoing analysis accommodates the intuition that threats, and the difficulty of performing options, are generally accompanied by reductions in freedom, as well as the republican intuition that freedom is 'resilient non-interference'. It is the failure to perceive these implications that best explains the opposition of so many political philosophers to the 'physical impossibility' view of constraints on freedom, despite the greater consistency of that view with certain basic intuitions (e.g. that offers do *not* decrease freedom) and its greater conduciveness to measurement. In my view, this failure of perception is very often brought about by a failure to concentrate seriously enough on questions of *overall* freedom. What may appear, on the usual analyses of the notion of 'a specific freedom', to be descriptions of different and incommensurable dimensions of constraint turn out, in the light of a full analysis of 'overall freedom', to be different descriptions of a single dimension: that of the expected availability of sets of compossible actions.

9

Group Freedom

WE can now move on from the account of individual freedom given in the previous two chapters, and attempt to give an account of the attribution of degrees of overall freedom to groups. This means extending the analysis of freedom in terms of the availability of sets of compossible actions from the case of one person to that of many persons. To illustrate the need to do this, let me begin with an example which not only shows the usefulness of our analysis so far, but also raises one of the central questions yet to be addressed. The example is reported in a newspaper article entitled 'Price of Freedom':

pay first, and demonstrate later is the new rule in Moscow. Fed up with supplying extra policing and diverting traffic, the city authorities are demanding a fee for demonstrators and a council permit on each occasion.[1]

Are Muscovites free to demonstrate or not? The answer provided by our analysis so far is that they are (or rather, that they have a certain probability of being so), but that, as a result of the 'new rule', they nevertheless have less freedom overall than before. The reduction in their freedom will be represented in our measurements by a reduction in the number of sets of compossible actions that are left physically possible for them, of which demonstrating (on any one occasion) is a member (see ss. 7.2 and 8.2). This reduction is brought about by changes in the two variables of cost and probability (see ss. 7.5, 8.3, and 8.4). If Muscovites try to demonstrate without a permit, they are likely to be physically prevented from doing so (either by the police or by the traffic). But in order to obtain the permit, they must expend resources in terms of time and money; hence, demonstrating is physically impossible in combination with any group of actions which is sufficiently large necessarily to involve spending that time and money in a different way. In addition, there is a certain probability that the council will refuse in any one case to grant the permit; hence, there is a further reduction in the freedom of Muscovites, to be represented in our measurements by the probability, for each set of actions of which demonstrating on a particular occasion is a member (*after* taking into account the costs of doing so), of that set being physically possible. (Perhaps, for example, the probability of being awarded permits to demonstrate in the same

[1] *Guardian*, 14 Feb. 1992, p. 14.

place on two successive days is very low indeed, with the result that two such successive demonstrations are very likely to be impossible in combination.)

But who, or what, is suffering the unfreedom described above? Is 'the freedom to demonstrate' something that can be characterized in terms of the freedom of *individuals* to do certain things? How are we to characterize the loss in the freedom of *any one individual* brought about by the 'new rule'? Is each individual not free to go through all of the motions that she would have gone through at the demonstration (for example, walking down the street and making certain noises), only *alone*, and without paying a fee or requiring a permit? We seem, so far, to have ignored the question of the compossibility or otherwise of the actions of *more than one individual*, which may be thought to be relevant to the overall freedom of a *group* of individuals.

In this chapter I shall address two broadly distinct but closely related questions. The first, which I address in sections 1 to 3, is the question of whether there can be constraints on the freedom of groups that are not reducible to constraints on the freedom of individuals. Those who answer in the affirmative believe that measuring freedom should involve assessing not only the compossibility of actions of single individuals, but also the compossibility of actions of *different* individuals, where to render the actions of two or more individuals impossible in combination is to reduce their freedom as a group. On this view, to adopt G. A. Cohen's terminology, unfreedom can be *collective* as well as individual. Cohen makes use of the notion of collective unfreedom in attempting to show that the proletariat is an 'enslaved class'. I believe, however, that it is a mistake to appeal to the idea of collective freedom in arguments about comparative extents of group freedom. One reason for this is that such an idea turns out on reflection to be of little use (or even to be counter-productive) in attempting to achieve isomorphism with Cohen's Marxist (or neo-Marxist) intuition that disadvantaged and exploited groups (like proletarians) lack freedom.

The second question of this chapter, dealt with in section 4, regards the effects on freedom of the structure and distribution of enforced property rights. Here, we shall assess Hillel Steiner's 'zero-sum thesis', according to which overall group freedom can never be increased or decreased (except where one group's freedom increases at the expense of that of another). I shall argue against the zero-sum thesis. I believe that the communalization of resources within a given group can affect the degree of overall freedom of that group. As we shall see, there is a connection between the two questions addressed in this chapter, given that some counter-arguments to my view that property rights can affect overall group freedom appear to rest on a confusion of group freedom, understood as the sum total of individual freedom, with collective freedom in Cohen's sense.

i and j are	separately possible	separately impossible
possible in combination	(*a*)	(*c*)
impossible in combination	(*b*)	(*d*)

FIG. 7

My discussion of the freedom–property relation ought to have useful implications regarding the likely direction of a fruitful freedom-based debate between libertarians and egalitarians. I should say at the outset, however, that neither side will emerge victorious from my discussion. This is because the freedom–property relation is as much an empirical question as a conceptual one. I cannot assess any of the relevant empirical claims here; I aim only to show how far and in what ways they are relevant. If we endorse an empirical conception of overall freedom, we must accept that there can be no easy conceptual answer to the question of what structures of property rights best guarantee a society of justly distributed freedom (that is, one with maximal freedom, maximal equal freedom, or whatever). As we saw in Chapter 3 (s. 3.1), those who do try to provide an easy conceptual answer inevitably 'moralize' the concept of freedom, so betraying the very reasons they had in the first place for being interested in levels of overall freedom.

9.1 GROUP FREEDOM AND COLLECTIVE FREEDOM

Let the term 'collective freedom' describe the freedom of a *group* of individual agents to perform a *set* of agentially distinct actions (agent A being free to perform action i, agent B being free to perform action j, and so on) *in combination*. 'Collective *un*freedom' therefore means the lack of freedom *of that group* to perform that set of actions in combination. A and B may be said to possess or lack either individual or collective freedom with regard to the performance of their respective actions i and j. This means that the group A+B can be in one of four possible situations, as is made clear in Fig. 7.

The dimension of collective freedom and unfreedom is represented by the entries on the left-hand side of Fig. 7 ('possible in combination' and 'impossible in combination'). This means that (*a*) and (*c*) in Fig. 7 represent a situation in which A and B are collectively free to do i and j, whereas (*b*) and (*d*) represent a situation in which they are collectively unfree to do so. As regards individual freedom, (*a*) and (*d*) clearly represent the presence and lack of it respectively. Either of (*b*) or (*c*), on the other hand, may or may not represent a situation in which A and B are individually free to do *i* and *j*. In the case of (*b*), they will both have individual freedom only if *neither will as a matter of fact perform her respective action*; in the case of (*c*), *neither* of them will have individual freedom *unless both will as a matter of fact perform their respective actions*. In other words, in the case of (*b*), A's freedom to do *i* depends (among other things) on B's *not performing j*, whereas in the case of (*c*), A's freedom to perform *i* depends (among other things) on B's *performing j*.

The concept of collective unfreedom figures importantly in the work of G. A. Cohen, who claims that proletarians are individually free, but collectively unfree to 'exit' from the proletariat.[2] And the concept of collective unfreedom clearly has possible applications other than this Marxist one. It might indeed be applied to any situation in which one class exercises power over another, and the former is seen as exploiting the latter, as, for example, in the case of the feminist claim that men render the class of women unfree.[3] But the Marxist application is the one that most interests Cohen,[4] and it is this application on which I shall concentrate my attention, although I believe that my conclusions will also be relevant to the other cases.

In Cohen's view, while it may be possible for *some* proletarians to escape from the situation in which they are forced to sell their labour power, through hard work, saving, and risk-taking, it is nevertheless a consequence of the structure of the constraints to which they are subject as a group that only a limited number of them can do this, and therefore that 'the freedom of each is contingent on the others not exercising their similarly contingent freedom'.[5] Cohen clarifies this argument with an example, in which there are ten people locked in a room, from which one, and only one, is free to escape. They possess a key which will open the locked door, but only one person (any person) may use the key and leave, after which all the others must remain in the room. As it happens, none of the ten people is disposed to leave the room (say, out of solidarity or laziness). In such a situation, each is individually free to escape. For it is true of any one person that, should she try to pick up the key and leave the room, no one will stop her. Nevertheless, the group as a whole suffers collective unfreedom with regard to escaping, for the simple reason that not more than one of the ten people is free to escape.

---

[2] G. A. Cohen, 'The Structure of Proletarian Unfreedom', *Philosophy and Public Affairs*, 12 (1983); id., 'Capitalism, Freedom and the Proletariat'.

[3] Cf. A. Mason, 'Workers' Unfreedom and Women's Unfreedom: Is There a Significant Analogy?', *Political Studies*, 44 (1996).

[4] Despite the Marxist motivation behind Cohen's interest in collective unfreedom, the conception of a 'constraint on freedom' with which he works is, for the purpose of the argument under consideration, essentially a liberal one (cf. G. G. Brenkert, 'Cohen on Proletarian Unfreedom', *Philosophy and Public Affairs*, 14 (1985)).

[5] Cohen, 'The Structure of Proletarian Unfreedom', 11.

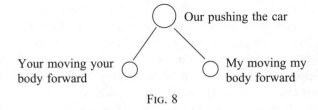

FIG. 8

Cohen's example fits case (*b*) in Fig. 7. What of situations represented by (*c*)? An example can be found in Alvin Goldman's analysis of power, where we are asked to imagine a stationary car (e.g. a stalled Buick) which will only move if pushed by two people rather than by one. (In this case, my 'pushing of the car at time *t*' is only possible *in combination* with your 'pushing of the car at *t*', and vice versa).[6] Since Goldman's example forms part of an analysis of 'power', he does not concern himself with the question of the source of the obstacle preventing the car from being pushed by one person. But if we wish we can easily make this a case of social unfreedom by imagining that there is a third person at the other end of the car who is as strong as either of us and who will apply his own weight in the opposite direction whenever we push. In Goldman's example, *i* and *j*, taken together, can be said to constitute a *joint action*. In calling them parts of a joint action, I mean that while *i* and *j* are, in the Davidsonian sense, two separate actions of two separate people, they nevertheless constitute, in Goldman's sense, a single action that is causally generated by the separate coordinated basic actions of two individuals. (On the difference between Davidson's and Goldman's theories of act individuation, see s. 7.2.) Thus, our joint action of pushing the car can be represented by an adaptation of one of Goldman's 'act-trees',[7] as depicted in Fig. 8. Presumably, the degree to which this specific freedom increases my individual freedom will be represented by the number we assign to the combination of equal spatio-temporally specified event-units that constitute the moving of the car (see s. 7.3), divided by the number of agents whose basic actions are necessary in order for that movement to be brought about —in this case, two.

This is not to say that (*c*) need necessarily represent the freedom of a group to perform a joint action; *i* and *j* might simply be two separate individual

---

[6] Goldman, 'Toward a Theory of Social Power', 170.

[7] Goldman, *A Theory of Human Action*, 35. In Goldman's example, a single action ('signaling pilot to land') is (conventionally) jointly generated by two basic actions of the *same* person ('holding left flag extended outward' and 'rotating right flag'). Fig. 8 might *look* like an act-*root* (see Fig. 6 at s. 7.7), but it is not, because it does not represent alternative hypothetical ways in which one person might do the same thing.

actions that some external force is preventing from being performed separately. An example of the latter type might be 'going on a guided tour of a museum', where the museum can only be seen by a guided tour, and the guide refuses to conduct a tour without a minimum number of tourists. If not enough people will visit the museum, the group can be described as collectively free but individually unfree to visit the museum, and its situation will in this sense be an exact mirror image of that of the proletariat as described by Cohen.

Despite this exact symmetry between (c) and (b) in the case of the museum visit and Cohen's locked room, an asymmetry occurs when we consider (c) as instead representing the collective freedom to perform a *joint* action (like the car-pushing). While in (c), i and j might together constitute a joint action, in (b) they cannot. This is because to prevent a joint action—that is, an action which, like the car-pushing, can only be causally generated by the coordinated basic actions of the members of the group—is also to prevent the separate performance of at least one of its component actions. Therefore, while the components of a joint action can be possible in combination while separately impossible, the opposite cannot hold; those components cannot be impossible in combination but also separately possible, in the way that they are in Cohen's example.

It might be suggested that the freedom to perform joint actions is quite distinct from the collective freedom Cohen has in mind, where i and j are simply two unconnected actions of two individuals (as in the museum visit), and therefore that it would be wrong to place the car-pushing and the museum visit in the same category. But as far as the measurement of collective freedom is concerned, this suggestion is without a sound basis. For if we are interested in degrees of *overall* collective freedom, both of these kinds of specific collective freedom should be taken into account in our measurements. After all, the only reason for distinguishing between the two kinds of specific collective freedom representable by (c) (in Fig. 7) lies in the different answers we give to the question of whether or not actions i and j could conceivably be *separately* performable while also being unperformable in combination. The only difference, then, is the fact that in the case of the car-pushing, the actions consisting in a part of 'the pushing of the car' are actions that cannot be unperformable in combination while also separately performable, as they could conceivably be in the case of the museum visit—i.e. were the guide to allow individual visits and prevent group visits. But this distinction is only useful as a means to determining whether, *in addition to collective unfreedom*, there might also be *individual freedom*. As far as the presence of *collective* freedom or unfreedom is concerned, the additional presence of *individual* freedom or unfreedom is neither here nor there.

How should purely collective freedom be measured, and how is it to be compared with purely individual freedom? A partial but plausible answer to the first of these two questions is provided by Cohen, who suggests that the collective unfreedom to perform an act-type, A, 'is greater the smaller the ratio of the maximum that could perform [action] A to the total number in the group'.[8] What of the second question? Is collective freedom commensurable with individual freedom? How can we represent a gain in individual freedom (despite a loss in collective freedom), and a gain in collective freedom (despite a loss in individual freedom), such that the two combinations of gains and losses in freedom are commensurable in terms of the *overall freedom of a group*? This seems to be more difficult. As John Gray notes, Cohen provides no argument 'for the reducibility of collective freedom and unfreedom to individual freedom and its absence. . . . Nor is this surprising, since the two sorts of freedom seem on the face of it categorically distinct, and possibly even incommensurable notions of freedom.'[9] Cohen himself admits that 'collective unfreedom . . . is *irreducibly* collective when more can perform A *in sensu diviso* than can perform it *in sensu composito*'.[10]

Like Gray and Cohen, I can see no way of reducing degrees of collective freedom to degrees of individual freedom or of commensurating the two in terms of overall group freedom. Neither do I intend to pursue questions about the measurement of purely collective freedom any further here. Instead, I shall explain why I believe that measurements of the freedom of a group ought to involve only measurements of the *individual* freedom of its members. As in the previous two chapters, my strategy will consist in showing how this view of freedom is not as 'narrow', intuitively speaking, as might at first be suspected. In other words, I shall try to show that the price in terms of isomorphism with common-sense comparisons, of seeing group freedom as a function only of individual freedom, is much lower than might at first be supposed by those who are initially sympathetic to Cohen's introduction of the concept of 'collective freedom'. I shall present two arguments to this effect. The first argument, in s. 9.2, will show that Cohen's belief that the proletarian class has a relatively low level of overall freedom stands a much better chance of being reflected by measurements of individual freedom than by measurements of collective freedom. The second argument, in s. 9.3, will show that A and B in Fig. 7 *may*, in any case, both be more free *individually* if their situation is correctly represented by (*a*) rather than (*b*) (or by (*c*) rather than by (*d*)).

---

[8] Cohen, 'The Structure of Proletarian Unfreedom', 16.
[9] Gray, 'Against Cohen on Proletarian Unfreedom', 192.
[10] Cohen, 'The Structure of Proletarian Unfreedom', 16.

9.2 THE COLLECTIVE FREEDOM AND INDIVIDUAL UNFREEDOM OF PROLETARIANS

Proletarians have more collective freedom and less individual freedom than Cohen appears to believe. Let us look first at the level of their collective freedom and then at the level of their individual freedom.

When Cohen describes proletarians as collectively unfree to leave the proletariat he ignores the sense in which their situation can be represented by (*c*) in Fig. 7. As we have seen, in Cohen's example, there are ten people locked in a room. They possess the key to the door, but only one person may use the key and leave. In addition, no one is inclined to leave the room. In such a situation, the group can be described as individually free but collectively unfree to leave the room. But this example can be extended. Imagine that leading out of the same room there is a second locked door, to which there is no key, but which would be broken down if and only if ten people were to push at it with all their might. In such a situation, the group should be described as collectively free to leave through the second door. Suppose that not all of the ten people are inclined to push. Given Cohen's claim that the inclinations of the various individuals about whether or not to leave do not affect their collective *unfreedom* to leave (through the first door), he can hardly say that such inclinations affect their collective *freedom* to leave (through the second door). Instead, what we should say is that, because none (or at least, not ten) of the individuals wish to leave through the second door, none is *individually* free to leave through the second door. The freedoms and unfreedoms provided by the two doors are mirror images of each other: the people in the room are individually free but collectively unfree to leave through the first door, and they are collectively free but individually unfree to leave through the second door.

A clear analogy to the second door in this extended example is the possibility, according to classical Marxists, of a successful communist revolution leading to the abolition of capitalist exploitation. The first door referred to by Cohen only applies to the freedom of proletarians within the capitalist system. But Marxists also believe that, 'objectively speaking', capitalism can be overthrown. Add to this the premiss, affirmed, among others, by Cohen himself, that the main factor preventing a Marxist revolution has been a lack of proletarian solidarity,[11] and one is forced to conclude that the proletariat is collectively free (though by this means individually unfree) to escape its supposed confinement. Another possibility, which does not depend on this

[11] See G. A. Cohen's *Karl Marx's Theory of History: A Defence* (Oxford: Clarendon Press, 1978), 244–5.

Marxist belief in a successful communist revolution, might be that of the formation, on a large scale, of workers' cooperatives.

Cohen attempts to avoid this conclusion by distinguishing, in the way I
already have, between collective freedom as the freedom of a group to perform a set of separately performable actions and collective freedom as the
freedom of a group to perform a joint action. In the first case, Cohen says,
'the relevant agents are individuals, not a group as such', and therefore 'the
freedom or lack of it which the proletariat has to overthrow capitalism falls
outside our scope, since no individual proletarian could ever be free to do
so, even when the proletariat is free to do so'.[12] Here, however, Cohen has
simply described a situation analogous to the example of the car-pushing. It
is impossible for any one individual to overthrow capitalism, just as it is impossible for either individual to push the car alone. But this is a fact about *individual* freedom, not about collective freedom. All it shows is that the
situation of proletarians with regard to the freedom or unfreedom to overthrow capitalism cannot conceivably be represented by (*a*) or (*b*) in Fig. 7.
It does not therefore show that proletarians do not enjoy a *collective* freedom
(represented by (*c*) in Fig. 7), which should at least be balanced against the
collective unfreedom identified by Cohen (and represented by (b)). This leaves
us with Cohen's belief that, in the case of his own claim about proletarian
collective freedom, 'the relevant agents are individuals, not a group as such'.
But why should this be so? As we have seen, Cohen himself says that where
there is no individual unfreedom, collective unfreedom is 'irreducibly' collective. In what sense, then, can an agent that suffers such a collective
*un*freedom be said to be an individual? Only in so far as that agent '*shares
in*' that collective unfreedom.[13] Why, then, should an individual member of
the group that is collectively free but individually unfree to push the car not
be said in a similar way to *share* in the collective *freedom* to push the car?
Is collective freedom without individual freedom any less a thing which a
member of a group 'shares in' than collective unfreedom without individual
unfreedom?

Cohen's distinction between these two kinds of situation seems to rest on
the intuition that my 'sharing' in the collective unfreedom to leave the room
(through the first door) does not depend on the inclinations of the other members of the group, but that my 'sharing' in the collective freedom (to leave
through the second door) does, since I cannot leave unless all the others are
inclined to do so. But if this is so, then he has confused collective freedom

---

[12] Cohen, 'The Structure of Proletarian Unfreedom', 17.

[13] Cohen's definition of collective unfreedom specifies that 'x *shares in* a collective unfreedom with regard to a type of action A if and only if...' (ibid. 16, my emphasis).

with individual freedom. I 'share' in the collective freedom to leave through the second door *regardless* of the inclinations of the others. It is my *individual* freedom to leave that depends on the inclinations of the others.

If we accept Cohen's concept of collective freedom (together with various revolutionary or reformist empirical hypotheses), then, we must conclude, *contra* Cohen, that proletarians are collectively free to stop being proletarians. What of the proletarian's degree of *individual* freedom? In fact, an analysis of unfreedom in terms of an individual's available sets of compossible actions ought to allow us to describe proletarians as each suffering a great deal of individual unfreedom. This is not because only a limited number of proletarians can escape from the proletariat within the capitalist system (although, as we shall see below, it *may* also be *partly* for that reason), but simply because it is extremely difficult for even one individual to escape from the proletariat. In line with the analysis presented in the previous chapter, the difficulty of doing *x* can be taken into account in our measurements of freedom either by reference to the cost of doing *x* or by reference to the probability of succeeding in doing *x* should one try. The point being made here is similar to that made in my argument against the 'republican challenge' to liberal conceptions of freedom (in s. 8.6). To take the example of cost, if escaping from the proletariat involves saving and working extremely hard, then doing so is impossible in combination with a great many actions which are performable by proletarians who do not try to escape.

It is not clear, then, that critics of capitalist exploitation must embrace the concept of collective freedom in order to describe proletarians as substantially less free than capitalists. Indeed, *if* such critics wish their measurements of freedom to be isomorphic with Cohen's common-sense comparison of the freedom of proletarians and non-proletarians, and *if* their commitment to that common-sense comparison of freedom is greater than their commitment to the concept of collective freedom as a dimension of overall freedom (as my second argument, below, may help to persuade them it is), then they ought, in reflective equilibrium, to abandon the belief that collective freedom is one of the dimensions of overall group freedom.

Perhaps Cohen has overlooked the important sense in which proletarians are individually unfree through a neglect of questions about *overall* individual freedom (as opposed to questions about specific individual freedoms), and thus of the fact that even if proletarians *are* individually free to leave the proletariat, this does not imply that they are individually as free *overall* as non-proletarians. Although Cohen has been more sensitive than most to the importance of making sense of the idea of degrees of overall freedom, the true reason for the lesser individual freedom of the proletarian only really becomes clear once we have seen the importance of measuring overall individual freedom in terms of the expected availability of sets of compossible actions, and this method is not considered by Cohen. The proletarian *is* individually free to become a bourgeois, but, given a general lack of access to resources, this particular freedom adds little to his overall individual freedom.

9.3 THE TRUTH IN CLAIMS ABOUT COLLECTIVE FREEDOM AND UNFREEDOM

I now come to my second argument in favour of measuring the freedom of groups only in terms of individual freedom, that argument being that even where we do so, as a matter of contingent empirical fact the individuals in question *may well* be correctly described as less free *individually* partly because they belong to a group suffering from what Cohen would call collective unfreedom. In other words, what Cohen calls 'collective unfreedom' can itself be one of the *empirical factors* that *contribute* to a reduction in individual freedom, despite it never being a sufficient condition for such a reduction.

It seems to me that the most felicitous way of characterizing propositions about 'collective unfreedom' is simply as counterfactual conditionals about individual actions (of some) and individual unfreedoms (of others) (*if* A does *i*, *then* B will be unfree to do *j*). These counterfactual conditionals will affect degrees of individual freedom when their antecedents are true. A counterfactual conditional implying the joint impossibility of certain actions of different people is certainly a *necessary* condition for the presence of unfreedom. But in order to become a *sufficient* condition, the action referred to in the antecedent of that conditional must be one that *will* be performed (or, more precisely, that will have a degree of *probability* of being performed). Even if A's and B's respective actions *i* and *j* are not possible in combination, it hardly makes sense to say that B is suffering any unfreedom, as long as A is certain not to try to perform *i*. You (a pedestrian) are not unfree to cross the road simply because of the fact that *if* I (a driver) were to accelerate, you *would* be run over. On the other hand, since the freedom of each depends on the probability that the other will perform her respective action, *if* there is some probability of A performing her respective action then B *does* have less freedom. If there is indeed some probability that I (the driver) will accelerate, then you (the pedestrian) are indeed less free. But this last fact will be represented in our measurements as a lack of *individual* freedom. For if *i* and *j* are impossible in combination, then the sum of the probability of *i* being successfully performed and of *j* being successfully performed (assuming both actions to be attempted) can never be more than 1.

The case of claims about collective freedom is no different from that of claims about collective unfreedom. As in the case of collective unfreedom, claims about collective freedom tell us nothing about the truth value of the antecedent of the counterfactual conditionals they imply. Does it really make sense to say that the 'collective freedom' of a group (of which I am a member) to push the car is something which I *enjoy*, unless there is *some chance* that the other member or members of the group will also perform the basic actions necessary for the performance of that joint, causally generated action? Surely, the extent to which this 'freedom' is something I *enjoy* (and thus, the extent to which it really is *freedom*) depends on the probability of the others cooperating with me. But then, to the extent that they *will* cooperate with me, this thing I enjoy can be characterized as individual freedom. My freedom to 'push the car' can be represented by the number assigned to (my part in) performing the action of pushing the car, multiplied by the probability of it being possible for me to do so (i.e. to perform that part)—that is, the combined probabilities of the others pushing if I push, and of our being unrestrained as a group from pushing.

The case of demonstrating in Moscow, mentioned in the introduction to this chapter, can be treated in the same way. Here, the freedom of the individual Muscovite is simultaneously increased (or likely to be, given that demonstrating may increase or safeguard individual freedom) by the inclination of others (if they have it) to demonstrate, and decreased, in the way described earlier, by the 'new rule' referred to in the newspaper report. Again, regardless of the presence or absence of the new rule, in the (unlikely) event of our being *sure* that none of the others is inclined to cooperate, why say that the individual is free to perform (her part of) the level-generated action of demonstrating? (This is not to deny that, in such a situation, the new rule may be what dissuades the others from cooperating, and therefore that there would be an increase in individual freedom were the rule to be abolished.)

I should mention the following complication in the case of the demonstration example. I say above that the overall freedom of the Muscovite is *likely* to be increased by the inclination of the others to demonstrate, and not that it is certainly increased. The reason for this is that while 'pushing the car' is *causally* generated by the coordinated actions of the group, 'demonstrating' is only *conventionally* generated (see s. 7.2), and so is identical, for the purposes of freedom measurement, to the set of coordinated actions (of the separate individuals) which generate it. But this need not be seen as counter-intuitive when one considers that in being free to demonstrate (that is, in being free to perform such actions in coordination with those of others), one is likely to be exercising, with the others, collective *power*, which itself has a certain likelihood of being accompanied by increases in (or the safeguarding of) certain levels of freedom, in the way described in s. 8.6. (The probability of others cooperating with me may in turn be affected by the degree of power *I* have over *them*. People may be more likely to accompany me on a demonstration if, for example, I exercise charismatic power over them. Hence, my having more power in this case may lead (empirically) to my (and their) having more freedom. On the other hand, the fear of imprisonment, or doubts about the likelihood of obtaining a permit (which result from govenmental power), may make the others less likely to cooperate.)

We can therefore conclude that (*a*) in Fig. 7 will in many situations describe a higher level of individual freedom than (*b*) in Fig. 7, and (*c*) a higher level than (*d*), partly by virtue of the presence, in the cases of (*b*) and (*d*), of the phenomenon Cohen calls 'collective unfreedom'. This partial correlation provides useful intuitive backing for my own view that while the compossibility of actions does directly affect degrees of freedom in the case of one person (i.e. where those actions are all actions of the same agent), it does not directly affect degrees of freedom in the case of many persons (i.e. where those actions are agentially distinct). As usual, it provides this intuitive backing by partly absorbing the common-sense comparisons that initially appear to conflict with such a view.

On my view, then, the phenomenon Cohen has spotted is more appropriately described as the truth of a counterfactual conditional regarding individual actions (of some) and individual freedoms (of others). Such a phenomenon provides useful information in assessing degrees of group freedom, but it does not itself constitute a dimension of group freedom.

9.4 GROUP FREEDOM AND COMMUNAL PROPERTY

I now turn to the second question mentioned in the introduction to this chapter —that which concerns the implications of the structure and distribution of enforced property rights for overall group freedom. This is a complex matter, depending not only on conceptual claims about the relationship between freedom and property, but also on empirical ones about the possibility of cooperation and about degrees of scarcity. Sometimes there will be nothing for it but to go out and actually measure group freedom. Nevertheless, it will be useful to see just how far purely conceptual reasoning about the freedom–property relation will take us, and to see in what ways, exactly, the implications of property structures for overall freedom will further depend on contingent factors not implied by those structures themselves.

The arguments I shall present here will assume that the degree of freedom of a group of individuals is nothing more than the sum of the degrees of freedom of its individual members, as argued in the previous two sections. It is important to make this clear, since, as we shall see, certain initially plausible objections to my arguments can be shown to rest on a confusion between group freedom and collective freedom (as I have defined them). I should also say that in what follows I shall assume a 'causal responsibility view' of the sources of constraints on freedom (see s. 8.1). A 'moral responsibility view' would complicate matters further, although I think that the general thrust of my conclusions would be upheld by such a view too.

The idea that the total freedom of a group can change as a result of changes in the distribution of that freedom has been challenged by Hillel Steiner, according to whom 'a universal quest for greater personal liberty is a zero-sum game'.[14] The truth of this claim would be of some consequence for freedom-based theories of justice, as it would imply that the principle of maximal societal freedom is entirely pointless (except where it refers to the maximization of the freedom of one society at the expense of the freedom of another, in which case, presumably, most would see it as an unjust principle). It would also imply that the policies of maximizing equal freedom, and of maximinning or leximinning freedom, are in practice equivalent to that of equal freedom. Hence Steiner's endorsement of the principle of equal freedom (see s. 3.2).

A challenge to the zero-sum thesis is to be found in an argument of Cohen to the effect that communalizing property can lead to an overall increase in the freedom of the group that has access to the communal property. The example Cohen gives is that of two neighbours who share their household tools while respecting the rule that either may use a tool belonging to the other on the condition that she returns it when the owner needs it. Assuming that each has tools that the other lacks, the gain in freedom for each neighbour, in terms of the possibility of using the tools of the other, outweighs any loss in freedom caused by having to allow the other access to her own tools. Thus, where the two neighbours relinquish their full liberal ownership rights in their tools in favour of a communal set-up involving the rule just mentioned, there should be an overall increase in the freedom of each, and thus in the freedom of the group.[15]

Let us try to get a more precise idea of the conceptual implications of communalization for overall group freedom. Take a simple example, involving only the sharing of space. Divide an empty room into ten equal spatial units, one unit being the maximum space a person can take up at any one time, and the set of ten units being in theory occupiable by ten people simultaneously.

---

[14] Steiner, *An Essay on Rights*, 54; cf. id., 'Individual Liberty', 49–50; id., 'How Free', 88–9.
[15] Cohen, 'Capitalism, Freedom and the Proletariat' (1991 version), 173–4; cf. Taylor, *Community, Anarchy and Liberty*, 154–5.

We can say, then, that my freedom with respect to these units of space when I occupy the room exclusively is 10/10, given that I can perform a certain set of basic actions in any one unit during any one time-slice. (This resultant measurement is made in accordance with the revised Steinerian formula set out in s. 7.2, except that, given the present simplified example, we are only looking at the freedom of a person with respect to the actions which may be performed within a single time-slice, and there is no set of compossible actions that has more than one member.)

Now imagine a different situation in which the room is no longer occupied exclusively by me, but is also occupied by you. Should we say that my freedom with respect to the list of these ten units of space is now 5/10 (and that yours is similarly 5/10)? This is what an advocate of the zero-sum thesis will have to say. However, this will only be so if my room is divided into two equally sized compartments, one belonging to me and the other to you, where you are physically denied access to my compartment and I am physically denied access to yours. If we think instead of my room as communally possessed by the two of us, surely we should say that my freedom (still with respect to the list of the ten units of space) is now 9/10 (and that yours is similarly 9/10). I do not know which units of space you will take up, or at what times, but I do know that you only have one body, that it is logically impossible for you to be in two places at one time, and therefore that at any one time it will only be impossible for me to be in one of the ten units. The room provides us with more individual freedom when we possess it communally than when we are each in exclusive possession of a half of it.

What happens when the number of people in the room increases further? If the above argument is correct, then maximal group freedom in the communalized room will obtain when there are five or six occupants. Here, the sum total of available spatial units provided by the communalized room (within the given time-slice) will be thirty (as opposed to ten if the room is divided into five or six compartments). As the number of people increases above six, the sum total of available units provided by the communalized room drops, until where ten people are in the room, as where a single person possesses it exclusively, the sum total is only ten. (Once we start imagining an even more crowded room, the sum total of freedom it provides will presumably drop yet further until, where the individuals' bodies are physically squashed up against one another, the sum total of freedom it provides will be near to zero.)

The formula for calculating the sum total of freedom (i.e. the sum total of alternative spatial units) which the communalized room makes available during a given time-slice will be

$$b\ (a-b+1)$$

where a is the number of units of space and b is the total number of occupants during the relevant time-slice. (Note, however, that the formula only applies where b is less than or equal to a.) Similarly, the formula for the optimum number of occupants during the time-slice (in terms of maximal group freedom) will be

$$(a+1)/2$$

In the above example I am of course assuming that the occupants of the room have nowhere else to go. If we relax this assumption and say that in addition to having access to the communal room, each also has access to her own private room, and can choose whether or not to enter the communal room, then the total amount of freedom the communal room makes available will depend on the empirical question of how inclined each individual is to enter the communal room. For now, in order to pursue the above conceptual point a bit further, I shall continue to hypothesize a closed system in which the total available set of resources is either pooled or privatized.

Things get more complicated if we extend the above analysis to cover physical objects as well as space, and to cover sets of act-sequences rather than a single set of co-temporal alternatives. But the general argument surely applies to such cases as well, so confirming Cohen's intuition about tool-sharing. Here, a (in the above formulae) should represent the number of alternative sets of compossible actions which the relevant set of physical objects makes available, such that those sets (i) are each as large as possible when hypothesized as being performed by an individual in exclusive possession of the objects and (ii) are also all separately performable by different individuals. These two characteristics of a are analogous to two characteristics of the number of spatial units in the room in the previous example. First, each set of actions—where the actions are performable in combination by one individual—should be as large as possible, being the most that any *one* person can do with the relevant set of physical objects, in the same way as each unit of space in the room was the maximum space that one person could take up at any one time; second, the various sets of actions must themselves be compossible for *different* people—i.e. it must be possible for *all* of the sets to be performed, where each set is hypothesized as being agentially distinct—in the same way as the units of space in the room could all be simultaneously occupied by different people. This figure might well be difficult to estimate in practice, but there do not seem to be any conceptual reasons against the possibility of doing so, given the analysis of the idea of quantifying available actions set out in Chapter 7.

On what grounds might Steiner challenge the above argument against his zero-sum thesis? One way might be by pointing to the counter-intuitivity of saying that a physical component which provides ten possible actions at one time can be made to provide eighteen possible actions at another (as it did in the example of the room given earlier, where the number of occupants increased from one to two). But this doubt ought to be dispelled once it is emphasized that in measuring freedom we are counting *future possible* actions (which have not been performed) rather than past actions (which have). Action theorists like Davidson and Goldman, whose primary concern is with providing a basis for the explanation of *past* actions, would certainly agree that if you have performed a certain spatio-temporally specified action then I cannot have performed that action, and that if you have performed nine out of ten spatio-temporally specified actions then at most I can only have performed one of those ten. But it does not follow from this that if you are *free* to perform a certain spatio-temporally specified action, I cannot also be free to perform it. What we should say is that I am free to perform an action if we can be certain now that you will not perform it. (More precisely, we should say that the probability of my being free to perform the action is equal, *ceteris paribus*, to the probability of your not performing it.) This, of course, we may not know, if the physical component which allows the action is jointly possessed by the two of us. But if only two of us jointly possess a physical object which makes available three alternative actions (none of which is performable in combination by one person), then I can be sure that at least two of those actions will not be performed by you. It follows that my total freedom with respect to the physical object is equal to 2. To say otherwise is to confuse the number of *actions* that a possible world can contain with the number of *freedoms to act* that a possible world can contain. It is true that you and I cannot both be performers of a specific action, x, in the same possible world. But to be the performer of x is to be something more than just free to do x. We must be careful to distinguish between the conditions under which two actions are compossible and the conditions under which two *freedoms* are compossible.

The failure to distinguish in this way between the number of actions a world can contain and the number of freedoms it can contain seems to me to provide the best explanation of Steiner's insistence on the zero-sum thesis. Steiner claims that although it is true that 'both Becker and McEnroe were free to compete in the 1990 Wimbledon Men's Singles Tennis Championship, it cannot be true that they were both free to win it'. It may often be difficult, he says, 'to predict which one of many possible worlds will become actual', but 'there's no possible world in which two (or more) such attempters can both be unprevented'.[16] This is true. But the example trades on the fact that Becker

---

[16] Steiner, *An Essay on Rights*, 41.

and McEnroe are 'attempters'. Since both cannot win, if both attempt to win then at least one must be unfree to win. To make Steiner's example exactly analogous to Cohen's, where ten people are locked in the room and no one as a matter of fact chooses to leave, we should instead assume something that is in fact untrue of these two tennis players: that neither wants to win, nor will as a matter of fact attempt to win, and therefore that if one were to attempt to win, he would succeed. In this case, not only is it true that some third, weaker player will as a matter of fact win; it is also true that before the championship has been decided, Becker is free to actualize a possible world in which Becker is the winner, and McEnroe is free to actualize a possible world in which McEnroe is the winner. This is because, on our unrealistic assumption about their propensities to compete, neither Becker nor McEnroe is preventing the other from actualizing a world in which that other is the winner. As we have seen (at s. 8.2), Steiner characterizes freedom not only as the actual possession of physical things but also as the subjunctive possession of physical things. On our unrealistic assumption, this subjunctive possession is exactly what McEnroe and Becker both have: it is true both of McEnroe and of Becker (on our unrealistic assumption) that if he *were* to attempt to win the tennis championship, he would not be prevented from doing so. We can of course relax the unrealistic assumption: we can assume instead that at least one of the two players will attempt to win. But in that case, the example will no longer be analogous to that of Cohen, and neither Cohen nor I would then claim that both players are free to win. If it seems counter-intuitive to hypothesize that both McEnroe and Becker are free to win, this is only because it is unrealistic to suppose that neither will try to win. And if on the other hand we do assume that neither will try to win, then we should not let the fact that both *cannot* win stop us from affirming that both are *free to* win.

Clearly what *is* lacking as a result of the fact that Becker and McEnroe cannot both win the championship is their *collective freedom* to win the championship, in Cohen's sense of the term. But this does not make either Becker or McEnroe less free individually, and, if the arguments of the previous two sections are correct, we should not see it as affecting their overall group freedom. It is only the collective freedom of the group, and not the individual freedom of any of its members, that is limited by the number of options available to the group *as a whole*. Thus, in Cohen's example (discussed in s. 9.1), where there are ten people locked in a room from which only one may exit but from which no one *does* choose to exit, the overall *group freedom* of the ten people is equal to the sum of the separate *individual* freedoms of the ten to exit (=10). This remains true despite the fact that the group *as a whole* only has one such freedom of exit. Similarly, in the example discussed earlier in this section, when you enter my room (which we have divided into ten units), our overall *group freedom* is the sum of our separate *individual* freedoms to occupy the various units of space in the room (=9+9=18). This remains true despite the fact that the group as a whole has available only ten such units of space.

From the above argument, and from the fact that we have rejected appeals to the notion of collective freedom, we can see how there is a sense in which Cohen can turn the arguments of the previous two sections to his advantage. This ought to be clear from the fact that those who are most hostile to the communalization of property also happen to be those who are least likely to want to appeal to the notion of collective unfreedom in support of their political prescriptions. John Gray, for example, has argued not only against Cohen's thesis about the relationship between freedom and the communalization of property, but also against the notion of collective unfreedom. We do not normally suppose, Gray says, that 'unless any subscriber to a telephone system can use it at the same time as every other or most other subscribers, then the entire class of telephone users is rendered unfree by the system'. And this means that Cohen's appeal to the notion of collective freedom is 'at variance with much of our standard thought'.[17] Thus far, Gray would agree with my own arguments in ss. 9.2 and 9.3 against appeals to the notion of collective unfreedom. And yet this very fact seems to count in favour of Cohen's argument to the effect that tool-sharing can increase overall group freedom. For a number of the arguments used by Gray against this last idea appeal implicitly to the notion of collective unfreedom. Gray suggests, for example, that after communalization no individual is free to 'decide when the tools are to be replaced', or 'to engage in long-term planning about the use of tools', and that a general difficulty with Cohen's scheme is that 'it says nothing about what will be done under it when households "need", or wish to use, tools at the same time'.[18] But these appear for the most part to be problems that have to do with the compossibility of actions of different individuals, and thus with the degree of their *collective* freedom. Take, for example, the freedom to replace the tools. This freedom is not removed by Cohen's communist scheme; it is just that we may not be sure who will replace the tools, or indeed who wants to. Suppose that the money with which to buy new tools is now communally available, and may be used by anyone at any time for the purpose of tool replacement. *Someone* will replace the tools (it may just be the first person to decide to do so), and if they do so, it follows that they were free to do so. The fact that we may not know who will buy the new tools or when (and thus who is prevented from doing so and when), is a fact which, however

---

[17] Gray, 'Against Cohen on Proletarian Unfreedom', 91.   [18] Ibid. 81–2.

unpleasant or frustrating for the individuals involved, cannot be taken to imply that no one is free to do so. On the contrary, until someone does replace the tools, *each* individual is free to do so. What may be lacking is the *collective* freedom to replace the tools; one individual's replacing them precludes another individual's doing so. But this does not imply an overall reduction in individual freedom in terms of tool-replacement possibilities. As to Gray's more general point about the *use* of tools—i.e. that different households are not free to use a given tool 'at the same time'—we could hardly have been presented with a clearer appeal to the notion of collective unfreedom.

So it is possible for Cohen to answer Gray's objections to the communalization of property by rejecting the very notion of collective unfreedom that he has employed elsewhere. This move is of course not necessary to Cohen's defence; he need not himself reject the notion of collective unfreedom merely in order to answer Gray. In fact, he might reasonably feel unmoved by Gray's objection on the grounds that the collective unfreedoms noted by Gray appear to be equally present in a situation in which the household tools are privately owned. In other words, it seems that the communalization of property can increase the sum of individual freedom while leaving the sum of collective freedom unchanged. Nevertheless, it remains the case that as a rhetorical device, rejecting the notion of collective unfreedom immediately deprives the opponents of communalization of some of their favourite arguments.

Finally, we should note the additional conditions that are necessary for the communalization of resources to produce increases in group freedom. The first of these conditions has to do with the way people would be likely to behave toward one another in the event of communalization—in particular, how likely they would be to perform actions that limit the freedom of others in ways not yet taken into account. The second has to do with degrees of scarcity of resources.

The first condition in fact derives from a more general point. There is a class of actions the performance of which, regardless of the structure of property rights, is likely to decrease group freedom. Most obviously, as Bertrand Russell says, a community composed of individuals which constantly try to kill each other will certainly contain less freedom overall than a community where individuals do not try to do so.[19] Similarly, if each individual happens to shoot another individual in the leg, so that every individual ends up being shot in the leg, there will be a clear net loss in group freedom. These and other less serious freedom-limiting actions, involving various kinds of use, removal, or destruction of external resources, are actions that individuals must refrain from performing if group freedom is to be maximized.

---

[19] Russell, 'Freedom in Society', 173.

Group freedom is in part a function of the probability that individuals will refrain from performing such actions, and this probability might, for various reasons, be claimed to be higher where property is private than where it is communal.

The other necessary condition for communal property implying greater group freedom is, as we have already seen, that the ratio of individuals to the quantity of available resources (the number of 'units' represented by a in the formulae set out earlier in this section) be less than 1. This condition can be called 'non-scarcity', although we should bear in mind that 'non-scarcity' is here defined in a peculiar way: non-scarcity obtains when a (representing a measure of the resources) is greater than the number of individuals with access to the resources, regardless of the desirability of those resouces for those individuals.

Where these last two conditions do indeed obtain, maximal group freedom ought to be realized in a state of anarco-communism. By a state of anarco-communism, I mean simply a state in which resources are pooled and the rules of peaceful, freedom-enhancing cooperation that govern their use are obeyed voluntarily rather than being enforced.[20] In the case of either communal *or* private property, there are certain rules that individuals must follow regarding the treatment of others and of their (partly or exclusively owned) property if group freedom is to be maximized. Where those rules are *not* enforced at all but individuals will still *not* as a matter of fact break them, group freedom will be greater than where the rules are not enforced and individuals *will* break them. The level of group freedom achieved through the *enforcement* of the rules lies somewhere between these two levels.

To the extent that one is sceptical about the above two conditions (absence of freedom-limiting actions and non-scarcity of resources), one will be less inclined to see anarchy or communism as increasing freedom. Assuming non-scarcity, different freedom-based arguments in favour of certain kinds of property rights and their enforcement will depend on different opinions regarding the realizability of the first condition (the absence of freedom-limiting actions). In its most optimistic (but for many unrealistic) form, this condition implies that individuals voluntarily refrain from making excessive demands regarding their use of the resources available to them and cooperate peacefully in the use they do make of them. Just as the communist argument from group freedom flounders in the face of scarcity, so the anarco-communist argument from group freedom flounders (even assuming non-scarcity) once

---

[20] Forms of voluntary cooperation that involve resource-pooling as a means to the performance of *joint actions* (e.g. 'catching big game') increase group freedom by giving each individual the possibility of performing her share of those joint actions. This fact appears to be overlooked by Michael Taylor at p. 157 of *Community, Anarchy and Liberty*.

this possibility of peaceful voluntary cooperation is rejected on the grounds of human egoism or weakness of the will or collective action problems. If such grounds are valid, anarchism will be sub-optimal in terms of overall group freedom (and no doubt also in terms of the equitable distribution of freedom). Just how far we must go down this more sceptical road before rejecting communism as well as anarchism (still assuming non-scarcity) is unclear at this purely conceptual level of analysis. Nevertheless, even on the more pessimistic view of human nature and of collective action problems that non-anarchist liberals tend to endorse, maximal group freedom might still be guaranteed by the enforcement of 'pockets' of communally held property within an otherwise privatized world.

What is certainly clear is that those who favour liberalism over anarchism, or state-enforced private property rights over some system of state-enforced communal property rights, should admit that their favoured scheme of enforced property rights does not *as such* maximize group freedom (and does not, for that matter, maximize *equal* freedom, even given 'equal starts' in terms of amounts of property). Rather, it does so given a certain theory about human nature and/or collective rationality and/or scarcity.

Needless to say, there are other reasons for preferring private property to communal property, and vice versa. My concern here has been exclusively with freedom-based reasons, in particular where those reasons presuppose the aim of maximizing total group freedom. The most obvious alternative argument for private property is that it provides stronger guarantees of certain specific freedoms by making the individual sovereign over a given set of physical objects. The point, however, is that this argument does not appeal to increases in overall freedom, but to another, perhaps competing ideal: that of the security either of a given set of specific freedoms or of a given measure of overall freedom.

9.5 CONCLUSION

In this chapter I have defended an individualist view of group freedom. The freedom of a group is nothing other than the sum total of the degrees of freedom of its individual members. Thus, the prevention of a set of compossible actions is directly relevant to group freedom where the members of that set are the actions of a single individual (as argued in ss. 7.2 and 8.2), but not where they are the actions of many individuals (ss. 9.2 and 9.3). In support of this view, we have seen that Cohen's own intuitions regarding the degree of freedom of proletarians are confirmed, rather than contradicted, by an individualist account of group freedom.

From this individualist account of group freedom it follows that under certain circumstances, and making certain assumptions about human nature and the possibility of cooperation, the communalization of material resources brings about net increases in group freedom. Cohen's anti-communist opponents are wrong to think that they can uphold such an individualist account of group freedom and also provide conceptual arguments against the implication regarding the communalization of property. Thus, on both sides of the political divide, in terms of correspondence with common-sense comparisons of freedom and in terms of implications for property rights, the radical potential of an individualist account of group freedom has been greatly underestimated.

10

Indicators of Freedom

In this chapter I shall assess the prospects of estimating degrees of overall freedom once we have descended to a more realistic level of theorizing, as opposed to the purely conceptual level at which the main body of this book is pitched. Recall that when we descend from the level of purely conceptual theory to that of realistic theory (see s. 3.4), we start to take into account practical problems of measurement (such as problems of observation and information gathering), rather than only the conceptual problems considered in the previous three chapters (such as the problem of whether it makes sense to 'count' possible actions, or the problem of supposedly incommensurable constraint dimensions). I shall first illustrate the importance of such a theoretical move (section 1) and then assess the feasibility and acceptability of two possible metrics (sections 2 and 3). In the latter case, my remarks will necessarily be tentative. My aim is not to complete the search for indicators of freedom, but only to point that search in the right direction in the light of the conceptual analysis provided in the previous chapters.

10.1 THE NEED FOR A REALISTIC FREEDOM METRIC

The previous three chapters were aimed at making sense of the idea of overall freedom in a way that conforms to our reasons for seeing freedom as valuable and to our common-sense comparisons of freedom. I think that for many liberals the analysis I presented there stands a reasonable chance of being acceptable in reflective equilibrium: it fits most of their common-sense comparisons, despite the initial appearance of being 'narrow' or 'restricted', and those comparisons that it does not fit can be modified in reflective equilibrium, in the light of a stronger, more general commitment to a freedom-based theory of justice. But we saw in Chapters 3 and 4 that isomorphism with common-sense comparisons is not all that characterizes a definition of overall freedom in reflective equilibrium. We also require powers of measuring freedom that meet the demands made by our principle for the distribution of freedom.

How does the foregoing analysis fare in terms of implied powers of measurement? At the purely conceptual level, it appears to fare very well. The idea of measuring 'extents of available action' in terms the physical dimensions of the events agents are free to bring about allows, in theory, for absolute, cardinal measurements. This is because space, time, and matter are, as we saw in Chapter 7, 'extensive' qualities, and therefore ones on which we can in theory perform concatenation operations so as to be in a position to say 'how much' of those qualities is present. Moreover, none of the conceptual objections raised in the previous chapters (regarding the supposed incommensurability either of various constraint-types or of individual freedom with 'collective' freedom) has been sufficiently serious to overturn this favourable conclusion, given my accommodation of most of the common-sense comparisons of overall freedom that motivate those objections.

In the real world, however, we may well encounter practical problems regarding both the gathering of the information necessary for such measurements and the complex calculations that they require. If these practical problems turn out to be insuperable, then some more approximate metric will be needed. This more approximate metric can be found by looking for more simple *indicators* of empirical freedom. The previous three chapters told us what overall freedom *is*, and what its direct measurement would involve: namely the enumeration of individual agents' (more or less probably) available sets of compossible actions. The question that now arises is the following: if the practical realization of such an enumeration turns out to be too problematic, are there nevertheless more practicable, if indirect, methods of measuring overall freedom? I have said that in general I see the practical problems involved in measuring freedom as lying outside the scope of this book. This, however, does not excuse me from at least pointing in the direction of certain workable indicators of empirical freedom.

Why is this so? Why should the search for indicators be a part of my present concern? This book is, after all, a work on political philosophy. It tries to make sense of the idea of overall freedom as a quantitative attribute in so far as that attribute is an important *distribuendum* in a liberal theory of distributive justice. Is it not the job of the social scientist to tell us, once we know exactly what overall freedom *is* (and why we should be interested in its measurement), what practical steps can be taken in order to estimate the actual extents of overall freedom of individuals or groups? Unfortunately, the division between political philosophy and the social sciences is less clean-cut than this excuse makes out. The search for indicators of overall freedom is in fact an enterprise on which political philosophers and social scientists ought to cooperate.

The reason for this last claim can be illustrated by looking at the recent dispute between Rawls and Sen over the proper currency of distributive justice. For Rawls, this currency consists in the primary goods—that is, 'basic liberties' and 'all purpose means', such as income and wealth, together with the 'social bases for self respect'. According to Sen, on the other hand, Rawls is guilty of a form of fetishism, since what really matters is people's capabilities —the possibilities they have of doing and being certain valuable things, or, in Sen's terms, of achieving valuable functionings (see s. 2.5).[1] Some people are more efficient than others at converting primary goods into capabilities— to take an extreme example, a handicapped person needs much more income or wealth than an able-bodied person to do the same types of thing—and this means that it must be wrong to concentrate on people's primary goods rather than on what they are capable of doing with them. Rawls has answered this criticism by referring to the practical problems involved in directly measuring and distributing capabilities. Specifying principles of justice for the distribution of primary goods seems to be the best we can do, he says, in attempting to achieve a just distribution of Sen's 'effective freedoms'. Sen's work on capabilities has been useful because it has provided a test for the appropriateness of the primary goods metric. But the primary goods remain the proper *distribuendum* of our theory of justice.[2]

What Rawls is doing here is moving from the level of purely conceptual theory to that of realistic theory. This brings him, indeed, to a defence of what he has called a 'realistic utopia'. It remains a utopia, inasmuch as it is still articulated at the level of 'ideal' theory. I shall not concern myself here, at least directly, with the difference between ideal and non-ideal theory. But the distinction between purely conceptual theory and realistic theory is important for our present purposes. Theorists of justice, both ideal and non-ideal, ought to be interested in arriving at a realistic metric for freedom (though, as we saw in s. 3.3, the difference between ideal and non-ideal theory may affect whether we are interested in cardinal or only ordinal measurements). Rawls's central point is that practical problems of interpersonal comparability need to be taken into account *in theorizing about justice*, and not simply *after* theorizing about justice. And it seems to me that where the relevant practical difficulties really do come up consistently, this additional requirement of the political philosopher is quite reasonable. Thus, the search for indicators of overall freedom does not take us over a borderline between political philosophy and social science but, rather, into an area in which the two subjects overlap.

What is questionable about the development of Rawls's theory is the fact that he appears to have arrived *first* at the 'realistic' metric—i.e. that of primary goods—only *subsequently* acknowledging that these are in fact practical

---

[1] Sen, 'Equality of What?'; id., 'Justice: Means versus Freedoms', *Philosophy and Public Affairs*, 19 (1990); id., *Inequality Reexamined* (Oxford: Oxford Univerity Press, 1992), ch. 2.
[2] See Rawls, *Political Liberalism*, s. V:3.

indicators of something else, of what really matters—i.e. of Sen's notion of 'effective freedom'. The requirement of being realistic does not excuse us from the requirement of constructing a purely conceptual theory of justice; on the contrary, the former requirement *entails* the latter. Regardless of what either Rawls or Sen mean by 'freedom' in this context, we have no reason to think, in the absence of a prior analysis of that term, that Rawls happened to hit on the correct indicators. It is surely necessary *first* to have a clear idea of what is to be indicated, and *then* to look for indicators. As far as overall freedom is concerned, that prior analysis is something we have now gone through in Chapters 7, 8, and 9. Perhaps, in the light of that analysis, the primary goods will *not* be the most appropriate indicators of empirical freedom, or at least will not be so in the exact form they take in Rawls's theory.

It should be said, on the other hand, that at first glance the primary goods —or at least certain of them—are better candidates as indicators of overall freedom than are the 'achieved functionings' referred to by Sen as possible indicators of well-being. Sen admits the problem of information regarding the measurement of 'capabilities', but then appears to suggest that where we do lack this information, our measurements of individual well-being cannot include a freedom variable at all. 'Ideally', he says, 'the capability approach should take note of the full extent of freedom to choose between different functioning bundles, but limits of practicality may often force the analysis to be confined to examining the *achieved* functioning bundle only.'[3] But deciding to concentrate on achieved functionings cannot represent some sort of second best as far as the measurement of degrees of overall *freedom* is concerned, for there is no reason to suppose there to be a reliable correlation between the former and the latter. Achieved functionings might be thought to be a rough indicator of degrees of *value-based* freedom (as long as individuals usually choose to realize the options they prefer), although even this is dubious, given that individuals may vary greatly in terms of the number of valuable but incompatible options they each have available. But even assuming achieved functionings to be a rough indicator of value-based freedom, they will in any case not do as an indicator of *empirical* freedom. As we saw in Chapter 5, degrees of value-based freedom are reducible to the values of the specific things one is free to do, and hence have little to do with degrees of overall freedom properly defined. How much freedom people have, and the value of the specific things they are free to do, will often be quite independent variables. Thus, whatever Sen's reason for concentrating on achieved functionings, it is not a freedom-based reason—not, at least, in the absence of a search for more reliable indicators of freedom.

---

[3] Sen, *Inequality Reexamined*, 53, emphasis in original.

In the next two sections I shall examine two possible realistic metrics for overall empirical freedom based, respectively, on a list of freedom-types and on the exchange values of personal resources. In a subsequent section, I shall briefly consider the possibility of combining these two metrics.

10.2 THE FREEDOM-TYPE METRIC

Human rights measures are a good place to start in attempting to construct an index of freedom-types. Obviously, degrees of respect for human rights are not sufficient to tell us how free a society is *overall*, since freedom is constrained in many ways other than through the violation of human rights. We must also be careful not to appeal implicitly to a moralized definition of freedom (see s. 3.1), in the way that human-rights-based metrics of freedom appear to. But serious human rights violations (like torture, arbitrary arrest, and detention) are as a matter of fact often the most serious restrictions of freedom, in both the value-based and the empirical sense. Therefore, despite the inadequacies of human rights measures from the point of view of the empirical approach to measuring freedom, those measures do provide us with useful basis for further work.

The 1991 *Human Development Report* of the United Nations Development Program (hereinafter UNDP) contains a 'Human Freedom Index' (hereinafter HFI), which builds on the previous work of Charles Humana.[4] This is ostensibly a metric for ordering groups—here, countries—in terms of their relative degrees of overall freedom. The UNDP follows Humana in listing forty human rights, which include the right to travel in one's own country and abroad, the right to associate and assemble, freedom from capital and corporal punishment, freedom to publish books, freedom from arbitrary seizure of personal property, and so on.[5] The idea is that by reference to this list of rights one can arrive at a ranking of countries in terms of overall freedom by simply assigning the numeral '1' to a country which respects a particular right, and '0' to a country which violates it, so that each country is assigned marks out of forty.

Both Humana and the UNDP have been criticized for their methods of data collection. Certainly there are practical problems created by the limited availability of data. Above all, records of human rights violations are scarce, and what records there are may be kept secret. Some have also pointed out

---

[4] C. Humana, *World Human Rights Guide* (London: Hodder & Stoughton, 1986); cf. R. Gastil, *Freedom in the World: Political Rights and Civil Liberties* (London: Greenwood Press, 1987).
[5] UNDP, *Human Development Report* (Oxford: Oxford University Press, 1991), 20.

a problem of partiality in 'processing and interpreting the data' resulting from the interpreter's 'political orientation' or 'the relation of the country rated to his or her home country'.[6] Not wishing to embark on an empirical study myself, I am not in a position to investigate these problems of data gathering and interpretation. Instead, I shall limit myself to making a modest assumption: that such problems of data availability are not serious enough to prevent us from making at least *some* valid comparisons of overall freedom, even if they prevent us from achieving as much as Humana and the UNDP claim to have achieved—i.e. a complete ordering (in terms of respect for human rights) of eighty-eight countries.

Some writers on the measurement of human rights abuses would claim that even this last assumption is false, and that the data on human rights are too varied to allow for 'overall measures'. Michael Stohl and company quote an Amnesty International Report that is sceptical about such overall measures: 'prisoners are subjected to widely differing forms of harassment, ill-treatment and punishment, taking place in diverse contexts', and 'this fact would render any statistical or other generalized comparisons meaningless as a real measure of the impact of human rights abuses'.[7] But to the extent that this point is intended to be used as an objection to the possibility of measuring overall *empirical freedom*, it is misplaced. For the objection is pitched at the purely conceptual level and has, I believe, already been refuted in earlier chapters of this book. As I emphasized in Chapters 2 and 5, we must be careful not to confuse freedom with other good things, and, likewise, unfreedom with other bad things. The differences between the kinds of ill treatment referred to above are certainly important, but this does not mean that they must be relevant to a metric of unfreedom. They may indeed be incommensurable in terms of their overall disvalue, thus rendering meaningless the idea of a 'generalized comparison' of their 'impact' on people's lives (as the Amnesty Report seems to suggest). But, as the arguments of Chapters 7 and 8 showed, this does not make them incommensurable in terms of the amounts of empirical unfreedom they imply, given that the latter represent only a part of their 'impact' (see s. 5.6). Moreover, 'generalized comparisons' purely in terms of empirical freedom *are* meaningful, given that overall freedom is an attribute of agents (s. 1.5) and given that it has non-specific value (Chapter 2).

---

[6] These problems are mentioned in L. J. Bernt, 'Measuring Freedom? The UNDP Human Freedom Index', *Michigan Journal of International Law*, 13 (1992), 735; cf. R. J. Goldstein, 'The Limits of Using Quantitative Data in Studying Human Rights Abuses', *Human Rights Quarterly*, 8 (1986).

[7] M. Stohl et al., 'State Violation of Human Rights: Issues and Problems of Measurement', *Human Rights Quarterly*, 8 (1986), 594. Cf. 598–600.

The basic idea behind the UNDP's index—that we can make rough measurements of freedom on the basis of the presence or absence of certain rather broadly defined *types* of freedom—seems to me to be sound. It also seems to me that in order to arrive at an adequate realistic metric of such freedom-types, it will suffice to rely on Steiner's original formula (see s. 7.1), which sees overall freedom as nothing more than the proportion of freedoms, from a given list, that are as a matter of fact respected, rather than on my suggested revision of that formula (see s. 7.2), which directly incorporates the insight contained in Chapters 7 and 8 about the importance of the *compossibility* of freedoms. We can rely on Steiner's original formula for practical purposes because, as we shall see, the compossibility of specific freedoms can be taken into account indirectly, if approximately, by attaching different weights to different kinds of constraints on freedom.

As we shall also see, however, the HFI fails in a number of ways to put this basic idea into practice, even leaving aside the problems of data availability mentioned above. Perhaps this failure has been perceived by the UNDP, which, since 1991, has no longer included the HFI in its annual Development Reports. Should we conclude from this omission that they have now decided to drop the index in favour of some version of the specific-freedom thesis (see s. 1.4)? Whether or not this interpretation is correct, it should be clear in the light of my arguments so far that such a move would be premature. Let us now see, then, whether my purely conceptual refutation of the specific-freedom thesis cannot now be applied realistically to the task of eliminating the most glaring deficiencies in the UNDP's freedom metric.

My constructive critique will not take me as far as proposing an exact list of freedom-types; the nature of that list will in part depend on the degree of specificity that is practicable. It should be recalled from s. 7.3 that, in terms of accuracy, the more we are able to break the freedom-types down into their more specific component freedom-types (thus producing a longer list of freedom-types), the better. All that will be proposed here is a set of general guidelines for the listing and aggregation of the freedom-types, through an application of the arguments of the previous three chapters.

I shall make three preliminary points about the nature of the freedom-types, and then three points about how the freedom-types should be aggregated. Of the preliminary points, the first two concern the ways in which our list of freedom-types should differ from the list of rights on which the Humana and UNDP indexes are based. They explain why I prefer to call the metric under discussion a 'freedom-type' metric rather than a 'human rights' metric. The third preliminary point concerns the source of constraints on the freedom-types.

(a) *The nature of the freedom-types*

The first preliminary point is that we must, as I have said, be careful to avoid basing our measurements on a 'moralized' definition of freedom (see s. 3.1). The concept of a human right certainly contains a moral filter, as indeed does the Rawlsian concept of a 'basic liberty'. The set of human rights and basic liberties does include rights to do many things that the 'moral majority' in any given country might judge to be wrong, but it does not include the right, say, to steal or to murder. From the point of view of the *empirical* approach, then, rather than a list of human rights or basic liberties, what is needed, ideally, is a morally *neutral* list of freedom-types. The set of morally neutral freedom-types overlaps to a certain extent with the set of human rights. But, in so far as it does not contain a moral filter, the former set is larger.

Second, there is also a sense in which the set of freedom-types on our list ought to be *smaller* than the set of human rights listed by Humana and the UNDP. Some of the rights on their list cannot be included in our list of freedom-types, for the simple reason that they are not rights of individuals to *do* certain things, and cannot therefore be counted as among the specific types of empirical *freedom* people may or may not have. Certainly we should include 'the right to practise any religion', to practise 'homosexuality between consenting adults', and to 'travel in [one's] own country'.[8] But we should perhaps leave out such entries as 'the legal right to a nationality', and 'the legal right to being considered innocent until proved guilty'—unless, that is, the latter can themselves be shown to be indicators of reasonably discrete sets of available act-types. Another problem is that some of the rights listed by Humana and the UNDP, such as 'social and economic equality for ethnic minorities' and 'equality of [the] sexes during marriage and for divorce proceedings', clearly concern the *distribution* of freedom within a group (where they concern freedom at all), rather than the *total* freedom of the group. Perhaps some of these last rights will turn out to be useful indicators of equality of empirical freedom. We must be careful, however, not to confuse distributive and aggregative issues.

The third preliminary point is that the scores given to the various countries should presumably be based not only on restrictions of freedom carried out by the state (as is usually the case in studies like those of Humana and the UNDP), but also on the basis of restrictions of freedom imposed by other collective agencies or even by individuals. This point, in conjunction with the first preliminary point mentioned above, ought to lead to measurements that confirm a general conclusion reached at the end of s. 9.4 in the previous

[8] UNDP, *Human Development Report*, 20; cf. Humana, *World Human Rights Guide*, pp. xii–xiv.

chapter. We saw there that group freedom ought to be highest in an anarchic world where people cooperate peacefully. For it is in this kind of world that restrictions of empirical freedom both by individuals *and* by the state are at a minimum. The highest degree of empirical group freedom is to be found in a peaceful 'state of nature' in which individuals not only pool their resources (in conditions of non-scarcity) but also refrain from performing various freedom-reducing actions despite being free to perform them. State-enforced rules, to the extent that they are freedom-based, presuppose an unwillingness or inability of humans to cooperate peacefully in this way, and so remove some freedoms in order to guarantee others. Such rules are aimed at realizing a just principle for the distribution of freedom (maximal freedom, equal freedom, maximin freedom, etc.), *within* the limits imposed by the unwillingness or inability to cooperate.

Perhaps practical problems will limit the impact of these last three points. For example, we might, for practical reasons, nevertheless restrict our attention to state violations of the freedom-types. As a justification for this, it might be suggested that the degree of respect for these freedom-types on the part of the state will provide a reliable indicator of the general respect for such freedoms in a society. It might further be suggested that degrees of respect for something like the list of Rawlsian basic liberties, rather than for a set of morally neutral freedom-types, provides the most realistic indicator of approximations to a just distribution of freedom (maximal freedom, equal freedom, maximin freedom, etc.). However, both of these suggestions depend in turn on a series of empirical hypotheses. These include, in the first case, the claim that states with a bad record of respect for the relevant freedom-types tend also to be more tolerant of restrictions of those same freedom-types on the part of their citizens, and in the second case, claims about the failure of individuals and groups to cooperate peacefully and voluntarily in a way that is compatible with the existence of freedoms the exercise of which would endanger the Rawlsian basic liberties. If these suggested restrictions of our attention are adopted, we should always bear in mind that they refer to possible indicators of the presence or absence of what are in reality the members of a much wider set of freedoms.

(b) *The aggregation of the freedom-types*

Having made these preliminary points about the nature of the relevant freedom-types, we are now in a position to consider the method by which they should be aggregated. For simplicity's sake, let us assume the same aim as that ostensibly pursued by Humana and the UNDP—that is, the measurement, at the level of non-ideal theory, of the *group freedom* of various countries. What numerical value should we assign to the presence or absence of a given freedom-type in a given country? We have seen that the HFI involves assigning a '1' or a '0' to each country for each right, according to whether the right in question is respected or violated. According to the UNDP, adopting this simple 'one–zero' approach, which distinguishes between 'freedom guaranteed' and 'freedom violated', gives us 'an illuminating ranking of countries'.[9] It is likely, however, that the UNDP are here showing an over-eagerness to produce a nice evenly spread ranking of countries at the expense of really measuring their extents of freedom. Is the simple 'one–zero' approach really the approach that is most illuminating *about extents of freedom*?

I would suggest that the 'one–zero' approach needs to be abandoned in favour of the assignment of variable numerals to each country for each freedom-type. These numerals will be decided by reference to three factors: first, the 'weight' assigned to a freedom-type in terms of empirical freedom; second, the degree to which the freedom-type is restricted (taking into account the constraint-types by means of which it is restricted); and third, the probability of restrictions of the freedom-type in the foreseeable future. This alternative approach will have the added advantage of leading to cardinal measurements.

The need to weight each freedom-type in terms of the extent of empirical freedom for which it is a necessary condition arises out of two considerations, having to do, respectively, with the *extensiveness* and the *location* of possible actions. The first consideration (about the extensiveness of actions) is that under average circumstances, for the average individual, the complete restriction of one of the freedoms mentioned on the list may imply a much greater reduction in available action than the complete restriction of another of the freedoms. This fact needs to be reflected in our measurements. (On the notion of 'extents of available action', see ss. 5.5, 7.2, and 7.3.) Weighting the freedoms is in any case unavoidable. The UNDP claims to have abstained from weighting the human rights on its list, but this is false; in fact, they have simply assigned *equal* weights, in terms of implied degrees of freedom, to each right. The equal weights are assigned by default, so to speak. Humana, on the other hand, assigns variable weights to the rights on his list, but by recourse to *value-based* criteria.[10] Our own criterion for weighting a freedom-type should be the estimated extent of action that would be made available to the average individual in virtue of her being subject to no restrictions whatsoever on that particular freedom-type. If the arguments in s. 7.9 are correct, these weights will in part be a function of the proximity to the agent's body

---

[9] UNDP, *Human Development Report*, 19.
[10] Humana, *World Human Rights Guide*, 6.

of the physical components over which control would be necessary in order to remove the freedom. At the very least we should say that, *ceteris paribus*, where the removal of one freedom-type would involve direct control over the agent's body, or the threat of such direct control, and the removal of another freedom-type would not involve such direct control, the first freedom-type carries greater weight than the second. Such weightings will certainly often be rather impressionistic. But even impressionistic empirical weighting will be preferable both to value-based weighting and to the arbitrariness of a priori equal weighting.

The other consideration behind the need to weight the freedom-types (this time having to do with the location of actions) is that some freedom-types may overlap with others, to greater or lesser extents, in terms of the spatio-temporally described events they allow the agent to bring about. The freedom to 'travel in [one's] own country' and the freedom to 'travel abroad' certainly do not describe overlapping possible act-types. However, there might be a partial overlap between, say, the freedom to 'peacefully associate and assemble' and the freedom to engage in 'peaceful political opposition'.[11] Normally, when we give very broad definitions of freedom-types, we not only omit to specify the physical extensiveness of the possible actions they allow, but also leave underdetermined the physical *location* of those possible actions. Where these locations have, as a matter of fact, a good chance of overlapping to a certain degree, the weights assigned to the relevant freedom-types should presumably be reduced accordingly, and to the relevant degree, in order to minimize double counting. It may prove convenient that, given the arguments of s. 7.8, the degree to which two freedoms overlap in spatio-temporal terms will to some extent be indicated by the degree of perceived qualitative similarity of the options they respectively imply.

The second factor affecting the numeral to be assigned to a country in terms of its respect for a given freedom-type is that of the extent to which the freedom is *restricted*, including the extent of the population subjected to such a restriction. The HFI is insensitive in important respects to degrees of individual freedom (as opposed to group freedom), and one reason for this lies in the UNDP's adoption of the 'one–zero' approach even when measuring *group* freedom. The freedom-types listed are freedoms that are possessed or not possessed by different numbers of individuals, and those who possess them do so to certain degrees, depending on which spatio-temporally specified instances of those types they possess. More accurate measurements of group freedom would surely therefore attempt to take into account (*a*) the *proportion* of individuals in a country for whom a particular freedom-type is

---

[11] UNDP, *Human Development Report*, 20.

restricted,[12] and (*b*) for those individuals, the *degree* to which each specific freedom-type is restricted.[13] These two variables may not be independent of one another,[14] but this does not stop us from combining them into overall measures. They could be combined by producing a fraction for each freedom-type representing the *average degree* to which it is restricted. Instead of a simple 1 or 0, each country would be assigned a number between 1 and 0 for each freedom-type, and these numbers could then be weighted in the way described above. Once again, in practice, the values of these variables might have to be assigned impressionistically on the basis of limited data. But here, as before, an impressionistic empirical judgement is better than a value-based judgement or an arbitrary one.

An assessment of the above variable—the 'average degree to which a particular freedom-type is restricted'—will have to take into account the *constraint-types* by means of which agents' freedom is restricted. Here we might be thought to encounter a problem. It should be recalled that, given the arguments of Chapter 8 (in particular, at ss. 8.2 and 8.3), obstacles such as threats of punishment or the creation of physical difficulty do not remove the freedom to perform the action the threatener aims to deter or the action that is rendered difficult. Only the physical impossibility of doing *x* removes the freedom *to do x*. Were this not the case, we would be faced, even at the purely conceptual level, with problems of incommensurability between constraint-types. For example, if the threat of punishment for 'travelling to a neighbouring town' were to be seen as constituting a removal or reduction of the freedom to travel to a neighbouring town, we would face the problem of commensurating such a removal or reduction of the freedom to travel to a neighbouring town with the degree of unfreedom implied by the *physical impossibility* of travelling to a neighbouring town.

Do the arguments of Chapter 8 imply that we must limit our attention to restrictions of freedom-types that render actions physically impossible? They do not. For we also saw in Chapter 8 that while the above-mentioned threat does not itself constitute a constraint on the freedom to travel to a neighbouring

[12] This variable is taken into account by Humana, though in a rather crude way, by giving marks out of three for each right.

[13] In a similar vein, Stohl et al. suggest that adequate human rights measures would need to take account of three dimensions: the *scope* of human rights violations (i.e. the seriousness of 'what is done to the victims'), their *intensity* (i.e. their 'frequency of occurrence'), and their *range* (i.e. 'the size of the population targeted') ('State Violation of Human Rights', 600–1). In my own terms, (*a*) roughly corresponds to Stohl's 'range', (*b*) to Stohl's 'intensity', and the 'weight' of a freedom-type to Stohl's 'scope'. Part of Stohl's 'scope' may also be reflected in (*b*).

[14] Nicola Abbagnano provides a useful analysis of the mutual effects of variables (*a*) and (*b*) in 'Condizioni, dimensioni e razionalità delle scelte', in his *Fra il tutto e il nulla* (Milan: Rizzoli, 1973), 352–3.

town, it nevertheless provides a fairly reliable *indicator* of a reduction in *overall freedom*. The reason for this is that threats are fairly reliable indicators of reductions in the numbers of sets of compossible actions available to agents. The same can be said of the constraint variable 'difficulty', also discussed in Chapter 8. Although we saw in Chapter 8 that there are exceptions to the rule that threatened agents suffer reductions in freedom, we also saw that these exceptions will be quite rare (s. 8.2): threateners who are bluffing do not restrict the freedom of the threatened, but it is generally rather difficult for a government to sustain bluffs over extended periods of time; and while the threat to punish someone other than the threatened agent does not reduce the freedom of the threatened agent, the arguments of Chapter 9 imply that it does nevertheless often reduce group freedom.

We need to bear in mind, however, that each constraint variable will indicate a greater or a lesser reduction in numbers of available sets of compossible actions. It is a conceptual truth that the physical impossibility of doing x indicates a greater reduction than any threat against doing x (in terms of the resultant number of sets of compossible actions available to the agent), and threats themselves will vary in the degree of unfreedom they indicate, normally in proportion to the severity of the sanction, where 'severity' is estimated not in terms of the disvalue of the sanction but in terms of the extent of action that it would prevent. The different constraint variables therefore need to be weighted in order to produce valid (though indirect) measurements of degrees of overall freedom.

The third and final factor to be taken into account is that of probability, as outlined in ss. 7.5, 8.4, and 8.6. Here, we re-encounter the problem of commensurating probabilistic judgements with judgements about the degree of freedom to perform given act-types. This problem was avoided at the purely conceptual level by denying that the freedom to do a specific thing is a matter of degree, and simply assigning probabilities to the freedom to perform given sets of spatio-temporally specified actions. In the case of a realistic metric of freedom-types, on the other hand, the notion of degrees of respect for a specific freedom *is* employed, because it provides us with a rough *indicator* of degrees of overall freedom. What is needed, then, is a pragmatic solution to the problem of combining degrees of freedom and degrees of probability which somehow approximates the results that would have been arrived at on the basis of direct measurements. One such approximation might consist in dividing the future into equal time-slices (say, years or months), and assigning to each time-slice a fraction representing the degree to which the freedom-type in question is *most likely* to be restricted. In this case, we could avoid the problem of combining the dimensions of 'the degree of freedom to do x' and 'the probability of being free to do x', by simply aggregating those (temporally specified) degrees of freedom to do x that have the highest probability of being realized.

Even rough probabilistic judgements of this kind will require extensive empirical research about the stability of regimes—both of those with a greater tendency to guarantee given freedom-types and of those with a greater tendency to deny them. But such judgements must be employed if we are really to provide measurements of *overall* freedom. Their importance is highlighted by the fact that those who ignore the dimension of probability often overestimate *fluctuations* in degrees of overall societal freedom. Both Humana and the UNDP suggest that political volatility represents a practical problem for the freedom measurer, implying as it does that freedom 'can appear or vanish abruptly'.[15] This may often be true, but the point can also be exaggerated if one's measurements of current degrees of freedom fail to take into account the relevance of the presence or absence of stabilizing factors that guarantee the persistence or absence of given freedom-types over time (see s. 8.6).

10.3 THE EXCHANGE-VALUE METRIC

Given the arguments of ss. 3.1 and 8.5, it would seem that another useful indicator of an individual's degree of overall freedom is to be found in the size of the bundle of resources in her possession. How are we to measure the size of a bundle of resources? The normal way is by reference to that bundle's exchange value. This brings us to the 'exchange-value metric' for freedom, most notably adopted in the theories of justice of Hillel Steiner and Philippe Van Parijs.[16]

Now it might at first be doubted whether this kind of metric can be available to us if we adopt the empirical approach to measuring freedom. Does not the exchange value of a person's resource bundle simply represent the *utility* of that resource bundle? Will we not therefore be falling back on the value-based approach if we adopt this metric?[17] Not necessarily. Exchange values do not *only* tell us the utility of resources, but are also useful indicators of the extent of action that resources make available to those who possess them. Consider the following example. If I have an apple, I am free to make apple juice. And if an apple exchanges for an orange, then as long as I have

[15] UNDP, *Human Development Report*, 21.

[16] See, in particular, Steiner, *An Essay on Rights*, 271 n. 11, and Van Parijs, *Real Freedom for All*, 50–1.

[17] Van Parijs, indeed, explicitly grounds his adoption of the exchange-value metric on the *preference*-based approach to measuring freedom.

the apple, I am also free to make orange juice. Possession of the apple is a *means* to making orange juice. Given this, we can say that the apple and the orange are each a means to performing *the same (spatio-temporally specified) set of actions* (more precisely, they are both means to performing one of two sets of (spatio-temporally specified) compossible actions described by the phrases 'making apple juice' and 'making orange juice'). Therefore, if A has an apple and B has an orange, and an apple and an orange have the same exchange value, we can say that in this respect A and B are equally free in the *empirical* sense, since each is free to make either apple juice or orange juice.[18] Thus, it seems that we can produce a cardinal representation of the degree of freedom offered by a particular resource bundle (although only relative to the freedom offered by other resource bundles) by reference to its total exchange value—and this, without worrying about the intricacies, complexities, and epistemic problems involved in enumerating available actions.

So the exchange-value freedom metric is not necessarily a value-based metric. As the above objection makes clear, on the other hand, the relationship between exchange values and degrees of empirical freedom might help to explain the intuitions which draw some people towards the value-based approach to measuring freedom. After all, we have discovered that it *is* true that where an object's value increases in the eyes of society, the amount of freedom it provides its owner with is very likely to increase with it.

Notice that if we are interested in taking into account all of an agent's personal resources, we must include the agent's own body as one such resource. The exchange value of a person's body is not always obvious, but the assignment of values to human bodies on the basis of a hypothetical body market should not be such a difficult task, and is indeed one in which insurance companies already engage. This point ought to be sufficient to overcome any objections of resource fetishism that might be raised by Sen and his followers. For the fact of one body being more efficient than another at converting resources into functionings ought to be reflected in their respective prices. Sen might object that this solution fails to distinguish adequately between capabilities that are 'basic' and those that are not, and therefore fails to take into account the greater importance of the former. But—apart from the fact that basic capabilities are likely to have a higher market value than non-basic ones—we must once again recall the arguments of Chapter 2: to be concerned more about basic capabilities than about non-basic ones is to be concerned with their *specific* value, rather than with their *non*-specific value; while we should not deny the specific value of capabilities, the particular good that we are here interested in measuring is their *non*-specific value.

---

[18] This argument was originally suggested to me by Hillel Steiner.

In case the idea of assigning exchange values to bodies is for some reason thought to be monstrous, it should be recalled that my aim here is *not* to place values on bodies but, rather, to find indicators of extents of available action. Neither does the fact of my attaching an infinitely high value to my own body prevent it from having a finite exchange value. This is because the particular kind of value we are interested in here is not the asking price of the owner of the resource in question, but the highest price other people are prepared to pay for it. Hobbes said: 'let a man (as most men do) rate themselves at the highest value they can; yet their true value is no more than it is esteemed by others.'[19] Hobbes may or may not have been right about the nature of men's 'true value'; my point is simply that what Hobbes describes as men's true value happens to provide a useful indicator (in a relative but not absolute sense) of their extents of available action.

There are nevertheless three further objections to the exchange-value metric which, though not conclusive, I am unable to answer fully. The first is that exchange values do not necessarily take account of the range of goods made available on the market. That is to say, they do not necessarily reflect the fact that if a good is taken off the market, owing, say, to the choice of a manufacturer, or to government intervention, one's freedom has been decreased, for in such cases the exchange value of one's own resources might not have changed.

The second objection is that the exchange-value metric fails to tell us how much freedom is provided by an object that has no price—that is, by an object that is valued only by its owner, or indeed by no one at all. Such an object cannot be said to provide 'no freedom'—not at least if the arguments of Chapter 5 are sound—since, despite its having an exchange value of 'zero', there will be things that its owner is free to do with it. It is true that the possibility of an object having an exchange value of 'zero' may be rare. However, even if this particular shortcoming turns out to be a minor one, it brings out a more general problem with the exchange-value metric, which is that the market value of an object tells us nothing about the amount of action that its possessor can perform *with that object itself*. We may say that an object provides freedom both 'extrinsically' and 'intrinsically'. The freedom which an object provides one with *intrinsically* consists in the possibility one has of performing actions of which that object is itself a physical component. The freedom that an object provides one with *extrinsically* consists in the possibility one has of performing actions the physical components of which can be acquired by means of that object. For example, part of the quantity of freedom which my orange provides me with intrinsically is the freedom to make

---

[19] Hobbes, *Leviathan*, ch. 10, p. 152.

orange juice, and part of the quantity of freedom it provides me with extrinsically (if I can exchange it for an apple) is the freedom to make apple juice. To measure an object's exchange value is to measure only the (relative degree of) freedom which that object provides *extrinsically*. But objects provide freedom intrinsically as well as extrinsically. Therefore, the fact that the total exchange value of my resources equals the total exchange value of yours is not sufficient grounds for saying that our degrees of freedom are precisely equal. The only way we seem to have of determining the degree of freedom that a set of resources provides intrinsically is by actually enumerating the possible actions it makes available, and this absolute freedom metric seems to be incommensurable, in terms of degrees of freedom, with the wholly relative exchange-value metric.

The damage caused by these first two objections may be limited by noting that exchange values nevertheless still provide us with a *rough* indicator of extents of available action. They at least provide a useful guide to the sets of compossible actions available to an agent apart from those of which her currently owned resources are physical components. And in the average market economy, the amount of freedom a resource provides one with intrinsically is negligible compared with the amount of freedom it provides one with extrinsically.

A third, and perhaps more serious objection, is that the exchange-value metric seems to be unable to accommodate the argument of the previous chapter regarding the communalization of property. The most that I can suggest here is that we might consider weighting the exchange value of the relevant communalized resource bundle, depending on the presence or absence of the various freedom-enhancing and freedom-diminishing factors discussed in s. 9.4. Presumably, for this purpose one would need a scale measuring the propensity of agents in communal set-ups to cooperate in freedom-enhancing ways.

10.4 COMBINING THE TWO METRICS

Let us assume that these last difficulties can be overcome, and that we have arrived at a version of the exchange-value metric that adequately reflects agents' relative cardinal extents of available action. Will this be enough to indicate individuals' degrees of overall freedom? It would seem not. For such a metric will still fail to take into account preventing conditions other than those imposed by the structure and distribution of property rights. Income and wealth are necessary conditions for freedom (see s. 8.5), but not sufficient ones. It is an elementary point that we can well imagine two individuals in two different societies whose resources have equal exchange values, but where a number of activities are prohibited by state-enforced rules in one society but not in the other. For example, the car of a resident of country A might have the same exchange value as that of a resident of country B, but this will not be sufficient to imply that each of these two individuals is free (or equally probably free) to drive down a motorway at 120 m.p.h., since the speed limits in the two countries might be different, or enforced with different degrees of efficiency. Assuming a lack of complete freedom of movement between countries A and B, there will be a difference in extents of freedom that the exchange-value metric will fail to take into account.

It seems, then, that even if we decide to adopt the exchange-value metric for freedom, this will need to be combined in some way with the freedom-type metric discussed earlier.[20] The most obvious way of combining the two metrics is by taking the fraction representing the overall degree of respect for the set of (pre-defined) freedom-types in any given society (or for any given individual)—where '1' represents total respect for all the freedom-types and '0' represents their total absence—and multiplying this fraction by the number already assigned to an individual or group on the basis of the exchange-value metric. The basic intuition here is that we should first look at the agent's personal resources—itself an indicator of various preventing conditions or their absence—and then go on to ask what the agent is prevented and unprevented from doing *with those resources*. In other words, we start by considering how much freedom an individual or group has on the basis of the exchange value of their resource bundle and assuming complete respect for a list of specific freedom-types (which is not, of course, to assume that 'complete respect' for the whole set of freedoms for all individuals is possible, even conceptually). And we then take that figure and multiply it by the fraction reflecting the actual extent to which the freedom-types of the individual or group are restricted. Thus, where the freedom-type measure is 1/2, the figure will be halved, and so on. The exchange-value metric provides us with a cardinal freedom value, and the freedom-type metric then allows us to *subtract* from that value.

A problem might be thought to arise in connection with this dual metric once we consider that we shall not be dealing with independent variables, given that restrictions on the use or sale of resources may affect their market value. To take an obvious example, the high price of hard drugs is often put down to their illegality. As we saw earlier, however, the non-independence

---

[20] This suggestion is apparently supported by Philippe Van Parijs's definition of 'real freedom', which includes not only 'opportunities' (as measured by the value of personal resources), but also 'formal freedoms' (*Real Freedom for All*, 22–3).

of two variables does not itself prevent us from combining them into an over-all measure, and this is well illustrated in the case laws against hard drugs. Such laws have the effect of (i) curtailing the freedom of all to sell or use hard drugs in certain (mostly public) places at certain times, (ii) increasing the freedom of those in possession of hard drugs in terms of the resources they can nevertheless acquire (illegally) in exchange for those drugs, and (iii) reducing the freedom of those not in possession of drugs in terms of the relative exchange value of their resources. The freedom-type metric is meant to take account of the first effect and the exchange-value metric of the second and third. The fact that the first effect may not be possible except in combination with the second and third does not constitute an objection to our taking all three into account in our measurements of overall freedom.

10.5 CONCLUSION

Given the empirical problems left unresolved in this chapter, my conclusion cannot be more than tentative. I do believe, however, that the preceding discussion gives grounds for optimism in the search for workable indicators of empirical freedom. Given adequate information, such workable indicators can be found in a freedom-type metric (if attention is paid to the particular freedom-types listed and to the way in which they are aggregated), and in the exchange values of the resources over which agents have control. We have also seen that an overall indicator might be provided by combining these two metrics.

My main concern in Part III of this book has been with the purely conceptual elaboration of an intuitively acceptable notion of overall freedom as a quantitative attribute. Without that elaboration, we would not know what our indicators were meant to indicate. Here, I have tried on the basis of that elaboration to show where such indicators might be found. We have seen in previous chapters that the concept of overall freedom does have a determinate meaning, and that intuitively acceptable measurements of it are indeed conceptually possible. Various practical difficulties notwithstanding, we can now also envisage the construction of a realistic metric for overall freedom capable of meeting the demands made by a realistic freedom-based theory of distributive justice.

Conclusion

ONE of the central concerns of this book has been to argue against what I have called the 'specific-freedom thesis'—the view that all we need talk about, or indeed all we *can* coherently talk about, is the freedom to do one or another specific thing—and thus in favour of what I have called the 'overall-freedom thesis'. We have seen that the specific-freedom thesis is mistaken on three counts. It is mistaken as an ontological thesis, because there is also such a thing as overall freedom, however measurable or unmeasurable such a thing might be. It is mistaken as a normative thesis, because freedom is non-specifically valuable. And it is mistaken as an epistemic thesis, because it is possible to aggregate the specific actions an agent is free to perform and the specific preventing conditions to which she is subject in a way that fits, in reflective equilibrium, both with the comparisons of overall freedom that common sense sanctions, and with the requirements of a freedom-based theory of justice. These three points, taken together, allow us to construct coherent conceptions of justice and overall freedom in reflective equilibrium. They allow us to treat freedom as one of the *distribuenda* of a liberal theory of justice and as measurable in the ways required by such a theory.

We should perhaps have been surprised if we had found the specific-freedom thesis to be mistaken on one count and yet correct on another. In particular, there would, in my view, have been something strange in the conclusion that liberals see freedom as valuable as such, but that the comparisons of overall freedom they normally make or presuppose are in fact meaningless. It was much more likely, from the start, that when liberals claimed or assumed freedom to be valuable as such, they had already perceived—even if only unconsciously—the nature of overall freedom that has now been made explicit in Part III of this book.

Nevertheless, it is still possible that those who have had the patience to follow my whole train of thought from the beginning to the end of this book will feel the result to be something of a let-down. Are the inspiring arguments of the noblest of our liberal forefathers in favour of the ideal of freedom to be cashed out into nothing more than the possibility of performing various physical movements? Has something not been lost along the way? Can such a normatively significant premiss lead to such a 'philistine' conclusion?

One way of answering this objection is by saying 'so much the worse for the premiss'. For what cannot be denied is that my conclusion is its logical outcome. The only basis we have for seeing comparisons of degrees of over-all freedom as normatively significant lies in freedom's non-specific value. And in order to make room for freedom's non-specific value, we must under-stand degree-of-freedom judgements as having a purely empirical basis. We should not see such judgements as 'value neutral'; for they are, after all, judgements in terms of freedom's non-specific value. But neither should we see them as referring to the value of specific freedoms in terms of the things those freedoms allow us to do.

Perhaps, then, some will see Part III of this book as implying that the non-specific value of freedom is not so important after all, and that we should therefore abandon our interest in comparing the degrees to which people are free. If my book has this effect, I shall be disappointed, but I shall not feel that I have wasted my time. Ridding our political discourse of all talk of 'more' or 'less' freedom would be no mean feat, and is unlikely to be achieved with-out first showing what degree-of-freedom judgements *would* amount to *were* they worth making, as well as what they *cannot possibly* amount to. I have attempted to do both of these things in some detail: I have argued that if degree-of-freedom judgements are worth making (given freedom's non-specific value), they amount to empirical comparisons of expected extents of available action; and I have further argued that degree-of-freedom judgements cannot possibly amount to value-based comparisons of specific freedoms—that is, comparisons of the value of the things that freedom allows us to do—even where a value-based conception of overall freedom is interpreted as nothing more than a rhetorical device.

The view that attributions of degrees of overall freedom should be expunged from political discourse and theorizing is not one that I share. I think that attributions of degrees of overall freedom, understood in purely empirical terms, are a matter of great moral and political importance. Thus, rather than going back to our analysis of the value of freedom and embrac-ing the normative version of the specific-freedom thesis, I prefer to reason in the other direction: the importance of freedom's non-specific value itself teaches us the importance of having a measure of freedom, understood in purely empirical terms. The Dworkinian thought that empirical freedom is 'flat' or 'uninteresting' is merely a hangover from the initial confusion that led so many philosophers to endorse a value-based interpretation of degree-of-freedom judgements, and ought, on the basis of my arguments, to be rejected. That erroneous thought is brought about by something like the following line of reasoning: 'because freedom is a valuable thing, the question of how free I am must be a normative one, and must therefore be answered by reference to the valuable things in life.' But such a line of reasoning is inconclusive. For it ignores my arguments to the effect that empirical freedom is *itself* one of the valuable things in life.

Convincing oneself of the value of empirical freedom is not as difficult as the propagators of the above-mentioned confusion seem initially to have thought. To underline this fact, let me here refer to two broad claims sustained in this book. The first claim is that our initial premiss—the idea of freedom's non-specific value—is a relatively weak one. The second claim is that our conclusion is not as 'philistine' as some have thought, given the intuitive acceptability of judgements of degrees of empirical freedom.

First, the weakness of the premiss: recall that 'non-specifically valuable' does not mean anything as strong as 'intrinsically valuable' (although intrinsic value is a form of non-specific value), and that it certainly does not mean 'unconditionally valuable'. It is quite consistent to say that freedom is only instrumentally or constitutively valuable, while at the same time saying that freedom has non-specific value. Neither does freedom's having non-specific value rule out its also having *specific* value. It would indeed be foolish to say that having a measure of empirical freedom is all that matters about one's freedom, and that one should be indifferent between various specific freedoms. Some freedoms clearly are more valuable than others in terms of goods *other* than freedom, and it can indeed be interesting to compare the different degrees of specific freedoms in different social systems. The empirical approach to measuring freedom does not take account of all the important aspects of our freedom. For not all of the important aspects of our freedom serve to determine 'how much freedom' we have (either overall or of a specific kind), just as not all of the important aspects of the gold in one's possession (aspects which might include the aesthetic value of a gold necklace or the symbolic meaning of a gold ring) serve to determine 'how much gold' one has (either in total or in the form, say, of rings).

Secondly, in order to deflect the accusation of 'philistinism', we should bear in mind the arguments presented in Parts II and III of this book to the effect that resultant measurements of empirical freedom need not, in reflective equilibrium, clash in any major way with the comparisons of freedom that common sense sanctions. For example, measurements of empirical freedom are usually isomorphic with those common-sense comparisons that have mistakenly motivated some theorists to endorse a value-based approach to measuring freedom, and they usually reflect our perception of degrees of qualitative variety among options. Our common-sense judgements of degrees of freedom are indeed important normative judgements. They are judgements about the greater or lesser presence of a valuable quantitative attribute. And these judgements are generally reflected in measurements of overall empirical freedom.

We have seen that the empirical conception of overall freedom is not reductionist, in the sense of implying a 'physicalist' or, more generally, a 'preference-based' theory of action. And from what has just been said, it should be clear that it is not reductionist in a normative sense either. The empirical conception of freedom does involve treating freedom as a homogeneous quantitative attribute, in a way analogous to that in which Bentham conceived of utility. But the analogy with Bentham's utility calculus stops here. Nothing I have said in this book implies that the freedom to play pushpin is as good as the freedom to read poetry. While those who initially oppose the empirical conception may do so because they see that conception as somehow 'reducing away' the special value freedom has, the truth of the matter is exactly the opposite. A truly reductionist conception of overall freedom is a value-based conception. Such a conception reduces claims about overall freedom to claims about the value of the specific things one is free to do, when in fact overall freedom is a distinct good, embodying freedom's *non*-specific value. A value-based conception of freedom therefore 'reduces away' freedom's non-specific value. Only the empirical conception is consistent with freedom having all the different kinds of value that it actually has—including non-specific value.

The upshot of this more positive reaction to the arguments of my book is that the notion of overall freedom can do significant work in political argument. As is to be expected from an empirical conception of overall freedom, much of this work will itself be of the empirical kind. It is an empirical question, for example, whether private or communal property is better for freedom. Being neither 'moralized' nor in any way value-based, the empirical conception of overall freedom provides no easy conceptual answers to questions about the relationship between freedom and other goods (or between freedom and other things that are *presumed* good on the grounds that they are good for freedom). This is an inevitable result of freedom's independent, non-specific value.

How, exactly, will normative political philosophy be affected by my conceptual conclusions? There may be many erstwhile 'specific-freedom theorists' for whom my conclusions need not imply any direct changes in their resultant political prescriptions. For example, if we interpret Rawls's theory of justice as implying a commitment to a guaranteed minimum of empirical freedom (given a particular interpretation of Rawls's commitment to a 'fully adequate scheme of basic liberties'), we are unlikely to bring about any changes in the prescriptions resulting from that theory. But this need not always be so. For example, if Rawls were to renew his original commitment to the principle of maximal equal freedom, he might indeed find in the light of this that some 'fully adequate schemes of basic liberties' are 'more fully adequate' than others. To give another, perhaps more dramatic example, we have seen that a genuine commitment on the part of libertarians to maximal freedom or to maximal equal freedom is unlikely to result in the political prescriptions that many libertarians endorse.

In any case, we should not underestimate the importance of the *justificatory* change that this conclusion necessarily brings with it. It supplies us with a justificatory basis for liberalism that differs both from that of contemporary liberal egalitarians, who generally go no further than compiling a list of specific freedom-types, and from that of contemporary libertarians, who generally appear to have used the language of more and less freedom in an elliptical way, to refer to the greater or lesser realization of some other good (usually, the non-violation of a given set of property rights). At the very least, this means that where liberals are arguing with non-liberals, the former will be armed with a powerful additional reason for condemning unjust regimes. Freedom in China is indeed distributed less equally than in Denmark, and for some individuals sinks below a bare minimum. This is true in a *literal* sense. For liberals, literal truths like these can and should constitute reasons for preferring one kind of society to another.

The impact of my conclusion, in both practical and justificatory terms, will in part depend on how far-reaching our principle for the distribution of freedom is. Clearly, the principle of maximal equal freedom reaches further, in terms of its degree of impact on liberal theory and policies, than the principle of a (fairly low) guaranteed minimum of freedom for all. Its impact will also depend on the degree of priority we give to that principle in relation to principles for the distribution of other goods. And these two factors will in turn partly depend on the kind or kinds of non-specific value we attribute to freedom. Pronouncing on these last questions has not been among my present concerns. If the arguments of this book are to be taken seriously, addressing them will presumably be among our next tasks. Any specific institutional implications will depend on this further reasoning about our freedom-based theory of justice. What we do know, at this point, is that whatever the answers we give to such questions, there is a coherent conception of overall freedom on which they can be based and which will partly determine their meaning.

I have tried in this book to make sense of claims about 'more' and 'less' freedom, and to show why they are important. To the extent that I have failed in this enterprise, we can at least now say that we have found good reasons for eliminating such claims from the language of freedom, however difficult that might appear to be. To the extent that I have succeeded, we have a justificatory basis for liberalism that is importantly different from those of many contemporary liberals, yet truer to the liberal tradition of seeing freedom as a distinct and independent ideal.

BIBLIOGRAPHY

ABBAGNANO, N., *Fra il tutto e il nulla*, Milan: Rizzoli, 1973.

ANNAS, J., 'How Basic are Basic Actions?', *Proceedings of the Aristotelian Society*, 78 (1977–8), 195–213.

ANSCOMBE, G. E. M., *Intention*, Oxford: Blackwell, 1957.

—— 'Under a Description', *Noûs*, 13 (1979), 219–33.

ARMSTRONG, W. E., 'Utility and the Theory of Welfare', *Oxford Economic Papers*, 3 (1951), 259–71.

ARNESON, R. J., 'Freedom and Desire', *Canadian Journal of Philosophy*, 3 (1985), 425–48.

ARROW, K. J., 'A Note on Freedom and Flexibility', in K. Basu, P. K. Pattanaik, and K. Suzumura (eds.), *Choice, Welfare and Development: A Festschrift in Honour of Amartya K. Sen*, Oxford: Oxford University Press, 1995.

AUSTIN, J. L., *Philosophical Papers*, Oxford: Oxford University Press, 1979.

AYER, A. J., *Russell and Moore: The Analytical Heritage*, London: Macmillan, 1971.

BARBER, B. R., 'Justifying Justice: Problems of Psychology, Measurement, and Politics in Rawls', *American Political Science Review*, 69 (1975), 663–74.

BARNETT, R., 'Pursuing Justice in a Free Society: Part One—Power vs. Liberty', *Criminal Justice Ethics* (1985), 50–72.

BARRY, N., 'Hayek on Liberty', in Z. Pelczynski and J. Gray (eds.), *Conceptions of Liberty in Political Philosophy*, London: Athlone Press, 1984.

BEARDSLEY, M., 'Actions and Events: The Problem of Individuation', *American Philosophical Quarterly*, 12 (1975), 263–76.

BECCARIA, C., *On Crimes and Punishments*, trans. H. Paolucci, Indianapolis: Bobbs-Merrill, 1963.

BELLAMY, R., *Liberalism and Modern Society: An Historical Argument*, Cambridge: Polity Press, 1992.

BENN, S. I., *A Theory of Freedom*, Cambridge: Cambridge University Press, 1988.

—— and PETERS, R. S., *Social Principles and the Democratic State*, London: Allen & Unwin, 1959.

—— and WEINSTEIN, W. L., 'Being Free to Act and Being a Free Man', *Mind*, 80 (1971), 194–211.

BENNETT, J., *The Act Itself*, Oxford: Clarendon Press, 1995.

BERLIN, I., *Four Essays on Liberty*, Oxford: Oxford University Press, 1969.

—— *The Crooked Timber of Humanity*, London: HarperCollins, 1991.

BERNT, L. J., 'Measuring Freedom? The UNDP Human Freedom Index', *Michigan Journal of International Law*, 13 (1992), 720–38.

BLACKBURN, S., *The Oxford Dictionary of Philosophy*, Oxford: Oxford University Press, 1994.

BOBBIO, N., *Left and Right: The Significance of a Political Distinction*, trans. A. Cameron, Chicago: Chicago University Press, 1996.

BOSWELL, J., *The Life of Samuel Johnson LL.D.*, London: Everyman, 1906.

BRENKERT, G. G., 'Cohen on Proletarian Unfreedom', *Philosophy and Public Affairs*, 14 (1985), 91–8.

BUCHANAN, J., *Liberty, Market and the State*, Brighton: Wheatsheaf, 1986.

CAMPBELL, N. R., *An Account of the Principles of Measurement and Calculation*, London: Longmans, Green, 1928.

CARTER, I., 'Is Analytical Action Theory Reductionist?', *Analyse & Kritik*, 8 (1991), 61–6.

—— 'The Independent Value of Freedom', *Ethics*, 105 (1995), 819–45.

—— 'The Concept of Freedom in the Work of Amartya Sen: An Alternative Analysis Consistent with Freedom's Independent Value', *Notizie di Politeia*, 43–4 (1996), 7–22.

CAUDWELL, C., *The Concept of Freedom*, London: Lawrence & Wishart, 1965.

CHARLES, D., 'Perfectionism in Aristotle's Political Theory: Reply to Martha Nussbaum', *Oxford Studies in Ancient Philosophy*, Suppl. Vol. (1988), 184–206.

CHARLTON, W., *The Analytic Ambition*, Oxford: Blackwell, 1991.

CHARVET, J., *A Critique of Freedom and Equality*, Cambridge: Cambridge University Press, 1981.

CHISHOLM, R. M., 'Intrinsic Value', in A. I. Goldman and J. Kim (eds.), *Values and Morals*, Dordrecht: Reidel, 1978.

CHRISTMAN, J., 'Liberalism and Individual Positive Freedom', *Ethics*, 101 (1991), 343–59.

—— 'Autonomy and Personal History', *Canadian Journal of Philosophy*, 20 (1991), 1–24.

CODY, A. B., 'Can a Single Action Have Many Different Descriptions?', *Inquiry*, 10 (1967), 164–80.

COHEN, G. A., *Karl Marx's Theory of History: A Defence*, Oxford: Clarendon Press, 1978.

—— 'Capitalism, Freedom and the Proletariat', in A. Ryan (ed.), *The Idea of Freedom*, London: Oxford University Press, 1979. Revised version in D. Miller (ed.), *Liberty*, Oxford: Oxford University Press, 1991.

—— 'Illusions about Private Property and Freedom', in J. Mepham and D. H. Ruben (eds.), *Issues in Marxist Philosophy*, iv, Hassocks: Harvester, 1981.

—— 'The Structure of Proletarian Unfreedom', *Philosophy and Public Affairs*, 12 (1983), 3–33.

—— *History, Labour and Freedom: Themes from Marx*, Oxford: Clarendon Press, 1988.

—— 'Equality of What? On Welfare, Goods and Capabilities', *Recherches Économiques de Louvain*, 56 (1990), 357–82.

—— *Self-Ownership, Freedom, and Equality*, Cambridge: Cambridge University Press, 1995.

COHEN, M. R., and NAGEL, E., *An Introduction to Logic and Scientific Method*, New York: Harcourt Brace, 1934.

CONDORCET, M. J. A. N., *Sketch for a Historical Picture of the Progress of the Human Mind*, trans. J. Barraclough, Westport, Conn.: Hyperion Press, 1955.

CONNOLLY, W. E., *The Terms of Political Discourse*, 2nd edn., Princeton: Princeton University Press, 1983.

COOMBS, C. H., DAWES, R. M., and TVERSKY, A., *Mathematical Psychology: An Elementary Introduction*, Englewood Cliffs, NJ: Prentice Hall, 1970.

COOPER, W. E., 'Taking Reflective Equilibrium Seriously', *Dialogue* (Canada), 20 (1981), 548–55.

CROCKER, L., *Positive Liberty*, London: Nijhoff, 1980.

DANIELS, N., 'Equal Liberty and Unequal Worth of Liberty', in N. Daniels (ed.), *Reading Rawls*, Oxford: Blackwell, 1975.

—— 'Wide Reflective Equilibrium and Theory Acceptance in Ethics', *Journal of Philosophy*, 76 (1979), 256–82.

—— 'Reflective Equilibrium and Archimedean Points', *Canadian Journal of Philosophy*, 10 (1980), 83–103.

DANTO, A. C., *Analytical Philosophy of Action*, Cambridge: Cambridge University Press, 1973.

DAVIDSON, D., *Essays on Actions and Events*, Oxford: Clarendon Press, 1980.

—— 'Reply to Quine on Events', in E. LePore and B. McLaughlin (eds.), *Actions and Events: Perspectives on the Philosophy of Donald Davidson*, Oxford: Blackwell, 1985.

DAY, J. P., 'On Liberty and the Real Will', *Philosophy*, 45 (1970), 171–92.

—— 'Threats, Offers, Law, Opinion and Liberty', *American Philosophical Quarterly*, 14 (1977), 257–72.

DE MARNEFFE, P., 'Liberalism, Liberty, and Neutrality', *Philosophy and Public Affairs*, 19 (1990), 253–74.

DEN UYL, D., 'Freedom and Virtue', in T. R. Machan (ed.), *The Libertarian Alternative*, Chicago: Nelson-Hall, 1974.

DOWDING, K., 'Negative Liberty and its Value', unpublished paper, London School of Economics.

—— 'Choice: Its Increase and its Value', *British Journal of Political Science*, 22 (1992), 301–14.

DWORKIN, G., *The Theory and Practice of Autonomy*, Cambridge: Cambridge University Press, 1988.

DWORKIN, R., *Taking Rights Seriously*, London: Duckworth, 1977.

—— 'We Do Not Have a Right to Liberty', in R. L. Cunningham (ed.), *Liberty and the Rule of Law*, College Station: Texas A. & M. University Press, 1979.

—— 'What is Equality? Part II: Equality of Resources', *Philosophy and Public Affairs*, 10 (1981), 283–345.

—— *A Matter of Principle*, Cambridge, Mass.: Harvard University Press, 1985.

—— 'What is Equality? Part 3: The Place of Liberty', *Iowa Law Review*, 73 (1987), 1–54.

FEINBERG, J., 'The Interest in Liberty on the Scales', in A. I. Goldman and J. Kim (eds.), *Values and Morals*, Dordrecht: Reidel, 1978.

—— *Social Philosophy*, Englewood Cliffs, NJ: Prentice-Hall, 1979.

—— *Rights, Justice and the Bounds of Liberty*, Princeton: Princeton University Press, 1980.

FLATHMAN, R. E., *The Philosophy and Politics of Freedom*, Chicago: Chicago University Press, 1987.

FLEW, A. (ed.), *A Dictionary of Philosophy*, London: Pan Books, 1979.

FØLLESDAL, D., 'Analytic Philosophy: What Is It and Why Should One Engage in It?', *Ratio*, NS 9 (1996), 193–208.

FRANKFURT, H. G., 'Freedom of the Will and the Concept of a Person', *Journal of Philosophy*, 68 (1971), 5–20.

GABOR, A., 'The Measurement of Freedom', *International Journal of Social Economics*, 6 (1979), 429–39.

GABOR, D., and GABOR, A., 'An Essay on the Mathematical Theory of Freedom', *International Journal of Social Economics*, 6 (1979), 330–71.

GASTIL, R., *Freedom in the World: Political Rights and Civil Liberties*, London: Greenwood Press, 1987.

GIBBS, B., *Freedom and Liberation*, London: Chatto & Windus, 1976.

GINET, C., *On Action*, Cambridge: Cambridge University Press, 1991.

GOLDMAN, A. I., *A Theory of Human Action*, Englewood Cliffs, NJ: Prentice Hall, 1970.

—— 'Toward a Theory of Social Power', in S. Lukes (ed.), *Power*, New York: New York University Press, 1986.

GOLDSTEIN, R. J., 'The Limits of Using Quantitative Data in Studying Human Rights Abuses', *Human Rights Quarterly*, 8 (1986), 607–27.

GOODMAN, N., *Fact, Fiction and Forecast*, 3rd edn., Hassocks: Harvester Press, 1979.

GORR, M. J., *Coercion, Freedom and Exploitation*, New York: Peter Lang, 1989.

GRAY, J., 'Against Cohen on Proletarian Unfreedom', *Social Philosophy and Policy*, 6 (1988), 77–112.

—— *Liberalisms: Essays in Political Philosophy*, London: Routledge, 1989.

—— *Enlightenment's Wake: Politics and Culture at the Close of the Modern Age*, London: Routledge, 1993.

GRAY, T., *Freedom*, London: Macmillan, 1991.

GRIFFIN, J., *Well Being: Its Meaning, Measurement and Moral Importance*, Oxford: Clarendon Press, 1986.

HALDANE, J. B. S., 'A Comparative Study of Freedom', in R. N. Anshen (ed.), *Freedom: Its Meaning*, London: Allen & Unwin, 1942.

HART, H. L. A., 'Rawls on Liberty and its Priority', in N. Daniels (ed.), *Reading Rawls*, Oxford: Blackwell, 1975.

HATTERSLEY, R., *Choose Freedom: The Future for Democratic Socialism*, London: Joseph, 1986.

HAUSMAN, D. M., and MCPHERSON, M., *Economic Analysis and Moral Philosophy*, Cambridge: Cambridge University Press, 1996.

HAYEK, F. A. VON, *The Road to Serfdom*, London: Routledge & Kegan Paul, 1944.

—— *The Constitution of Liberty*, London: Routledge & Kegan Paul, 1960.

—— *Law, Legislation and Liberty*, London: Routledge & Kegan Paul, 1982.

HEES, M. VAN, 'On the Analysis of Negative Freedom', *Theory and Decision*, forthcoming.

—— 'An Axiomatic Analysis of Freedom', unpublished paper, University of Twente.

—— and WISSENBURG, M., 'Freedom and Opportunity', *Political Studies*, forthcoming.

HIRSCH, A., and DE MARCHI, N., *Milton Friedman*, London: Harvester Weatsheaf, 1990.

HITLER, A., *Hitler's Table Talk*, trans. N. Cameron and R. H. Stevens, Oxford: Oxford University Press, 1988.

HOBBES, T., *Leviathan*, London: Penguin, 1985.

HOBHOUSE, L. T., *Liberalism*, London: Greenwood Press, 1911.

HORNSBY, J., *Actions*, London: Routledge & Kegan Paul, 1980.

—— 'Actions and Identities', *Analysis*, 39 (1979), 195–201.

HUMANA, C., *World Human Rights Guide*, London: Hodder & Stoughton, 1986.

HUMBOLDT, W. VON, *The Limits of State Action*, Indianapolis: Liberty Classics, 1993.

HURKA, T., 'Why Value Autonomy?', *Social Theory and Practice*, 13 (1987), 361–82.

JONES, P., and SUGDEN, R., 'Evaluating Choice', *International Review of Law and Economics*, 2 (1982), 47–65.

KALLEN, H. M., *Patterns of Progress*, New York: Columbia University Press, 1950.

KANT, I., *The Metaphysical Elements of Justice*, trans. J. Ladel, New York: Macmillan, 1965.

—— *Political Writings*, trans. H. B. Nisbet, Cambridge: Cambridge University Press, 1991.

KERLINGER, F. N., *Foundations of Behavioural Research*, Austin, Tex.: Holt, Rinehart & Winston, 1964.

KLEMISCH-AHLERT, M., 'Freedom of Choice: A Comparison of Different Rankings of Opportunity Sets', *Social Choice and Welfare*, 10 (1993), 173–89.

KRAMER, M., SIMMONDS, N., and STEINER, H., *A Debate over Rights: Philosophical Enquiries*, Oxford: Oxford University Press, 1998.

KRANTZ, D. H., LUCE, R. D., SUPPES, P., and TVERSKY, A., *Foundations of Measurement*, i, London: Academic Press, 1971.

KRIPKE, S., 'Identity and Necessity', in S. P. Schwartz (ed.), *Naming, Necessity and Natural Kinds*, London: Cornell University Press, 1977.

KRISTJÁNSSON, K., *Social Freedom: The Responsibility View*, Cambridge: Cambridge University Press, 1996.

KYBURG, H. E., *Theory and Measurement*, Cambridge: Cambridge University Press, 1984.

KYMLICKA, W., 'Liberalism and Communitarianism', *Canadian Journal of Philosophy*, 18 (1988), 181–204.

—— *Liberalism, Community and Culture*, Oxford: Oxford University Press, 1989.

—— *Contemporary Political Philosophy*, Oxford: Oxford University Press, 1990.

LARMORE, C., *The Morals of Modernity*, Cambridge: Cambridge University Press, 1996.

LEONI, B., *Freedom and the Law*, Los Angeles: Nash, 1961.

LEWIS, D., 'Counterpart Theory and Quantified Modal Logic', *Journal of Philosophy*, 65 (1968), 113–26.

LOCKE, J., *Two Treatises of Government*, London: Everyman, 1924.

LOEVINSOHN, E., 'Liberty and the Redistribution of Property', *Philosophy and Public Affairs*, 6 (1976–7), 226–39.

LOMBARD, L. B., 'Actions, Results and the Time of a Killing', *Philosophia* (Israel), 8 (1978), 341–51.

LUKES, S., 'The Contradictory Aims of Action Theory', in G. Seebass and R. Tuomela (eds.), *Social Action*, Dordrecht: Reidel, 1985.

—— *Marxism and Morality*, Oxford: Clarendon Press, 1985.

—— 'Equality and Liberty: Must They Conflict?', in D. Held (ed.), *Political Theory Today*, Cambridge: Polity Press, 1991.

—— and GALNOOR, I., *No Laughing Matter: A Collection of Political Jokes*, Harmondsworth: Penguin, 1987.

MACCALLUM, G., 'Negative and Positive Freedom', *Philosophical Review*, 76 (1967), 312–34.

MACINTYRE, A., *After Virtue: A Study in Moral Theory*, London: Duckworth, 1981.

—— *Whose Justice? Which Rationality?*, London: Duckworth, 1988.

MAGRI, T., 'Negative Freedom, Rational Deliberation, and Non Satiating Goods', *Topoi*, 17 (1998), forthcoming.

MASON, A., 'Workers' Unfreedom and Women's Unfreedom: Is There a Significant Analogy?', *Political Studies*, 44 (1996), 75–87.

MILL, J. S., *Collected Works*, ed. J. M. Robson, London: Routledge & Kegan Paul, 1969.

MILLER, D., 'Constraints on Freedom', *Ethics*, 94 (1983), 66–86.

—— 'Reply to Oppenheim', *Ethics*, 95 (1985), 310–14.

—— *Market, State, and Community: Theoretical Foundations of Market Socialism*, Oxford: Clarendon Press, 1989.

MILNE, A. J. M., *Freedom and Rights*, London: Allen & Unwin, 1968.

MISES, L. VON, *Human Action: A Treatise on Economics*, New Haven: Yale University Press, 1949.

MOORE, G. E., *Ethics*, London: Oxford University Press, 1965.

MOYA, C. J., *The Philosophy of Action: An Introduction*, Cambridge: Polity, 1990.

NARVESON, J., 'Equality vs. Liberty: Advantage, Liberty', in E. Frankel Paul, F. D. Miller, Jr., and J. Paul (eds.), *Liberty and Equality*, Oxford: Blackwell, 1985.

NG, Y. R., *Welfare Economics*, London: Macmillan, 1979.

NIELSEN, K., *Equality and Liberty: A Defence of Radical Egalitarianism*, Totowa, NJ: Rowman & Allanheld, 1985.

—— 'Rawls and the Socratic Ideal', *Analyse & Kritik*, 13 (1991), 67–93.

NORMAN, R., 'Liberty, Equality, Property', *Proceedings of the Aristotelian Society*, Suppl. Vol. 55 (1981), 193–209.

—— *Free and Equal*, Oxford: Oxford University Press, 1987.

NOZICK, R., *Anarchy, State and Utopia*, Oxford: Blackwell, 1974.

—— *Philosophical Explanations*, Oxford: Oxford University Press, 1981.

—— *The Examined Life*, New York: Simon & Schuster, 1989.

NUSSBAUM, M., 'Nature, Function, and Capability: Aristotle on Political Distribution', *Oxford Studies in Ancient Philosophy*, Suppl. Vol. (1988), 145–84.

—— 'Reply to David Charles', *Oxford Studies in Ancient Philosophy*, Suppl. Vol. (1988), 205–14.

—— 'Non-Relative Virtues: An Aristotelian Approach', in M. Nussbaum and A. Sen (eds.), *The Quality of Life*, Oxford: Clarendon Press, 1993.

OLSARETTI, S., 'Freedom, Force, and Choice: Against the Rights-Based Definition of Voluntariness', *Journal of Political Philosophy*, 6 (1998), 53–78.

O'NEILL, O., 'The Most Extensive Liberty', *Proceedings of the Aristotelian Society*, 80 (1980), 45–59.

—— *Constructions of Reason: Explorations of Kant's Practical Philosophy*, Cambridge: Cambridge University Press, 1989.

—— 'Autonomy, Coherence and Independence', in D. Mulligan and W. Watts Miller (eds.), *Liberalism, Citizenship and Autonomy*, Aldershot: Avebury, 1992.

—— 'Justice, Capabilities, and Vulnerabilities', in M. Nussbaum and J. Glover (eds.), *Women, Culture, and Development: A Study of Human Capabilities*, Oxford: Clarendon Press, 1995.

—— *Towards Justice and Virtue: A Constructivist Account of Practical Reasoning*, Cambridge: Cambridge University Press, 1996.

OPPENHEIM, F. E., *Dimensions of Freedom*, New York: St Martin' s Press, 1961.

—— *Political Concepts: A Reconstruction*, Oxford: Blackwell, 1981.

—— 'Constraints on Freedom as a Descriptive Concept', *Ethics*, 95 (1985), 305–9.

—— 'Social Freedom and its Parameters', *Journal of Theoretical Politics*, 7 (1995), 403–20.

—— 'La libertà sociale ed i suoi parametri', *Sociologia del Diritto*, 22 (1995), 5–37.

—— 'Si può misurare la libertà complessiva? Nota critica agli scritti di Ian Carter', *Quaderni di Scienza Politica*, 2 (1995), 455–61.

ORWELL, G., *1984*, Harmondsworth: Penguin, 1954.

PAGE, B. I., *Choices and Echoes in Presidential Elections*, Chicago: University of Chicago Press, 1978.

PARENT, W. A., 'Some Recent Work on the Concept of Liberty', *American Philosophical Quarterly*, 11 (1974), 149–67.

PASSMORE, J., *The Perfectibility of Man*, London: Duckworth, 1970.

PATTANAIK, P. K., and XU, Y., 'On Ranking Opportunity Sets in Terms of Freedom of Choice', *Recherches Economiques de Louvain*, 56 (1990), 383–90.

—— —— 'On Preference and Freedom', *Theory and Decision*, forthcoming.

PETTIT, P., 'The Freedom of the City: A Republican Ideal', in P. Pettit and A. Hamlin (eds.), *The Good Polity*, Oxford: Blackwell, 1989.

—— 'A Definition of Negative Liberty', *Ratio*, NS 2 (1989), 153–68.

—— 'Negative Liberty, Liberal and Republican', *European Journal of Philosophy*, 1 (1993), 15–38.

PETTIT, P., *Republicanism: A Theory of Freedom and Government*, Oxford: Oxford University Press, 1997.

PFEIFER, K., 'A Problem of Motivation for Multipliers', *Southern Journal of Philosophy*, 20 (1982), 209–24.

—— *Actions and Other Events: The Unifier–Multiplier Controversy*, New York: Peter Lang, 1989.

PONTARA, G., *Filosofia pratica*, Milan: Il Saggiatore, 1988.

PUPPE, C., 'An Axiomatic Approach to "Preference for Freedom of Choice" ', *Journal of Economic Theory*, 68 (1996), 174–99.

PUTNAM, H., *The Many Faces of Realism*, La Salle, Ill.: Open Court, 1987.

QUINE, W. V. O., *From a Logical Point of View*, Cambridge, Mass.: Harvard University Press, 1953.

—— 'Events and Reification', in E. LePore and B. McLaughlin (eds.), *Actions and Events: Perspectives on the Philosophy of Donald Davidson*, Oxford: Blackwell, 1985.

RAE, D., 'Maximin Justice and an Alternative Principle of General Advantage', *American Political Science Review*, 69 (1975), 630–47.

RAWLS, J., 'Outline of a Decision Procedure for Ethics', *Philosophical Review*, 60 (1951), 177–97.

—— *A Theory of Justice*, Cambridge, Mass.: Harvard University Press, 1971.

—— 'The Independence of Moral Theory', *Proceedings and Addresses of the American Philosophical Association*, 47 (1974–5), 5–22.

—— *Political Liberalism*, New York: Columbia University Press, 1993.

RAZ, J., 'The Claims of Reflective Equilibrium', *Inquiry*, 25 (1982), 307–30.

—— *The Morality of Freedom*, Oxford: Clarendon Press, 1986.

RESCHER, N., *A Theory of Possibility: A Constructivistic and Conceptualistic Account of Possible Individuals and Possible Worlds*, Oxford: Blackwell, 1975.

RICHARDS, N., '*E Pluribus Unum*: A Defense of Davidson's Individuation of Action', *Philosophical Studies*, 29 (1976), 191–8.

RORTY, R., *Contingency, Irony and Solidarity*, Cambridge: Cambridge University Press, 1989.

ROSENBAUM, E. F., 'On Measuring Freedom', unpublished paper, Darwin College, Cambridge.

ROTHBARD, M. N., *The Ethics of Liberty*, Atlantic Highlands, NJ: Humanities Press, 1982.

RUSSELL, B., 'Freedom in Society', in *Sceptical Essays*, London: Allen & Unwin, 1935.

—— 'Freedom and Government', in R. N. Anshen (ed.), *Freedom: Its Meaning*, London: Allen & Unwin, 1942.

—— *Logic and Knowledge*, London: Routledge, 1988.

RYAN, C. C., 'Yours, Mine, and Ours: Property Rights and Individual Liberty', in J. Paul (ed.), *Reading Nozick: Essays on Anarchy, State and Utopia*, Oxford: Blackwell, 1982.

SCARPELLI, U., 'La dimensione normativa della libertà', *Rivista di Filosofia*, 55 (1964), 449–67.

SCRUTON, R., *The Meaning of Conservatism*, Harmondsworth: Penguin, 1980.

SEN, A., *On Economic Inequality*, Oxford: Clarendon Press, 1972.

—— 'Equality of What?', *Tanner Lectures in Human Values*, 1 (1980), 197–220.

—— *Commodities and Capabilities*, Amsterdam: North Holland, 1985.

—— 'Well-Being, Agency and Freedom', *Journal of Philosophy*, 82 (1985), 169–221.

—— *On Ethics and Economics*, Oxford: Blackwell, 1987.

—— 'Freedom of Choice: Concept and Content', *European Economic Review*, 32 (1988), 269–94.

—— 'Welfare, Freedom and Social Choice: A Reply', *Recherches Economiques de Louvain*, 56 (1990), 451–86.

—— 'Justice: Means versus Freedom', *Philosophy and Public Affairs*, 19 (1990), 111–21.

—— 'Welfare, Preference, and Freedom', *Journal of Econometrics*, 50 (1991), 15–29.

—— *Inequality Reexamined*, Oxford: Oxford University Press, 1992.

—— 'Capability and Well-Being', in M. Nussbaum and A. Sen (eds.), *The Quality of Life*, Oxford: Clarendon Press, 1993.

—— 'Freedom, Capabilities and Public Action: A Response', *Notizie di Politeia*, 43–4 (1996), 107–25.

SHUE, H., 'Liberty and Self Respect', *Ethics*, 85 (1975), 195–203.

SKINNER, Q., 'The Paradoxes of Political Liberty', *Tanner Lectures on Human Values*, 5 (1984), 227–50.

—— 'The Republican Ideal of Political Liberty', in G. Bock, Q. Skinner, and M. Viroli (eds.), *Machiavelli and Republicanism*, Cambridge: Cambridge University Press, 1990.

—— *Liberty before Liberalism*, Cambridge: Cambridge University Press, 1998.

SOMERVILLE, J., 'Toward a Consistent Definition of Freedom and its Relation to Value', in C. J. Friedrich (ed.), *Liberty* (*Nomos*, 4), New York: Atherton Press, 1962.

SPECTOR, H., *Autonomy and Rights*, Oxford: Clarendon Press, 1992.

SPENCER, H., *Social Statics*, rev. and abridged, London: Williams & Norgate, 1892.

STEINER, H., 'The Natural Right to Equal Freedom', *Mind*, 83 (1974), 194–210.

—— 'Individual Liberty', *Proceedings of the Aristotelian Society*, 75 (1974–5), 33–50.

—— 'The Structure of a Set of Compossible Rights', *Journal of Philosophy*, 74 (1977), 767–75.

—— 'How Free: Computing Personal Liberty', in A. Phillips-Griffiths (ed.), *Of Liberty*, London: Cambridge University Press, 1983.

—— 'Capitalism, Justice and Equal Starts', *Social Philosophy and Policy*, 5 (1987), 49–71.

—— *An Essay on Rights*, Oxford: Blackwell, 1994.

—— 'Choice and Circumstance', *Ratio*, NS 10 (1997), 296–312.

STEVENS, S. S., 'Mathematics, Measurement and Psychophysics', in S. S. Stevens (ed.), *Handbook of Experimental Psychology*, New York: Wiley, 1951.

STOHL, M., CARLETON, D., LOPEZ, G., and SAMUELS, S., 'State Violation of Human Rights: Issues and Problems of Measurement', *Human Rights Quarterly*, 8 (1986), 592–606.

STRAWSON, P., *Logico-linguistic Papers*, London: Methuen, 1971.

SWANTON, C., *Freedom: A Coherence Theory*, Indianapolis: Hackett, 1992.

TARTT, D., *The Secret History*, Harmondsworth: Penguin, 1992.

TAYLOR, C., *Hegel and Modern Society*, Cambridge: Cambridge University Press, 1979.

—— 'What's Wrong with Negative Liberty', in A. Ryan (ed.), *The Idea of Freedom*, London: Oxford University Press, 1979.

TAYLOR, C., 'The Diversity of Goods', in A. Sen and B. Williams (eds.), *Utilitarianism and Beyond*, Cambridge: Cambridge University Press, 1982.

—— 'Kant's Theory of Freedom', in Z. Pelczynski and J. Gray (eds.), *Conceptions of Liberty in Political Philosophy*, London: Athlone Press, 1984.

TAYLOR, M., *Community, Anarchy and Liberty*, London: Cambridge University Press, 1982.

TEMKIN, L., *Inequality*, Oxford: Oxford University Press, 1993.

THOMSON, J. J., 'The Time of a Killing', *Journal of Philosophy*, 68 (1971), 115–32.

UNDP (United Nations Development Program), *Human Development Report 1991*, Oxford: Oxford University Press, 1991.

VAN PARIJS, P., *Real Freedom for All: What (If Anything) can Justify Capitalism?*, Oxford: Oxford University Press, 1995.

WALSH, J., *Growing up Catholic*, London: Macmillan, 1989.

WILLIAMS, B., *Problems of the Self: Philosophical Papers 1956–1972*, Cambridge: Cambridge University Press, 1977.

WORSTHORNE, P., 'Too Much Freedom', in M. Cowling (ed.), *Conservative Essays*, London: Cassell, 1978.

INDEX